Adventuring in British Columbia

THE SIERRA CLUB
ADVENTURE TRAVEL GUIDES

Adventuring in British Columbia

**ISABEL NANTON
and MARY SIMPSON**

Sierra Club Books
San Francisco

For Lloyd, David, Danielle and Katie, without whom adventuring would not be nearly so much fun.

The Sierra Club, founded in 1892 by John Muir, has devoted itself to the study and protection of the earth's scenic and ecological resources — mountains, wetlands, woodlands, wild shores and rivers, deserts and plains. The publishing program of the Sierra Club offers books to the public as a nonprofit educational service in the hope that they may enlarge the public's understanding of the Club's basic concerns. The point of view expressed in each book, however, does not necessarily represent that of the Club. The Sierra Club has some sixty chapters coast to coast, in Canada, Hawaii, and Alaska. For information about how you may participate in its programs to preserve wilderness and the quality of life, please address inquiries to Sierra Club, 730 Polk Street, San Francisco, CA 94109.

Originally published in Canada by Douglas & McIntyre Ltd., 1615 Venables Street, Vancouver, British Columbia, Canada V5L 2H1.

Library of Congress Cataloging-in-Publication Data
Nanton, Isabel, 1951-
Adventuring in British Columbia / Isabel Nanton & Mary Simpson.
p. cm. — (A Sierra Club adventure travel guide)
Includes bibliographical references (p.   ) and index.
ISBN 0-87156-674-5
1. Outdoor recreation—British Columbia—Guide-books. 2. British Columbia—Description and travel—1981- , —Guide-books. I. Simpson, Mary, 1947- . II. Title.
III. Series: Sierra Club adventure travel guides.
GV191.46.B74N36 1991
790'09711—dc20   91-10193
                    CIP

Quote from Miles Richardson appears with the permission of *Beautiful B.C.*

Design by Robert MacDonald / MediaClones
The cover photograph by Graham Osborne was taken on Idaho Peak, part of the Selkirk Mountains in the Kootenays.
Photographs by Lloyd Twaites, Michael Mong, Mary Simpson and Sam Whitehead
Maps by Werner Gruenwald
Printed and bound in Canada by D. W. Friesen & Sons Ltd.
Printed on acid-free paper

10 9 8 7 6 5 4 3 2 1

Contents

ACKNOWLEDGEMENTS

To research this book we travelled extensively throughout British Columbia asking incessant questions, taking copious notes and reading insatiably. Along the way, friends, acquaintances, fellow adventurers and experts in the field were very generous with their time and energy. With them we shared our enthusiasm for the province and traded insights, anecdotes and travel secrets. We are extremely grateful for everyone's input and in particular would like to thank: Werner Gruenwald for his detailed work on the maps; Helen and Philip Akrigg for helping with B.C. place names; Jean McTavish for sharing her provisioning expertise; Michael Mong for his photographic input; Dr. Nigel Mathews for his tips on first aid on the West Coast Trail; Jan Turnbull and Dee Miller of F.A.S.T. for bush first-aid advice; Suzie Sims for sharing her kayaking knowledge; Donna Hayes for her cross-country ski tips; Dr. Peter Belton for the word on bug repellent; Chris and Jenny Harris for their Bowron Lakes and Mount Robson insights; Richard T. Wright for being the authority on canoeing in our province; John Morgan for his fishy advice; Jim Ross and Marjorie Morrison for their Broken Islands input; Anne Tempelman-Kluit for giving us some tips on the North; the folks at the main branch of the Vancouver Public Library, history, science and geography divisions, for their patience while we fact-checked; Noel van Sandwyk at B.C. Rail, our favorite railway; Vicky Haberl and Don Macauley at the BC Parks office in Victoria for checking the park information; the folks at the Computer Clinic for being such efficient computer doctors; Ken Twaites for his help with disk conversions; Louise Robbins for her diligent proofreading; Gerald Gilbey-Gold for photo research, and friends Cindy Low, Denise Gross and Jo-Anne Birnie Danzker for moral support. Heartfelt thanks to our husbands, David and Lloyd, for putting up with us during all those hours of researching, writing and polishing the final manuscript. You said that we would finally get it done and we did! Special warm thanks to our editor, Barbara Pulling.

HOW TO USE THIS BOOK

We had mixed feelings about doing this book. We wanted to share the beautiful, wild places of the province with others who would appreciate them, but at the same time we hoped not to spoil the one thing we value most—British Columbia's very remoteness, the feeling that you are the only person for miles around. Increasing population in the urban centres is putting a big strain on those wilderness areas, such as Garibaldi Park, nearest to the cities. Over the last few years, we have seen a staggering increase in the number of people enjoying the trails of this and similar parks. Some are not properly equipped for mountain trips and, unfortunately, not everyone respects the fragile mountain environment— its waters, flora and fauna. It is our hope that this book, in exploring the wild areas of the province, will bring about an appreciation of their uniqueness, encourage preservation and promote the kind of exploration that leaves the wilderness intact.

Descriptions of British Columbia's 10 regions form the bulk of this guidebook. A map and a general introduction highlighting the region's history, physical geography and climate precede our detailed coverage of each of these 10 major areas. Short "Useful Information" sections throughout include important addresses and telephone numbers; the area code for the whole of British Columbia, unless otherwise stated, is 604, so all you need to do is dial 1 before any out-of-town number. In the "Useful Addresses" section at the back of the book, you will find a master list of the province's regional park headquarters, the main Forest Service offices and regional tourist associations, together with information on where to get maps. A selective bibliography includes some of the titles we most recommend about various aspects of British Columbia.

Although we have tried to list only those operators who have established a good reputation for interesting and well-organized trips, inclusion in the book does not imply endorsement of a company's tours. However, the exclusion of a company may just mean that we haven't heard about them. It is a good idea to ask some questions of an operator before you commit to a tour: find out how long they have been in business, what kinds of qualifications their guides have, what their safety record is, whether they are members of a professional association and whether or not they can provide personal references from previous clients.

While the material in the book is accurate as of print time, information does change, particularly addresses and phone numbers. Please alert us to changes and share your insights on areas you have explored by writing to us c/o Douglas & McIntyre, 1615 Venables St., Vancouver, B.C., Canada V5L 2H1.

British Columbia

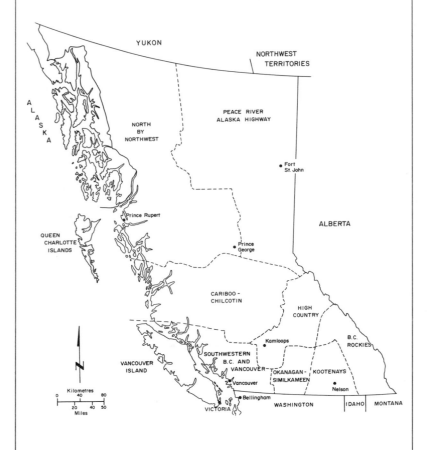

YUKON

NORTHWEST TERRITORIES

ALASKA

NORTH BY NORTHWEST

PEACE RIVER ALASKA HIGHWAY

● Fort St. John

ALBERTA

Prince Rupert

QUEEN CHARLOTTE ISLANDS

● Prince George

CARIBOO – CHILCOTIN

HIGH COUNTRY

B.C. ROCKIES

● Kamloops

VANCOUVER ISLAND

SOUTHWESTERN B.C. AND VANCOUVER

OKANAGAN – SIMILKAMEEN

KOOTENAYS

● Nelson

● Vancouver

● Bellingham

VICTORIA

WASHINGTON

IDAHO

MONTANA

Kilometres
0   40   80
   20   40   50
        Miles

N

CHAPTER 1

Discovering British Columbia

LOCATION

British Columbia, Canada's third largest and westernmost province, stretches in a great rectangle between the 60th and 49th parallels, containing an adventurers' paradise so diverse that few areas in the world can compete for sheer variety. Bigger than any of the U.S. states except Alaska, four times as large as Great Britain and more than twice the size of Japan, the province's 952,263 sq. km (367,669 sq. mi.) encompass mountains, rivers, lakes, forests, coastline and islands tailor-made for exploring. And what makes many of these wilderness treasures even more appealing is their remarkable accessibility to major urban centres.

To the northwest, a chunk of Alaska extends 893 km (563 mi.) down the western edge of the province. The Yukon and the Northwest Territories form a straight 1062-km (669-mi.) northern boundary, and, on the east, B.C. shares a 1545-km (973-mi.) border with Alberta. Washington State, Idaho and Montana make up the 650-km (409-mi.) border to the south. Pacific Ocean waters rim a grand total of 27,040 km (16,900 mi.) of mainland and island coastline, including that of Vancouver Island, which is half the size of Italy.

Victoria, on Vancouver Island, is the provincial capital, while Vancouver, located in British Columbia's Lower Mainland, is the biggest city and financial hub of the province.

GEOLOGY

British Columbia's varied landscape was created by a complex series of geological events. Most geologists accept the plate tectonics theory as the explanation for the movement of land masses over the earth's surface in this part of the world. The mid-Pacific rift zone, a long, north-south fracture in the earth's crust, runs along the west coast of Vancouver Island and is continuously forming new crust composed of basaltic lava. As this new rock is injected through the rift zone by convection currents deep within the earth, the Pacific plate is pushed towards the North American continent.

Although the movement is very slow, just a few centimetres per year, the results are dramatic where the plates are forced under the Continental Crust on the west coast. Earthquakes result from the sudden jolting as plates slide past each other. The movement is smooth where the plates are well lubricated, causing only slight tremors which do little or no damage. Serious damage can occur, however, where the plates are sticky and energy is released with a sudden jerk. British Columbia has had few strong shocks to date, but scientists expect that a major quake will occur sometime in the next 200 years.

Plates can also move in directions parallel to each other. The Pacific Plate moves northwards past the America Plate; this movement is most noticeable along the San Andreas Fault zone in California. Movement also occurs off the B.C. coast along the Queen Charlotte Fault, where the smaller Juan de Fuca Plate moves east and plunges beneath the America Plate. It is this action, called subduction, that creates mountains. The lower plate heats up as it is forced into the hot mantle, creating large bodies of magma that cool beneath the surface, then are uplifted and eroded over time. The Coast Plutonic Complex, which stretches from southwestern B.C. through the Yukon to Alaska, is still rising at the rate of about 1 centimetre per 100 years.

Some uplifted magma reaches the surface through weak areas in the crust, forming volcanoes. Many volcanic eruptions have occurred in B.C. over the last 5000 years. Examples can be seen in Garibaldi Park near Mount Garibaldi and Mount Price, where eruptions formed the wall of lava now known as the Barrier. The Mount Meager eruption many years ago was much more powerful than the one at Mount St. Helen's in Washington State in 1980, and layers of white volcanic ash can still be seen in the soil in the Bridge River area many miles away. Spatzizi Park, in northern B.C., contains other examples of volcanic activity.

Several mountain ranges run northwesterly through B.C., in a series of ranges and troughs that continue all the way from the Pacific rim to the Rocky Mountains at the Alberta border. The Outer Mountain area forming the Queen Charlotte Islands and Vancouver Island is separated from the Coast Range by the Coastal Trough, which contains Hecate Strait and Queen Charlotte Sound. The Coast Range combines large masses of older volcanic rock with younger volcanic peaks and consists largely of elevated plutonic rock. This makes for an area blessed with hot springs, lakes, cinder cones and alpine meadows.

A series of glacial events occurred in B.C. as long as 100,000 years ago. Glaciers form where the yearly snowfall exceeds the quantity that is melted during the summer months. The requirements are cold temperatures and high precipitation, which is why, in British Columbia, glaciers are found predominantly on the western slopes of the Coast Range where winter storms drop the bulk of their moisture in the form of snow. As the ice thickens on the mountains over the years, it begins to flow as a river of ice. The ice carries along with it

rocks that grind the land beneath, forming U-shaped valleys and other prominent features such as eskers and piles of glacial debris called moraines. As the
climate warmed, cooled and then warmed again, glaciers advanced and re-
ceded, leaving large valleys which are now occupied by lakes and rivers.
Fiords gouged out by glaciers as they flowed to the ocean cut through the Coast
Mountains in a westerly direction. Glacial action created countless kilometres
of bays, islands and estuaries along the Pacific coast; the ruggedness of the
B.C. coastline has left it sparsely populated by people but rife with wildlife.

The Central and South Plateau regions feature a series of plateaus and
mountain ranges, including the Stikine, Skeena, Cascade, Monashee, Purcell
and Columbia mountains. These in turn are divided from the Rocky Mountain
Range by the Rocky Mountain Trench, a fault formed 20 million years ago that
extends from the United States border to the northern reaches of the province.

The Rocky Mountains are blocks of sedimentary rock thrust upward east of
the fault. They contain fossils of creatures that lived in shallow oceans up to
500 million years ago. Some of these fossils now lie at 4000 m (13,000 ft.)
above sea level! A combination of glacial activity and rain has eroded the land
and carved valleys, now filled with rivers and fast-flowing creeks.

Today 57 per cent of B.C. is forest land. Fresh-water surfaces cover 2 per
cent of the province. In such a varied landscape adventuring opportunities are
endless. The infinitely indented coastline provides a haven for kayakers and
sailors; the mountains host summer hikers and winter skiers, while the lakes
and forests offer exciting possibilities for boaters and walkers.

CLIMATE

The only certainty about weather in British Columbia is its variety.
Because the landscape is so varied, areas in relative proximity to each other,
often separated merely by a mountain range or stretch of water, enjoy very
different climates. Vancouver Island's west coast is, for instance, very wet:
over 300 cm (118 in.) of rain falls on some parts annually. Yet only 69 cm
(27 in.) falls on the Sunshine Coast, less than 200 km (122 mi.) due east on the
B.C. mainland.

Winters on the Pacific coast and in the coastal valleys are generally mild
and wet, December being the rainiest month in the two main southern cities of
Vancouver and Victoria. In January, Victoria's temperature averages 4° C
(39° F); July temperatures hover around the 15° C (60° F) level, though they can
soar as high as the record of 35° C (95° F). Final spring frosts occur during the
first week in April, while the first ones in the fall appear, appropriately enough,
at Halloween. Victoria's average total annual precipitation is 64 cm (25 in.).
By contrast, Prince Rupert, at the northern tip of the B.C. coast, has average

January temperatures of 1.7° C (35° F), enjoys relatively warm summers, experiences spring frosts up to the third week in April and gets much more precipitation (240 cm/94 in. a year).

Lush rain forests characterize much of the coast, where tourism, logging and fishing are the primary sources of income.

As you move west into the southern interior of the province, winters become colder and summers hotter. In Princeton, residents can expect the mercury to hover around the -8° C (17° F) mark in January, shifting to 18° C (65° F) in July. Spring frosts occur until the beginning of June, while fall frosts move in in mid-September. The southern interior receives only half Victoria's annual rainfall, resulting in a land of scrub, ponderosa pines and sagebrush ideal for fruit orchards, vineyards and ranch range land. Another bonus of the short, warm summer months are the spectacular alpine areas above the timber line that metamorphose into blooming meadows. The southern interior contains Canada's only true desert, south of the Okanagan around Osooyos. The driest place in the province is Ashcroft, where only 15 cm (6 in.) of rain falls annually.

The central interior covers a vast region ranging from the grassland plateau of the Cariboo-Chilcotin north to the mining areas around Barkerville. Here prospecting gold rushers had to contend with spring frosts occurring up to the last week in June and fall frosts beginning the second week of August. The January mercury here hovers in the -10° C (14° F) range, while at least 538 cm (212 in.) of snow falls annually. Lillooet holds the provincial record for heat: 44° C (112° F) in midsummer.

The farther north you go, of course, the more severe the winters. The northern settlement of Smith River has recorded temperatures as low as -58.9° C (-74° F), with frosts occurring as early as the second week in August. Until very recently Tide Lake, about 50 km (31 mi.) north of Stewart, Canada's most northerly ice-free port, held the Guinness Book world record for annual snowfall, a whopping 2760 cm (1104 in.).

In our experience, whether you are slogging through the heavy rains of Cape Scott on northern Vancouver Island or sweltering among the kangaroo rats of the Pocket Desert near Osoyoos, it's best to be prepared for any eventuality. As they say in Ireland, another country with a notoriously fickle climate: "If you don't like the weather, stick around. It will change in half an hour!"

For current weather information wherever you are in the province, go to the blue pages at the back of the telephone directory. In the "Governments: Canada" section, you will find weather information listings for the area under Environment Canada and in the "Frequently Called Numbers" section.

The information available will vary from region to region. In the Vancouver area, for example, there is a telephone number for obtaining daily forecasts for the city and vicinity, numbers to call for marine, aviation and mountain forecasts, and numbers for general weather and climate information. We have found the aviation weather predictions to be the most reliable; after all, pilots depend on them. In any event, weather forecasting in B.C. is no more exact a science than it is anywhere else in the world, so it's always a good idea to be prepared for the worst.

HISTORY

Recent radiocarbon dating at Charlie Lake Cave in northeastern B.C. shows evidence of human habitation in the province as long as 10,600 years ago, predating by centuries European "discovery" of the land at the close of the eighteenth century.

Down the years the province we know today as British Columbia has been home to many distinct aboriginal cultures. While there are several theories about the origins of the native peoples of the Pacific Northwest, most non-native anthropologists agree that the earliest people crossed the Bering Strait land bridge from Asia looking for fresh hunting grounds. Not all native people accept this idea, however, since each group has its own creation story. What is agreed is that native peoples lived for a long time in this vast land before European arrival.

The Tlingit Indians inhabited the extreme northwestern corner of B.C. as well as the Alaska Panhandle. Farther down the coast lived the Tsimshian, whose territory extended inland along the Nass and Skeena rivers. Around a little pocket at Bella Coola lived the Bella Coola people, who spoke a Salish dialect. Farther south, on the coastal mainland, the Haisla, the Heiltsuk and the Southern Kwakiutl (Kwakwaka'wakw) all shared a common language. On the southern coast lived the Coast Salish. Both the Coast Salish and the Kwakwaka'wakw people also inhabited Vancouver Island, along with the Nootka (Nuu-chah-nulth). The Haida people made their home on Haida Gwaii (the Queen Charlotte Islands).

The northern and central interior of the province was home to the Athapaskan (or Dene) peoples, while three main groups lived on the southern interior plateau—the Plateau Athapaskans (including the now extinct Nicola, the Chilcotin and the Southern Carrier), the Interior Salish (the Lillooet, the Thompson, the Okanagan and the Shuswap), and the Kutenai.

While each culture was separate and distinct, all native peoples of the Pacific Northwest had highly developed and complex social structures and a profoundly spiritual relationship with the environment. Natural resources and other forms of life were not dominated and subdued but allowed to live with the people in harmonious coexistence.

The now famous words of Chief Seattle of the Squamish people probably most eloquently summarize the prevailing philosophy of the native peoples of the Pacific Northwest. In 1852, in response to a United States government request to purchase some tribal lands for arriving pioneers, he said, "Every part of this country is sacred to my people. Every hillside, every valley, every plain and grove, has been hallowed by some fond memory, by some sad experience of my tribe."

Early European explorers travelled to this land from Spain and Britain. In 1774 Juan Pérez made the first recorded glimpse of the Queen Charlotte Islands. In 1775 Captain Bodega y Quadra again glimpsed what is today B.C. while sailing up the coast to Alaska to strengthen the Spanish claim in the area. He was followed in 1778 by Captain James Cook representing the British. Cook's discoveries of prime sea-otter pelts at Nootka Sound precipitated a fur-trading rush that lasted 25 years.

Captain George Vancouver accepted, for Britain, the surrender of the Spanish claim in 1793 and immediately set about charting the intricate coastline. His journals record his first impression of the city which today bears his name: "A swampy flat, that retires several miles, before the country rises to meet the rugged snowy mountains."

That same year, Alexander Mackenzie, a young Scottish employee of the North West Company (rival to the Hudson's Bay Company), became the first white man to reach the coast travelling overland. He travelled briefly on the upper Fraser River, then, on the advice of his native guides, set off overland to reach the coast at Bella Coola. From the Fraser River near Quesnel he followed the centuries-old Grease Trail, used by native people to transport oolichan oil into the interior.

Explorer Simon Fraser was the first European to explore the Fraser to its mouth, reaching the sea in 1808. Fraser and his voyageurs traded with native peoples and battled the elements, all the while coping with terrifying river conditions. At one moment on his voyage, the river, in freshet in June, rose 2.5 m (8 ft.) within 24 hours. His companion voyageurs were reduced to eating berries, moss and dog flesh. Explorer David Thompson named the river after Simon Fraser in 1813.

Thompson himself travelled the Columbia River to its mouth in 1811, after initially exploring the Kootenays in southeastern B.C. with his wife and three small children.

As the river arteries opened up the West to trade, Hudson's Bay Company forts sprang up en route. The company ran the colony of Vancouver Island from 1849 until 1851 when their Chief Factor, James Douglas, became governor.

Life in 1858 Fort Victoria is superbly recorded by Margaret Ormsby in her now out-of-print book *British Columbia: A History*. She draws a vivid picture of Songhee Indians hawking clams, salmon, grouse, duck, venison and berries while long-pigtailed Chinese people "jog-trotted through the mire as they balanced on their shoulders the long poles to which they tied their bundles of tea, fresh vegetables and laundry. Late at night, more than one drunken miner stumbled into the gutter."

The year 1858 marked the first of B.C.'s many gold rushes. The Fraser River gold rush attracted over 5000 prospectors (mostly Americans) who passed through Victoria on their way to the lower reaches of the Fraser around Yale. Some drowned crossing Georgia Strait in vessels resembling bathtubs; others survived to make the inland hike.

From 1861 to 1865, the Cariboo gold rush opened up the B.C. interior from Yale to Barkerville. The biggest town north of San Francisco and west of Chicago, Barkerville bustled with swaggering prospectors and ladies of the night frequenting the many saloons. American prospectors were joined by European adventurers, many of whom never found the mother lode but succumbed to tough winters and now lie buried in the Barkerville cemetery.

In May 1862, 53 Royal Engineers sappers under Captain J. M. Grant started construction of the first major road into the interior: the Cariboo Wagon Road, complete with its many milehouses. Miners and road builders subsisted on "cariboo turkey" (bacon) and "cariboo strawberries" (beans). In 1865 the road, with Lillooet as Mile Zero, was completed. Concurrently, other trails, such as the Whatcom and Dewdney trails, opened up the southern interior.

Immigrant settlement of British Columbia had a radical impact on the lives of its aboriginal peoples. Indians had been indispensable partners in the fur trade, but once that was abandoned, the settlers wanted land. Indians succumbed in such large numbers to smallpox and tuberculosis that by 1900 the population of the Northwest Coast had been reduced from 50,000 to 10,000. The famous potlatch feasts, central to the social and economic structures of many Northwest Coast Indian groups, were outlawed by the Canadian government in 1885 in a misguided attempt to assimilate native people into the dominant culture.

Relentless "progress" resulted in the incorporation of Vancouver in 1886 when it was selected as the site for the western terminal of the Canadian Pacific Railway. Prior to that time, economic activity had centred around Hastings Mill on the north shore. Gassy Jack Deighton's saloon on the south shore of Burrard Inlet, situated in a grove of maple trees at today's Water and Carrall streets, became Vancouver's entertainment hub. Gassy Jack, a former river pilot addicted to lengthy monologues, made his saloon the focal point of the settlement of Gastown, subsequently named Granville.

From early days the three main centres of Victoria, Vancouver and New Westminster enjoyed a healthy rivalry. In 1867 the Victoria-based *British Colonist* newspaper pronounced New Westminster "a pimple on the face of creation" and the Fraser River "a stream of liquid mud." The editor of the Vancouver paper *The British Columbian* later retaliated by referring to Victoria as being "located on a frogpond."

When B.C. entered into Confederation in 1871, the understanding was that a railway would connect the B.C. coast with eastern markets. The Canadian Pacific Railway did just this, cutting west from Field through the Rockies, following the Thompson and Fraser rivers to the coast. Settlements opened up all along the line, stepping up the pace of immigration.

By the turn of the century a multicultural mosaic of immigrants was starting to settle the province. Chinese labourers had come in to build the railway. Groups such as Mennonites and Doukhobors, fleeing prejudice and religious persecution, farmed settlements in the Kootenays and beyond. English, Irish and Scottish settlers helped open up interior ranchlands, while Italian and German immigrants gravitated to farming in the fertile river valleys. Many East Indian immigrants worked at logging trades. On the coast, Japanese fishermen pioneered commercial salmon canneries and market gardens, cultivating such productive spots as Mayne Island, where they produced huge tomato crops.

During World War II, when the Sitka spruce forests of the Queen Charlotte Islands supplied material for the light wooden frames of Mosquito bombers, B.C. residents of Japanese descent were interned and their property confiscated. In 1989, the Canadian government formally apologized to Japanese Canadians who had been affected by the government's wartime actions and agreed to compensate these people for some of the financial losses they had suffered.

Since the 1970s, many people from Asia, particularly southeast Asia, have immigrated to B.C., strengthening the province's connections with the other Pacific Rim countries. Today, it is not uncommon at the citizenship court in downtown Vancouver for B.C.'s newest citizens to come from as many as 135 different countries, making for a rich ethnic and racial potpourri where individual cultures are respected and enjoyed.

Native people in B.C., as in the rest of Canada, are currently working actively to sustain their cultures and to win the right to self-determination. Many native groups and individuals have been instrumental in the struggle to save precious wilderness areas of the province, such as the Stein Valley, Meares Island and South Moresby Island. In many parts of B.C., native groups have made land claims due to the government's failure to honour rights entrenched in original treaties or to the absence of treaties covering specific areas. Some of these claims are currently being heard in the courts, while many more have yet to be recognized. The issue of native land claims is the source of much political and legal discussion today.

B.C. is one of 10 Canadian provinces. Its citizens are governed by 4 levels of government: the federal government in Ottawa, the provincial government in Victoria and regional district and municipal governments in different areas of the province.

Economically, forestry provides the highest source of revenue in the province, followed by tourism, fishing and mining. English is the main spoken language, while 6 per cent of the province speaks French—Canada's other official language—as a first language.

HOW TO GET THERE

Main road access to British Columbia is via the Trans-Canada Highway (Highway 1) from the Prairies and central Canada or the Yellowhead Highway (Highway 5) from Edmonton, Alberta. Interstate 5 leads north from Washington State, the Alaska Highway (Highway 97) south from the Yukon.

Visitors coming from the United States may also travel by ferry from either Seattle or Alaska.

Vancouver International Airport services traffic from the rest of Canada, the entire Pacific Rim, Australia, Europe and continental U.S.A. It is also possible to fly into the Calgary and Edmonton airports and from there drive a rented vehicle on to B.C. A popular method of travelling to, and within, the province is by recreational vehicle (RV). The Recreation Vehicle Dealers Association in Langley, B.C., can provide a cross-Canada list of RV rental opportunities. Contact them at 533-4200 or by fax at 533-0795.

FLORA AND FAUNA

Trees and Flowers

Trees dominate the landscape of more than half of British Columbia and rainfall determines distribution of the various species. On the coast thrive red cedar, western hemlock and coastal Douglas fir. In the warmer interior, ponderosa pine and Engelmann spruce mix with interior Douglas fir. Stands of lodgepole pine and spruce are interspersed with deciduous trembling aspen growth in the Cariboo region. Farther north, large trees give way to more stunted species such as willow, birch and black spruce.

Handy books on B.C. trees include *Native Trees of Canada* by R. C. Hosie, *Trees, Shrubs and Flowers To Know in British Columbia* by C. P. Lyons and Randy Stoltmann's *Hiking Guide to the Big Trees of Southwestern B.C.*

Any traveller to the province who is interested in the spectacular summer alpine and subalpine flower showings should pick up the excellent guidebook *Wildflowers of the Canadian Rockies* by George W. Scotter and Halle Flygare. Arranged into categories by colour with good, clear photos, this guide works well in the field. Other useful books include Lewis Clark's six field guides to the wildflowers of the Pacific Northwest. The provincial flower is the Pacific dogwood.

Birds

British Columbia is a bird-watcher's paradise. Over a million birds use the Pacific Flyway for migration routes, including tiny rufous humming-birds that travel north from California every spring to hatch their bumblebee-sized chicks. Snow geese fly from Wrangel Island, in the Russian arctic, south to the Fraser Delta in early November to congregate en masse at the George Reifel Bird Sanctuary. Thirty-four species of raptors alone live in the province, including ospreys and peregrine falcons.

Wayne Campbell's *The Birds of British Columbia: Volume I, parts I and II* has locator maps and precise information on 266 species of water birds, hawks, grouse, owls, hummingbirds and woodpeckers in the province. (Volume II is scheduled for publication in 1992.) Roger Tory Peterson's *Western Birds* is also good, as is the National Geographic Society *Field Guide to Birds of North America*.

Twenty-eight of the species found in B.C. are endangered, threatened or of special concern. Three species—the western grebe, the American white peli-can and the spotted owl—have virtually run out of nesting habitats. B.C. is home to 75 per cent of the world's murrelets, 80 per cent of Cassin's auklets and 90 per cent of Barrow's goldeneye. The highest density of red-throated loons in the world breed on the Queen Charlotte Islands.

One of our favourite species is the blue grouse, the second largest grouse in North America, whose booming mating hoots resound throughout coastal forests from late April to mid-May. During display, the male grouse fans his splendid tail and blood flows to the eye combs, changing them to a kaleido-scope of red, yellow and orange.

Bald eagles, another favourite, sometimes nest as close to urban areas as Vancouver's Stanley Park, building massive homes of moss, sticks and straw up to 3 m (10 ft.) across and 5 or 6 m (16-19 ft.) deep. Great pirates, bald eagles use their 2-m (7-ft.) wingspan most efficiently to prey on other fishing species and loot their catch. The birds mate for life, use the same nest year after year and, when full-grown, can stand as high as 1 m (3 ft.) and weigh up to 6 kg (15 lb.).

An estimated 16,000 to 20,000 adult eagles inhabit B.C. In the southern part of the province, a prime viewing spot for them is the B.C. Ferries route through Active Pass in the Gulf Islands. During the fall months, fish runs such as the Adams River sockeye run also provide ample opportunities for viewing these magnificent birds.

Another interesting species is the ptarmigan, an above-timber-line dweller with white winter plumage and mottled brown feathers in summer. The large black and dark-blue Steller's jay, the provincial bird, is the only jay west of the Rockies with a crest. Gray jays, also known as Canada jays or whiskey jacks, hop around campsites and can be enticed to land on your hand to get a treat.

Sea Life

Sea life in B.C. coastal waters is as prolific as fauna is on land. Whales swim along the shores on annual migration patterns or in the resident pods that permanently inhabit the waters off the B.C. coastline. Eighteen resident pods of black-and-white killer whales (orcas) live in the east-coast waters of Vancouver Island, and Johnstone Strait, which runs between northeast Vancouver Island and the mainland, contains the densest concentration of killer whales anywhere in the world. Robson Bight, just south of Telegraph Cove on Vancouver Island, is the site of unique rubbing beaches, where whales congregate to massage themselves in shallow waters.

On the west coast of the island, Pacific gray whales migrate north from mating and calving lagoons in Baja, California, and Mexico to feeding grounds in Alaska in March and April, passing close to shore. Some spend the summer in B.C. waters.

Occasionally, minke whales are seen feeding on salmon runs alongside the killer whales in Johnstone Strait. Another group of minkes summers in the San Juan Islands off the south coast of Vancouver Island. In recent years, humpback whales have been sighted in the waters of Hecate Strait between the coastal town of Prince Rupert and the northern tip of Vancouver Island.

Harbour seals are common on the west coast, often following spawning salmon upstream to take up residence in interior lakes. Sea otter colonies are making a comeback on the west coast of Vancouver Island, while Steller and California sea lion colonies thrive in such places as Cape Scott Provincial Park on northern Vancouver Island.

Five species of salmon travel Pacific waters, swimming up major B.C. rivers to spawn after 1 to 4 years at sea. In all species, the homing instinct is so strong that mature salmon from hatcheries will attempt to push themselves up the same pipes they were fed through as fingerlings. The biggest salmon caught in B.C. weighed 57 kg (126 lb.). Lingcod and giant halibut also inhabit B.C. waters. Inland lakes and streams contain populations of cutthroat, rainbow and Dolly Varden trout and kokanee salmon. Dedicated fishers enjoy the winter sport of ice fishing. As a rule, "ice-off" on inland lakes occurs by May 1.

Back on shore, shellfish proliferate along the B.C. coastline. The federal government monitors the shoreline for toxic red tides that cause paralytic shellfish poisoning and posts warning signs in affected areas. Do not harvest shellfish from these areas, since the toxin, which inhibits transmission of nerve impulses, can be fatal. Symptoms include tingling lips and tongue, numb extremities and loss of muscle control. Induce vomiting immediately if you suspect one of your group has eaten contaminated shellfish.

Animals

Twenty-five per cent of the world's grizzly bears (*Ursus arctos horribilis*) inhabit British Columbia, in addition to a large population of black bears (*Ursus americanus*). Subspecies of the black bear include the white Kermode bear of the Terrace-Kitimat area and the glacier bear of the far northwest corner of the province. Black bears may weigh up to 250 kg (600 lb.) and are seldom more than 1.5 m (5 ft.) long. Grizzlies can be identified by their larger size (up to 500 kg/1100 lb.), white-tipped hair and distinctive shoulder hump.

Measuring up to 2.4 m (8 ft.) long, a grizzly can outrun a race horse. These bears are currently being intensively studied in the Flathead Valley of southern B.C. The Border Grizzly project has ascertained that grizzlies can gain and lose up to 113 kg (250 lb.) from summer to winter. Their highly developed sense of smell extends for 3.2 km (2 mi.) and females breed only every 3 or 4 years. Cubs weigh 2.2 kg (1 lb.) at birth in the hibernating den, nursing to 4.5 kg (10 lb.) before emerging in the spring. Mainly herbivores, grizzlies also eat salmon, ground squirrel and some carrion.

Grizzly or other bear attacks usually only occur in defence of cubs or in territorial defence of carrion. Since 1900, in all of North America, there have been only 45 documented fatal attacks by grizzlies and 23 by black bears. Bee stings, lightning strikes, falls and drownings account for 97 per cent of park fatalities.

As a rule, bears will avoid people if they can. They are notoriously short-sighted, so the best way to warn them is by making noise, talking, whistling or singing. Many hikers attach "bear bells" to their packs; others find the constant jingling annoying. Be particularly noisy when travelling near a stream bed since a bear may not hear you over the sound of water. Carry a whistle (around your neck, not in your pack). Keep it handy at night.

Watch for fresh tracks, droppings and diggings. Never approach a bear, especially a cub; if it approaches you, always ensure you leave the bear an escape route. Leave your pets at home: a dog can often provoke a bear attack, and, even worse, lead a bear back to its owner!

Food is the main reason bears come into conflict with humans. Do not keep food or items smelling of food—cooking utensils, stove, etc.—in or near your tent. Put food into a strong, waterproof bag and suspend from a tree, preferably between two trees and at least 3.6 m (12 ft.) off the ground. Some campgrounds, particularly in the Rockies, have food poles especially designed to discourage bears and other animals. **Use them.** Do not discard food or bury scraps: either burn garbage thoroughly or carry it with you.

If you spot a bear in the distance, try to make a wide detour. If you are in a close encounter, try to stay calm, either standing still or moving slowly backwards. Flailing arms excite and antagonize bears. Move backwards, preferably towards a tree, undoing the hip belt on your pack. Bears have a critical territorial range of 45 m (150 ft.) so try to get outside this range. This will enable the bear to feel less threatened and it may decide to leave on its own.

A bear may rear up on its hind legs and swing its head from side to side to get a better scent of you. This does not always mean it will attack. Preliminary aggressive behaviour may consist of a series of "whoofs," jaw chomping and a mock charge. If the worst happens and the bear actually charges, drop your hat or jacket to distract it (this can work in elephant charges too!), then get off the trail and "play dead." Drop to the ground on your stomach or curl up into a ball. Clasp your hands behind your neck and stay still (this is easier said than done). Don't drop your pack as it may provide some protection. Usually a bear will retreat immediately after an attack.

In B.C., park rangers monitor grizzly areas for potentially dangerous situations and post warning signs in sensitive areas. Other areas are closed if bears have been particularly active or a sow with cubs has been spotted. Always obey trail closure signs. A few years ago, a Rocky Mountain hiker was fined a substantial amount for ignoring a trail closure sign, then becoming involved in an encounter with a sow and her cub.

Cougars live in B.C., especially on Vancouver Island, but are very rarely seen. Since males and females do not live together, their mutual territories vary in size from 13-65 sq. km (5-25 sq. mi.). Cougars feed on deer, young elk, mice and insects.

Mountainous B.C. is excellent country for bighorn sheep. Rocky Mountain bighorns inhabit the southeast parts of the province, with Dall sheep in the north-central mountains and Stone sheep in Stone Mountain Provincial Park. California bighorns live in the Okanagan, Similkameen and Chilcotin. Unlike antlers, sheep's horns do not shed, and they can weigh, in the case of the Rocky Mountain bighorn, up to 20 kg (44 lb.). They are used as shields, as symbols of rank and for smashing each other during rutting rites.

Mountain goats (*Oreamnos americanus*) are actually more like goat-antelopes, closely related to the chamois of the Alps. The resident population of 20,000 in B.C. are distinguished by their white coats and short black horns, which they do not shed. Look for them particularly in the Nass Valley.

Several species of deer proliferate in the province. Black-tailed deer, the smallest species, lack the characteristic ears and rump patches of mule deer. Rocky Mountain elk, distinguished by a large white rump patch and a mane of

Mountain goats in Cathedral Lake Park. *Photo by Lloyd Twaites*

coarse dark hair, may be spotted in the mountains. A moose, the largest member of the deer family, is easily recognized by its size (bigger and heavier than a horse) and distinctive skin flap or "bell." Moose eat willow, aspen, maple and birch twigs, supplemented by aquatic plants in summer. Woodland caribou range the northern portion of B.C. and are the main species of deer to be spotted in herds.

Another interesting B.C. creature, the hoary marmot, is found in rocky areas of the alpine ridges, living in deep burrows. Marmot coats range from light orange to dark brown, and marmot "sentries" emit a high-pitched whistle to warn other marmots of potential danger. These curious little creatures will often pose nicely on rocks for photos. But don't get too close or they will quickly disappear into a convenient burrow.

Porcupines, in their constant search for salt, have been known to chew on sweaty backpack straps. Since they are nocturnal, be especially careful what you leave out around the camp at night. The normal porcupine diet is vegetarian and includes tree bark, especially pine.

The best time to watch beavers is during their dawn and dusk work hours. Clues to their existence in an area are their distinctive lodges at the edge of a lake or pond and the chewed stumps of trees they leave in their wake. They

Moose spotted north of Prince George. *Photo by Lloyd Twaites*

make a distinctive sound when slapping the water with their fleshy tails.

Shy little pikas, sometimes called rock rabbits, look like small guinea pigs. Very difficult to photograph since they move quickly in and out among rocks, pikas emit a high nasal squeak and seldom leave the safety of their boulder fields. They harvest summer flowers and grasses for their winter food supply, placing them to dry in neat little haystacks on sunny rocks.

An underground plougher, the pocket gopher is hardly ever seen. It packs snow tunnels full of diggings in the winter, and those long ridges of earth above the ground are exposed when spring sun melts the snow.

Mosquitoes and Other Pests

If you travel B.C. in July and August, mosquitoes can be pesky. Their larvae hatch in June and, of the province's 36 mosquito species, only about 4 or 5 can create eggs without blood. Many species, however, rely on birds and large animals for blood supply. In the alpine areas, *Aedes hexodontus* is the species most interested in humans.

Mosquitoes seem to gravitate towards dark colours, damp, and, some claim, people who eat a lot of bananas. Your best defence is to wear repellents containing N-N-diethylmetatoluamide (deet) as the active ingredient. Products containing as little as 50 per cent deet are effective in lab tests for up to 8 hours. By comparison, Avon Skin-So-Soft bath oil, which enjoys a popular reputation as an active bug repellent, lasts for 30 minutes. The practice of "loading" vitamin B supplements prior to an extended trip in the bush does not prevent the bugs biting, but suppresses the immune response, so you won't itch as much. Repellents work with varying degrees of efficiency against blackflies, no-see-ums and horseflies.

Ticks can be a nuisance in areas where herds of large animals live. Again, repellent works well, but if you are bitten always remove the whole creature. Spring and early summer are tick season.

Bees and wasps emerge in summer months, and anyone with an allergy to insect stings should carry their medication with them at all times. Otherwise, haul a little meat tenderizer (active ingredient: MSG!) on your outdoor trips. If you are stung, make a paste of the tenderizer and apply to the affected area; this will draw out the sting and relieve pain. Another handy sting-pain reliever is roll-on deodorant (active ingredient: aluminium chloride). If you are concerned about allergic reactions to insect bites, always carry an Anakit (insect sting emergency kit), available at pharmacies. The kit will deal with symptoms of anaphylactic shock, such as wheezing and restricted breathing. It contains tablets and a preloaded doubleshot syringe.

The only poisonous snake in B.C., the northern Pacific rattler, is found in hot, dry interior climates. Though it is a fairly lethargic species, you can exercise caution in desert territory by wearing boots and gaiters if you are nervous ofbites. Snakebite fatalities in B.C. are extremely rare. If someone is bitten, however, the Poison Control Branch recommends that you do not make an incision. Instead, apply a pressure dressing above the site of the puncture, immobilize the limb and keep it below the level of the heart, then get the person to an emergency medical facility as quickly as possible.

Anti-snakebite serums are hard to come by but several professional guiders in B.C. use Snake Doctor, which we recommend as a kit if you are bitten by poisonous insects or snakes hours away from medical help. Snake Doctor, also used by physicians, hospitals, zoos and snake handlers, can be carried in your pocket or pack and delivers 25V of electric DC current to the bite area. A small gismo resembling a radio, Snake Doctor zaps the venom's toxicity and relieves pain by dispersing protein breakdown. This product is available from J & K Industries, Box 1205, Claremore, Oklahoma 74098 (918-341-6715) for $49.95 U.S.

If you are going to be hiking in the bush, be sure to familiarize yourself with poison ivy, a green plant with tree leaves that turn red in fall. Whitish berries close to the stem also characterize this bush, whose poisonous oil causes inflammation, blisters and itchiness on skin contact. Even the smoke of burning poison ivy is highly irritating to the skin. After contact, wash your clothes and affected areas thoroughly, then use zinc oxide lotion or calamine lotion to reduce discomfort.

Although pets are allowed on trails in provincial and national parks if they are on a leash, they should be left at home whenever possible. They can annoy other hikers, harass wildlife and anger bears that might otherwise avoid you.

PARKS

Both the Canadian federal government and the provincial government of British Columbia have set aside park areas to preserve natural and cultural features and provide recreational opportunities. These areas are designated as follows:

1. World Heritage Sites

The UNESCO World Heritage Convention was created to recognize and preserve the cultural and natural heritage areas of the world, regardless of national boundaries. There are currently 217 World Heritage Sites, 9 of which are in Canada. Two of these are in B.C. They are Anthony Island (Ninstints), at the southern tip of the Queen Charlotte Islands (now part of Gwaii Haanas/ South Moresby National Park Reserve), and the Rocky Mountain parks of British Columbia and Alberta, which include Kootenay and Yoho national parks in B.C. and Banff and Jasper national parks in Alberta.

2. National Parks

These are parks managed by the Canadian federal government through the Canadian Parks Service under the Ministry of Environment. The national parks within B.C. are Yoho, Kootenay, Glacier, Mount Revelstoke, Pacific Rim and, the most recent addition, Gwaii Haanas/South Moresby National Park Reserve. Information on any of these parks can be obtained by contacting the park superintendents in the appropriate area. (Check the "Useful Addresses" section at the back of the book for details.)

3. Provincial Parks

There are approximately 390 provincial parks, recreation areas and wilderness conservancies in B.C. These areas are managed by the provincial government through the Ministry of Parks. Provincial parks are categorized according to the use for which they are intended.

Class A parks are intended to preserve natural or historic features and are for recreational use only. No commercial or industrial use is allowed. Included in this classification are 38 coastal and several inland marine parks. Marine parks provide essential facilities while maintaining natural surroundings; some have mooring buoys, landing floats, campgrounds or picnic facilities.

Class B parks are intended primarily for recreational use, but resource use is permitted if it is considered by the ministry not to be detrimental to natural values.

Class C parks are community parks where no industrial use is allowed.

Recreation areas are tracts of Crown land designated under the Park Act and are really "park reserves" in which mineral evaluation is being undertaken prior to a government decision on park status. No commercial logging is allowed, and these lands may become Class A parks upon completion of the mineral evaluation.

Wilderness conservancy and nature conservancy areas are roadless tracts in which the natural ecological community is preserved. No development of any kind is permitted in these areas.

Another aspect of the provincial park system is the maintenance of the Ecological Reserve Program. An ecological reserve is an area of Crown land, or sometimes donated or leased private land, where the natural ecosystem is preserved for the purposes of scientific study and educational use. Some limited use by hikers, bird watchers, photographers and others is permitted in most of these areas. Other, more delicate areas are closed to public use. The 132 ecological reserves in B.C. cover a total of 157,666 ha (389,597 a.) with approximately one-third of this in marine waters.

Information on any of these provincial areas can be obtained from the Ministry of Parks or regional/district park offices. (See the "Useful Addresses" section at the back of the book for details.)

WHERE TO STAY

Accommodation in B.C. runs the gamut from $5-a-night campground sites to hotel suites costing over $1000. To make your choices, the best resource is the B.C. Ministry of Tourism's annual *Accommodation Guide*, available free from tourist information centres throughout B.C. or by writing to Tourism B.C., 1117 Wharf St., Victoria, B.C. V8W 2Z2.

The guide includes information on hotels, motels, lodges, guest ranches, commercially operated campgrounds and trailer parks in the province. Inclusion in the guide indicates that the accommodation has met the Ministry of Tourism's standards of courtesy, comfort and cleanliness. Each establishment also displays a blue "Approved Accommodation" sign or window decal. A summary of provincial and national park campgrounds is also included at the back of the guide.

There are several regional bed-and-breakfast guides to the province.

Campsites

Provincial parks and recreation areas offer various levels of service depending on their size, the remoteness of their location and other factors. Camping fees at provincial parks run from $5 to $13 a night depending upon site amenities. Reservations cannot be made at provincial park campgrounds; however, most commercial campgrounds do accept them. During the summer months, provincial campsites can fill up by Thursday for the weekend, so always have a contingency plan in case the site you are aiming for proves to be full. Back-country wilderness sites in provincial parks are usually free, although some of the more popular areas now charge a fee. Information on provincial campgrounds can be obtained from the Ministry of Parks or from the regional/district offices listed in the "Useful Addresses" section at the back of the book.

All national park users must pay for a park entry permit. The cost is $20 for an annual permit (good for all national parks), $6 for a 4-day limit at any one park and $3 for a daily permit. Campgrounds charge an additional user fee which varies depending upon amenities and the time of year. Back-country users pay only for the park entry permit. Information on national parks can be obtained from the appropriate park superintendents; see the "Useful Addresses" section at the back of the book for details.

Most parks can be used at any time of the year. The exceptions are those where weather limits access, such as Mount Revelstoke Park. A park's opening and closing dates indicate when park staff are on hand to maintain facilities and provide various services.

Areas designated as Forest Service recreation sites are sometimes areas that the public is already using on a regular basis. In other cases, the Forest Service works with logging companies to maintain attractive sites for recreational use within a forest management area. These sites are usually small—no more than 2-5 ha (5-12 a.)—and simple. Services are generally limited to basic facilities such as pit toilets, fire rings and picnic tables. In some cases, boat ramps are provided. Signs saying "User Maintained" indicate that visitors are expected to carry out their own garbage and help keep the site in good condition. No campsite fees are charged.

Maps and further information on Forest Service campsites can be obtained from the regional Forest Service offices listed in the "Useful Addresses" section at the back of the book.

Alpine Huts and Cabins

In some scenic back-country areas, huts and cabins are maintained by the provincial and federal parks departments or by such groups as the Alpine Club of Canada (ACC). They range from cozy and comfortable wood-heated cabins with cookstoves, fully equipped kitchens and padded sleeping platforms to unheated aluminum boxes perched on the edge of a cliff. But the price is right—usually between $6 and $15 a night per person—and even a tin box is a welcome haven in a storm.

Some of the more popular huts, such as the Slocan Chief Cabin in Kokanee Glacier Provincial Park and the Naiset Cabins in Mount Assiniboine Provincial Park, require advance reservations, especially in winter. The Alpine Club's Stanley Mitchell Hut in Yoho National Park and the Elizabeth Parker Hut at Lake O'Hara are also very popular.

Most alpine huts can be booked through Parks Canada, the B.C. Ministry of Parks or the Alpine Club of Canada, based in Banff. ACC huts are usually locked and require a key, which is available to members. Membership fees for 1991 are $45 for a single person, $78 for a couple and $23 for juniors.

Logging Road Travel

Logging operations produce mixed benefits. They provide access to areas otherwise accessible only via a several-day bushwhack. But clear cuts remain areas of tangled devastation that create ugly scars on the mountainside and make hiking difficult since they obscure existing trails.

If you plan to travel on logging roads, it is always wise to check first with the B.C. Forest Service or with the local logging company to find out which areas are being actively logged and where logging trucks might be expected. These immense, heavily laden vehicles are perhaps the most serious hazard to exploring B.C.'s back roads. A truck coming downhill with a 27,000-kg (30-ton) load of logs has little manoeuvrability and no way of stopping suddenly. A logging truck always has right of way. When you see one approaching, get to a turnout and let it by. Don't stop on the road to sightsee or take photos. If you must stop, park well off the road and away from corners. Watch for "sweepers"—extralong logs, up to 21 m (70 ft.), that overhang the back of the truck by as much as 6 m (20 ft.). On a steep road with tight curves, these logs can literally sweep a car over the edge. It is because of the hazard posed by sweepers that signs will occasionally direct you to drive on the left-hand side of the road.

While travelling logging roads, drive with your lights on and always obey the speed limit and road signs. Don't rely on your CB radio. It does not always use the same frequency as logging truck radios, and can give you a false sense of security. Stay alert and always be ready to take evasive action. Remember, you will never win in a confrontation with a logging truck.

Visiting Native Land

Several trips described in our guide, such as the Stein Valley and the west coast of Vancouver Island, include passage through or time spent near native Indian land. We cannot emphasize too strongly how important it is that visitors to land belonging to native people ask for permission in all instances, and treat carvings, house timbers, skeletal remains, petroglyphs and all other signs of native Indian habitation with the respect due to very old cultures that have survived in the face of incredible obstacles. Indian reserves are private property and are clearly marked on federal and provincial topographical maps.

Many of the interesting abandoned village sites are on reserve property. Before visiting any of these sites, permission should be requested from the local band council by phone or letter. A better alternative is to apply personally at the band council office. Addresses for all of the 196 bands in B.C. can be obtained from Legal & Statutory Requirements, Lands, Revenues & Trusts, Suite 300, 1550 Alberni St., Vancouver, B.C., V6G 3C5 (666-5132).

OUTDOOR ACTIVITIES

Being Prepared

Wilderness travel requires that you plan your trip carefully. Study the area you plan to visit to get an understanding of the terrain and climate. Make sure that your equipment is adequate for the trip and always prepare yourself for the worst possible weather conditions. Finally, let someone else know of your plans: where you will be starting from, how many days you will be gone and your approximate route. Water, food and a change of clothing should be kept in the car for use on your return.

Even on a day trip, a number of essential items should be carried:
Water bottle: 1-2 l (32-64 oz.) size
Extra clothing or space blanket: enough to spend a night out
Extra food: high-energy stuff like dried fruit, nuts and chocolate
Swiss Army knife (or similar model)
Basic first aid and emergency kit, containing a whistle, nylon cord, space blanket or emergency shelter such as a tube tarp, moleskin, Band-Aids, bandages, antiseptic cream and aspirin

Wading a stream in Golden Ears Park. *Photo by Lloyd Twaites*

Sunglasses for both summer and winter trips
Fire starter: a piece of candle or some chemical fuel for starting fires with wet wood
Matches in a waterproof container (an empty film canister works well)
Flashlight with extra bulb and batteries
Map: know how to read it
Compass: know how to use it
    For longer trips or even day trips into more rugged country, the first aid and emergency survival kit should be more comprehensive.

Suggested Equipment

Clothing
Boots: Light- or medium-weight hiking boots are needed for most back-country travel. Boots that provide ankle support and have lug soles for traction on rocky or slippery ground are best. Waterproof the seams and leather, and break them in before you go on a long trip. Running shoes are suitable only for

day hiking on well-maintained, dry trails. A pair of gaiters can protect your feet and keep you drier in wet or muddy areas. In winter, they keep the snow out of your boots.

If your route will take you through shallow creeks, you may wish to take along a pair of old sneakers. They dry out quickly in front of a campfire and make comfortable camp slippers, too.

Socks: Most people prefer to wear two pairs: a thin, inner sock of polypropylene or light wool and a thicker, wool outer sock.

Long Underwear: For activities such as cross-country skiing or kayaking in cold waters, polypropylene is best; it's light, yet keeps you warm. For sleeping in tents in the mountains, woollen long johns and top save you from shivering in your sleeping bag.

Pants: Long, loose-fitting pants made of synthetic blends are best. They breathe and dry quickly. Never wear jeans—they are heavy when wet, chafe your skin and can contribute to hypothermia. Shorts are great in summer. It's a good idea to carry along a pair of wind or rain pants at all times. The kind with zippers up the side work best, as they can be slipped on over your boots.

Shirts: T-shirts are standard. Long-sleeved cotton or flannel shirts are useful in buggy areas, and, combined with a light sweater, will provide sufficient layers to add or take off as temperature dictates. Any outdoor travel in B.C. requires layering of your clothing to meet temperature fluctuations.

Jackets: A wind- and rain-proof jacket is essential on almost any trip. Gore-Tex jackets are waterproof yet breathable, but they are more expensive than the basic, coated nylon wet-weather gear. Make sure your jacket has a hood. Some people prefer ponchos, but these don't work well in windy areas—unless you are into hang-gliding! A down or synthetic vest or jacket will be needed in the mountains. The nights can get chilly, even in summer.

Gloves: A pair of mitts or gloves is useful, especially high in the mountains, even in summer. And they are obviously essential in winter anywhere in the province.

Hat: A wool toque. Up to 60 per cent of body heat is lost through your head, so putting on a hat when your feet are cold makes sense. Wear your toque at night to keep you warm while sleeping. In summer, a cotton hat with brim may be needed to protect you from the sun.

Shelter

Tent: A lightweight model with a good rain fly and bug-proof netting is ideal.

Sleeping bag: Down or synthetic? It is hard to choose, especially since today's bags are similar in quality and weight. Price will often be the determining factor. However, if you plan to be travelling on water, a synthetic bag is probably best as it retains some of its insulating property even when damp;

down just goes lumpy and provides no insulation at all. Whichever type you have, carry it in a heavy-duty plastic garbage bag that has been placed inside the stuff bag.

Sleeping pad: The cheapest option is a closed-foam pad like Ensolite. The more expensive Therm-a-Rest pad is a luxury mattress consisting of an inflatable mat with a foam pad inside.

Packs

The kind of pack you choose—internal or external frame—is usually a matter of personal preference. Internal frame packs provide more stability during activities such as cross-country skiing and climbing. We prefer an external frame pack in summer as it allows some air circulation between your sweaty back and the pack. To be sure that your belongings stay dry, it is also a good idea to have a waterproof pack cover tucked into a pocket ready for use.

Cooking

Firewood, particularly in alpine areas, can be in short supply, and fires are becoming less acceptable since they scar the area. A lightweight, reliable backpacking stove is the best way to protect the environment. Two cooking pots, a pot holder, a spare fuel container, a nylon pad or J cloth, biodegradable soap and a cup, bowl and spoon are the other necessary items.

Other Items (some more essential than others):

Insect repellent

Toilet paper

Sunscreen

Lip protection cream

Fishing gear: a lightweight collapsible rod and reel is best

Camera and film

Binoculars: it's a good idea to use a brightly coloured strap so that they are easy to spot if left on the ground

Book (for when you are tent-bound due to bad weather)

Notebook and pencil

Rope for hanging up food or crossing strong creeks

Personal toilet articles: toothbrush and toothpaste, dental floss, biodegradable soap, comb, etc.

It is a good idea to line the inside of your pack with a heavy-duty plastic garbage bag to keep things dry. We also separate items into individual plastic bags; it not only keeps them dry but makes them easier to locate. We always have a complete change of clothing ready in the car for when we return from a trip. Even a grubby, showerless body feels better in clean, dry clothes after a few days in the bush.

Provisions

Outdoor cooking doesn't have to be a monotonous fare of bland-tasting freeze-dried food. Many campers have marvelled at what professional outfitters are able to produce in the bush—cheesecakes and fresh baking spring to mind—but we are all under the same constraints, professional travellers or not. We deal with limited carrying capacity, lack of cooling facilities and a small range of cooking equipment. But with a little imagination and a certain amount of planning, there is no reason why you can't whip up a pineapple upside-down cake or apple pie on your next safari into the outback.

Breakfasts basically fall into two categories: cold or hot, fast starts or slow starts. Granola provides quick, easy morning fuel, while pancakes are good when you are not in a hurry to start your day. If you like meat for breakfast, spiced sausage makes a fine change from the high fatty content of canned bacon, although neither is a good idea to use in bear country.

Eggs will last up to a month as long as they are not sitting in the sun; if you are kayaking, your craft can act as a cooler for these and other perishables. The key to making meals interesting is to take along little extras that you can toss in as treats—dried apples or apricots, for example. And on hiking trips in B.C. you will invariably have access to many berries. Huckleberries make a great topping for cheesecakes. Take plenty of powdered milk; all you have to add is water. We also like to brew up mint tea from wild mint.

Rehydration is the key to making some really imaginative food on over-night treks. Take along dried food and then just add water. Many a fine dessert has been made using rehydrated apples and plenty of cinnamon. And double-bag everything. For extended trips, buy rolls of heavy-duty plastic bags. Baby-bottle bags are useful for bagging small amounts of spices, dried herbs, etc.

Professional guides have found that herbal teas are good fluids to take on safari, and we like them too. Many people develop sores after protracted drinking of powdered fruit juices, which can also cause diarrhea. Frozen orange juice will last 10 days in its container and, while heavy for hiking, it is great for camping.

Remember that in hot weather your butter or margarine will likely turn to liquid during the day, so we tend to use mayonnaise in a tube as a spreader.

Make up your own "goodie bags" for that time in between breakfast and lunch. Dried fruits, wrapped candies and Smarties (in cold climates) are good possibilities, and so are nuts, although they can become stale on long treks. Fruit roll-ups are fine if the weather is not too hot.

Fruit and vegetables are ideal for lunch on the early days of your trip, especially if you are kayaking. Otherwise, have on hand a selection of mixes such as pilafs, couscous, soups (Mayacamas does a good range with no MSG), jams, salamis, crackers and peanut butter. Once again, it's the extras that will make the difference. Pack in some pickles, a tube of mustard, some garlic, a variety of spices, a tube of anchovy paste or a small can of pink razor clams.

For supper, it is handy to premix food and have it ready to use. If you have access to a food drier, you can make stews, chilis and fruit leathers in advance and then rehydrate them on the trail. No-bake cheesecake mixes are delicious; just check the package beforehand to make sure that the mix you choose doesn't require whipping. Popcorn is easy to pop up on the trail, and Jell-O makes a nice hot syrup. If you take along a bottle of liqueur, you can have a thimbleful each night around the campfire. And don't forget the marshmallows!

Put some thought into the containers you take on your trip, since some plastics are easily tainted. Most good outfitting stores stock Nalgene, a line of plastic containers that don't absorb any tastes or smells. If you are buying a screw-top container, be sure to choose one with lots of screws to hold the top down. The plastic tubes with screw tops are really great for things like margarine, peanut butter and jam. Tape down the tops of other problem foods like pancake syrup and oil. And remember that you can always improvise. If those ginger snaps you'd planned for tea crumble, just throw them on top of a dessert. Enjoy!

A personal bible for menu planning on long trips is *The Well-Fed Backpacker* by June Fleming. It contains a large variety of one-pot meal ideas as well as tips on packaging and preparation. Another useful book to consult before a trip into the woods is John G. Ragsdale's *Camper's Guide to Outdoor Cooking*. It includes 200 easy recipes and interesting tips such as how to boil water in a paper cup or bake a potato wrapped in mud.

Wilderness Photography

The amount of camera equipment you can carry on a trip depends on how much space you have and how much other equipment you need to carry. If weight is not a major factor, opt for one SLR (single lens reflex) body with 4 lenses: a 24mm wide-angle lens; a 35mm lens (which many photographers prefer over the standard 50mm because it offers slightly wider angle coverage); a 105mm micro lens (this versatile telephoto lens allows you to take close-ups without extension tubes), and a 180mm telephoto lens, which provides a 3x magnification over a 50mm. You might also want to carry a tabletop tripod, a small flash, a polarizing filter (to increase colour saturation and reduce reflections) and a spare set of batteries. A skylight filter protects the front element of your lens, reducing the blue from UV (ultraviolet) rays, and is particularly useful in shade and at high altitudes.

If weight *is* a factor, you can still get superb results using a compact automatic focus camera. Some contain a built-in flash, others a zoom lens (usually 35mm to 70mm) with close-up capability. Some are also weatherproof. These cameras are ideal for carrying on ski trips and kayaking or mountaintop expeditions.

Store your camera equipment in resealable plastic freezer bags to protect it from moisture. In cold weather, try to keep the equipment at ambient temperature, avoiding drastic temperature changes. Condensation will occur if you take the equipment from a very cold environment into a warm environment, so leave it in the plastic bag and allow it to warm up slowly. To prevent your hands from freezing onto the metal camera body, wear thin gloves that allow good dexterity. In a wet environment like the Queen Charlottes, use a powerful flash and shield your camera with plastic garbage bags while photographing.

Dust and wet are the enemies of outdoor photography, so be sure to clean the camera frequently. If you are unlucky enough to drop your camera overboard, as we did on one canoe trip, bear in mind that rust is the major enemy when this happens. Our camera was ruined. However, when a wildlife photographer friend of ours dropped his Hasselblad into a river, he fished it out and immediately immersed it in a bucket of water. Still in water, the camera was flown to the Hasselblad laboratories in West Germany where it was restored to mint condition. If he had attempted to dry out the camera himself, rust would have set in.

In the bush, look for a solid platform, such as a tree branch, a stump, a rock or even a backpack, on which to rest the camera rather than attempting to handhold at long shutter speeds.

If you shoot slide film and hope one day for publication, always use ASA (ISO) 50 or 64 film. Slide film provides finer grain and better colour saturation. While it is also available in ASA 100, 200, 400 and up, remember that with higher film speeds the grain pattern increases and colour saturation is reduced. Print film rated at ASA 100 and 200 is starting to rival the image quality of slower slide film.

You can buy film on sale and store it in your deep-freeze to retard the expiry date. Allow it to thaw in the canisters before using. As a general rule, the best times for outdoor photography are usually before 10:00 A.M. and after 3:00 P.M. In low-light situations such as woods, remember that you can use your flash to provide some light, even during daylight hours.

Try to store your film in a cool, dry place. Don't leave it in hot places like a car's dashboard or glove compartment since heat will cause colour shifts and may even melt the film.

Maps

"The map," wrote veteran travel writer Paul Theroux in *Sunrise with Seamonsters*, "is the oldest means of information storage, and can present the most subtle facts with great clarity.... A map can do many things, but I think its chief use is in lessening our fear of foreign parts and helping us anticipate the problems of dislocation. Maps give the world coherence." A good map, Mr. Theroux concludes, is better than a guidebook.

B.C. explorers can obtain provincial and individual park maps from MAPS BC, Surveys and Mapping Branch, Parliament Buildings, Victoria, B.C., V8V 1X5 (387-1441). Tourism B.C. offices provide general provincial maps and travel guides free of charge. The Canada Map office in Ottawa sells the federal National Topographic (NTS) maps (1:50,000 scale). This office will provide an NTS map index as well as a list of map distributors in B.C. The addresses of both the Ottawa office and the main map distributors in B.C. can be found in the "Useful Addresses" section at the back of the book. Sporting goods and outdoor equipment stores also often have a supply of NTS maps of local areas on hand.

The most useful and detailed road maps to the province are put out by the B.C. Automobile Association. Members of B.C.A.A. and affiliated automobile associations are entitled to free travel information, maps and route-planning kits as well as emergency road service. Membership costs $47 a year for renewal, $64 for new members. Information can be obtained from local B.C.A.A. offices or from the head office at 999 West Broadway, Vancouver, B.C., V5Z 1K5 (732-3911).

The Ministry of Parks publishes very good brochures on many of the provincial parks. These brochures may be obtained from local tourism centres and regional and district parks offices listed in the "Useful Addresses" section at the back of the book. B.C. Forest Service Recreation Site maps and forestry company maps can also be obtained from the addresses given in this section.

Marine charts, tide tables and boating guides are published by the Canadian Hydrographic Service. They can be obtained from most marine supply stores or by writing to Canadian Hydrographic Service, Department of Fisheries and Oceans, Institute of Ocean Sciences, 9860 West Saanich Road, Box 6000, Sidney, B.C., V8L 4B2 (356-6358).

The Outdoor Recreation Council of B.C. publishes an excellent series of maps and is also a centre for information on any number of recreational activities. Many provincial outdoor recreation groups maintain offices at the council, so it is a good central place to go for information on kayaking, skiing, camping, nature study or back-roads travel. Contact them at 1367 West Broadway, Vancouver, B.C., V6H 4A9 (737-3000).

Hypothermia/Hyperthermia

Hypothermia is a lowering of the body core temperature below the normal 37.4° C (98.6° F). A drop of only 5 degrees is very serious. Hypothermia—also known as exposure—most commonly occurs in wet and/or windy conditions, often in combination with fatigue. Most accidents involving hypothermia occur when the outdoor temperature is between -1° C and 10° C (30°-50° F).

The first symptom of hypothermia is shivering. Don't decide that you can keep warm by moving on without stopping to put on extra clothes or rain gear.

If you start to shiver, stop at once, put on warmer gear and have a high-energy snack.

A person in the later stages of hypothermia is often not capable of recognizing the symptoms. Her speech will be slurred or incoherent, and she will stumble around, unable to think clearly. She may often deny that she needs help, so it will be up to her companions to figure out what is happening and take steps to warm her. Get the person into warm, dry clothes, and give her a sweetened hot drink (not alcohol) and some high-energy food. If possible, build a fire to warm her. If her condition is serious, put her in a sleeping bag with another person. In general, "believe the symptoms, not the victim."

To prevent hypothermia, stay dry. Keep your head covered and warm, and eat frequent high-energy snacks. Boaters should always wear approved life jackets. They should also be aware of improved survival equipment such as the UVIC Thermofloat jacket, which provides extra buoyancy and helps retain body heat, or the one-piece UVIC survival suit. A boater accidentally dumped overboard can survive only a short time in the extremely cold waters of B.C.'s lakes or the ocean. Survival time varies depending upon the temperature of the water; in the summer, with an ocean temperature of approximately $10°$ C ($50°$ F), the survival time averages between 2 and 3 hours.

Hyperthermia, the opposite of hypothermia, is the raising of the normal body temperature. It can occur at any altitude in hot, dry weather but is more common at high altitudes, where the air is drier and the sun hotter. Loss of fluids and salt due to excessive sweating can bring on hyperthermia. The symptoms are dizziness, headache, inability to sweat, muscle cramps and high body temperature. The affected person should be taken to a shady spot, cooled with water or snow and given a cold, slightly salted drink. We recommend drinking lots of fluids, even when not particularly thirsty, to prevent this type of dehydration.

Frostbite

Frostbite usually occurs in the extremities of the body: fingers, toes, nose and ears. As the body gets cold, it shuts off the blood supply to these areas, and they freeze. The symptoms of frostbite are numbness and pale, waxy-looking skin.

For superficial frostbite, warm the affected area with body heat. Put your hands under your armpits, between your thighs or on your bare stomach. For feet, remove your boots and warm your feet in your hands. A better method is to place your bare feet in someone else's armpits, between their thighs or on their bare stomach—what else are friends for! Hold warm hands over affected areas on the face. Never rub the frozen area, as rubbing damages the skin and can cause infection.

When frostbite is severe, do not attempt to rewarm the frozen area since it will be extremely painful for the victim and further damage could be done if the area is later refrozen. Get a person with severe frostbite to a hospital as quickly as possible.

Drinking Water

That clear, bubbling mountain stream may not be as good to drink as it looks. It is an unfortunate fact that, with an increasing number of people using the back country, the incidence of contaminated water has multiplied.

A relatively new menace to back-country users—*Giardia lamblia*—is an intestinal parasite that causes giardiasis or "beaver fever." Common throughout the western United States, it is now infecting the back country areas of B.C.

Infection by this parasite causes diarrhea, cramps, bloating, weight loss and nasty burps. In severe cases, vomiting and dehydration may cause serious problems. The acute stage of the disease often does not last long—although it may seem like forever to the victim—but it may recur periodically for months until treated correctly. Many people who contact giardiasis do not have any symptoms at all, but they carry and spread the disease through poor hygiene. Dogs and beavers are also to blame for spreading the disease. Once the condition has been diagnosed, there are several effective drugs that will provide immediate relief.

Proper water treatment will kill the giardia bugs as well as other little microbes that are up to no good. The question of when and how to treat is a difficult one. Any water coming directly from a snow field or found in a relatively untravelled area above the tree line is probably fine to drink. However, to be really safe, all water should be treated. There are several ways to do this.

The first method of treatment is to boil water for at least 10 minutes. This kills all bacteria, viruses and parasites. However, this method is only practical when you are preparing a meal. It is not very convenient when you need additional water during the day, and it also uses fuel.

The second method, one commonly used by hikers, is to add chlorine, usually in the form of Halazone tablets, to the water. This is not effective in the case of badly polluted water, and is useless against amoebic cysts and certain viruses. While better than nothing, this method is not recommended.

The third method is to use iodine. There are several ways to do this. One is to add 8 drops of a 2 per cent tincture of iodine solution to 1 l (32 oz.) of water, stir and wait 10 minutes. If the water is cloudy to begin with, then twice the amount of iodine should be used. We find a plastic dropper bottle is the most convenient way to carry the iodine. The main drawback to this method is that the water has a noticeable taste.

You can also use tetraglycine hydroperiodide pills, also called iodine water purification tablets. Add one tablet to 1 l (32 oz.) of water, let it dissolve, stir the water and then leave it for 10 minutes before use. The main drawback with these pills is that they lose their effectiveness when exposed to air.

The best, cheapest and easiest method of using iodine is outlined by Frederick Kahn and Barbara Visscher in the May 1975 issue of *The Western Journal of Medicine*. A 30-cc clear glass medicine bottle with a hard plastic cap is required. Add 5 to 7 grams of crystal iodine in chunk form; most pharmacies will be able to provide this for a small cost. This amount will treat 500 1 (528 qt.) of water. To use it, fill the bottle with water, shake for a minute or two and then let the crystals settle to the bottom. A portion of the solution can then be added to your water bottle to purify the water in it.

The amount of solution to be added to 1 1 (32 oz.) of water depends on the temperature of the water. Use 20 cc to purify 1 1 (32 oz.) of water at 3° C (37° F), 15 cc for water at 20° C (68° F) and 10 cc for water at 40° C (104° F). The standard medicine bottle cap, which holds 2.5 cc, can be used as a measure. The water will be ready to drink in 20 minutes. If the water is heavily polluted, wait 40 minutes or double the amount of iodine solution added. Although this method has the least effect on the taste of the water, those who object to the lingering iodine flavour may wish to add some flavoured juice crystals.

Commercial water filters, such as Katadyne, First Need and Timberline, are also available through some outdoor stores.

Back-country users should also do their bit to prevent the spread of disease by selecting toilet sites well away from any water sources.

Campfires

Because forests are B.C.'s greatest natural assets and the mainstay of the economy, protecting them from fires is crucial.

Spells of hot, dry weather exacerbate forest fire conditions and, on average, firefighters in the province combat 3000 fires every year. At such times, the Ministry of Forests may impose restrictions on travel and the lighting of campfires in forested areas. If no such restrictions apply, a campfire may be lit providing that it is not started within 3 m (10 ft.) of any log, stump, dead snag or tree, within 15 m (50 ft.) of any flammable building or debris, or when strong winds are blowing.

To make a campfire, remove all leaves, twigs and flammable material from the fire site, making sure that the area has been cleared down to the mineral soil and extends at least 1 m (3 ft.) around the fire.

Always have a shovel and pail of water on hand, and attend to the fire at all times, completely extinguishing all embers on departure. When the fire appears to be out, we always doublecheck by sifting the ashes through our fingers. Try to be as discreet as possible about campfires. We try to avoid making them unless absolutely necessary, since they do leave unsightly scars that are difficult to hide.

Should you spot a forest fire, dial "O" and ask for Zenith 5555, the free province-wide forest fire emergency telephone number. The B.C. Forest Service has been fighting forest fires for more than seventy years and aims to bring every forest fire under control within 24 hours of its discovery. Using a combination of ground and helicopter-borne forces, they manage to accomplish their objective in 86 per cent of wildfires.

Camping Tips

Camping mottos in B.C. are "Take only photographs, leave only footprints" (on land), "Take only photographs, leave only bubbles" (underwater) and "Pack it in, pack it out." Essentially, they mean the same thing—try not to leave any evidence of your presence. Each group of travellers should experience the wilderness untouched by others' leftovers. Carry a garbage bag with you to collect your rubbish.

Burn only paper; plastic emits dangerous fumes and aluminium foil does not burn completely. Don't bury your garbage—animals have better noses than we do, and will dig it up and strew it all over the place. Remember to hang up your garbage bag with the food bags at night in bear country. A bear can't tell the difference between dried-up leftovers and your gourmet beef stew for tomorrow's supper. Pack out banana skins and orange peels, since they are not instantly degradable.

Avoid polluting water sources and be considerate of others over sanitation matters. A lightweight plastic trowel will enable you to dig a cat-hole, 15-20 cm (6-8 in.) deep, for human waste. Toilet paper, preferably white, should be burned; keep a lighter or matches with the roll and ignite the paper before filling in the hole. In very dry conditions, bury the toilet paper rather than risk starting a forest fire. Locate your cat-hole several hundred metres (250 yards) from any water source. Carry a pot of water away from the lake or stream for the washing of pots, bodies and clothes. Use biodegradable soap, since it is a little easier on the environment. Don't throw leftovers into a stream; they decompose slowly and the next camper may not enjoy looking at your old macaroni shells.

When walking in alpine areas, stay on established trails. Alpine plants grow slowly and are easily disturbed, especially when the ground is wet. If you do have to walk off trail, avoid walking in single file, as this causes more damage to plants by creating a path. When on a switchback trail, resist the temptation to cut the corners. This leads to bank erosion and, eventually, to trail erosion.

Keep groups small. There is less impact on the wilderness this way, and less chance of leaving someone straggling behind.

Hiking

British Columbia's hiking opportunities are limitless and varied. Whether you are travelling on relatively new provincial or national parks trails, or historic ones like the Chilkoot, the Alexander Mackenzie "Grease" and the West Coast trails, the landscape begs superlatives, delivering pristine blue lakes, snow-covered mountains, active glaciers and wild, tumbling rivers. Many hiking guides cover specific parts of the province, and references to these can be found in the appropriate chapters of this book.

Trails vary in quality from rough routes, marked with flagging tape, to well-graded pathways. In grasslands and above tree line, cairns, posts or orange paint on rocks often mark the route. Most hiking trails should be considered wilderness areas, and hikers should have adequate equipment and experience to be self-sufficient. Even on a day trip, always be prepared for a change of weather. It is a good idea to carry the appropriate topographic maps and to check your position every so often.

If you prefer to join a group, there are several well-established companies who offer hiking trips of varying lengths to a variety of destinations in the province: some well known, others well kept secrets.

Tourism B.C. and the Outdoor Recreational Council's annual "Adventure Travel" brochure highlights some of the best hiking possibilities in the province. A copy can be obtained from Tourism B.C. (see "Useful Addresses" section at the back of the book for details). Maggie Paquet's *Parks of British Columbia and the Yukon* is also a good general reference.

Whether choosing a short day hike in local mountains or a strenuous back-packing trip, research the route, leave a copy of your plans with a responsible person and then head out. You will be rewarded with outstanding scenery, abundant wildlife and, above all, a marvellous sense of peace and solitude.

For information on hiking clubs, backpacking and wilderness survival courses, contact either the Outdoor Recreation Council of B.C. or the Federation of Mountain Clubs of B.C. at 1367 West Broadway, Vancouver, B.C., V6H 4A9 (737-3058).

Canoeing/Kayaking

It is widely recognized that B.C. offers some of the finest paddling in the world—for the beginner setting out across a placid, protected lake, for the fine-tuned athlete willing to tackle one of the heart-stopping challenges presented by the province's more remote and demanding white-water rivers, and for the seasoned wilderness camper, equipped with canoe or touring kayak, looking for secluded beaches and coves. As a sport, paddling is rapidly gaining devotees. At last count, there were 50,000 participants in the province.

During the past ten years, developments in the design and manufacture of items specific to kayaking and canoeing have made life much easier for paddlers. Gone are the days when the only kayaks available were homemade, basement-built fibreglass boats weighing 18 kg (40 lb.) or more. Long gone is the time when just one or two designs were available through clubs, designs

Kayaking on the Chilliwack River. *Photo by Michael Mong*

that were used both for white-water competition and for touring. Now the choice of equipment is awesome and has grown to include touring wheels, high-tech life jackets, safety helmets actually designed for kayaking, a variety of paddles, and myriad other bells and whistles.

Clothing and equipment choices should be made from both a comfort and a safety standpoint. Most of B.C.'s waters are directly glacier-fed and even the ocean—despite warming currents—is basically cold. Dress comfortably, sensibly and with the unexpected in mind! Your old T-shirts, running shoes, long underwear and shorts will generally be fine for what can be a very wet sport. The only essential piece of gear is a life jacket.

You should always carry a bailer, a spare paddle, and bow and stern lines. Canoeists may also appreciate knee pads. Get to know your canoe or kayak. Kayakers should try to master the Eskimo roll, and both canoeists and kayakers should practice deep-water rescue techniques. For detailed discussions on preparation, equipment and routes, refer to the popular *Sea Kayaking Canada's West Coast* by John Ince and Hedi Kottner or to the three books by Betty Pratt-Johnson on white-water trips in various areas of the province: *Whitewater Trips for Kayakers, Canoeists and Rafters on Vancouver Island, Whitewa-*

ter Trips for Kayakers, Canoeists and Rafters in British Columbia and *White-water Trips and Hot Springs, West and East Kootenays.* An excellent reference guide for canoeists is Richard Thomas Wright's *Canoe Routes British Columbia*, unfortunately no longer in print, but worth checking for at second-hand bookstores and local libraries.

On most canoe or kayak trips, weight is no object. So eat well! For a long trip, freeze-dried ingredients may be a necessity, but it is also possible to eat fresh avocados and alfalfa sprouts in a salad at the end of a 3-week ocean kayak trip. Be creative with your food—the rewards are worth the planning. There is nothing magic about baking fresh muffins and cinnamon buns over a one-burner backpacking stove.

Last, but not least, it pays to know where you're going. A few dollars spent on a map or chart can make the difference between mental comfort and extreme anxiety. In order to save money, some friends of ours decided not to include one map that covered a very small portion of the white-water river they were travelling. As a result, they completely lost track of where they were in relation to the Grade 4 rapids they knew were somewhere ahead! They survived, but not without a few anxious moments.

Marine charts and tide tables can be obtained from Canadian Hydrographic Services or from marine supply stores. Topographical maps can be obtained from MAPS BC, the Canada Map office or local sporting goods stores. Charts should be protected from the water, either by carrying them in a waterproof plastic pouch or by coating them with liquid plastic or clear plastic shelf covering.

One of the immense joys of paddling anywhere in B.C. is the possibility of spotting wildlife. This can be harbour seals in English Bay in the heart of Vancouver, dozens of bald eagles a day in the Queen Charlotte Islands, orcas and gray whales off Vancouver Island, beavers on the Chilcotin River, salmon spawning on the major river systems, migrating birds, deer wandering through campsites—we've seen them all and more besides! The area does not have to be remote for wildlife spotting, but if you do travel for remoteness, you also gain solitude—the solitude of a natural silence broken only by the sound of waves, wind and wildlife.

There is an international standard for classifying the difficulty of rivers and rapids for kayaks and canoes. The following is taken from the safety brochure published by the Outdoor Recreation Council of B.C.:

Grade 1: Suitable for novices in kayaks and decked canoes. Easy. Waves small and regular; passages clear; occasional sand banks and artificial difficulties like bridge piers.

Grade 2: Suitable for intermediate paddlers in kayaks and decked canoes. Quite easy. Rapids of medium difficulty; passages clear and wide. Occasional boulders in stream.

Grade 3: Suitable for experienced paddlers in kayaks and decked canoes. Medium difficulty. Waves numerous, high and irregular. Rocks and narrow (clear) passages. Considerable experience in manoeuvring required. Advance scouting usually needed. Kayaks must be equipped with spray covers.

Grade 4: Suitable for experts in kayaks and decked canoes. Difficult. Long rapids, powerful irregular waves; dangerous rocks, boiling eddies; passages difficult to reconnoitre; advance scouting mandatory; powerful and precise manoeuvring required. Spray decks mandatory.

Grade 5: Suitable for expert paddlers only in kayaks and decked canoes with specific white-water training under expert leadership. Very difficult. Extremely demanding long and very violent rapids, following each other almost without interruption. River bed extremely obstructed; big drops; very steep gradient; advance scouting mandatory and usually difficult due to nature of terrain.

Grade 6: Suitable for teams of expert paddlers only in kayaks and decked canoes at favourable water levels and only after careful study with fully trained and experienced rescue team in position. Extraordinarily difficult. The difficulties of Grade 5 carried to extremes. Nearly impossible and very dangerous.

A wealth of options awaits the adventurous. Do your research, plan carefully, take the necessary instruction to fine-tune your skills, pick your companions and begin adventuring in B.C.—by kayak or canoe.

For further information on courses, kayak or canoe routes and clubs, contact the Recreation Canoeing Association of B.C., the Whitewater Canoeing Association of B.C. or the Sea Kayaking Association of B.C., all at 1367 West Broadway, Vancouver, B.C., V6H 4A9 (737-3058).

Rafting

Many wild rivers can provide exciting white-water rafting experiences. The most popular rivers for this activity in British Columbia include the Thompson, the Fraser, the Chilko, the Chilcotin and the Kootenay rivers. Several well-established companies offer safe yet exhilarating rides on these rivers. Trips range in length from 1 to 10 days. The rafting company will provide you with the necessary safety gear, including a mandatory life jacket.

After a series of river rafting fatalities in B.C. during 1988, an investigative commission recommended stringent safety precautions. Now all operators have to carry a provincial licence and are more safety-conscious than ever before, particularly about not running rivers if conditions are considered too dangerous. In our experience, white-water rafting is one of the most thrilling sports in the province, absolutely guaranteed to induce a feeling of euphoria that we've seldom experienced in any other sport.

The River Outfitters Association of B.C. puts out an excellent rafting safety brochure that should be compulsory reading for anyone contemplating rafting in the province. The association represents commercial rafting companies who aim to maintain a high standard of white-water experience while reducing the risks associated with rafting. Be sure that the company you choose is a member of this association. For information, contact them at 1367 West Broadway, Vancouver, B.C., V6H 4A9 (737-3058).

Cross-country (Nordic) Skiing

B.C. offers some of the best groomed trails and back-country skiing in Canada. The sheer variety of experiences makes nordic skiing here unique, and aficionados may own 3 to 6 pairs of skis in order to take advantage of every skiing opportunity. It is not unheard of for the same skier to do a 30-km (18.6-mi.) marathon one day, put in another 10 km (6 mi.) of night skiing on groomed trails, then do an overnight back-country mountain tour, all in one week.

B.C.'s varied terrain provides the nordic skier with groomed trails set for classic skiing (traditional diagonal stride) and "skating" (the more recent go-fast technique). Excellent groomed trails lie minutes away from the down-towns of many of the province's major cities. For example, Vancouver nordic skiers can be gliding around 25 km (16 mi.) of groomed trails within 30 minutes of escaping the city centre. A lovely bonus is that over 5 km (3 mi.) of these trails are lit for night skiing. Kamloops and Prince George also boast great trails very close by.

In addition, many downhill ski resorts, such as Whistler Mountain, have capitalized on nordic enthusiasm and established groomed trails for varying capabilities. Silver sliders and grey gliders (seniors) are just as likely to lead the cross-country pack as are 8-year-old youngsters racing along with Olympic biathlons in mind.

Long before the professionally groomed trails existed in B.C., nordic skiers took to the logging roads and hiking trails.Many skiers still prefer this kind of back-country experience, while others head to the high peaks and alpine meadows found in provincial and federal parks.

The rebirth of the telemark turn (developed by Sondre Norheim of Tele-mark, Norway, in the mid-1800s) has caused a revolutionary expansion in back-country touring. Whereas 10 years ago tourers would cautiously traverse a steep, powder slope, today the same skiers carve graceful telemark turns straight down the fall line. In fact, many telemarkers ski side by side with downhill skiers in alpine areas.

Extra winter gear to add to your pack should include a spare ski tip, a spare pole basket, extra mitts and a down vest or jacket. With short winter days and the possibility of changing weather conditions, we recommend a back-country skier always carry adequate emergency equipment for spending an unexpected night out in the woods.

Avalanches, both large and small, have a tremendous force and pose a serious threat to any back-country winter traveller. Even experienced people are not always able to predict an avalanche with any degree of certainty. However, it is recognized that avalanches are more likely to occur during or just after a heavy snowstorm, during or after a wind greater than 24 km (15 mi.) per hour, after any great temperature variation and during hot sun on south-facing slopes in spring. Stay clear of gullies, open slopes of 20° or more and cornices. Select a route that follows a ridge or valley bottom, staying on the windward side of the ridge.Tree-covered slopes are usually safer than steep, open slopes.

If you are planning to travel in an area where avalanches are a possibility, you should carry an avalanche rescue transceiver, an avalanche probe and a shovel. Before setting out, you might want to enrol in a course that shows you how to analyze the snow pack and how to read a slope. Avalanche rescue techniques are also taught.

If one of your group does get buried by an avalanche, remember that the buried victim has only a 50 per cent chance of survival after one hour. So, wherever possible, stay in the vicinity and mark the place where you last saw him or her. Don't go for help unless help is very close.

A valuable reference guide is Richard and Rochelle Wright's *British Columbia Cross Country Ski Routes*, now unfortunately out of print but available in public libraries and used bookstores. *Ski Trails in the Canadian Rockies* by Rick Kunelius and Dave Biederman contains excellent advice on equipment and winter survival techniques as well as trail information for the national parks of the Rockies.

For information on courses, avalanche safety and cross-country ski clubs, contact Cross Country B.C. at 1367 West Broadway, Vancouver, B.C., V6H 4A9 (737-3058).

Caving

Caving is starting to gain popularity as more and more people realize that it is indeed one of the last frontiers. Spelunkers (*spelunca* is the Latin word for cave) can expect to explore a limestone world riddled with caverns—some as big as football fields, others mere crevices in the wall—where depigmented creatures such as white trout and sticky crickets roam. Prime areas in the province include the Quatsino system around Gold River on Vancouver Island and the Cody Caves in the Kootenays.

Of all the environments in the province, caves are among the most fragile. Formations in caves grow at the rate of about one cubic centimetre (0.06 cu. in.) a century and are so susceptible to deterioration that even human sweat and oils can spoil this environment. The caves themselves are extremely old, dating from the laying down of limestone beds 600 million years ago and the subsequent mountain building forces. Underground time is measured in hundreds of thousands of years; in this time frame, entire civilizations come and go on the surface with seeming insignificance, which makes the sight of old beer cans in some of the more accessible caves in the province all the more abhorrent. Prepare for your caving expedition carefully. Take the necessary precautions, and treat the need for preservation of the caves very seriously. A serious spelunker's basic checklist should include a tight-fitting, pocketless caving suit made of tear-resistant nylon, a hard-hat with a chin strap, a miner's lamp attached to a rechargeable battery pack and a sound pair of good climbing boots. The hard-hat protects a caver against falling rocks and overhead rock formations. Experienced cavers relish wriggling through tight, muddy, belly-squeezing crawlways and tunnels, some so restricted that cavers must exhale before entering. For such outings cavers wrap their equipment in rip-proof sacks, attaching the load to their boots and dragging it behind them.

For more information, contact the B.C. Speleological Federation, Box 733, Gold River, B.C., V0P 1G0 (283-2691).

Bicycling

From March to October, recreational cyclists fan out across the province, usually led by prairie dwellers escaping a long winter. Local clubs offer weekend tours of the Gulf Islands and the Sunshine Coast, two of the most popular areas for cycling in B.C. Relatively peaceful, and usually low on traffic, both areas lend themselves to interesting trips that begin with a spot of ferry hopping.

The strenuous "Golden Triangle"—west from Golden, B.C., through Yoho National Park to Lake Louise in Banff National Park, south to Radium Hot Springs and then back to Golden—is another favourite with cyclists. The Kootenay route is more gentle but no less spectacular, with mountains, deep-blue lakes and old mining towns providing highlights along the way.

Before beginning a bicycle tour, have your bike professionally checked out to make sure that the tires have good tread and that wheel spokes and axle nuts are tight. Replace the brake pads if they are worn, and check brake cables for signs of fraying, kinking or sticking. Your drive chain should ride smoothly and lubricate regularly. Your front reflectors should be white, your rear reflectors red for night riding. Side reflectors should be white or amber on the front wheels and white or red on the rear. It is also a good idea to use reflective tape and safety flags. If you plan to camp on your trip, do make use of pannier bags, since loading everything into a backpack can lead to severe back pain.

The B.C. Bicycle Association's resource library contains bike routes, maps and books for members' use. For information, contact them at 1367 West Broadway, Vancouver, B.C., V6H 4A9 (737-7433).

Sailing

The coastline of British Columbia, in particular the Strait of Georgia between Vancouver Island and the mainland, is unequalled in the world for sailing options. The "drowned" coastline offers many bays and inlets protected from the Pacific Ocean by Vancouver Island. The Gulf Islands and Desolation Sound, with their many marine parks, are popular summer sailing territory. And for the more experienced sailor, a trip around the outside of Vancouver Island can prove to be an unforgettable experience.

Opportunities for sighting wildlife, both mammals and birds, abound. Killer whales, porpoises, sea lions and harbour seals enjoy the B.C. coastal waters and are often spotted by boaters. During the spring and fall migrations, numerous birds use the Pacific Flyway. Birds inhabiting the coastal areas include beautiful harlequin ducks, scooters, mergansers, grebes, great blue herons, several members of the cormorant family, tufted puffins and the extraordinary-looking rhinoceros auklets, which breed in the Queen Charlotte Islands. Observant sailors can see 4 different birds of prey: bald eagles, peregrine falcons, ospreys and turkey vultures. Seventeen species of gulls also live around coastal waters.

A wide variety of marine parks set aside by the B.C. government provide unspoiled settings for boaters and homes for scores of birds.

If you are unfamiliar with sailing in coastal waters, several well-established companies offer skippered cruises in the Gulf Islands, Desolation Sound and the Queen Charlottes. The same companies also give short courses for those who need to brush up on their coastal navigation skills. Knowing how to read tide and current charts is an important aspect of coastal sailing. Skippers with proven coastal sailing experience can opt for the bare-boat charter experience: renting a boat and skippering it themselves.

Canadian Hydrographic Service publishes the *British Columbia Small Craft Guide* (2 volumes) and *Sailing Directions—British Columbia Coast* (2 volumes), both of which contain valuable reference information on passes, anchorages, etc. These books, along with marine charts and tide and current tables, can be obtained directly from the Canadian Hydrographic Service or from local marine supply stores. Weather forecasts are broadcast by the Canadian Coast Guard over several frequencies and often by VHF channels. The coast guard issues small-craft warnings from April to November as well as gale, storm and hurricane warnings year-round.

Sailors, neophyte or otherwise, would be well advised to pack plenty of Gravol if motion sickness is a problem. Another handy product, but often difficult to obtain, is Transderm-V bandages, which are placed behind the ear and slowly release anti-nausea drugs into your bloodstream.

There is an excellent series of cruising guides to four areas around the southern B.C. coast; see the bibliography at the back of the book for details.

Climbing

The difference between hiking and climbing is merely a matter of vertical feet, and while it is not within the scope of this book to detail the myriad climbing possibilities in B.C., it goes without saying that in such a mountainous province climbing opportunities are limitless.

Climbing terrain ranges from the sheer rock face of the Stawamus Chief outside Squamish, north of Vancouver, to the steep mountainsides of the Bugaboo Range and the Rockies in the interior. Like rafting, climbing is an exhilarating sport that can induce a feeling of euphoria. And like rafting, climbing requires stringent safety precautions.

The secret to successful climbing is to pace yourself and always carry a day pack that includes survival items. Mountains demand respect, so if you are a novice, go out with someone who is experienced. Several organizations in the Lower Mainland conduct climbs in the mountains. The B.C. Federation of Mountain Clubs represents more than 30 clubs and associations geared to mountain recreation, from walking groups to rock-climbing clubs. Call them for information at 737-3053 or write Suite 336, 1367 West Broadway, Vancouver, B.C., V6H 4A9. A good resource book for recreational climbers and rock climbers is Bruce Fairley's *A Guide to Climbing and Hiking in Southwestern British Columbia*.

Diving

The 27,040 km (16,900 mi.) of coastline in B.C. make for prolific marine life and some of the most exciting diving in the world. According to *Equinox*, a Canadian naturalist publication, at least 450 fish species, 600 plant species and over 4000 invertebrates live in these cold waters. Some of the more intriguing creatures include giant sea whips more than 2.6 m (8.5 ft.) tall, multiarmed sunflower sea stars, foot-long sea slugs and 2-m (6.5-ft.) wide sponges. The sheer variety of sea anemones, starfish, urchins, sponges, abalone, octopuses, crabs, rockfish, wolf eels and hundreds of fish make diving in British Columbia a treat. Diving is particularly good in winter, when visibility can extend up to 45 m (147.6 ft.).

Popular diving spots include the "Diving Capital of Canada" off Powell River on the Sunshine Coast north of Vancouver, Campbell River and Port Hardy on northern Vancouver Island, the passages between the Gulf Islands and the west coast of Vancouver Island, particularly around the Broken Island group. "The Graveyard of the Pacific," off the west coast of Vancouver Island, provides an underwater museum for wreck divers. Some of these shipwrecks have been designated as historic sites to prevent removal of artifacts. Wrecks on the periphery of Pacific Rim National Park are also protected. Saltery Bay, just south of Powell River, boasts its own mermaid—the first underwater statue in Canada. Closer to Vancouver, and convenient for weeknight dives, are Whitecliff, Copper and Telegraph coves in West Vancouver.

If you dive to collect edibles such as delicious Dungeness crabs or sea cucumbers, be aware of local regulations regarding minimum size of creatures you may harvest and daily limits. While it is quite safe to dive in red-tide conditions, since you are breathing compressed air, be sure not to harvest bivalves when a red tide warning is in effect.

Be sure your equipment is in good order and always consult the local weather office for diving conditions. The best resources in B.C. for divers are individual commercial dive shops such as the Diving Locker at 2745 West 4th Ave., Vancouver, B.C., V6K 1P9 (736-2681) and Diver's World, 1523 West 3rd Ave., Vancouver, B.C., V6J 1J8 (732-1344). When diving any waters in B.C., remember that your most important piece of equipment is your buddy.

Betty Pratt-Johnson's *141 Dives in the Protected Waters of Washington State and British Columbia* is the local divers' bible, providing detailed information on the province's best diving areas. *Shipwrecks of British Columbia* by Fred Rogers describes numerous wreck dives. *Diver* magazine, published monthly, is another source of local information. Each issue includes a directory of diving stores and resorts offering scuba instruction and charters.

For general information about diving in the province and addresses of dive shops and charters, contact Dive BC, 5824 Ash St., Powell River, B.C., V8A 4R4 (483-9740).

Fishing

A major chunk of the adventure travel industry in B.C. is devoted to fresh-water and salt-water fishing, and with good reason. Five salmon species, giant halibut and cod inhabit the sea while inland lakes and rivers are home to fresh-water trout. Unique among them is the migrating sea-run rainbow trout, the steelhead.

Trophy fishers invariably head to floating fishing camps at Rivers Inlet or Hakai Pass, south of the Queen Charlottes, to angle for Chinook salmon, known as tyee salmon once they reach a weight of 13.6 kg (30 lb.). Deep-swimming fish and notoriously difficult to catch, tyee provide a challenge for everyone from ordinary folks to Hollywood film stars.

This book will tell you the whereabouts of good fishing holes in B.C. (some of them anyway—anglers are very secretive!). Any angler in B.C., unless of native Indian birth, must buy a B.C. fishing licence, available from most sporting goods stores, and catch limits are in effect at all times. A growing trend among anglers to release, unharmed, a portion of their allowable catch is heartily endorsed by real sportspeople and by fisheries management staff.

Because of stock depletion some species, such as steelhead, are subject to mandatory catch-and-release programs. If you do intend to catch and release, don't play your fish too long and exhaust it. Keep it in the water, which acts as a protective cushion. Take out the hook, as gently and as rapidly as possible, with long-nosed pliers, and if the fish is deep-hooked, leave the hook in and cut the leader. When returning the fish, always hold it in the water, propelling it back and forth to pump water through its gills. When it revives and begins to struggle, then it is ready to swim off.

The B.C. inland fishing season starts at ice-off time, about May 1, on inland lakes. Campbell River, Cowichan River, the Queen Charlotte Islands, Face Lake in the Kamloops/Merritt area and Bulkley River are popular fishing areas.

Anglers should contact the B.C. Fishing Resorts and Outfitters Association, Box 3301, Kamloops, B.C., V2C 6D9 (828-1553) with fishing queries, and invest in the indispensable *B.C. Fishing Directory and Atlas*, available at major tackle stores.

Tourism British Columbia, in conjunction with the B.C. Fishing Resorts and Outfitters Association, puts out two free annual guides, *Freshwater Fishing* and *Saltwater Fishing*. These include information on fishing in the province, including tips on equipment, locations and lodge operators.

Out-of-province anglers can call Tourism B.C. at 1-800-663-6000 toll free for further information on fishing destinations, outfitters, guides, lodges and licences.

Vancouver Island and the Gulf Islands

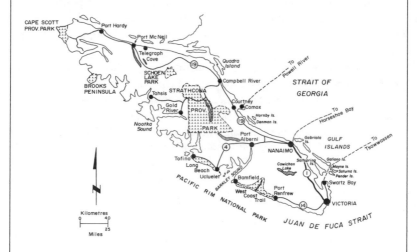

CAPE SCOTT PROV. PARK

Port Hardy

Port Mc Neil

Telegraph Cove

SCHOEN LAKE PARK

⑲

Quadra Island

Campbell River

STRAIT OF GEORGIA

To Powell River

BROOKS PENINSULA

Tahsis

STRATHCONA

Courtney
Comox

To Horseshoe Bay

Gold River

PROV.

Hornby Is.
Denman Is.

⑲

Nootka Sound

PARK

Port Alberni

Gabriola Is.

GULF ISLANDS

To Tsawwassen

④

NANAIMO

Tofino

Long Beach

Ucluelet

BARKLEY SOUND

Cowichan Lake

Saltspring Is.

Galiano Is.

Mayne Is.
Saturna Is.
Pender Is.

①

Swartz Bay

Bamfield

West Coast Trail

Port Renfrew

PACIFIC RIM NATIONAL PARK

⑭

VICTORIA

JUAN DE FUCA STRAIT

Kilometres
0   40
0   25
Miles

N

CHAPTER 2

Vancouver Island and the Gulf Islands

For thousands of years before European exploration, Vancouver Island was home to several distinctly different Pacific Northwest groups. In the north lived the artistic Kwakiutl, who today call themselves Kwakwaka'wakw. The whaling Nootka (now known as the Nuu-chah-nulth) inhabited the west coast of the island. To the south lived the Coast Salish. Communities thrived at selected sheltered beaches along the coast. At high tide, often as many as 20 or 30 cedar canoes lay pulled up on the sand, backed by a row of houses that followed the curve of the beach well back from the water. The Kwakwaka'wakw traditionally raised totem poles, as did the Nuu-chah-nulth and Coast Salish in later years.

Ample, reliable salmon runs provided a staple food, and rain forests burgeoning with cedar yielded wood for homes, clothing, storage chests, plank drums and food trays. Native people twisted the inside bark of the cedar into rope for harpoon lines, wove blankets, capes and baskets from it, and made its roots into thread or twine. In a prayer of homage to the young cedar tree, the Kwakwaka'wakw would intone, "There is nothing for which you cannot be used..."

Most of the coastal peoples had no real taste for land mammals but valued seal meat highly. Fresh or dried salmon provided the bulk of coastal diet and other fish products were highly prized too. When herring shoals came to shore to spawn, they encountered weighted cedar boughs that had been lowered into the water. The boughs were later raised, complete with masses of spawn clinging to the fronds. This spawn was mashed with stones and made into balls to be dipped into oil and eaten. Salmon heads were buried for six weeks in boxes, to be relished when highly flavoured. Beaches brimmed with clams; mussels (called "little birds") were prised from tidal rocks. Men constructed elaborate salmon weirs. Women dug for camass lily roots as vegetables and picked berries in season.

The potlatch was of central economic and social importance to many Northwest Coast groups. A ceremonial distribution of property used to validate or reinforce status and to mark certain life passages, the potlatch was outlawed by the Canadian government in the late 1800s. When the law dropped from the books in 1951, the potlatch reemerged as a vital part of contemporary native life.

The Kwakwaka'wakw had the greatest artistic achievements of the Vancouver Island peoples. Painters, sculptors and weavers had to apprentice for years before producing highly sophisticated, technically perfect works such as elaborate totems, masks, potlatch dishes, raven rattles and spoons. Kwakwaka'wakw ceremonial art displays brilliant colours and often depicts supernatural beings with beaks or mouths that open and "clash" shut and masks that "transform." One striking sea monster mask that we have seen is made of wood painted red, white, black and green and has obsidian eyes and a moveable jaw.

The Nuu-chah-nulth were the preeminent whalers of the west coast. They regularly headed out in impressive canoes over the open ocean to hunt migrating gray and humpback whales. Harpoon blades were made of mussel shell or the barbs of elk antler. Sealskin floats were used on the line as drags to tire the whale and bring it to the surface where it could be harpooned.

The Coast Salish on both Vancouver Island and the mainland constructed elaborate weirs to catch fish. In addition to salmon, rock clams, razor clams, bent nose clams, butter clams, cockle clams and horse clams were Coast Salish staples. Clambaking was done by digging a hole in the sand, filling it with clams and steaming them under a covering of earth or seaweed. The Coast Salish also netted birds for food, using poles 12 m (40 ft.) high strung with fine nets.

Captain James Cook and the Spanish explorers before him made first contact with the people of this part of the Pacific Coast. Cook tells of anchoring in Nootka Sound in the spring of 1778; canoes came out to meet his ship, elaborate incantations were intoned and the spreading of eagle down took place prior to trading. In exchange for pelts, the Nuu-chah-nulth particularly coveted iron.

Fourteen years later, Captain George Vancouver, arriving at this large island fresh from a twenty-year scout of Tahiti, New Guinea and the Antipodes, decided that it was "the most lovely country that can be imagined." The island bears his name in recognition of his circumnavigation of it.

James Douglas, chief factor of the Hudson's Bay Company and later governor of the colony of Vancouver Island, called the area "the perfect Eden." Colonization brought commerce in the form of the fur trade and the city of Victoria subsequently became a base to service the gold rushes into the interior.

Today, forestry is the mainstay of the island's economy; also important are the fishing industry, a strong tourist trade and some agriculture. Half a million people live here, the most heavily populated area being on the east coast south of Campbell River.

In their time off, islanders love to hike, fish and generally explore their lovely island, which stretches 451 km (282 mi.) from Cape Scott in the north to Race Rocks in the south. Victoria, the provincial capital, lies well below the 49th parallel. Highway 19, Vancouver Island's main road, runs almost the entire length of the east coast. Feeder roads leading west from Highway 19 include Highway 4, which cuts across the island from Parksville through Port Alberni to the coastal town of Tofino, on the edge of Pacific Rim National Park.

Studded with forests of cedar, hemlock, Douglas fir and Sitka spruce, the island rises to 2200 m (7219 ft.) at Mount Golden Hinde in Strathcona Provincial Park. An intricate, 3400-km (2150-mi.) coastline stretches around Vancouver Island, and over 2000 lakes lie inland.

More than 10,000 black bears still inhabit Vancouver Island, as well as, at last count, 700 cougars and over 100,000 black-tailed deer. Approximately 150 species of birds use the Pacific Flyway to travel between summer breeding grounds in the north and winter homes in the southern U.S.A. Five species of Pacific salmon and 28 kinds of marine mammals, including gray whales, killer whales and sea lions, live in the sea.

Vancouver Island's climate is kept mild by both the Pacific Ocean and the Kuroshio Current. Since much of the east coast lies in a rain shadow, there is considerably less rainfall there than on the west coast just 100 km (62 mi.) away. Victoria receives only 68 cm (27 in.) of rain a year, the west coast at least 254 cm (100 in.). Winter snows do fall on the island's mountains but frost and snow seldom linger at altitudes below 600 m (1970 ft.). The average January temperature in Victoria hovers around the 4.1° C (39.3° F) mark, while July averages 15.4° C (60° F). December is the rainiest month. Its temperate climate makes the island a major year-round travel destination for B.C. residents and out-of-province visitors.

Access to Vancouver Island is by ferry or by air. Harbour Air runs a regular service between Vancouver and Victoria. Flights leave from Coal Harbour, adjacent to Canada Place and the Convention Centre in downtown Vancouver. For more information, call Harbour Air at 688-1277.

Ferries depart hourly (less frequently during winter months) from Tsawwassen, 30 km (19 mi.) south of Vancouver, to land at Swartz Bay, 32 km (20 mi.) north of Victoria. You can take your car onto the ferry, take a bus from downtown Vancouver to Victoria or board the ferry at the Tsawwassen terminal as a foot passenger.

The 44-km (24-mi.) trip, which takes 1 hour and 35 minutes, passes through scenic Active Pass between Galiano and Mayne islands. To get more information, call B.C. Ferries at 669-1211 in Vancouver, 386-3431 in Victoria or 206-441-6865 in Seattle. For a recorded message that gives you the ferry schedule 24 hours a day, phone 685-1021 in Vancouver, 656 0757 in Victoria or 753-6626 in Nanaimo. B.C. Ferry Corporation headquarters are at 1112 Fort St., Victoria, B.C., V8V 4V2.

Pacific Coach Lines (385-4411) runs buses between Vancouver and Victoria. On Vancouver Island, Island Coach Lines (385-4411) connects Victoria with Port Hardy in the north and links up at Port Alberni with Orient Stage

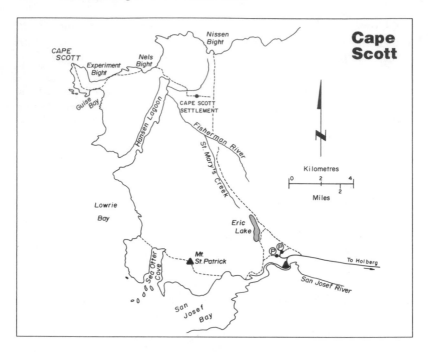

Lines (723-6924), which provides bus service to the west-coast towns of Ucluelet and Tofino near Long Beach.

We will mention some of the unique places to stay on the island, but also recommend that prospective visitors call Tourism B.C. toll free at 1-800-663-6000 to get a free copy of *Accommodations*, the annual guide to accommodation in the province. Tourism B.C. can also provide a good map of Vancouver Island and its provincial parks.

Our guided tour of adventures on Vancouver Island will start with the remote north, then work south via Highway 19 to Victoria, with side trips along Highways 28, 4, 18 and 14 into the interior and out to the west coast.

CAPE SCOTT

Since Highway 19 ends at the northern community of Port Hardy, 65 km (40 mi.) from the tip of Vancouver Island, the only people who get a glimpse of marine life off the northwest coast are hikers in remote Cape Scott Park and kayakers paddling in from Queen Charlotte Strait to the east or the open Pacific to the west.

In recent years, travellers here have reported increased sightings of humpback whales *(Megaptera novaeangliae)*. These leviathans nearly became extinct during the professional slaughter that lasted from the mid-1800s until the closing of the last whaling station in 1968. Humpbacks belong to the *Balaenopteridae* family, whose biggest member, the blue whale, has a heart the size of a Volkswagen Beetle and arteries as large as plumbing pipes. Humpbacks themselves can measure up to 19 m (62 ft.) in length and weigh 48,000 kg (53 tons). Their wide, graceful tail flukes distinguish them from other whales and they are famous for their "singing"—a beautiful, high-pitched series of squeaking sounds, which according to researchers is the whales' way of communicating.

Early immigrant settlers write of humpbacks regularly breeching in Georgia Strait, swimming into harbours and giving inhabitants of floating homes a scare by rubbing up alongside houseboat pontoons. One account tells of school being cancelled in a float-home community because humpbacks were making such big waves that the school water taxi couldn't function!

The northeast coast of Vancouver Island faces a cluster of islands known collectively as the Duke of Edinburgh Ecological Reserve. Access is by boat only and you must obtain permission from the Ministry of Parks in Victoria. Permission is usually granted only to people who are doing scientific or educational work.

The reserve includes Pine Island, Storm Island, Treet Islets, the Buckle Group, Reid Islets and Naiad Islets. They contain the nesting grounds of one million sea birds, making the area the second largest colony of breeding sea birds in Canada. Three main species breed here: fork-tailed storm petrels, Leach's storm petrels and the rhinoceros auklet. Petrels, incidentally, were named for St. Peter because of their uncanny ability to walk on water.

Cape Scott Sand Neck, which juts out from the northwestern tip of Vancouver Island, is the only place from which you can see both sides of the island simultaneously. To reach the neck, you must hike the primitive trails of Cape Scott Provincial Park, a wilderness park where it frequently rains torrentially, making for muddy conditions. Even in summer, periods of prolonged sunshine are rare.

Before European immigration, the halibut rich banks off Cape Scott provided food for the Kwakiutl. But even these people retreated from their summer village of Ouchton (meaning "foam palace") to more protected villages on the east coast when winter storms hit.

The first European settlement of Cape Scott took place in 1893 when a Dane, Rasmus Hansen, recruited ninety followers from Seattle to head to Goose (now Hansen) Bay, where they established a Scandinavian colony based on cooperative principles. Despite the shipwreck of their boats on arrival and their abortive attempts to tame the land with a series of dikes (all of which succumbed to the heavy downpour and violent windstorms), the colony subsisted until a second wave of settlers arrived in 1909.

But Cape Scott, which receives 375-500 cm (150-200 in.) of rainfall annually, defied development. Today the 15,070-ha (37,000-a.) park contains only remnants of the Scandinavian colony. Established in 1973, the park is rimmed by 64 km (40 mi.) of rugged coastline, including 23 km (14 mi.) of scenic, sandy beaches stretching from Nissen Bay in the north to San Josef Bay in the south.

Wildlife includes elk, deer, black bears and cougars on land, and waterfowl, seals, sea lions and otters off the coast. Cape Scott is one of the best places in B.C. to watch peregrine falcons and there are hundreds of shore birds here too. Natural edible foods include orange huckleberries, scarlet salmonberries and sweet, coarse salal berries. Some tenacious apple trees, strawberry plants, monkey puzzle trees (*Araucaria araucana*) and rhododendrons remain from settler days.

Access to the park is from the town of Port Hardy. A logging road leads 46 km (28 mi.) due west to the community of Holberg. Just past Holberg, turn right and continue another 16 km (10 mi.) to the end of the road and the San Josef Bay campground, shaded by tall red cedars on the banks of San Josef River.

From a San Josef base, you have a number of options. You can hike to Sea Otter Cove and Lowrie Bay by way of Mount St. Patrick, kayak right around Cape Scott, canoe or hike down the San Josef River for 4 km (2.5 mi.) or hike out to the cape.

Many of the trails in the park can be extremely muddy. Logs and boardwalks have been placed across many of the worst stretches but these can be very slippery when wet. So, when hiking anywhere in the park, you'll find a hiking staff very useful for probing quagmire and mud and for maintaining your balance. Hikers should also be equipped with good boots and rain gear. Torrential rain can be expected at any time, even in summer, so make sure your food, clothing and sleeping bags are well protected in waterproof bags. Hang your food at campsites because of mice and don't worry if you get bitten by sand spiders at some of the beaches—their bites are itchy but harmless.

The San Josef campground is close to the trailhead to San Josef Bay. There is also a boat launch nearby for canoeists or kayakers who paddle down the river to the bay. The 2.5-km (1.5-mi.) trail passes through some marshy areas to an old roadway built by the Danish settlers in the early 1900s. At the northwest end of the beach, a 10-km (6.2-mi.) trail leads to Sea Otter Cove via the summit of Mount St. Patrick. The trail continues for another 2 km (1.2 mi.) to Lowrie Bay. The BC Parks brochure recommends 5 hours one way for this strenuous hike.

The major hiking trail of Cape Scott Park accesses both Nels Bight and Nissen Bight as well as the cape itself. From the trailhead just past the San Josef Bay campground, the 19.4-km (12-mi.) hike to northern Nels Bight takes one long day (or two more leisurely days). Nels Bight, one of the most lovely beaches in the Pacific Northwest, stretches 3.5 km (2.17 mi.) and is 2 km (1.24 mi.) wide. Drinking water is available en route at Eric Lake and Fisherman River. Just before the trail splits between the Nissen Bight and Nels Bight routes, a path leads east into the woods. Here potbellied stoves, bathtubs and other paraphernalia bear silent witness to "the Cape of Lost Dreams" and the tough pioneering life. A 3-m (6-ft.) high granite obelisk marks the grave of the local schoolteacher's 12-year-old son, who died of blood poisoning after treading on a rusty nail—the closest medical help lay 115 km (72 mi.) away by sea.

At the trail junction, head left for Nels Bight and Cape Scott. The trail passes through the remains of the old settlement to Hansen Lagoon, which is bordered by a wide expanse of wet meadows reclaimed from the sea by the Danish pioneers. Continuing west along the head of the lagoon, the hiker soon arrives at the long stretch of sandy beach at Nels Bight. Most hikers choose to set up camp here near the stream at the western end of the beach and day-hike the 8-km (5-mi.) trail to the cape.

The trail from the beach continues west to Experiment Bight, Guise Bay and the Cape Scott Sand Neck, where breakers crash dramatically on both sides. The remains of a wooden plank road lead across the sand and climb the headland to the end of the trail at the Cape Scott Light Station.

The original light station, situated on nearby Triangle Island, was washed into the sea during a 1912 storm. Today, the two families stationed at the lighthouse provide weather reports to meteorologists across North America. When visibility is low, the only sound hikers hear is the hoot of foghorns, warning ships of land nearby. While the wind and rain at Cape Scott can at times seem unrelenting, patches of sunshine do occur from June through August.

Below the lighthouse bluff, carpets of pink and yellow wildflowers border the sea. If you peer the 72 m (236 ft.) straight down into the kelp beds, you can often glimpse some of the Steller sea lions (*Eumetropias jubata*) who breed in this area. Colonies of these lumbering animals range from the Commander Islands off the Siberian coast as far south as the northern coast of California. They are rarely seen in captivity.

The largest of all sea lions, a Steller bull can weigh up to 907 kg (a ton), measuring 3.6 m (12 ft.) from top to tail. Cows average about half that weight and length. Feasting on skate, hake, sculpin, rockfish, cod, flounder, squid and occasionally salmon, northern sea lions create a thick layer of fat or blubber as insulation against cold water. During mating season on the rocks off Cape Scott, the bulls set up harems containing ten to twenty cows, staking out their territory with great roars and bellows and occasionally kidnapping cows from a neighbouring harem. Females give birth in May or June, after a 51-week gestation period, then mate again in about a week. In the general pandemonium the mortality rate among new pups is high; some fall off the rocks into the water and are too weak to clamber ashore, while others are crushed by warring bulls. Those that do survive suckle for 3 months, building up blubber before heading south with the troop at the end of summer. Now that they are protected from hunters, the Steller sea lions' main enemy is the nomadic type of killer whale, which occasionally kills sea lions. It has now been firmly established that there are two types of orcas (killer whales)—those that roam and kill other sea mammals, seemingly just for fun, and those that concentrate purely on eating salmon.

Useful Information

A brochure and map of Cape Scott Provincial Park and information on the Duke of Edinburgh Ecological Reserve can be obtained from the Ministry of Parks, 4000 Seymour Place, Victoria, B.C., V8V 1X5 (387-5002).

Pacific Sunset Nature Tours, #305-4559 Imperial St., Burnaby, B.C., V5J 1B7 (437-3150) offers excellent hiking tours of the cape, originating in Port Hardy.

The Outdoor Club of Victoria's *Hiking Trails III—Central and Northern Vancouver Island* and *Island Adventures* by Richard Blier contain good descriptions of the trails in and around Cape Scott Park.

THE NORTH COAST

Port Hardy to Port McNeill

A relatively new (1979) paved extension to Highway 19 connects Port Hardy, the end of the road on northern Vancouver Island, with Campbell River 237 km (147 mi.) to the south. Port Hardy faces the salmon-rich waters of Queen Charlotte Sound, giving its population of 5400 easy access to numerous Chinook and tyee, some in excess of 22 kg (50 lb.). Known as "King Coho Country," Port Hardy's seas are also rich in large bottom fish such as halibut, lingcod and yelloweye rockfish. The Chinook season starts at the end of May and peaks in August. The best season for halibut is April, just prior to the commercial opening. Most halibut in the area are in the 13-22 kg (30-50 lb.) range. However, halibut as big as 120 kg (267 lb.) have been caught on lines, while fish up to 180 kg (400 lb.) have been snagged in nets.

Diving is also prime in the waters around north and northeastern Vancouver Island. Visibility is best between November and March when plankton and sediment levels are low. Colourful underwater species include strawberry coral, hooded nudibranches and wolf eels, as well as vast colonies of sea anemones that live in the many shipwrecks in the area. Charter firms in such communities as Port Hardy, Port Alice, Port McNeill, Alert Bay, Sointula and

Telegraph Cove provide a range of services for divers, including compressed air, gear rental, tour guides and dive masters.

The former air force base and whaling station of Coal Harbour is a 20-minute drive south of Port Hardy. Signs on the main highway indicate the route. In Coal Harbour take time to look at the large jawbone of a blue whale and an early harpoon gun in an informal outdoor display. The southern-exposed village lies on Holberg Inlet. From here, you can launch a canoe or kayak for fishing and exploring in the immediate area or in Quatsino Sound, south of the inlet, which contains many coho salmon.

From June to September, on alternate days of the week, the B.C. Ferry Corporation's *Queen of the North* leaves Port Hardy's Bear Cove for a scenic 15-hour daytime cruise of the Inside Passage. This route takes passengers north through the sheltered fiords of B.C.'s west coast, past steep-sided forested slopes with distant views of the snow-capped Coast Mountains. The ferry boasts reclining seats, cocktails, movies and dancing. You can go as a foot passenger but you can also take your vehicle if you plan to drive east from Prince Rupert, the ferry's mainland destination, or continue north to Alaska. Ferry links can also be made at Prince Rupert for the Queen Charlotte Islands.

Forestry companies have established a number of campgrounds, picnic sites and boat launches in the Port Hardy area. Travelling south, you can take a signposted road branching southwest off the highway for 30 minutes to the pulp mill town of Port Alice, situated on the shores of Neroutsos Inlet. Logging roads radiate out from Port Alice to places like Link River Regional Park. Other highlights of the area include Beaver Lake, long a favourite north Vancouver Island swimming hole, and Marble Lake, popular with swimmers and water-skiers. A 2-hour drive along a logging road rising high above Neroutsos Inlet takes you to the shores of Side Bay or Klaskino Inlet over on the west coast of Vancouver Island.

If you have a sturdy vehicle, you may want to visit the natural cave features of this region, which include Devil's Bath, Eternal Fountain and Vanishing River, all on the east side of Alice Lake. Get logging road maps and directions from the nearest tourist information centre.

Follow the same road back from Port Alice, turning south when you get to Highway 19. Soon you will reach Port McNeill, home to 3000 people and regional headquarters for three major logging companies.

Whale watchers and native Indian history enthusiasts will want to stop in Port McNeill to see the killer whales of Robson Bight or view Kwakwaka'-wakw native art at the Alert Bay Cultural Centre and Museum.

Useful Information
For further information about campgrounds, charter fishing and diving contact the **Port Hardy Charterboat Association** at 949-2628.

Killer whale at Robson Bight. *Photo by Lloyd Twaites*

Several Vancouver companies offer diving trips in the Port Hardy area: **The Diving Locker**, 2745 West 4th Ave., Vancouver, B.C., V6K 1P9 (736-2681); **Adrenalin Sports**, 1512 Duranleau St., Granville Island, Vancouver, B.C., V6H 3S4 (682-2881), and **Diver's World**, 1523 West 3rd Ave., Vancouver, B.C., V6J 1J8 (732-1344).

Island Adventures by Richard Blier contains good descriptions of backroads trips in this area.

Robson Bight

Southeast of Port McNeill, the road leads to the tiny, mist-shrouded town of Telegraph Cove. A former salmon saltery and sawmill junction built on stilts, the cove now capitalizes on its proximity to some of the best orca-watching waters in the world.

Of the thirty orca pods that exist between Washington State and Alaska, 19 pods—a total of 170 *Orcinus orca*—summer over in the Johnstone Strait south of Telegraph Cove. These magnificent black-and-white mammals, generally known as killer whales, feast on migrating salmon as well as other fish. They travel in pods containing 5 to 20 bulls, cows and calves.

On average, an orca male measures 8 m (25 ft.), a female 6 m (20 ft.), and they weigh 8130 and 7110 kg (8 and 7 tons) respectively. Newborn calves are 2-2.5 m (7-8 ft.) long. Life expectancy for orcas is from 60 to 80 (or more) years.

On an excellent day of orca watching you can expect to see them breach (leap out of the water and land on their bellies), fluke (slap their tails or flippers on the surface) and spyhop (lift their heads and torsos out of the water for a quick look around). Typically, whale watchers will see the pod do three or four short dives, followed by a long dive lasting several minutes. Unless orcas approach a boat, by law the vessel must keep a distance of 100 m (330 ft.). However, hydrophonic systems enable whale watchers to tune in to whale chat. Their sophisticated communication system consists of squeaks, whistles and moans, sounds that can travel and be heard up to 11 km (7 mi.) away, and every pod has its own unique dialect. The sci-fi-type clicks of the mammals' sonar systems indicate they are determining the size and location of objects in their path and locating prey before zeroing in at speeds of up to 40 kph (25 mph).

Whale-watching ethics require that boats do not speed, that watchers in boats make no noise and that boats make no sudden, irrational changes in direction.

The undisputed highlight of a whale-watching trip in Johnstone Strait is the whales' massage parlour at Robson Bight, a short trip down the coast from Telegraph Cove. For centuries, for reasons unknown, orcas have approached the shallow bight waters to rub themselves against the underwater pebble beaches. Destined at one time to be a log dump for timber companies, Robson Bight was declared a B.C. Ecological Reserve in 1982. It consists of 412 ha (1018 a.) of dry land and 1300 ha (3212 a.) of subtidal territory, and is off-limits to overnight campers. Boats and kayaks are not permitted in the bight when the whales are rubbing, unless whales arrive while your craft is there.

Johnstone Strait featured strongly in Kwakwaka'wakw legends. Stories focussed on BaxbakualanuXsiwai ("the cannibal at the north end of the world") who, along with his mythical attendant beasts, swept down from his smoky lair to prey voraciously upon villagers.

Kayaking is prime in Johnstone Strait between Port McNeill and Robson Bight. A good launching area and a campsite exist at Cayoosh Creek (check your area map for exact location). If you set up camp here on a summer evening, you might be lucky enough to hear the rhythmic, whooshing breathing of travelling orcas. If you are out on the water when whales appear, tap your boat gently with the paddle to let them know you are a craft. You may then be rewarded with the sight of an orca torpedoing under your kayak and resurfacing on the other side.

Kayakers should exercise caution when travelling between Robson Bight and Telegraph Cove because of the heavy traffic caused by deep-sea freighters, tugboats, cruise ships, fishing boats, barges and log booms pulled by towboats.

Useful Information

The **University of British Columbia's Continuing Education Department** offers a 3-day summer course on killer whales and native culture, including an orca-viewing visit in Johnstone Strait. For more information, contact them at the Centre for Continuing Education, University of British Columbia, 5997 Iona Drive, Vancouver, B.C., V6T 2A4 (222-2181).

Several companies offer whale-watching trips: **Stubbs IslandCharters**, Box 7, Telegraph Cove, B.C., V0N 3J0 (928-3185 or 928-3117); **Robson Bight Charters**, Box 99, Sayward, B.C., V0P 1R0 (282-3833); **SeaSmoke Sailing Charters & Tours**, Box 483, Alert Bay, B.C., V0N 1A0 (974-5225), and **Bluewater Adventures**, 202-1676 Duranleau St., Granville Island, Vancouver, B.C., V6H 3S4 (684-4575).

Kayaking trips are offered by **Discovery Kayaking**, 2775 Departure Bay Road, Nanaimo, B.C., V9S 3W9 (758-2488), who runs 5-day kayaking trips in Johnstone Strait from July through September; **Pacific Rim Paddling**, Box 1840, Station E, Victoria, B.C., V8W 2Y3 (384-6103); **Geoff Evans Kayak Centre**, Box 97, Cultus Lake, B.C., V0X 1H0 (858-6775), and **Ecosummer**, 1516 Duranleau St., Granville Island, Vancouver, B.C., V6H 3S4 (669-7741).

Sea Kayaking Canada's West Coast by John Ince and Hedi Kottner gives a detailed description of the area for kayakers.

Alert Bay

Cormorant Island, a short ferry ride from Port McNeill, houses the village of Alert Bay. Cyclists and hikers come over for the day to shop for native handicrafts and art, as well as to visit the Kwakwaka'wakw longhouse and the U'mista Cultural Centre's collection of potlatch masks. If you plan a bit in advance, you may be able to attend some native ceremonies on Cormorant Island. Contact the cultural centre at Box 253, Alert Bay, B.C., V0N 1A0 (974-5403) for information on hours and programs.

Mamalilaculla, an abandoned Indian village on Village Island due west of Alert Bay, was at one time renowned for its potlatch ceremonies. To visit Mamalilacula, kayakers must obtain permission from the band office in Campbell River.

Another 20-minute ferry ride from Port McNeill takes travellers to the quiet fishing village of Sointula on Malcolm Island. The word "sointula" means harmony, and the island was given its name by Finnish settlers who hoped to create a utopian colony here at the turn of the century.

Little Hustan Cave Park

Nestled in the Nimpkish Valley, just a 20-minute drive along an unpaved route leading west from the Island Highway, lies Little Hustan Cave Park. This park marks the start of the island's most exciting caving areas, which stretch southeast towards Gold River and on to the northwestern boundaries of Strathcona Park.

Little Hustan offers just a small taste of the many caves and other limestone features of the Quatsino System, the underground of much of north Vancouver Island. A short trail leads from the parking lot through woods to a platform overlooking a rock bridge and deep pools filled with green water.

Travellers keen to spelunk (cave) further in this vast subterranean world, along ancient limestone corridors that lead to a maze of lakes, rapids, football-field-sized halls and chambers loaded with stalagmites and stalactites, can explore some of the 1050 known caves on Vancouver Island. The longest one, Thanksgiving Cave, is 5.5 km (3.4 mi.) long, and several other island caves exceed 2 km (1.2 mi.) in length.

Limestone solution caves are formed by the action of water combining with carbon dioxide to produce a weak solution of carbonic acid. This acid slowly dissolves the limestone to form passageways. A fist-sized cave formation will take up to a thousand years to grow.

When caving deep into internal systems, you can expect to experience another world, one carved out by fast-flowing underground streams and sluggish runnels of ice. Caves are consistently 7° C (45° F). Their limestone formations are broken down into various types: pencil-thin "soda straws" or snow stalactites; "moon milk" (actually calcium carbonate too water-logged to solidify), which cascades like cottage cheese from crevices; "popcorn," consisting of calcified kernels, and "fried eggs," mounds of smooth limestone deposit.

In some caving areas, waterfalls cascade through caverns into intertidal pools that are often littered with fish bones. The sepulchral creatures of this underworld include white frogs, salamanders, spiders and depigmented trout. Cave-dwelling crickets have adapted to their damp environment by developing unusually long antennae and fish-hooked feet that enable them to cling limpet-like to slimy walls.

Caving is a dangerous sport. Entrances are usually vertical pits or steep muddy slopes, and the most beautiful sections of most caves lie deep underground. Caves are also extremely sensitive environmentally. Bacteria, body oils, skin flakes, lint from clothing, food crumbs and other evidence of human contact will leave indelible imprints. Nevertheless, enthusiasts find spelunking a matchless sport that allows them the thrill of exploring one of the last frontiers on earth.

Useful Information

For more information on Little Hustan, contact the Regional District of Mount Waddington at 956-3161, or the Ministry of Forests, Campbell River District, 370 Dogwood St., Campbell River, B.C., V9W 6Y7 (286-3282). Helmets and lights can be rented at **Joe's Hardware** in Gold River (283-2544). **Mostly Caves Enterprises**, Box 897, Gold River, B.C., V0P 1G0 (283-2691), offers guided cave trips.

West Coast Sounds

Along the west coast of Vancouver Island, 5 "sounds" dig right into the coastline, starting with Quatsino Sound in the north and culminating in Barkley Sound to the south.

The detour off the Island Highway that leads through caving country terminates 42 km (26 mi.) later at the west coast village of Zeballos. Ocean kayakers put in here to explore the Zeballos and Esperanza inlets, or slightly farther north at Fair Harbour to explore the islands and inlets of Kyuquot Sound.

Between Kyuquot Sound and Quatsino Sound, just south of Cape Scott Park, juts the thumb of land that is the Brooks Peninsula Recreation Area. Brooks Peninsula forms the northern boundary of Checleset Bay, home to the only colony of sea otters in Canadian waters.

By 1900 sea otters had been virtually eradicated by traders who sold their fine, soft pelts to the fashion-conscious Chinese. The current sea otter colony numbers about 500, all descendants of otters brought in from Alaska in the 1960s and early 1970s. A member of the weasel family, the sea otter is protected under Canada's Fisheries Act.

The otters here in Checleset Bay love to "raft-up," just like their cousins much farther south in Monterey Bay, California. This involves wrapping themselves up in kelp and snoozing on calm seas, in between diving bouts to the ocean floor to collect abalone and sea urchins. Before diving for food, mother sea otters fashion playpens out of kelp for their pups. Even if they resurface some distance away, moms locate the tots by following the squeaks emitted by their safely contained babies.

The delights of Brooks Peninsula are particularly apparent to kayakers. One good route starts just north of Quatsino Sound at Winter Harbour, skirts Brooks Peninsula, then crosses Checleset Bay to end at Kyuquot or Fair Harbour. Drop-off and pick-up by float plane can be arranged with local airlines such as Pacific Rim Airlines. This trip should only be done by experienced ocean kayakers, who must be prepared for weather-related delays.

Paddlers can also set out from the village of Kyuquot to explore the Bunsby Islands in Checleset Bay. Acous Peninsula and Battle Bay, across from the Bunsby Islands, are explorable on this particular trip.

Kyuquot is accessible by air, by local charter boat from Fair Harbour or via the M. V. *Uchuck III* from Gold River. The *Uchuck*, a converted minesweeper, makes regular trips through Nootka Sound, Esperanza Inlet and Kyuquot Sound, and can serve as a drop-off and pick-up service for kayakers.

An alternative to kayaking is to take advantage of the trips offered by West Coast Expeditions from their base camp on Spring Island. Daily excursions by boat take adventurers to a variety of destinations, including the Brooks Peninsula and the Bunsby Islands, with opportunities for observing sea otters, beachcombing and exploring old-growth forests.

Useful Information

Pacific Rim Airlines, Box 1196, Port Alberni, B.C., V9Y 7M7 (724-4495) and **Air Nootka**, Box 397, Tahsis, B.C., V0P 1X0 (283-2255) can provide float plane drop-off and pick-up services.

Discovery Kayaking, 2775 Departure Bay Road, Nanaimo, B.C., V9S 3W9 (738-2488) offers guided kayak trips of the area. **Strathcona Park Lodge**, Box 2160, Campbell River, B.C., V9W 5C9 runs similar trips.

Contact **West Coast Expeditions**, 1348 Ottawa Ave., West Vancouver, B.C., V7T 2I15 (926-5268 or 298-0575) for more information on their camping/boat trips.

For information on schedules, fares and reservations for the M. V. *Uchuck*, contact **Nootka Sound Service**, Box 57, Gold River, B.C., V0P 1G0 (283-2515 or 283-2325).

Sea Kayaking Canada's West Coast by John Ince and Hedi Kottner describes several excellent west-coast trips.

Nimpkish Area

South of Port McNeill, Highway 19 runs inland from Johnstone Strait, skirting the east coast of the Nimpkish River and the Nimpkish River Ecological Reserve. Created in May 1988, the reserve comprises an 18-ha (44 -a.) stand of giant Douglas firs, some as old as 600 years and reaching as high as 96 m (315 ft.).

As you head down island on Highway 19, you will be close to two good hiking and nordic skiing areas: Mount Cain Alpine Park and Schoen Lake Provincial Park.

Mount Cain Park, just east of Woss, contains a relatively new nordic ski area with 20 km (12 mi.) of unmarked trails, plus a day lodge with a snack bar and ski rentals.

A signposted gravel road east of Woss leads 12 km (7.5 mi.) to the 8170-ha (20,188-a.) wilderness park at Schoen Lake. Mount Schoen, a 1802-m (5900-ft.) peak, abuts its namesake lake, a narrow 5-km (3-mi.) stretch good for canoeing. In summer, hikers prepared for a rugged trail can enjoy the park's Nisnak Meadows, with its superb showing of subalpine wildflowers and resident wildlife—Roosevelt elk, black bears, beavers, wolves, cougars and black-tailed deer.

Useful Information

For information on skiing, contact **Mount Cain Alpine Society**, Box 1225, Port McNeill, B.C., V0N 2R0 (281-0244).

Randy Stoltmann's *Hiking Guide to the Big Trees of Southwestern B.C.* gives general information about the Nimpkish River Ecological Reserve as well as being a trail guide. Both *Island Adventures* by Richard Blier and the *Outdoor Club of Victoria's Hiking Trails III—Central and Northern Vancouver Island* have trail descriptions for the Schoen Lake area.

Sayward

The Sayward Forest Canoe Route provides one of the most extensive canoeing opportunities on the island. Its total 46.7 km (29 mi.) of paddling waters are located northwest of Campbell River, within the Sayward Provincial Forest. You can reach the circuit either from Highway 28, via the Camp 5 Road, or from Highway 19 via MacMillan Bloedel's Menzies logging road. Use car headlights at all times when travelling on these industrial roads and exercise caution.

The canoe route runs through a series of lakes joined by a number of portage trails constructed by the British Columbia Forest Service. Maps of the route can be obtained from forest service offices in Vancouver, Port McNeill and Campbell River.

Summer and early fall are prime times to canoe Sayward, and most paddlers follow the route counterclockwise, from any one of the many available starting points. If canoed in its entirety, the route takes 3 to 4 days to complete, but excellent access roads to most of the lakes mean it can be canoed in sections as well. The numerous Forest Service Recreation Sites located along the canoe route provide many areas for overnight camping. Most paddlers put in at Gosling Bay on Campbell Lake and then portage to Gosling Lake before continuing on the well-marked route. Other points of entry are Loveland Bay, Strathcona Dam, McIvor Lake and Forbes Landing.

The rolling countryside through which paddlers travel is covered mainly with immature second-growth timber dotted with numerous lakes and creeks. Anglers should take along their rods, but be sure to bury all fish cleanings as well as food remains to avoid attracting bears. We recommend paddlers avoid disturbing beaver dams, since they help maintain water levels.

Useful Information

Sayward Forest Canoe Route maps can be obtained from the Ministry of

Forests, Campbell River District, 370 Dogwood St., Campbell River, B.C., V9W 6Y7 (286-3282).

Island Adventures by Richard Blier gives a description of the Sayward Forest Canoe Route.

CENTRAL VANCOUVER ISLAND

Campbell River

Campbell River (pop. 17,000), a.k.a. Salmon Capital of the World, is situated on Discovery Passage, on northeastern Vancouver Island, facing the islands of Quadra, Cortes, Read, Sonora and Thurlow. For centuries 6 seasonal Indian villages moved into the Campbell River area, capitalizing on the 5 different salmon runs that make fishing here a year-round proposition.

Canada's first Pacific coast public fishing pier, Discovery Pier, was built at Campbell River in 1987. Complete with weather shelters, fish-cleaning stations and lighting for night fishing, the pier extends 48 m. (160 ft.) offshore. Several anglers have landed 18-kg (40-lb.) fish from its heights. All this activity takes place minutes from downtown Campbell River.

Where Discovery Passage narrows to a 2-km (1.2-mi.) passage between Campbell River and Quadra Island, it forces migrating salmon through the compressed channel, creating some of the richest fishing grounds in B.C. (Beware the tides, however, which can run from 7 to 16 knots in places.) One of the most beautiful sights we've ever seen from our fishing boat was orcas feasting on salmon in kelp beds in the passage, while sunset light turned the kelp pink and the surrounding waters turquoise-blue.

The lure of Campbell River salmon fishing is the possibility of catching a tyee (a Chinook weighing over 14 kg/30 lb.). Tours are available in Campbell River for short or extended fishing expeditions, and there are plenty of U-Drive boats with tackle for do-it-yourselfers. Famous fishing billets in Campbell River include Painters Lodge and April Point Lodge.

Keen fish people visiting Campbell River might also enjoy something unique to the area—float-and-snorkel trips down the Campbell River. Once made primarily by fisheries people and occasional scuba enthusiasts, these trips to view homing salmon and steelhead are gaining popularity. Huge fish that have escaped anglers' lures sweep upriver, some still dangling lures ... the ones that got away! It's like being inside a giant aquarium, except that the continually changing riverscape beneath, the variable current and the sheer numbers of fish are features lacking in an artificial environment. Wet suits will allow even nonswimmers to make the trip. As experienced scuba divers know, you seldom see salmon at sea, so this is an ideal opportunity to study them eye to eye. But only tackle the trip with capable assistance from such companies as Beaver Aquatics in Campbell River.

Quinsam Salmon Hatchery, located 5 km (3.1 mi.) west of downtown Campbell River (turn left off the Gold River Highway after passing the junction to Port Hardy and follow the signs), explains the salmon's life cycle and gives visitors the chance to view thousands of salmon fry. The hatchery is open from 8:00 A.M. to 4:00 P.M. year-round.

Campers and hikers can also head to Elk Falls Provincial Park, just northwest of town, for a forest walk near the river. The Campbell River Museum and Archives displays a wide selection of artifacts from native people of the area and runs nature tours and other events. The Campbell River Chamber of Commerce puts out an excellent guide to day hikes in the Campbell River and Quadra Island area, including 6 underwater trips for scuba divers.

Quadra Island, a 10-minute ferry ride from Campbell River, is well worth a visit for a variety of reasons. The ferry lands at Quathiaski Cove, one of the island's two main centres. (Heriot Bay is the other.) A typical tour of Quadra might include a stop at Cape Mudge Lighthouse, located on the historical 1792 landing site of Captain Vancouver's voyage to the Coast Salish village of Tsquloten. After viewing the petroglyphs that are clearly visible on the rocks here, you could do some tide pooling, then return to Quathiaski Cove for a meal at the Landing Pub.

The Kwagiulth Museum and Cultural Centre, located in Cape Mudge Village on the southern tip of Quadra Island, provides a fascinating stop-off point. The spiral-shaped cedar building resembles a sea snail, symbolizing the Kwagiulth people's strong connection with the sea. The museum houses a superb collection of Kwagiulth potlatch regalia, including masks, whistles, rattles and a totem pole.

Rebecca Spit Provincial Park, a marine park on Quadra's west coast, provides good summer swimming and beachcombing, plus splendid views of the Inside Passage islands backed by the snow-capped mountains of the Coast Range.

From Quadra, you can catch another ferry to Cortes Island. Cortes, at the head of Desolation Sound, is a favourite summer hideaway for urban Vancouverites.

From Campbell River, Quadra or Cortes, you can pay private boat owners to take you to Mitlenatch Island Provincial Nature Park. This park is a prime destination for ornithologists, who come to view hundreds of nesting pairs of the glaucous-winged gulls, pelagic cormorants and pigeon guillemots that cover this large rock island in season. The din of birds staking out their territory is nonstop. Be sure to use bug repellent, as summer mosquitoes at Mitlenatch can be a nuisance. Volunteer naturalists are available in summer to explain the birds' habits to visitors.

Back on Vancouver Island, Campbell River provides a natural jumping-off point for boaters heading into the lovely marine park of Desolation Sound just off the coast.

Useful Information

For details about hiking, scuba trips and ferry schedules as well as other general information about the area, visit the Tourist Information Centre in the main square of downtown Campbell River.

For information on snorkelling along Campbell River, contact **Beaver Aquatics** at 287-7652. Contact the **Quinsam Salmon Hatchery**, Box 467, Campbell River, B.C., V9W 5C1 (287-9564) for further information about their programs.

Cruising Guide to British Columbia: Volume II—Desolation Sound and the Discovery Islands by Bill Wolferstan is an indispensable guide for boaters travelling in this area.

Gold River

Travellers can reach the logging town of Gold River, a spelunking centre and the dock for the M. V. *Uchuck III*, by driving southwest from Campbell River on Highway 28.

The *Uchuck*, a converted U.S. minesweeper, offers a freight and passenger service in Nootka Sound, Esperanza Inlet and Kyuquot Sound. In July and August, the vessel also makes twice-weekly cruises down the Muchalat Inlet, around Bligh Island (named after the famous *Bounty* captain) and into Friendly Cove on Nootka Sound. The *Uchuck* is the ideal vehicle for transporting canoes, kayaks and camping gear into this area. Its name stems from the Nootka word *uchucklesit*, meaning "there inside the bay."

Captain James Cook landed in Friendly Cove in 1778 with his ships *Discovery* and *Resolution*; Bligh was Cook's navigating officer. According to some historians, the native people tried to guide Cook into the cove's sheltered waters by shouting "Noot-ka eh, noot-ka-eh," meaning "Come around here." Cook thought they were identifying themselves, and the name Nootka stuck. (Nootka people today prefer to be known as Nuu-chah-nulth, which translates roughly as "all along the mountains.") While trading took place, Cook brewed up spruce beer to combat scurvy among his crew.

Hikers keen to explore Nootka Sound can either charter helicopters from Tofino, 80 km (50 mi.) to the south, or arrange in Gold River for a boat to drop them off for a week-long hike that runs from Escalante Beach, within sight of Friendly Cove, south to Hot Springs Cove. The hike, which takes hikers past the Estevan Point Lighthouse, leads along the relatively sheltered shores of Hesquiat Harbour. Driftwood beaches are fringed by foreshore flowers and covered with seashells and the occasional Japanese glass fishing float. On this trek you can harvest little neck clams on the lower tides and rockfish, trout or crab can be caught from the shore. Permission to do this hike should be requested by visiting the native band office in Hesquiat.

The Upana Cave System lies 25 minutes west of Gold River along the Head Bay Forest Road. This system provides travellers with the opportunity to view limestone caves on a self-guided tour. Administered by the B.C. Forest Service, the caves were used for underground sequences of the TV series "Huckleberry Finn and His Friends."

Useful Information

For information on schedule, fees and reservations for the M. V. *Uchuck III*, contact **Nootka Sound Service**, Box 57, Gold River, B.C., V0P 1G0 (283-2325 or 283-2515).

Contact the Gold River Travel Infocentre, Village Square Plaza, Box 39, Gold River, B.C., V0P 1G0 (283-7123) for information on companies who will provide drop-off services to Escalante Beach.

For general information about the Upana Cave System, contact the **B.C. Speleological Federation**, Box 733, Gold River, B.C., V0P 1G0 (283-2691). **Mostly Caves Enterprises**, Box 897, Gold River, B.C., V0P 1G0 (283-2691) offers guided cave trips.

Strathcona Park

The 231,434 wilderness ha (571,880 a.) of Strathcona, B.C.'s oldest provincial park, form a massive wedge in the north-central part of Vancouver Island.

Named after Lord Strathcona and Mount Royal, a Canadian pioneer and one of the driving forces behind the building of the Canadian Pacific Railway, the park stretches from salt water (at southwestern Herbert Inlet) to alpine meadow. Its nickname, "Little Switzerland," derives from the fact that it contains 6 of the 7 highest peaks on the island. Strathcona also harbours the vast Comox Glacier, Vancouver Island's last remaining icefield.

At one time, provincial authorities had hoped tourism in Strathcona would rival that in Banff National Park in Alberta, but the Great War years put paid to that scheme, leaving this varied park mainly for B.C. residents.

Activities of choice here include hiking, backpacking, wilderness camping, nordic and alpine skiing, ski mountaineering, and boating and canoeing on 32-km (20-mi.) long Buttle Lake, which contains cut-throat, rainbow and Dolly Varden trout.

Campbell River and Courtenay are the primary access points to Strathcona Park. Highway 28 leads to the park headquarters at Buttle Lake, 48 km (30 mi.)

west of Campbell River. Park interpreters are on hand from June to September. Family hikers tend to head in from Courtenay in the Comox Valley (a 25-minute drive in summer on the Mount Washington road) to the subalpine Paradise Meadows trailhead near the nordic skiing lodge. Trails through the meadows provide access to the numerous lakes of the Forbidden Plateau area. As native legend has it, the plateau was inhabited by evil spirits who consumed women and children who dared venture into the area. This route is also the starting point for longer hikes into the alpine meadows and lakes towards Mount Edward Albert.

In summer months, blooming heather, violets, Indian paintbrush, monkey flower, lupines, phlox, moss campion and a dozen other varieties of flowering plants cover the hillsides with a palette of brilliant blues, reds and yellows.

In winter, skiers enjoy both the plateau and Mount Washington, Vancouver Island's premier alpine and nordic skiing area. There are over 30 km (19 mi.) of groomed trails, which, together with the abundant snowfall and extensive back-country routes, make for some of the best nordic skiing in the province. In March, Mount Washington hosts its annual cross-country ski marathon.

Drive-in campgrounds at Buttle Lake and Ralph River accommodate overnight visitors. People using the park can also stay at Strathcona Lodge, situated on the lake just outside the park boundary. The lodge's international reputation stems from its outdoor education centre, which offers apprenticeships in wilderness leadership as well as adventure holiday packages. Dedicated to providing an environment that fosters "growth of the human spirit and integration with the natural world," Strathcona Lodge capitalizes on its prime location. Courses are available on everything from advanced rock climbing and mountaineering to white-water canoeing and kayaking, orienteering, survival skills, sailing and wildlife photography. Guided tours include kayak trips to Nootka and Kyuquot sounds.

Hiking trails in the park radiate from Buttle Lake, with Flower Ridge, the Elk River Trail and Marble Meadows being some of the best-known hikes. Once off established trails veteran hikers should take to the high ridges to avoid rock slides, thick underbrush and the mosquitoes of the valley bottoms. These high ridges often interconnect, making circular alpine tours easier by reducing tedious retracing of steps. A map of Strathcona put out by the provincial government delineates all the park's trails with sensible time and distance estimates.

Gear for Strathcona should include gaiters to keep pant legs dry, an ice axe and rope for tricky slopes and a barometer or altimeter. Always get the most up-to-date information available about your routes. And be very careful. Injuries resulting from slipping on wet heather have necessitated several helicopter evacuations over the years.

Climbers can scale the island's highest peak—the 2200-m (7219-ft.)

Golden Hinde, a high pyramid of volcanic rock whose summit dominates lower granite-shouldered peaks. Many climbers start from Burman Lake, where the elevation gain from base to summit is 1200 m (3936 ft.). The best route up Golden Hinde is from the south. The final approach up steep scree and unstable rock requires extreme caution, but the view from the top is worth it!

Another fine hike in Strathcona, one very popular with visitors from Europe, is the trail leading from the head of Great Central Lake to the 460-m (1443-ft.) Della Falls, the highest free-falling falls in North America and the sixth highest in the world. Della drops in three separate cascades and is particularly impressive in May and June during spring runoff.

The 36.8-km (23-mi.) paddle up Great Central Lake from the south (outside park boundaries), followed by the 16-km (10-mi.) hike in to the falls, makes a leisurely one-week trip. Campsites dot the lake and the well-maintained trail. You can rent canoes from the Ark Resort at the southeastern end of the lake. (Access to the resort is signposted on Highway 4 west of Port Alberni, just before the Sproat Lake Park turnoff.) The resort offers 15 campsites, trailer accommodation for 6 people, a store where you can purchase supplies and a water taxi service in summer to take hikers to the start of the trail. Hiking season to Della is from the beginning of May to the end of October.

Another way to get to Della Falls is to pick up a Pacific Rim Airlines or Coastal Airlines charter flight in Port Alberni for a 20-minute scenic jaunt to the top of the lake and the start of the hiking trail. On the return trip, be sure to peek out over Sproat Lake and you may notice the Mars Water Bombers, the largest forest-fire-fighting planes in the world.

Experienced mountaineers can come overland to Della Falls via Mount Septimus.

Useful Information

A map and brochure about Strathcona Park are available from the Visitor Services Coordinator, BC Parks, Strathcona District, Box 1479, Parksville, B.C., V0R 2S0 (755-2483) or from the park headquarters at Buttle Lake.

Contact **Strathcona Lodge**, Box 2160, Campbell River, B.C., V9W 5C9 (286-3122) for information on accommodation and wilderness adventure trips.

Contact the **Ark Resort**, R. R. #3, Site 306, C-1, Port Alberni, B.C., V9Y 7L7 (723-2657) for information on camping, canoe rentals and water taxi service to the Della Falls trailhead.

For information on charter flights, contact **Pacific Rim Airlines**, Box 1196, Port Alberni, B.C., V9Y 7M1 (724-4495 or 1-800-663-6679, toll free within B.C.) or **Pacific Coastal Airlines**, 4440 Cowley Crescent, Richmond, B.C., V7B 1B8 (273-8666).

Mount Washington ski information can be obtained by writing to Box 3069, Courtenay, B.C., V9N 5N3 (338-1386).

Benno's Country Adventure Tours, 1958 West 4th Ave., Vancouver, B.C., V6J 1M5 (738-5105), offers nordic ski tours to Mount Washington. The Outdoor Club of Victoria's *Hiking Trails III—Central and Northern Vancouver Island* provides trail descriptions of most hikes in the park. *Island Adventures* by Richard Blier provides the canoe route and trail description of the Great Central Lake and Della Falls trip.

Courtenay and Comox

Courtenay and its sister community, Comox, a few miles east on the peninsula that forms Courtenay's harbour, are centres for the rich farming areas of the Comox Valley. Both towns are an easy drive away from the prime skiing areas at Mount Washington and Forbidden Plateau. Comox makes a good base from which to charter boats for the exquisite marine park of Desolation Sound, just a day's sail away across the Strait of Georgia.

One of the nicest swimming holes on the island is situated just outside of Courtenay. The town has begun to promote Nymph Falls as a local point of interest, and you can get details from the tourist information office on Highway 19 near the north end of town.

Nymph Falls can be reached by taking the road leading to Forbidden Plateau and Mount Washington. When the road divides, keep on the Forbidden Plateau fork alongside Browns River. A marked trail leads to the Nymph Falls rapids and deep pools where you can picnic, swim and do some natural water sliding.

Desolation Sound Yacht Charters, 201-1797 Comox Ave., Comox, B.C., V9N 4A1 (339-4914 or 339-7222) offers bare-boat, skippered and cruise-and-learn courses in the area.

Denman and Hornby Islands

Ferries depart regularly from the Buckley Bay terminal just south of Courtenay for the 15-minute trip to Denman Island. From Denman, another ferry makes the 15-minute journey to nearby Hornby Island. Both islands are quasi-tropical in summer and count many artists among their permanent populations of 590 and 690 respectively.

Denman, an island of 50 sq. km (19 sq. mi.), is rimmed with oyster and clam beds. Campers here tend to make tracks for Fillongley Provincial Park or Sandy Island Provincial Park. Both bicycles and canoes are available for rent.

Ferries for Hornby leave from Gravelly Bay on Denman and arrive at Shingle Spit. Though there are no provincial campgrounds on Hornby, 30 sq. km (11.5 sq. mi.) in size, campers can chose from a variety of commercial campgrounds. Windsurfers congregate on Tribune Bay during summer.

Day tours, excursions and kayak rentals on Hornby can be organized through Zucchini Ocean Kayak Centre. A full-day safari with Zucchini ends with a meal at the local pub. Sunset cruises are popular, too.

The diving off Hornby is superlative, rated by *National Geographic* magazine as better diving than the Red Sea. The cold waters surrounding the island contain very large specimens of some species. One example is the world's largest sea urchin, the giant red, which can reach 18 cm (7 in.) in diameter. Commercial divers harvest geoduck (burrowing clams) which can weigh up to 4 kg (10 lb.) and are sliced into steaks. One vast mussel from Hornby waters is often enough to make a chowder.

An added bonus when diving between mid-June and mid-September is the possibility of viewing docile sixgill sharks around the Flora Islets off Hornby. These primitive sharks (*Hexanchus griseus*), recorded in B.C. waters at a size of 4 m (13 ft.), can be recognized by their distinctive oval-ringed eyes, which loom very large in the low light situations. A huge mouth extends almost the full length of the sixgill's head. Although oceanographers at the University of Victoria are researching the theory that cold water makes sharks and other creatures more docile, seasoned divers advise treating these benign sharks with the respect they deserve. (No fin-pulling or tail-tweaking!) These fish may be "primitive"—they still have six gills, while most modern sharks have five—but they are armed with standard attack equipment.

Bob Zielinski, who runs Hornby Island Diving, also owns an informal bunkhouse that sleeps 28 people and contains a restaurant-style kitchen. Groups can book the whole cabin, rent diving equipment, get their tanks filled and join guide Bob in his 8-m (26-ft.) aluminium herring skiff for a trip out to dive this marine-rich area. Just bring your sleeping bags and food.

Useful Information
For information on ferry schedules and facilities on the islands, contact Denman/Hornby Tourist Services, Denman Island, B.C., V0R 1T0 (335-2293).

Zucchini Ocean Kayak Centre, Hornby Island, B.C., V0R 1Z0 (335-0045) offers day tours, bicycle and kayak rentals.

Contact **Hornby Island Diving**, c/o Bob Zielinski, Hornby Island, B.C., V0R 1Z0 (335-2807) for information on diving trips.

Bicycling Vancouver Island and the Gulf Islands by Simon Priest has detailed cycling route descriptions for both islands.

Lasqueti Island

Lasqueti Island, accessible by foot-passenger ferry from the foot of Lee Road off Highway 19, sits right in the middle of the Strait of Georgia. Its sheltered coves, offshore reefs and islets, and copious bird and sea mammal life make it ideal for paddlers. Since it is largely undeveloped, mountain bikers and hikers enjoy its traffic-free terrain. The island can also be reached from Powell River, on the mainland coast, via Texada Island.

THE WEST COAST

Highway 4 begins at Parksville, on the east coast of Vancouver Island, then cuts west, taking in Port Alberni, at the head of Barkley Sound, and ending at Tofino, on the northwestern periphery of Pacific Rim National Park.

Initially, Highway 4 heads through the hamlet of Coombs, known for the goats grazing on the rooftop of the local store, and for Butterfly World, where you can look at hundreds of free-flying butterflies (call 248-7026 for more information). The highway skirts Cameron Lake (good fishing for big lake trout), then leads through MacMillan Park's Cathedral Grove, a stand of 800-year-old Douglas fir trees that survived a forest fire 300 years ago. The largest tree measures 3 m (10 ft.) in diameter and is 75 m (240 ft.) high. A walk in the park is lovely at any time of day, and particularly so when the sun slants down through the branches high overhead.

The 50-km (31-mi.) drive from Parksville to Port Alberni skirts the tip of the Beaufort mountain range. Visitors come to Port Alberni year-round to fish Alberni Inlet and Barkley Sound for sockeye and coho salmon. An annual salmon festival on Labour Day weekend awards in excess of $40,000 in prizes.

From Port Alberni, hikers can take canoes the full length of Great Central Lake to the trailhead for the 16-km (10-mi.) hike to Della Falls in Strathcona Park. You can also catch a 20-minute flight from Port Alberni to the head of the lake if you don't have time to paddle. (See the Strathcona Park section in this chapter for details.)

One of the most enjoyable ways of getting to the southwest coast of the island from Port Alberni is to take the M. V. *Lady Rose*, a Scottish-built packet freighter that travels down Alberni Inlet to Barkley Sound and the coastal villages of Bamfield and Ucluelet. (Our section on the M. V. *Lady Rose* later in this chapter carries a full description of the trip.)

Highway 4 runs west from Port Alberni along the shores of Sproat Lake, then continues south through the Mackenzie mountain range. Once the highway reaches the coast, travellers can head south for the town of Ucluelet, or continue to Tofino, 42 km (26 mi.) to the north.

Tofino

Tofino lies just beyond the northern boundary of Pacific Rim National Park. Between the park campgrounds and the town (pop. 1000), there are numerous motels, beachfront cabins and private campgrounds, and there is also good accommodation in Tofino itself. An unusual place to stay is Clayoquot Lodge, located on a private island accessible by motor launch from Tofino.

Tofino has made its name not only as a thriving base for the west-coast fishing industry but also as a relaxed destination for whale watchers, visitors to the park and folks interested in the area's rich native heritage.

Tofino is accessible by boat and float plane as well as by car. Paddlers can reach the town by travelling down the Kennedy River to Tofino Inlet. Parks Canada's launching ramp and picnic site at Grice Bay, 19 km (12 mi.) from the mouth of Clayoquot Arm on Kennedy Lake, is the ideal place to put in. The mere 6-m (20-ft.) elevation drop between lake and ocean makes for a negligible river current, and the only portage is a 1-km (.6-mi.) detour around Kenfalls Rapids near the mouth of the river. Fishing for cutthroat and steelhead trout is excellent near the rapids.

Tofino is a year-round destination. Storm watching is prime between November and February. (Go to the Blue Heron Pub, overlooking Clayoquot Sound, to hear some good storm yarns!) From mid-March to mid-April, visitors flock to Tofino for whale watching. During these months, 20,000 gray whales (*Eschrichtius robustus*) swim north from Baja California to breeding grounds in Alaska, passing close to shore at this point in their migration.

The Pacific Rim Whale Festival, held every spring, attracts about 6500 avid whale watchers to the area. The most popular whale-watching sites are Schooner Cove, Green Point, Wickaninnish Centre (where it is possible to view the whales from shore), Wye Point and Amphitrite Point (near Ucluelet). Ocean-boat tours cost from $20 to $30 per person for a 2- to 3-hour trip. Pacific Rim National Park offers free, guided whale-spotting hikes, lectures, films and displays. And, since one pod of gray whales summers over near Tofino before heading south with the troop for winter, whale watching is also possible throughout the summer months.

For an interesting outing from Tofino, take a water taxi over to beautiful Meares Island and walk its rough-cut trails. The island, currently the subject of a land claims trial, was declared a tribal park in 1984 by the native Clayoquot and Ahousat peoples, and as recently as 1988 Tofino residents chained themselves to Meares' big trees to prevent the logging of this ancient forest. Many of the 8000-ha (19,768-a.) island's trails wind among the world's largest known western red cedars as well as some of the biggest hemlock and spruce trees in Canada. Though Carmanah Valley Sitka spruces are taller, those on Meares Island are no pygmies, some reaching 70 m (230 ft.) in height. One of the 1500-year-old red cedars measures 19 m (62 ft.) in circumference.

Meares Island's 3 trail systems run past bald eagle nests and bear dens. A good spot from which to survey the island is the 753-m (2417-ft.) top of Lone

Cone Mountain. Expansive mud flats ring Meares, making for pleasant beach-combing. A useful book to consult before a hike on the island is Randy Stoltmann's *Hiking Guide to the Big Trees of Southwestern British Columbia*. The whole of Clayoquot Sound, including Vargas and Flores islands to the north and west of Meares Island, is popular kayaking territory from April to October. Plentiful beaches and superb scenery make for pleasant 6- to 12-day paddles. Keep an eye out for harmless basking sharks, which sift plankton off Flores Island. Though 13 m (45 ft.) long, they are very shy and we've seen them spooked just by the shadow of a sail.

Native art connoisseurs will enjoy visiting the Eagle Aerie Gallery on the main street of Tofino. Featuring the work of Tsimshian artist Roy Vickers, the gallery smells sweetly of cedar. The whales, cormorants and eagles of the area have inspired some of Vickers's most striking pieces.

Tofino Air uses Tofino as a base from which to fly adventurers to otherwise inaccessible destinations off the west coast. Both the sea lion colony of Plover Reef and the famous bird-nesting area on Cleland Island are popular with naturalists.

Another increasingly popular destination from Tofino is Maquinna Provincial Park, named after Chief Maquinna of the Nootka. Established in 1955 after local store owner Ivan Clarke donated the land, Maquinna Park is real wilderness. Its best-known asset is Hot Springs Cove. Flanked on the east by the Openit Peninsula, Hot Springs Cove is on a narrow, 3-km (1.8-mi.) inlet often used by fishing boats holing up during winter storms. Main day-trip access to Hot Springs Cove is via regular float-plane service from Tofino. The 37-km (23-mi.) flight skims the sea at 300 m (1000 ft.). Planes dock at the government wharf, a deserted cannery. From here, a 1.9-km (1.2-mi) boarded trail leads through lush, dense rain forest to the hot springs. The trail is an easy stroll for adults as well as children.

For the three summer months of June, July and August, the Hesquiat Indian Band runs a twice-daily ferry service to Hot Springs Cove from the government dock in Tofino. Their aluminum boat, which holds 14 people, hugs the shore during the one-hour cruise to the hot springs.

The smell of sulphur fumes and the sight of steam rising over the salal bushes signal the presence of the cove's pools, which many fans believe have therapeutic effects on rheumatism and arthritis. Visitors bathe in the 6 rocky pools, each about 75 cm (30 in.) deep, which cascade in a line down to the ocean, getting progressively cooler closer to the sea. Temperatures range from 27° C (80° F) to 50° C (122° F). Gurgling waters contain sulphur, mineral salts, iron oxides and calcium to soothe hikers' and paddlers' aching muscles.

Take a pair of running shoes to wear in the pools and a large plastic bag for your dry clothes and towel, in case of rain. Allow half an hour for the stroll through dripping rain forest to the springs.

Kayakers make Hot Springs Cove a destination after paddling through the Flores and Vargas islands between Openit and Tofino. Unless you are an experienced paddler, plan on joining one of the summer paddling trips offered by commercial operators. Flores Island boasts good beaches. Ahous Bay, on Vargas Island, is a good viewing spot for gray whales during migration from March to July, and many birds nest on nearby Blunden Island.

Useful Information

For flights to Hot Springs Cove, contact **Tofino Air**, Box 424, Tofino, B.C., V0R 2Z0 (725-4454) or **Pacific Rim Airlines**, Box 1196, Port Alberni, B.C., V9Y 7M1 (724-4495).

For information on whale-watching trips, ferry-boat service to Hot Springs Cove, kayak trips and other services in the Tofino area, contact **Tofino Adventures Booking Centre**, Box 620, Tofino, B.C., V0R 2Z0 (725-4222).

Tofino Expeditions, 114-1857 West 4th Ave., Vancouver, B.C., V6J 1M4 (926-9904 or 725-4200/summer only); **Pacific Rim Paddling**, Box 1840, Station E, Victoria, B.C., V8W 2Y3 (384-6103), and **Five Seasons Adventure Tours**, 3201 Kingsway, Vancouver, B.C., V5R 5K3(435-5444) all offer kayaking trips in the area.

Nootka Charters runs sailing trips to Hot Springs Cove, Nootka Sound and Clayoquot Sound. Contact them at General Delivery, Tofino, B.C., V0R 2Z0 (725-3318) for further information.

Contact **Clayoquot Lodge**, Box 188, Tofino, B.C., V0R 2Z0 (725-3284) for information on accommodation at the lodge.

Long Beach

South of Tofino and north of Ucluelet, Long Beach is the first of three distinctive sections that form the Pacific Rim National Park. The others—the Broken Island Group and the West Coast Trail—are covered later in this chapter.

Popular with Canadians from coast to coast and with American and European visitors, Pacific Rim Park was dedicated in 1970 by Princess Anne. The park's great appeal lies in its long, windswept beaches, strong seas and moist Pacific air. Long Beach itself stretches for 11 km (6.8 mi.), its rocky points pounded by surf and its sands often yielding Japanese fishing floats. A good overview of the park is provided by films and exhibits offered at the Wickaninnish Centre on Wickaninnish Beach (named after the influential Nootka chief who lived among the Clayoquot people in the late 18th century).

The popular park campground above Green Point charges a daily fee from Easter to mid-October, but camping is free for the remainder of the year. We have fond memories of camping one February at Long Beach, when we had the snow-dusted beaches and resident whiskey jacks to ourselves. The heated women's washroom was the warmest spot around!

Parks Canada puts out an excellent *Hiker's Guide* to 9 marked trails in the Long Beach area. The pamphlet "Exploring the Seashore," published by Environment Canada, is another valuable resource. You can get both at the park information centre along with material on the geology, wildlife and other important features of the area. Ask at the centre about shellfish harvesting restrictions because of red tide.

According to Parks Canada's booklet *Birds of Pacific Rim National Park*, 54 species of birds breed in the park, and bird watchers have spotted 249 species here, ranging from albatrosses to waxwings.

Other natural highlights of the park include the sea arches, huge surge channels and rocky bluffs on the South Beach Trail near the Wickaninnish Centre. At South Beach the trail culminates in a boardwalk close to a fine winter storm watching perch, dubbed "The Edge of Silver Thunder" by local residents.

South of South Beach Trail along the Wickaninnish Trail, keep an eye out for minuscule sundew plants, lying on top of the colourful red, green and brown mats of sphagnum (peat moss). The sundew's tiny, sticky red droplets trap insects.

At the northern end of Long Beach, the Schooner Trail bridges a small salmon-spawning stream. As the *Hiker's Guide* points out, this is a good place for looking at the rich Sitka spruce fringe that skirts the entire outer coast of Vancouver Island and the Queen Charlotte Islands; the Sitka is especially adapted to daily bombardments by salty sea mists and beach sands.

Intertidal life along Long Beach runs the gamut from bull kelp to brilliant sea anemones. But do exercise caution on promontories, where isolated storm waves as high as 10 m (32 ft.) can roll in unannounced from Japan.

A relatively new sport on the beaches of the park is surfing. Clad in black and fluorescent orange, blue and green wet suits, surfers, mainly from Vancouver Island and the Lower Mainland, bring their boards to these Pacific waters. More than 90 per cent of the surfing is done between June and August; winter yields the best waves, however. The park, with 600,000 visitors a year, employs a surf guard from June to September at Incinerator Rock, a popular surfing location off Long Beach.

Useful Information

For park information and maps, contact Park Superintendent, Pacific Rim National Park, Box 280, Ucluelet, B.C., V0R 3A0 (726-7721 or 726-4212).

Bruce Obee's *The Pacific Rim Explorer* is a good general guide to the area. *Hiking Trails II—Southeastern Vancouver Island*, put out by the Outdoor Club of Victoria, is also useful.

Ucluelet

Ucluelet (pronounced you-cloo-let) is ranked third in B.C. in terms of annual total commercial fishing catch. The community, which takes its name from the Nootka word meaning "people of the sheltered bay," lies on the northwest side of Barkley Sound. Fishing, whale watching, nature cruises and diving can all be done out of Ucluelet. Accommodation is cozy, ranging from motels to resorts. Seafood, of course, is prime.

Useful Information

For information on whale watching and local sightseeing cruises, contact **Subtidal Adventures**, Box 78, Ucluelet, B.C., V0R 3A0 (726-7336 or 726-7061) or **Canadian Princess Resort Whale Watching & Nature Tours**, Box 939, Ucluelet, B.C., V0R 3A0 (726-7771 in Ucluelet, 598-3366 in Victoria or 1-800-663-7090 toll free).

The Broken Islands of Barkley Sound

"Unit two," as the federal government prosaically calls the middle part of the Pacific Rim National Park sandwich, consists of the Broken Island Group, which lies south of Ucluelet and north of Bamfield in Barkley Sound. Covering an area of about 130 sq. km (52 sq. mi.), the roughly 100 islands come in various shapes and sizes, none larger than 2 km (1.3 mi.) across.

Diving and kayaking are excellent in the area. The rich marine life, numerous reefs and old shipwrecks provide endless opportunities for divers and there are a large number of designated dive sites for everyone from novice to expert. Relentless weather batters the Broken Group during winter, so the canoeing and kayaking season here lasts only from April to October. Expect crowds in July and August, as the area is very popular with family groups.

Kayakers can either put in at Toquart Bay, north of the Broken Group, or travel down Alberni Inlet to the sound from Port Alberni on the M. V. *Lady Rose*, a trip described in detail in the section on the M. V. *Lady Rose* later in this chapter. The *Lady Rose* drops paddlers, divers and gear on a floating dock near Gibraltar Island at the northeast corner of the Broken Group. Travellers heading to the Toquart Bay launch site should turn off Highway 4 at Kennedy Lake onto the logging road heading down to the bay.

The picturesque scenery and abundant marine life make paddling the Broken Group a joy. Bring plenty of fresh water, as supplies vary. The largest island, Effingham, contains the only fresh-water lake. There are fresh water sources on Gibraltar, Benson, Clarke and Willis islands, as well as on a tiny islet northeast of Hand Island, but because of human contamination it is no longer considered safe to consume any of this water without boiling or treating it first.

Try to paddle in groups of two to three kayaks. You should be prepared to stay put for a while if summer fog rolls in, but early morning mist usually burns off when the sun reaches the hilltops. Essential gear should include a compass and a marine chart that delineates the many treacherous reefs.

Seven authorized camping areas dot the Broken Group. There are also emergency shelters on Clarke and Jacques islands that are adequate for use during stormy weather. Each campsite is unique: some are by sandy shores, others in grassy glades, still others in the giant cedar stands. Since the islands are so well utilized, please be sure to pack out all garbage. Use outhouses where available on Hand, Turtle, Turret and Benson islands. Otherwise, please dig deep latrines.

Basically, you can crisscross the channels between islands as the mood—and the weather—strike you. You can expect to glide over oyster beds, paddle past rocks covered in black mussels and inspect zillions of tide pools. Take time in the kelp beds to look at the crabs clinging to kelp fronds. Anglers can expect to catch spring salmon up to around 20 kg (44 lb.), coho around 7.5 kg (16.5 lb.) and plenty of cod. Mammals who live close to shore include minks, martens, river otters and raccoons, while harbour seals, porpoises, whales and sixgill sharks can be spotted in the water. Sea lions like to sun on the rocks by Wonwer Island, but don't get too close or return their calls too often as they are extremely territorial and have been known to charge kayaks.

In the lagoon between Jacques and Jarvis islands, you can spot the stone-wall traps used by native people to catch fish on retreating tides. On Turtle Island, a rather tangled garden serves as a memorial to Salal Joe, a hermit who lived here with his cat on a float home. He went fishing one day in 1980 and was never seen again, a not uncommon occurrence in these parts.

Other sites to explore are the large sea caves on the southwest side of Dempster Island, caves on Dicebox and Gibralter islands, which feature stalactites, and a number of sea caves near Meares Bluff on Effingham Island. Predeaux Island and Hand Island carry remnants of copper mining and logging operations.

Some of the most magical moments in the Broken Islands occur during dusk paddles, when the movement of your kayak activates bioluminescent streams and fish make similar trails deeper in the water.

Useful Information

For information on kayaking trips to the Broken Islands, contact **Discovery Kayaking**, 2775 Departure Bay Rd., Nanaimo, B.C., V9S 3W9 (758-2488); **Ecosummer**, 1516 Duranleau St., Granville Island, Vancouver, B.C., (669-7741); **Five Seasons Adventure Tours**, 3201 Kingsway, Vancouver, B.C., V5R 5K3 (435-5444) or **Pacific Rim Paddling**, Box 1840, Station E, Victoria, B.C., V8W 2Y (384-6103).

Betty Pratt-Johnson's book *141 Dives in the Protected Waters of Washing-*

ton and British Columbia contains detailed information on diving in the Broken Islands. Area 14 of Ince and Kottner's *Sea Kayaking Canada's West Coast* is devoted to kayaking in the Broken Island Group. *The Pacific Rim Explorer* by Bruce Obee also covers kayaking in this region.

The West Coast Trail

British Columbia's most famous hike, a 77-km (44-mi.) trip along the southern part of Pacific Rim National Park, originated in 1907 as a lifesaving route for shipwrecked mariners. More than 60 ships had gone down in this section of the ocean, dubbed "the Graveyard of the Pacific."

In 1906, the steamship *Valencia*, inbound from San Francisco for Victoria and Seattle, took two days to sink off the 18-24 m (60-80 ft.) cliffs of ill-named Shelter Bight. One hundred and thirty-six passengers and crew members drowned. The tragedy precipitated construction of the West Coast Trail, which now stretches from Port Renfrew in the south to Pachena Bay, near the town of Bamfield, in the north.

Shipwreck enthusiasts should get hold of a little booklet entitled *A Guide to Shipwrecks along the West Coast Trail* by R. E. Wells. We found copies at the Beachcomber gift shop in Port Renfrew for $3.95. This collection of drawings of 24 major west-coast shipwrecks includes a brief account of each wreck and a map showing its location relative to the trail.

Today, hikers check in with park wardens at either end of the trail. The hike, which ideally should be done between mid-May and the end of September, takes a good week to complete at the rate of 10 km (6.25 mi.) per day. All supplies must be packed in and garbage packed out, so count on carrying a pack that weighs about 20 kg (44 lb.).

The key ingredients for hiking the West Coast Trail are stamina, planning and caution. An excellent guidebook by the Sierra Club of Western Canada, *The West Coast Trail and Nitinat Lakes*, contains the best trail descriptions and provides comprehensive lists of necessary supplies and equipment. Two very handy items we would add to their lists are a crescent wrench, for dealing with such setbacks as a malfunctioning camp stove, and a short-handled axe for chopping driftwood for beach fires. A tide table (in a plasticized container) is also essential, since the trail hugs the coastline along much of the route. Tide tables and a map of the trail are available from the BC Parks offices at both the Port Renfrew and Bamfield ends of the trail. The provincial contour map splits the route into two sections: Port Renfrew to Nitinat Lake and Nitinat Lake to Bamfield. Very specific information is given for shoreline routes, river cross-ings (several of which are made by boat after paying a fee to the local native band), points of interest and camping along the way. This hike, it should be emphasized, is for the fit. Fatalities have occurred on the trail, so be very careful and always hike with a buddy.

Most hikers start at Port Renfrew, hiking the difficult part of the trail first. Bus service from Victoria to Port Renfrew is provided by Knight Limousine. At trail's end, Pachena Bay, a local taxi company provides transportation into Bamfield. From there, you can take a bus back to Victoria, drive along the logging road that skirts Alberni Inlet or—the most pleasant option—take the 4-hour boat trip up the inlet on the M. V. *Lady Rose* to Port Alberni.

Your journey from Port Renfrew begins with a boat ride to either Thrasher Cove or the mouth of the Gordon River, the official start of the West Coast Trail. Keep a lookout for ocean birds—pigeon guillemots, marbled murrelets and pelagic cormorants are often seen swimming in the waters nearby.

Steep cliff-side ladders and paths on the early part of the trail should be negotiated carefully. Conditions can be treacherously slippery on the huge logs that form walkways across some particularly muddy sections. The larger gorges can be crossed using cable trolleys that span the chasms at a reasonable height above the rivers.

Do use a hiking staff. Be particularly careful when fording what appear to be shallow streams, since deep crevices may be concealed by unreliable evening light. One friend of ours fractured his leg by stepping into one of these. Luckily, his travelling companion, a doctor, was able to set the leg in a makeshift splint before attracting the attention of the Coast Guard helicopter by waving a bright orange garbage bag. Although the Coast Guard do fly over the trail daily, hikers are cautioned to flag them down only in an extreme emergency of this nature.

The early section of the trail offers plenty of lookouts, and if you encounter good weather the evening stars will never seem brighter. One of the trail's greatest attractions is the primeval urge it can release in many hikers, especially in the early stages when morale is still high. You may feel like letting out a Tarzan-like yell from sheer joie de vivre, but do remember to conserve some energy for the days ahead!

The most picturesque portion of the West Coast Trail runs from Carmanah Creek to the Klanawa River and includes what many hikers consider the highlight of the trip—Tsusiat Falls. A reward for persevering hikers coming from the south and an inspiration for those tackling the trail from the Bamfield end, Tsusiat's 18-m (60-ft.) falls pack plenty of volume over their 24-m (80-ft.) lip. The falls drop down cliffs in a series of cascades, creating super swimming holes near the shores. You can also sit in behind the falls for a cool shower on a hot day. Many hikers make a day trip in from Pachena Bay just to take a dip in Tsusiat.

Bird watchers at the falls can expect to see several species of ducks, gulls and shore birds. Steller's jays, black oyster catchers and chestnut-backed chickadees have all been spotted here. Three species of woodpecker—downy, hairy and pileated—occur fairly regularly, as do both rufous and Anna's hummingbirds. Vegetation in the area includes many varieties of ferns and mosses, Indian paintbrush, goatsbeard, salmonberry, Oregon grape, miniature dogwood and masses of skunk cabbage and salal.

About 1.6 km (1 mi.) before the Pachena Bay Lighthouse, low tide at Michigan Creek reveals the boiler of the S. S. *Michigan*, wrecked in 1893. The last freighter to go down in this patch of ocean sank in 1972, complete with a hold full of Toyotas.

Near Pachena Bay, hikers will pass the chaotic remnants of the cabins used by linemen who maintained the trail in its early years. Shipwrecked sailors used to take refuge from bad weather in these cabins. Winter storms here often send spray over the top of the lighthouse 60 m (200 ft.) above sea level.

Some people like to combine hiking the West Coast Trail with canoeing part of the Nitinat Triangle, the chain of lakes known collectively as the Nitinat Lakes. Groups who do this usually prearrange to swap canoes for hiking boots with another group somewhere along the way.

Together with the West Coast Trail, the Nitinat Triangle makes up the southernmost section of Pacific Rim National Park. The lakes, ringed by virgin red cedar and hemlock rain forest, provide some of the best wilderness canoeing in southwestern B.C.

The Nitinat Triangle can be reached from Duncan, on the east side of the island, by following Highway 18 west to Cowichan Lake. The road running along the lake's north shore leads to the turnoff for the Nitinat Lake launch site just before Caycuse.

Since Nitinat Lake empties into the sea, both salt-water and fresh-water species of birds and mammals live here. The village of Whyac, located where the lake narrows at its seaward end, contains an old cannery. As the Akriggs point out in their book *British Columbia Place Names*, Whyac comes from an old Nitinat Indian word meaning "open mouth," which was used for the openings of fish traps. Northwest of Carmanah Point sits the village of Clo-ose, once a favourite resting spot for halibut fishermen and, prior to World War I, site of a Victorian real-estate promotion scheme that saw many rich English families build fine homes in the area.

Useful Information

For maps, tide tables and information on hiking the West Coast Trail, contact the Park Superintendent, Pacific Rim National Park, Box 280, Ucluelet, B.C., V0R 3A0 (726-7721) or phone the Pacific Rim National Park West Coast Trail Information offices at 728-3234 at Bamfield or 647-5434 at Port Renfrew between mid-May and the end of September.

Bus service to Port Renfrew is offered by **Knight Limousine Ltd.** of Victoria (361-9080 or 383-7311).

For schedules and reservations on the M. V. *Lady Rose*, contact **Alberni**

Marine Transportation, Box 188, Port Alberni, B.C., V9Y 7M7 (723-8313). **Hummingbird Nature Tours**, 31-22374 Lougheed Highway, Maple Ridge, B.C., V2X 2T5 (467-9219) and **Pacific Sunset Nature Tours**, 305-4559 Imperial St., Burnaby, B.C., V5J 1B7 (437-3150) offer guided backpacking trips of the trail.

The West Coast Trail and Nitinat Lakes by the Sierra Club of Western Canada provides the best trail description of the area. Another detailed (and humorous) book on the trail is *Blisters and Bliss* by David Foster and Wayne Aitken. Bruce Obee's *The Pacific Rim Explorer* also has a section on the trail.

Bamfield

Split in half by the waters of Bamfield Inlet and rimmed by salt-water lagoons, the small (pop. 260) village of Bamfield is a 4-hour trip from Port Alberni on the packet freighter M. V, *Lady Rose* or a 2-hour, 100 km (63 mi.) drive over logging roads.

Known as "the Venice of Vancouver Island" since residents travel everywhere by boat, Bamfield is home to the highest proportion of university-educated people of any community in Canada. This is in part due to the existence of the Bamfield Marine Station, maintained for research by five western universities.

Residents and visitors alike enjoy Bamfield's fishing-village charm, boardwalks, pastel-coloured homes and general store, which sells everything from fish bait to video tapes. Hikers can rest up in Bamfield before or after tackling the West Coast Trail. A favourite place to stay is Aguilar House, which offers lodge accommodation and charming self-catering cottages, all a short walk from the Canada Customs office in the village. From Aguilar, a 3-km (2-mi.) hike leads to Brady's Beach, Bamfield's best.

In spring, Bamfield plays host to a large chunk of the west-coast whale-watching traffic. Spring is a busy time in the air, too; the mating rituals of bald eagles resemble the manoeuvres of fighter pilots. Steller's sea lions speed like freight trains into the waters of Bamfield Inlet, gulping down great mouthfuls of the squid that residents jig for off the wharves.

Kelp has been an integral part of the west-coast Indian diet for years, and B.C.'s first kelp farm was established near Bamfield a few years ago. While kelp is relatively high in sodium, soaking it for a few hours will remove much of the salt. It makes a great broth, a tasty tea or a healthy main course; 28.4 g (1 oz.) provides 40 per cent of the dietary fibre and 10 per cent of the protein recommended for daily intake. Kelp can be easily incorporated into kayaking meals. Boil it in fresh water for thirty minutes to remove much of the salty taste, then toss in butter or margarine with seafood, garlic and herbs for a quick meal.

Useful Information

The **University of British Columbia's Continuing Education Department** runs an annual springtime Gray Whales and Seabirds trip to Bamfield. Contact them at the Centre for Continuing Education, University of British Columbia, 5997 Iona Drive, Vancouver, B.C., V6T 2A4 (222-5207) for more information.

Contact **Aguilar House**, Bamfield, B.C., V0R 1B0 (728-3000) for information on accommodation.

For information on tours of the **Bamfield Marine Station**, contact them at Bamfield, B.C., V0R 1B0 (728-3301).

The M. V. Lady Rose

The scenic 4-hour journey down Alberni Inlet from Port Alberni to Bamfield on the colourful packet freighter the M. V. *Lady Rose* gives travellers a keen sense of the lifestyles on this part of the island. Paddlers stack canoes, kayaks and camping gear on board and then sit back with fellow travellers as the boat's crew delivers goods to salmon fish farms, shoreline bush camps and floating post offices en route. On one of the trips we took, the *Lady Rose* dropped off boxes of Lifestage Diets ("If it swims, we feed it") to aquaculturists at Mateo Bay, then picked up a load of dirty laundry farther down the inlet. For many years, the boat's crew made weekly deliveries of groceries to one recluse with a horror of supermarkets.

Built in 1937 in Scotland, the privately owned and operated *Lady Rose* (passenger limit 100) became the first diesel-powered single propeller craft to cross the Atlantic. After wallowing in storms for sixty days, it finally reached Vancouver Island to work as a packet freighter serving military personnel between Port Alberni and Ucluelet.

Now strictly a passenger, freight and mail craft, the *Lady Rose* sails Tuesdays, Thursdays and Saturdays year-round to Bamfield and points along the way. Stopover time in Bamfield is anywhere from 40 minutes to 1½ hours; listen for the captain's announcement prior to disembarking. On Sundays the *Lady Rose* makes an excursion run to Bamfield. The 3½-hour stopover allows passengers to hike to Brady's Beach or explore the village. On alternate days in the summer, the *Lady Rose* sails to Ucluelet and the Broken Islands Group.

Useful Information

For information on specific itineraries and days of operation for the M. V. *Lady Rose*, contact **Alberni Marine Transportation**, Box 188, Port Alberni, B.C., V9Y 7M7 (723-8313). In summer, reservations are highly recommended for all sailings. The boat's coffee shop serves modestly priced cooked breakfasts and light meals.

THE SOUTH COAST

Qualicum Beach and Parksville

North of Nanaimo lie the resort communities of Qualicum Beach and Parksville, close to some of the most popular camping spots on the island. Parksville (pop. 3000) is famous for its beaches, where water warmed by hot sand makes for extra pleasant summer swimming.

At Qualicum Beach campers and hikers can enjoy the deep forests of Little Qualicum Falls Provincial Park. Appropriately enough, fishing is good in the area, since qualicum means "where the dog salmon run." The mountain streams west of Parksville also provide good trout and steelhead fishing.

Two extremely popular provincial parks lie south of Parksville: Rathtrevor Beach and Englishman River Falls. At the latter, visitors can look at two petroglyphs showing a bear and two whales. Park information guides can also give directions to an ecological reserve of wild rhododendrons dating from before the last ice age. The reserve is 7.2 km (4 mi.) south of Parksville on Highway 4, then a further 13.6 km (8 mi.) along a forestry road.

Parksville Travel Infocentre, Box 99, Parksville, B.C., V0R 2S0 (248-3613) can provide information on camping and fishing in the area.

Nanaimo

The second largest city on the island, Nanaimo (pop. 52,000) is the terminus for ferries travelling to Vancouver Island from Horseshoe Bay on the mainland north of Vancouver.

Until 1852, Nanaimo contained five separate Sneymo ("the great and mighty people") villages. Following the discovery of coal, Nanaimo was inundated with miners from England, who were followed at the turn of the century by loggers. Nanaimo's last coal mines closed in 1953, giving way to an economy now based on fishing, agriculture, forestry and tourism. The Centennial Museum in downtown Nanaimo showcases interesting exhibits covering the history of the region.

Recreationally, the city is well placed for boating in the Gulf Islands to the south and Desolation Sound to the north. Skippered and bare-boat charters are available. And while monster salmon tend to congregate farther north, in Campbell River, it is not unusual for anglers to hook into 14-kg (30-lb.) Chinook in Nanaimo.

A good time to plan a visit to Nanaimo is during Bathtub Week, held around the third week in July. This seven-day round of festivities culminates in the famous Nanaimo-to-Vancouver bathtub race across Georgia Strait. Another attraction from November until the end of April is a thriving colony of

Sandstone undercut by the waves, Gabriola Island. *Photo by Lloyd Twaites*

California and Alaskan northern sea lions in the Northumberland Channel off Nanaimo.

Hikers and campers may want to head offshore to Newcastle Island, via private boat or, from May through September, a small ferry that leaves from behind the Nanaimo Civic Arena. Newcastle Island, a 306-ha (756-a.) provincial marine park, is steeped in history, and its 9 km (6 mi.) of self-guided nature trails provide an easy introduction to the past. Coast Salish burial caves and archaeological sites exist alongside evidence of the Hudson Bay Company's coal-mining operations on the island, which was named after England's famous coal-mining town.

Japanese Canadians ran a herring saltery and shipyard on Newcastle from the early 1900s until 1941, when the Canadian government confiscated their property. During the subsequent twenty-year ownership by the Canadian Pacific Steamship Company, Newcastle Island operated as a resort. A dance pavilion, tea house, soccer field and wading pool made the island a favourite destination for company picnics and Sunday outings. In its heyday, up to 1500 people would congregate there at one time. In 1955 the island was sold to the City of Nanaimo. Nowadays, overnight docking is available for more than 50 boats.

Gabriola Island, a 20-minute ferry ride from Nanaimo, provides good cycling and beachcombing opportunities. Year-round accommodation ranges from beach cottages to such well-known places as Surf Lodge.

Useful Information

Schooner Cove Resort and Marina, just north of Nanaimo, provides facilities for sailors. They also offer Canadian Yachting Association (CYA) qualification packages and cruises of the Gulf Islands and Desolation Sound. Contact them at Box 12, Nanoose Bay, B.C., V0R 2R0 (468-7691 or toll free at 1-800-663-7060).

The following Nanaimo-based companies offer day-long wildlife boat tours out of Nanaimo: **Bastion City Wildlife Cruise,** Box 413, Nanaimo, B.C., V9R 5L3 (753-2852) and **Scenic Ferries,** 661 Hunter, Nanaimo, B.C. (753-5141). The **Vancouver Aquarium** runs an annual trip to view the sea lions. Contact them at Box 3232, Vancouver, B.C., V6B 3X8 (682-1118).

Contact **Surf Lodge,** Gabriola Island, B.C., V0R 1X0 (247-9231) for information about accommodation.

Mary and Ted Bentley's book *Gabriola: Petroglyph Island* provides interesting information about one of the island's features.

Southeast Vancouver Island

Visitors travelling south from Nanaimo on Highway 1 may want to stop in at Yellow Point Lodge, a short distance north of Ladysmith. Long a favourite with mainlanders, this magnificent log lodge is set on 73 ha (180 a.) of private parkland and forest, and boasts 1.6 km (1 mi.) of waterfront, a large salt-water swimming pool, reasonable rates, hearty meals served at communal tables, and even a sprung dance floor. Yellow Point's no-kids policy makes it an attractive getaway for harried urban parents and other adventurers.

Yellow Point is close to Quennell Lake, popular with canoeists for its 32 km (20 mi.) of shoreline. What makes Quennell particularly interesting paddling is the wide variety of herons, eagles, loons, ducks, swans and songbirds that live in its backwaters and channels. While only 8 km (5 mi.) long, the lake has lots of good fishing areas around its five different arms and long middle island. Visitors to the lake can stay at the Zuiderzee Campsite.

The town of Ladysmith sits right on the 49th parallel. It served as a shipping port for coal from the Nanaimo mines, a slice of history preserved appropriately enough in the Black Nugget Museum in the town's old Jones Hotel building.

South of Ladysmith and five minutes off of Highway 1 lies the community of Chemainus (pop. 3500). As Helen and Philip Akrigg explain in their excellent book *British Columbia Place Names,* the town's name derives "from the Island Halkomelem word meaning 'bitten breast.' The horseshoe shape of the bay reminded Indians of the bite that a frenzied shaman during certain tribal ceremonies would inflict upon a spectator."

Chemainus, once a one-industry town, faced economic disaster when its only sawmill closed in 1981. A local resident came up with a novel way of attracting tourists, and today the walls of downtown buildings sport 24 huge, colourful murals that depict the area's history: loggers felling a giant fir, steam locomotives hauling timber, dignified native chiefs. Now billed as "The Little Town That Did," Chemainus caters to 370,000 visitors annually.

From Chemainus, a ferry travels to Thetis Island and Kuper Island, two of the less heavily populated Gulf Islands.

Located 51 km (32 mi.) south of Nanaimo on Highway 1, the town of Duncan is home to 60 authentic totem poles and the excellent British Columbia Forest Museum, with its steam-train ride and displays of early logging techniques. The museum opens daily from May to September. Duncan makes a good base from which to cruise the Gulf Islands and Desolation Sound.

Just north of Duncan, Highway 18 heads west into the Cowichan Valley— fishing, hiking and paddling country. Still home to many members of the Cowichan Indian band, the valley's name comes from the Halkomelem word meaning "warm country" or "land warmed by the sun." As the authors of *British Columbia Place Names* explain, the name was given to the area because of a huge rock formation on the side of Mount Tzuhalem that resembles a frog basking in the sun.

The Cowichan Indian sweaters originating in these parts are, along with smoked salmon, the most popular souvenirs of the province. Made from raw fleece in soft greys, browns and blacks, and traditionally woven with family crests of raven and bear (though now other motifs do exist), the sweaters' water-repellent qualities make them popular with outdoorspeople.

The 64-km (40-mi.) Cowichan River rises in Cowichan Lake and flows west into the Strait of Georgia. Famous among fisherpeople, the Cowichan provides opportunities for some superb angling for rainbow, steelhead, brown trout and salmon along the well-maintained, 30-km (19-mi.) Cowichan River Footpath. Highlights of the footpath hike include the Skutz Falls swinging bridge and Banallacks and Summer pools.

Both Cowichan Lake and the Cowichan River are popular for paddling. You can spend anywhere from a few hours to 3 days canoeing the lake, but watch out for power boats. Put-in is at Gordon Bay Provincial Park on the lake's south shore.

A canoe or kayak trip down the Cowichan River takes 2 days. Hazards include rapids, log jams and quick fluctuations in water levels. Paddlers tend to put in at Lakeview Park in the village of Lake Cowichan, then travel the 10 km (6 mi.) to the Skutz Falls portage. Another portage around the 3 cascades at Marie Canyon may also be required depending upon the water level. The remaining 20 km (12 mi.) to Duncan are relatively easy.

The village of Lake Cowichan is also a starting point for access to the Carmanah Valley Provincial Park. Head northeast to Youbou, then on to the B.C. Forest Products Ltd. sawmill. Turn onto the logging road at the right-hand edge of the parking lot and follow signs for 70 km (44 mi.) to the Carmanah trailhead. It is best to travel on weekends because of heavy logging traffic on this road.

The Carmanah Valley is home to some of the tallest trees in Canada. Aged anywhere from 350 to 700 years, the more than 200 Sitka spruces here tower as high as city skyscrapers, many exceeding heights of 70 m (230 ft.). The Carmanah Giant, at 95 m (313 ft.), is believed to be the tallest tree in Canada and is the world's tallest recorded Sitka spruce; as a log on the ground, before processing, it would be worth $40,000. Numerous sightings of the little-known marbled murrelet have been made in the Carmanah Valley and in August 1990 a nest was found in the neighbouring Walbran Valley.

It takes approximately one hour to hike from the trailhead into the valley, where 20 km (12 mi.) of trails have been constructed through the forests of Sitka spruce and red cedar. Nothing quite prepares the hiker for the sogginess of it all! Three hundred and eighty cm (150 in.) of rain falls here annually, making for rife, interdependent growth of moss, salal, deer fern and huckleberries. Great yellow-and-black slugs gorge themselves on yellow, brown and purple mushrooms. Old-man's beard festoons the branches of young hemlocks, while moss envelops the spruce trunks. Tree foliage forms a canopy high overhead. We really caution all visitors to Carmanah to be properly equipped. This is a rain forest and running shoes are no substitute for sensible hiking boots and gaiters. Plan on getting very wet.

Park status was granted to the lower portion of the Carmanah Valley in the spring of 1990, and the provincial parks folks will eventually make available a guide to the area. In the meantime, use the Western Canada Wilderness Committee's detailed road access and hiking trail guide.

Drivers continuing south on Highway 1 from Duncan to Victoria travel the famous Malahat Drive, a scenic winding road that overlooks Saanich Inlet and the Saanich peninsula.

Useful Information
Contact **Yellow Point Lodge**, R. R. #3, Ladysmith, B.C., V0R 2E0 (245-7422) for information on accommodation.

Island Cruising, 6145 Genoa Bay Road, Duncan, B.C., V9L 1M3 (748-6575/748-7900) offers cruises of the Gulf Islands and Desolation Sound.

For information and hours of operation, contact the **British Columbia Forest Museum**, R. R. #4, Trans-Canada Highway, Duncan, B.C., V9L 3W8 (746-1251).

Contact the **Western Canada Wilderness Committee**, 20 Water St., Vancouver, B.C., V6B 1A4 (683-8220) for copies of the trail guide and informa-

Victoria harbour, with the Parliament Buildings in the background. *Photo by Mary Simpson*

tion on the Carmanah Valley. Their guide to Carmanah can also be purchased from several outdoor equipment stores in Vancouver.

Five Seasons Adventure Tours, 3201 Kingsway, Vancouver, B.C., V5R 5K3 (435-5444) offers weekend nature hikes into the Carmanah Valley.

GREATER VICTORIA

Much has been written about the provincial capital, home to 250,000 people and considered by many to be one of the most livable cities in Canada. In letters written home to his family in 1907, traveller Rudyard Kipling said: "To realize Victoria, you must take all that the eye admires most in Bournemouth, Torquay, the Isle of Wight, the Happy Valley of Hong Kong, the Doon, Sorrento, and Camps Bay; add reminiscences of the Thousand Islands, and arrange the whole round the Bay of Naples, with some Himalayas for the background."

The Olympic Mountains across Juan de Fuca Strait in nearby Washington State do provide a lovely backdrop to this beautiful city where annual rainfall is a mere 68 cm (27 in.) a year and flowers bloom almost all year round. Three municipalities—Oak Bay, Saanich and the navy base of Esquimalt—comprise the city. Float planes from Vancouver and Seattle and passenger vessels from Seattle and Port Angeles make regular trips to Victoria. The B.C. Ferry Corporation runs a regular service between Tsawwassen on the mainland and Swartz Bay, 32 km (20 mi.) north of Victoria.

A stroll along the inner harbour gives you views of Francis Rattenbury's neo-Gothic parliament buildings and his Empress Hotel, where afternoon tea is an institution. Just across from the provincial legislature sits the Royal British Columbia Museum, one of the most highly regarded museums in the world. No fusty place full of dusty relics, the museum is a real hands-on experience. You can admire a magnificent mastadon, then slip into an authentic native long-house and listen to a potlatch ceremony, while a fire glimmers and glows. Go down in a simulated diving bell and explore different levels of the ocean to the floor. Adventuring was never so easy, or such fun! The museum is open year-round.

Gardeners will want to make the short drive up the Saanich peninsula to Butchart Gardens, where the immaculate rose gardens, sunken gardens, fountain displays and displays of indigenous species are world famous. Be sure while there to look out for delicate Himalayan blue poppies. (You can buy the seed in the Butchart store, but we've never had any success growing them.)

Victoria's wide variety of restaurants, jazz clubs, shops and theatres make it a pleasant place to rest up between adventures.

Goldstream Provincial Park, located a mere 16 km (10 mi.) northwest of town on Highway 1, is a favourite picnic area of ours. Easy hiking trails traverse forests of massive 600-year-old cedars festooned with moss. If you visit Goldstream in spring, keep an eye out for the trilliums and calypso orchids that enjoy the area's benign climate. Another prime time to visit Goldstream is from mid-October to mid-December, when chum, coho and Chinook salmon spawn. During spawning season parks staff offer lecture tours (check with the park offices to see when these run, as it varies from year to year).

One of the most relaxing ways to explore the south coast is to take the one-day excursion from Victoria to Courtenay on the E&N Railiner train. The train operates daily year-round, leaving Victoria at 8:15 A.M. and arriving in Courtenay at 12:50 P.M. The train pulls out of Courtenay at 1:15 P.M., arriving back in Victoria at 5:45 P.M.

Useful Information

For general information about Victoria, contact Tourism Victoria Travel Infocentre, 812 Wharf St., Victoria, B.C., V8W 1T3 (382-2127 or toll free 1-800-663-3883).

Contact the **Royal British Columbia Museum**, 675 Belleville St., Victoria, B.C., V8V 1X4 (387-3701) for information on programs and hours.

Call **Butchart Gardens** at 652-4422 for information.

Contact the Visitor Services Coordinator, BC Parks, Malahat District, 2930 Trans-Canada Highway, R. R. #6, Victoria, B.C., V8X 3X2 (387-4363) for information on dates and times of the spawning-season lecture tours at Goldstream Park.

For information about the day-trip from Victoria to Courtenay, call **Via Rail** at 1-800-665-8630 (toll free from anywhere in B.C.).

Black Ball Transport Inc. (206-457-4491 in Port Angeles, 386-2202 in Victoria) provides a ferry link with Port Angeles on the Olympic Peninsula.

Washington State Ferries (1-800-542-7052 toll free in Washington or 381-1551 in Victoria) links Victoria with the San Juan Islands and Anacortes in Washington State. The **B.C. Ferry Corporation** (685-1021 in Vancouver, 206-441-6865 in Seattle or 386-3431 in Victoria) links Victoria (Swartz Bay) with the mainland.

Contact **Air B.C.**, 1000 Wharf St., Victoria, B.C., V8W 2Z2 (388-4521) for information on float-plane schedules between Vancouver, Victoria and other destinations.

The West Coast Road

The West Coast Road, Highway 14, skirts the south coast of Vancouver Island from Victoria to Port Renfrew. All but 8 km (5 mi.) of the route is paved, making for a scenic drive that passes through superb angling country at Pedder Bay, Becher Bay and Sooke. Campers and hikers also enjoy the area.

Between Sooke and Victoria lies Sooke Potholes Provincial Park, whose deep pools and river-carved potholes are some of our favourite swimming spots on the island. The water is so clear and, on a summer day, so cool and refreshing it tends to bring out Tarzan yells in all of us!

In Sooke, 34 km (21 mi.) west of Victoria, the Sooke Region Museum will give you a comprehensive introduction to early days in the area. Moss Cottage, a 19th-century home, comes complete with a contemporary "housewife" who will act as your guide to those times. The Sooke Travel Infocentre, located next to the museum, provides information on other tourist attractions in the area.

East Sooke Regional Park, on the opposite side of Sooke Inlet, offers 60 km (38 mi.) of wooded walks and beach trails that run along the exposed rugged coast on the Juan de Fuca Strait, then inland over Mount Maguire and Babbington Hill to the calm waters of Anderson Cove. Hikers can take a leisurely stroll down to Iron Mine Bay or embark on the 7-hour trip along the Coast Trail. Keep an eye out for the petroglyphs at Allridge Point.

Sooke is the best starting point for people planning to sail the west coast of Vancouver Island. A challenging journey for experienced sailors, the trip is described well in *Cruising Guide to British Columbia, Vol. IV: West Coast Vancouver Island, Cape Scott to Sooke* by Don Watmough.

The serviced campground at French Beach Provincial Park (46.4 km/29.2 mi. from Victoria) makes an excellent base for day trips in the area. Nearby Point-no-Point Resort provides lovely, reasonably priced accommodation. Sandcut Beach offers hiking and beachcombing west all the way to the Jordan River.

The highway junction leading to the Red Creek Tree is 2.4 km (1.5 mi.) out of Port Renfrew on the West Coast Road. Follow the Red Creek Mainline, as this logging road is known, east for 14.5 km (9 mi.) to this ancient Douglas fir. One of Canada's largest trees, it stands over 73 m (239 ft.) high and is estimated to be between 800 and 1000 years old.

Highway 14 ends in the fishing and lumbering community of Port Renfrew. One of the town's main attractions is Botanical Beach, famous for its tide pools and its huge variety of marine life. Set in a sandstone shelf riddled with potholes, the beach is home to mussels, goose and acorn barnacles, chameleon-like chitons, sea-robins and delicate pink coralline algae that fringe some pools, as well as hordes of purple sea urchins and primary-coloured sea anemones. Much of the kelp that washes up on Botanical Beach is *Renfrewia parbula*, a Port Renfrew namesake. Port Renfrew is also the access point to the southern end of the West Coast Trail.

Port Renfrew's waters contain plenty of halibut and crab. A one-lane bridge leads over the San Juan River to a campsite operated by the local native band. Paddlers can canoe up the river to Fairy Lake. Lizard Lake, which features a large newt population, also offers some campsites. Logging roads lead northeast back to Cowichan Lake, for a circle route back to Victoria via Duncan.

Useful Information

General information about the parks in the area can be obtained from the Sooke Travel Infocentre, Highway 14, Sooke, B.C., V0S 1N0 (642-6112).

EEPO Yacht Charters, 406-1755 Robson St., Vancouver, B.C., V6G 3B7 (290-8079) offers sailing trips around the west coast of the island from Sooke to Port Hardy.

For information on accommodation at **Point-no-Point Resort,** contact them at R. R. #2, Sooke, B.C., V0S 1N0 (646-2020).

The Outdoor Club of Victoria's *Hiking Trails I—Victoria and Vicinity* contains information on some interesting hikes in the southern Vancouver Island area. Detailed descriptions of many bicycling trips are contained in *Bicycling Vancouver Island and the Gulf Islands* by Simon Priest and Kimberley Klint. Bill Wolferstan's *Cruising Guide to British Columbia, Vol. I: Vancouver Island from Sooke to Courtenay* and Don Watmough's *Vol. IV: Cape*

Scott to Sooke are good general guides for sailors planning a trip on the west coast of Vancouver Island.

THE GULF ISLANDS

Prior to white settlement, the more than 250 islands that comprise the archipelago in the Strait of Georgia between Vancouver Island and the B.C. mainland were home to the Coast Salish people. Archaeologists sifting through shell middens on several of the Gulf Islands have traced human habitation back at least 5000 years before the arrival of the Europeans.

In 1792, Captain George Vancouver named the waters surrounding these islands the Gulf of Georgia. Later explorers, realizing it was not a gulf at all, renamed it the Strait of Georgia. But the Canadian islands located here are still called the Gulf Islands (as distinct from their American neighbours, the San Juans).

At one time Elvis Presley owned a Gulf Island. Another was given to Princess Margaret on a royal visit and is now a nature preserve. Still another remained a leper colony until 1924.

The popularity of the Gulf Islands as a recreation area is due mainly to a quasi-Mediterranean climate. They receive less than half the amount of the rainfall that deluges the mainland and enjoy eight frost-free months, making them a year-round destination.

Eight of the islands have permanent populations, but the southern islands of Galiano, Mayne, Pender (including North and South Pender), Saltspring and Saturna are the most visited. Tourist season runs from March onwards, when the first guests—migrating rufous hummingbirds from California—arrive on St. Patrick's Day. From then until late fall, ferries bring over day trippers, cyclists, kayakers, hikers and divers keen to sample the laid-back atmosphere so close to B.C.'s lower mainland. Boaters capitalize on sheltered waters to cruise in and out of the many bays.

The landscape of the islands typically consists of shoreline indented with idyllic little beaches and coves, many rimmed with sandstone cliffs. In many places, ochre-skinned arbutus trees overhang the Pacific waters that are home to the biggest colonies of sea anemones in the world. We love the grassy woodlands and placid country lanes, ideal for cycling; they remind us of the English countryside, an effect enhanced by the rural ambience and casual and friendly residents. Most islanders are devoted to keeping their islands as unspoilt as possible. The Islands Trust, established by the provincial government in 1974, is responsible for preserving and protecting the Gulf Islands in the face of the ever-increasing demand for more and larger tourist facilities and services. Because camping facilities are few and far between on the islands, we highlight a few popular bed-and-breakfast spots in this section. Some islands, like

Mayne and Galiano, do lend themselves to day tripping as well.

Regular ferry service links Galiano, Mayne, Pender, Saltspring and Saturna with the mainland and Vancouver Island. Ferries for the Gulf Islands depart from Tsawwassen Terminal, 40 km (25 mi.) south of Vancouver via Highways 99 and 17, and from Swartz Bay Terminal, 32 km (20 mi.) north of Victoria on Highway 17.

Reservations are required for vehicles travelling between the Tsawwassen Terminal and the Gulf Islands, but are not necessary for foot passengers or bicyclists. No reservations are accepted when travelling between the Swartz Bay Terminal and any of the Gulf Islands.

For schedules, reservations or further information, call B.C. Ferries at 669-1211 in Vancouver and 386-3431 in Victoria.

Harbour Air, at 1-800-972-0212 (toll free) or 278-3478 (in Vancouver), provides daily service between Vancouver and the major Gulf Islands.

We begin this section with an overview of the adventuring possibilities in the southern Gulf Islands, then zero in on the particular attractions of the five major islands.

Cycling

The Gulf Islands are ideal for cycle tours—ferry service is frequent, there is little traffic (except on weekends), most islands are not too hilly and there are plenty of scenic roads and beaches. Add to this a range of unique eateries and hostelries, and a tour becomes complete. Many out-of-province cyclists plan an itinerary that also includes the American San Juan Islands.

Early spring and fall are the best times to cycle, since accommodation is not at such a premium. In spring, expect to see fields of daffodils, lots of grazing sheep and cattle, and the delicate spring green of Garry oaks. Deserted bays complete with intertidal rock pools can provide pleasant breaks along the way. Your trip will be all the more enjoyable if you take good rain gear and use a cycle equipped with low hill-climbing gears.

Be prepared for narrow roads, not all of which are paved. If you're travelling in a group, don't ride abreast; it's not only dangerous but guaranteed to antagonize local residents and logging truck drivers.

Cyclists heading to Mayne Island should be aware there are no camping facilities, so book a hotel or bed-and-breakfast well in advance. Ride from the ferry terminal at Village Bay to Horton Bay, about 7.2 km (4.5 mi.), stopping for a picnic lunch at the government dock, or make the scenic 4.8-km (3-mi.) trip across the island to Campbell Bay.

On Galiano, a 72.4-km (45-mi.) route runs from the Sturdies Bay ferry terminal north to Porlier Pass Road and back. You can camp at Montague Harbour Provincial Park, about 10 km (6 mi.) from Sturdies Bay and about .5 km (.25 mi.) from the Montague Harbour ferry dock.

Most people take two days to meander around Saltspring's 100-km (62-mi.) circular route. Expect hilly roads, especially the first 8 km (5 mi.) heading south from Ganges towards Fulford Harbour and Ruckle Provincial Park. You can camp on cliffs overlooking the ocean at Ruckle Park on the south end of the island or in Mouat Provincial Park, not far from the island's hub at Ganges.

On Pender Island, a bridge links North and South Pender, creating a 41.8-km (26-mi.) route for cyclists. Start at the Otter Bay ferry terminal and head south on the east side of the island, making for Bedwell Harbour on South Pender. Public camping is available at Prior Centennial Park on North Pender, about halfway along the route. Unfortunately for cyclists, South Pender's Beaumont Provincial Park is accessible only by sea.

A northern route of about 33.8 km (21 mi.) gives cyclists on Saturna Island sweeping views of Georgia Strait and Mount Baker. Start at Lyall Harbour ferry terminal and continue along the northern half of the island to East Point. Come back along the same route. Since, like Mayne, Saturna does not have any designated camping areas or provincial parks, cyclists have to rely on bed-and-breakfast accommodation.

Useful Information

Benno's Country Adventure Tours hosts 2-day Gulf Island cycle tours combining the largest island, Saltspring, with the smallest inhabited island, Mayne. Contact them at 1958 West 4th Ave., Vancouver, B.C., V6J 1M5 (738-5105, fax: 738-9100).

Adventure Canada, c/o Northsouth Travel, 1159 West Broadway, Vancouver, B.C., V6H 1G1 (736-7447 or 1-800-387-1483 toll free) offers combined sailing and bicycling trips of the Gulf Islands.

Both *The Gulf Islands Explorer* by Bruce Obee and *Bicycling Vancouver Island and the Gulf Islands* by Simon Priest and Kimberley Klint are recommended.

Canoeing and Kayaking

The protected waters of the Gulf Islands are great for kayaking. Much of the sea-front property on the main islands is privately owned, however, making spur-of-the-moment camping tricky, so plan your accommodation well in advance. The joy of kayaking and canoeing in the Gulf Islands is that you can get to smaller islands not serviced by the ferries.

The marine parks on D'Arcy, Sidney and Portland islands are particularly attractive for canoeists and kayakers. (For an overview of the area, be sure to pick up a free copy of the *Coastal Marine Parks of British Columbia* map put out by BC Parks, available at tourist information offices.)

D'Arcy, parallel to the Saanich peninsula on Vancouver Island, is a former leper colony. Its 84-ha (207-a.) marine park contains many deer, otters and seals.

Sidney Spit Marine Park on Sidney Island's northeast tip offers 11 km (7 mi.) of sandy shore and is a popular day outing for Victoria residents. Native people used Sidney Island as a summer camp, naming it Mutcha, after a giant mink that the spirit god Swaneset transformed because of its uncontrollable greed. The long sand spit is Mutcha's tail, while the beaches are its belly and back. Sidney Island actually used to be known as the Pearl of the Gulf Islands, since some consider it the most lovely island of the lot. Once the domain of private boaters, Sidney can now be reached during the summer months by a regularly scheduled foot-passenger ferry from the town of Sidney, 5 km (3 mi.) away. Watch for killer whales and Dall's porpoises. In July and August, bird watchers can enjoy viewing large numbers of migratory shore birds stopping over in the park. Fallow deer on the land have become a bit of a pest.

Princess Margaret Park, which covers the whole of 194-ha (479-a.) Portland Island, is a destination for kayakers launching from the Swartz Bay ferry terminal. Once a farm where race horses were boarded, Portland's fine beaches, scenic hiking trails and fall fruit (from gone-to-seed orchards) make it very popular with boaters.

Kayakers can also head to Mandarte Island to view its colonies of glaucous-winged gulls, pelagic and double-crested cormorants, and pigeon guillemots, as well as the occasional tufted puffin.

The northern Gulf Islands, which range north of Saltspring Island to Gabriola Island, are not as well travelled as their counterparts to the south. A developed campsite at Pirates Cove on De Courcy Island, southwest of Gabriola, is popular in summer.

During the 1930s The Brother, XII, his mate Madame Z and their followers from the quasi-religious Aquarian Foundation made their home on De Courcy before moving later to the northern part of Valdes Island. The Brother, XII, and Madame Z raised many funds for the cause (partly through the Brother's seduction of affluent women). There is speculation that the more than $400,000 in gold they raised may be squirreled away on the island or just offshore. Beware if you go searching: open waters off De Courcy can be choppy and tidal currents, swift. Local mariners believe the Brother's spirit lurks in the vicinity of Brother XII's Rock, located off the east coast of De Courcy Island, and has been responsible for many recent sailboat groundings!

Other interesting spots for kayakers include the provincial park on Whaleboat Island, south of De Courcy; the ecological reserves of Rose Islets and Canoe Islets; the sandstone formations on Tent Island, Galiano Island and Valdes Island, and the salmon and cod populations of the Flat Top Islands.

Useful Information

Gulf Island Kayaking, R. R. #2, Porlier Pass Road, Galiano, B.C., V0N 1P0 (539-2442) offers various trips around the Gulf Islands as do **Ecosummer**, 1516 Duranleau St., Granville Island, Vancouver, B.C., V6H 3S4 (669-7741) and **Geoff Evans Kayak Centre**, Box 97, Cultus Lake, B.C., V0X 1H0 (858-6775). **Ecomarine Ocean Kayak Centre**, 1668 Duranleau St., Granville Island, Vancouver, B.C., V6H 3S4 (689-7575) provides kayak courses and rentals.

Sea Kayaking Canada's West Coast by John Ince and Hedi Kottner devotes two sections to kayaking the northern and southern Gulf Islands. Mary Ann Snowden's *Island Paddling* is another useful guide.

Sailing

One of our first introductions to adventuring in B.C. was an assignment to cover a flotilla weekend in the Gulf Islands. As landlubbers, we found it a delightful introduction to the joys of messing around on boats in lovely settings. After crossing the Strait of Georgia, we visited a pub at Pender Island's Bedwell Harbour before rafting up in an anchorage to swim, shuck oysters and exchange tall tales.

There are innumerable safe places to drop anchor in the calm waters of the Gulf Islands, including the many marine parks that dot the strait. Sailors should have, as a minimum, basic coastal navigation skills. You must be able to read tide and current tables, as well as marine charts, in order to negotiate these cluttered waterways.

According to Bruce Obee, a Gulf Islands expert, over a quarter of a million households in B.C. own boats, and 3000 own kayaks. In addition, 25,000 American boats enter B.C. waters each year.

Many come to fish the prime waters off Saturna Island's East Point, camping on shore or anchoring at Cabbage Island Park. Other prime fishing spots are Active Pass and Porlier Pass.

If you would like to sail the Gulf Islands but don't own a boat, you might want to contact one of the numerous companies that offer bare-boat charters to experienced skippers. Some companies offer summer flotilla weekends for sailors inexperienced with coastal waters, coping with tidal currents, etc. The flotilla consists of a small fleet of sailboats skippered by a Canadian Yachting Association–certified instructor in a pilot boat. Most companies also provide cruise-and-learn courses at various CYA proficiency levels. One company, Cooper Boating Centre, also offers an offshore cruise that runs north to Port Hardy, rounds the north end of Vancouver Island, heads 250 nautical miles west to the Cobb Seamount, then returns via Juan de Fuca Strait and Victoria.

Useful Information

Bare-boat, skippered and cruise-and-learn charters are all offered by the following companies: **Seawing Sailing School & Yacht Charters**, 1815 Mast Tower Rd., Granville Island, Vancouver, B.C., V6H 3X7 (669-0840); **Cooper Boating Centre**, 1620 Duranleau St., Granville Island, Vancouver, B.C., V6H 3S4 (687-4110); **Bosun's Charters**, Box 2464, 2240 Harbour Rd., Sidney, B.C., V8L 3Y3 (656-6644); **Gulf Islands Cruising School**, Box 2532, Sidney, B.C., V8L 4B9 (656-2628) and **The Island Cruising Group**, 6145 Genoa Bay Road, Duncan, B.C., V9L 1M3 (748-6575 or 1-800-661-1340 toll free in western Canada).

Skippered cruises of the Gulf Islands are also offered by **Bluewater Adventures**, 202-1676 Duranleau St., Granville Island, Vancouver, B.C., V6H 3S5 (684-4575) and **EEPO Yacht Charters**, 406-1755 Robson St., Vancouver, B.C., V6G 3B7 (290-8079).

Peter Chettleburgh's book *An Explorer's Guide: Marine Parks of B.C.* is a useful resource for prospective yachties, as is Al and Jo Bailey-Cummings's *Gunkholing in the Gulf Islands*. See also Bill Wolferstan's excellent *Cruising Guide to British Columbia, Vol. I: Gulf Islands and Vancouver Island from Sooke to Courtenay*.

Hiking

Hiking on the Gulf Islands is not the strenuous push to the alpine that characterizes so much of the hiking in the rest of the province. We once spent a very pleasant four-day holiday hiking around Mayne Island in the spring; our aim was more to clear out our lungs after a long city winter than to search out stunning vistas.

Still, there are some interesting and quite challenging hikes on the islands. Your best reference is Mary and David Macaree's *103 Hikes in Southwestern British Columbia*, which details some of the more interesting ones like Mount Maxwell on Saltspring Island and Mount Galiano on Galiano Island, with its superb views of Active Pass.

The Saltspring Chamber of Commerce puts out a comprehensive hiking map of the island, covering Ruckle Park, Beaver Point Park, Reginald Hill, Peter Arnell Park, Mount Bruce, Mount Maxwell, Mount Erskine, Mouat Park, Southey Point and Channel Ridge.

Useful Information

For maps of Saltspring, contact Saltspring Travel Infocentre, Box 111, Ganges, B.C., V0S 1E0 (537-5252). Galiano Island Travel Infocentre, Box 73, Galiano, B.C., V0N 1P0 (539-2233) can provide hiking guides to Galiano.

Diving

Some rich diving territory extends around the Gulf Islands. Good visibility and the wide variety of marine life make it a year-round activity. However, facilities for air and equipment are not plentiful on the islands, so it's best to make arrangements in Vancouver or on Vancouver Island before you go.

Popular spots are Beaver Point and Burgoyne Bay off Saltspring, where octopuses can sometimes be spotted lurking in their dens, and Alcala and Virago points on Galiano. Enterprise Reef and Georgina Shoals, off Mayne Island, have exceptional underwater scenery but are for experienced divers only, as the currents are swift and the marine traffic heavy in this area. Java Islets and Taylor Point, at the southeast end of Saturna, are also good diving areas.

Useful Information

Diving trips are organized by several diving shops in Vancouver and Victoria. Try **Adrenalin Sports**, 1512 Duranleau St., Granville Island, Vancouver, B.C., V6H 3S4 (682-2881), **Diver's World**, 1523 West 3rd Ave., Vancouver, B.C., V6J 1J8 (732-1344), **The Diving Locker**, 2745 West 4th Ave., Vancouver, B.C., V6K 1P9 (736-2681) and **Scubaland**, 102B, 1830 Island Highway, Victoria, B.C., V9B 1J2 (474-1134).

Betty Pratt-Johnson's book *141 Dives in the Protected Waters of Washington and British Columbia* gives detailed descriptions of many diving areas in the Gulf Islands.

Dive B.C., 5824 Ash St., Powell River, B.C., V8A 4R4 (483-9740) can also provide further information.

Each of the Gulf Islands offers its own unique variety of adventuring opportunities.

Galiano Island

Galiano is a one-hour ferry ride from Tsawwassen to Sturdies Bay or a half-hour flight from Vancouver. Long and thin, the island is 57 sq. km (23 sq. mi.) in size. Its permanent population of 850 people includes many artists, writers and artisans who display their work at places like the Dandelion Gallery of Fine Art. Part of Galiano's rustic charm is due to the fact that many of the hippies who settled here in the sixties have remained, never losing their faith in a more simple lifestyle.

Go to the Burrill Brothers General Store facing Sturdies Bay to find out about current events on Galiano. Local residents like to talk about their island, which is named after Commander Dionisio Alcala Galiano of the Spanish Navy, who explored the area in 1792. Talk may also be of the secret cave still hidden deep in Galiano Mountain. Local lore maintains that west-coast Indians would hole up safely in the cave, well out of range of Mounties' cannons, after a successful raid on another tribe's village.

Seventy-five per cent of the land on Galiano is under a tree farm licence, so logging roads make for easy hiking access. Visitors can refuel at places like Trincomali Bakery (get directions at Burrill Brothers) and take some cappuccino, cinnamon buns and cookies to the lookout over Trincomali Channel.

Gourmet eats exist at Galiano's famous Pink Geranium Restaurant on Porlier Pass Drive. The Hummingbird Inn on Sturdies Bay Road serves super fish and chips, and La Berengerie offers three rooms of accommodation as well as a prix fixe menu of French cuisine. La Berengerie is a 10-minute walk from the Montague Harbour ferry wharf and marina, and makes a good base for exploring the shell beaches and pristine forests of the provincial marine park at Montague Harbour.

Useful Information

Galiano Island Visitor Association can supply you with an up-to-date list of accommodations, camping facilities and local merchants. They can be contacted prior to your visit at General Delivery, Galiano Island, B.C. V0N 1P0.

The Galiano Island Chamber of Commerce's Infocentre for travellers (539-2233) is located at the ferry dock at Sturdies Bay.

Harbour Air makes daily flights to Galiano Island from downtown Vancouver; for more information call 1-800-972-0212 (toll free) or 688-1277 (in Vancouver).

Lake Union Air offers charter flights from downtown Seattle to Galiano (and free pick-up from Seattle's Sea-Tac airport). Call them at 1-800-826-1890 toll free.

For reservations and information, contact the **Pink Geranium Restaurant**, Porlier Pass Drive, Galiano Island, B.C., V0N 1P0 (539-2477) or the **Hummingbird Inn**, Sturdies Bay Road, Galiano Island, B.C., V0N 1P0 (539-5472).

Contact **La Berengerie**, Montague Harbour Road, Galiano, B.C., V0N 1P0 (539-5392) for information on accommodation.

Mayne Island

The second smallest of the populated Gulf Islands, Mayne's 21 sq. km (8 sq. mi.) are home to a permanent population of approximately 750 people and lots of sheep.

In early tourism posters, Mayne billed itself as "The Isle of Health and

Happiness." Certainly miners en route to the 1858 gold rush found it a welcome resting place, congregating in the area known today as Miners Bay. Subsequently, a big colony of Japanese farmers practised large-scale tomato cultivation until their lands were confiscated during the Second World War.

The lighthouse at Georgina Point, built in 1855, still guides vessels into the eastern entrance to Active Pass and is open daily to visitors from 1:00 P.M. to 3:00 P.M. The original oil lamp was supplemented by a foghorn in 1889.

Active Pass, which runs between Mayne and Galiano islands, is travelled by more than five million ferry passengers a year. Many spot bald eagles that gorge on the herring churned up by turbulent waters. Other feeders include Brandt's cormorants, arctic loons and Bonaparte's gulls. The salmon fishing in the pass is prime, but riptides are frequent so boaters must be extremely cautious.

Today Mayne Islanders consist of farmers, craftspeople and folks involved in the tourist trade. Island accommodation includes the Springwater Lodge, the oldest continuously operating hotel in the province, and some exquisite bed-and-breakfasts.

At Fernhill Lodge, a mid-island lodging and eatery, host Brian Crumblehume is an expert on herbs, growing 200 varieties in his Elizabethan garden. Meals at Fernhill run the gamut from Cleopatran to Renaissance and we consider the oysters in hot cumin sauce alone worth the trip to Mayne Island.

Popular with cyclists, the Blue Vista Resort on tranquil Bennett Bay offers fully equipped private cabins. The Springwater Lodge, the island's local pub, overlooks Active Pass.

Useful Information
Write the Mayne Island Community Chamber of Commerce at Box 160, Mayne Island, B.C., V0N 2J0 for a pamphlet on the island's attractions, or pick one up at the Miner's Bay General Store or at the realty office as you disembark at Village Bay.

Contact **Fernhill Lodge**, Box 140, Mayne Island, B.C., V0N 2J0 (539-2544); **Blue Vista Resort**, Bennett Bay, Mayne Island, B.C., V0N 2J0 (539-2463), or the **Springwater Lodge**, Mayne Island, B.C., V0N 2J0 (539-5521) for information on accommodation.

Pender Island

Pender Island is actually 2 islands, North and South Pender, which are joined by a one-lane wooden bridge overlooking Browning and Bedwell harbours. Medicine Beach in Bedwell Harbour and Hamilton Beach in Browning Harbour are both favourite spots for family outings and picnics.

Together, the islands cover 24 sq. km (10 sq. mi.). About 1300 people live on Pender Island, a one-hour-and-forty-minute ride by ferry from Tsawwassen, including a high proportion of writers and artists. Early residents included legendary gangsters Legs Diamond and Machine Gun Kelly, who used Pender as a base during Prohibition days. Bootleggers working for Al Capone, Kelly and Diamond capitalized on Pender's equidistance from the Canadian and American borders to store rum and whiskey in the island's barns.

Roads extend to the far reaches of both islands, but the majority of full-time residents live on North Pender, particularly in the Magic Lakes subdivision. Scenic lookouts include the 120-m (394-ft.) point on Bald Cone on North Pender and the 260-m (853-ft.) summit of Mount Norman on South Pender, accessible through Beaumont Park.

The Bedwell Harbour Resort, on South Pender, is near the customs office for visitors coming in from the United States by boat.

Ucoful Information

For information on accommodation at the **Bedwell Harbour Resort**, contact them at R. R. #1, South Pender Island, B.C., V0N 2M0 (629-3212). Other accommodation on Pender Island is available at **Pender Lodge**, MacKinnon Road, R. R. #1, Pender Island, B.C., V0N 2M0 (629-3221). Bed-and-breakfasts include **Cliffside Inn-on-the-Sea**, Armadale Road, North Pender Island, B.C., V0N 2M0 (629-6691) and **Corbett House**, Corbett Road, Pender Island, B.C., V0N 2M0 (629-6305).

The Canada Customs Clearance Office is at Bedwell Harbour on South Pender Island (629-3363).

Saltspring Island

By far the largest—180 sq. km (72 sq. mi.)—and most densely populated—7400 people—of the Gulf Islands, Saltspring has undergone much development in recent years. The 4 main centres of Ganges, Fernwood, Fulford and Vesuvius are linked to the rest of the world by fax machines and other technological aids, making it possible for many businesspeople to live full-time on the island.

Saltspring was originally home to the Coast Salish Indians. Its first non-native settlers were black pioneers escaping the persecution and slavery they faced in the United States. Agriculture became the island's mainstay, and today Saltspring lamb is a quality product. Like the other Gulf Islands, Saltspring numbers many artists and craftspeople among its residents, and many welcome visitors into their studios.

Adventure travel opportunities on Saltspring include hiking, cycling, scuba diving and sailing. St. Mary Lake, the largest fresh-water body on the island, is a favourite spot for boaters, anglers and windsurfers.

The usual variety of Gulf Island bed-and-breakfasts is complemented on Saltspring by such tony establishments as Hastings House, listed in Andrew Harper's *Hideaway Report* as one of the most peaceful unspoiled locations in the world.

Useful Information

Saltspring Island Information Centre, Box 111, Ganges, B.C., V0S 1E0 (537-5252) will provide further information together with a list of the island's many bed-and-breakfast places. For reservations at **Hastings House**, contact them at 160 Upper Ganges, Box 1110, Ganges, B.C., V0S 1E0 (537-3362 or fax 537-5333).

Saturna Island

Quiet and relaxing, Saturna is the southernmost of the Gulf Islands. Just 260 people inhabit its 31 sq. km (12 sq. mi.). Many people bypass Saturna because getting there involves a ferry transfer, but it's definitely worth a visit if you have time since its landscape is so untouched. Saturna's main claim to fame is the annual July the 1st (Canada Day) lamb bake held at a farm on Saturna Beach.

If you come for the day, you might want to plan to hike up Mount Warburton Pike to see the feral goats on the ecological reserve at the top. Winter Cove Marine Park, with its broad sandy beaches, is one of the few marine parks accessible from land. Cabbage Island Marine Park, off the east side of Saturna Island, is accessible only by boat, from either Georgia Strait or Tumbo Channel.

Cyclists usually take the East Point road beside Georgia Strait and visit the East Point lighthouse. The pub and the general store, near the ferry dock at Saturna Point, are prime information-gathering spots.

Useful Information

Accommodation on Saturna is limited. Try **Boot Cove Lodge**, Box 54, Saturna Island, B.C., V0N 2Y0 (539-2254) or **Breezy Bay Bed & Breakfast**, Box 40, Saturna Island, B.C., V0N 2Y0 (539-2937).

CHAPTER 3

Southwestern B.C.
and Vancouver

Southwestern British Columbia radiates out from the port city of Vancouver. It includes the Lower Mainland area and takes in Highway 101, which runs up the Sunshine Coast north of Vancouver to Lund, Highway 99 to Whistler and Highway 1, the Trans-Canada, which leads through Hope and north to Cache Creek. Rimmed on the west by the Strait of Georgia and containing the north shore mountains and part of the Coast Mountain range, southwestern B.C. offers plenty of adventuring opportunities. The lifeblood of the region is the Fraser River, which begins as a trickle in the Rockies, then flows west into the Pacific, where it empties into the ocean in a vast, lush delta.

Southwestern B.C. is served by Vancouver International Airport, and ferries run regularly between Tsawwassen, on the Lower Mainland, and Swartz Bay, on Vancouver Island, as well as between the Horseshoe Bay terminal and the Sunshine Coast. Highway I-5 leads into the province from Washington State, while the Trans Canada Highway brings traffic in from Alberta and points east.

For centuries, southwestern B.C. was the range of large populations of Coast Salish and Interior Salish people. Salmon formed the major part of their diet. Believing that five tribes of salmon lived in a great longhouse under the sea, the Salish were familiar with the behavioural patterns and breeding places of the Chinook (spring), sockeye (red), coho (silver), humpback (pink) and dog (chum) salmon.

The return of the first spring salmon each year was treated with the ritual and respect due the people's primary food source. The man who caught the first returning salmon laid its head facing upstream to ensure that a good run would follow. He would then call the village together for a ceremony. The fish was cleaned with fern leaves, cut laterally (not crosswise) with a knife of stone or mussel shell and then roasted on a split stick before a fire and eaten. An essential part of this ritual, which took place before sundown, involved returning the bones to the water so that the salmon could re-form and come again the next year. Fish were harvested with traps, spears and nets, each village using the particular method that best suited its location.

Hooks made of bent hemlock root were used to catch halibut. Giant sturgeon taken from the Fraser and Squamish rivers were hauled in on lines made from dried kelp, a single strand of which can stretch up to 46 m (150 ft.)

Southwestern B.C. and Vancouver

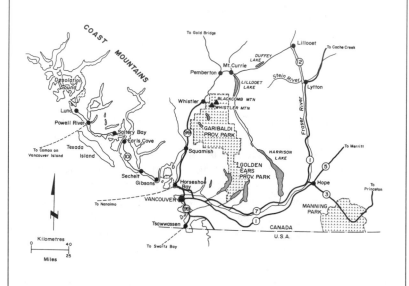

COAST MOUNTAINS

To Gold Bridge

Lillooet

To Cache Creek

DUFFEY LAKE

Mt.Currie

Pemberton

12

Stein River

Lytton

Desolation Sound

Whistler

BLACKCOMB MTN
WHISTLER MTN

LILLOOET LAKE

Fraser River

Lund

Powell River

99

GARIBALDI PROV. PARK

Saltery Bay
Earls Cove

Squamish

HARRISON LAKE

To Merritt

To Comox on Vancouver Island

Texada Island

10

GOLDEN EARS PROV. PARK

1

5

Sechelt

Gibsons

Horseshoe Bay

To Princeton

To Nanaimo

VANCOUVER

Hope

3

To Princeton

99

7

MANNING PARK

Tsawwassen

1

CANADA
U.S.A.

To Swartz Bay

N

Kilometres
0   40

Miles
0   25

in length. The Salish also relished clams and birds as other major protein sources.

Cedar provided building materials, its fine straight grain split into planks or slabs using wedges made of wood or elk antler. Cedar bark was woven into clothes.

Socially and economically the potlatch ceremony was very important to Salish life. Used to validate status and commemorate various significant rites of passage, the potlatch was outlawed by the Canadian government in 1885. Since the anti-potlatch law was dropped in 1951, the potlatch has experienced a revival.

The Fraser River, first explored by Simon Fraser in 1808, formed an artery for the 1858 gold rush in the interior of the province and was eventually spanned by a railway in 1885. The Trans-Canada Highway (Highway 1) now parallels it on its main canyon run.

Initially, business in the Lower Mainland centred around logging and servicing the needs of miners heading into the interior. Today, Vancouver and its suburbs still provide services, and heavy industry is minimal. The dairy farmers and the fruit and vegetable growers of the rich Fraser delta help feed the city.

Climatically, the area we cover in this section has warm summers and wet winters. Rain falls at lower elevations in southwestern B.C. fairly frequently from November through February, arriving as snow in cold years. The first spring buds appear in the middle of March, generally a blustery month. Southwestern B.C. residents can usually count on a stretch of sunny weather during July and August, when temperatures will hover around the 18° C (64° F) level. More often than not, September and early October will have warm and sunny spells as well.

Lower Mainlanders love the outdoors. Vancouver itself brims with opportunities, whether it's a picnic in one of the city's many parks, a quick fish off a wharf, board-sailing at a beach 10 minutes from downtown or just ambling through old forests. At some times of the year, it's actually possible to ski and windsurf on the same day! A couple of hours out of town you can rock climb sheer faces at Squamish, career down world-class ski runs at Whistler-Blackcomb, hike into alpine meadows or ride horses into the mountains.

If you are interested in exploring the Lower Mainland on foot, you can select from the variety of hikes outlined in the books *103 Hikes in South-western British Columbia* and *109 Walks in British Columbia's Lower Mainland. British Columbia Cross Country Ski Routes* includes descriptions of Lower Mainland nordic skiing routes; although the book is out of print, most Vancouver area libraries will have a copy. Canoe routes in the region are well documented in Richard and Rochelle Wright's *Canoe Routes British Columbia* (also unfortunately out of print) and Betty Pratt-Johnson's *Whitewater*

Playing cricket in Vancouver's Stanley Park. *Photo by Michael Mong*

Trips for Kayakers, Canoeists and Rafters in British Columbia: Greater Vancouver through Whistler, Okanagan and Thompson River Regions. Simon Priest's *Bicycling Southwestern British Columbia and the Sunshine Coast* is a good cycling reference book.

This section begins with adventuring possibilities in Vancouver. From the city, we move to the north shore mountains and then farther north up the Sunshine Coast. Next we cover the Howe Sound-Squamish region, including Garibaldi and Whistler mountains, and finally we explore the areas south and north of the Fraser River.

Before you begin to do any exploring in the Lower Mainland, we highly recommend that you get a free copy of the Ministry of Environment and Parks map, "Provincial Parks of the Lower Mainland." It can be obtained from Ministry of Environment and Parks, Parks and Outdoor Recreation Division, 1610 Indian River Drive, North Vancouver, B.C., V7G 1L3 (929-1291) and is also readily available at gas stations and in hotel lobbies.

VANCOUVER

Blessed with mountains, a clean ocean, low-density single-family neighbourhoods and parks galore, Vancouver has continued to escape the urban blight that plagues so many other big cities. A year-round temperate climate is a welcome change from the high humidity that characterizes most central Canadian cities in summer, and though it does rain quite a bit here during the winter months, extended periods of extremely cold weather are as rare as snow removal equipment in the work yards of the city's municipal crews!

This benign climate, along with plenty of eateries that feature cuisines from a wide variety of countries, accommodation ranging from the luxurious—the Pan Pacific Hotel is a favourite with Stevie Wonder and the Prince and Princess of Wales—to the ordinary, and the usual big-city mix of theatres, art galleries and shops, makes Vancouver a vibrant base from which to plan any adventures within the province.

Four hundred and fifty-one thousand folks live in the city of Vancouver, comprising a rich racial and ethnic mix. Many cultures are celebrated throughout the year with festivals ranging from international dragon boat racing to Caribbean feasts.

The city bus system runs frequently on major routes and, in our experience, the bus drivers are most helpful at alerting you to the stop you want if you are new in town.

The main adventure destination within city limits has to be the world-famous **Stanley Park** at the west end of the downtown core. Encircled by a seawall that is strolled and cycled by Vancouverites of every age, size and shape, the park is a 406-ha (1000-a.) peninsula of towering giant cedars, landscaped gardens, a cricket oval and stunning sea views.

Once the territory of the Squamish and Musqueam people, where groups of up to 2000 would attend potlatch feasts of berries and salmon in their ancient village of Whoi-Whoi, Stanley Park, as a plaque at the entrance proclaims, is dedicated "to the use and enjoyment of people of all colours, creeds and customs for all time."

The Vancouver Aquarium, in the heart of the park, opened in 1956 and is justifiably proud of being a forerunner of the many mega-aquariums now being built across North America. Canadian species form the core of its collection, and it is particularly well known for its killer whales, who perform remarkable leaps and dives several times daily for appreciative audiences.

About 8000 species altogether inhabit this living natural history museum. The aquarium's many public programs include beach walks, lectures on sea monsters and the annual Christmas tree lighting, using wattage from electric eels. The Amazon Rain Forest gallery is another of the aquarium's attractions and a great place to go to warm up on a cold winter's day. We also really enjoy the little petting pools where you can gently handle sea cucumbers, starfish and prickly sea urchins.

Students from the elementary to the graduate level use the aquarium's laboratories and library, and its vast data bank on animals is accessed by oceanariums across the continent. Dedicated to the challenge of making creatures thrive in captivity, the aquarium is a must-see for anyone remotely interested in the ocean beyond Vancouver's city limits.

The small Stanley Park zoo, located just alongside the aquarium, is worth visiting to see the otters and the children's petting zoo.

Another primary destination for visitors keen to understand and appreciate B.C. is the **Museum of Anthropology**, located on the University of British Columbia campus on the south side of Burrard Inlet. Designed by Canada's premier architect, Arthur Erickson (who is also responsible for the Vancouver Art Gallery, the new court house and Simon Fraser University), the MOA contains one of the world's finest permanent collections of Northwest Coast Indian art. Great towering totem poles, vast potlatch feast dishes, a hands-on drumming centre—the MOA has them all. Its centrepiece is master carver Bill Reid's stunning yellow cedar sculpture of the Haida creation myth, *Raven and the First Men*. Temporary exhibits feature the art and artifacts of cultures from around the world.

Granville Island Market, situated on False Creek under the girders of the Granville Street Bridge, is a 17-ha (42-a.) microcosm of Vancouver at its best. The market is a great place to provision for a trip or to return to for a spot of civilization after a spell in the bush. Restaurants, theatres, art galleries, studios: in all, 250 businesses operate on the island, which percolates with the smell of fresh-cut flowers, coffee and delicious market produce.

Granville Island is also headquarters for many adventure travel organizations. Visitors can learn to sail in eleven lessons through a program certified by the Canadian Yachting Association, arrange bare-boat and skippered charters for two to thirty people or make plans to visit wilderness destinations round the province.

Paddlers can canoe and kayak in False Creek or along the ocean shores. When the wind picks up off the beaches of Kitsilano, Jericho and Spanish Banks, windsurfing is the sport of choice. Vancouver's Surf City has the world's first computerized windsurfing simulator for novices.

Swimming is popular in Vancouver; summer water temperatures are around 18-20° C (64-68° F), dropping to 5-6° C (41-43° F) in winter. The beaches at Second Beach, Spanish Banks, Jericho, Kitsilano and Locarno all have lifeguards on duty during the summer months. Kitsilano Beach also boasts a large and very popular outdoor swimming pool that combines fresh and sea water.

Just offshore, the Strait of Georgia provides good fishing. Two hundred and twenty-two km (140 mi.) long and 28 km (18 mi.) wide, the strait is, on average, 155 m (500 ft.) deep and is home to a variety of salmon as well as many bottomfish such as flounder, sole, red snapper, rock cod, lingcod and perch.

Cyclists might enjoy the terrific 15-km (9.3-mi.) Seaside Bicycle Route that starts at Stanley Park, loops around False Creek and ends at Spanish Banks below Pacific Spirit Park.

Useful Information

The Vancouver Guide by Terri Wershler provides an excellent introduction to what the city has to offer. Tourism Vancouver, Four Bentall Centre, 1055 Dunsmuir St., Box 49296, Vancouver, B.C., V7X 1L3 (683-2000) can also answer many of your questions, as well as providing maps and brochures about places of interest.

The Stanley Park Explorer by Richard Steele is a useful resource. One of the most popular ways to explore the park is to rent a bicycle, moped or scooter. Stanley Park Rentals (681 5581) located near the park entrance provides this service. Contact the **Vancouver Aquarium** at 682-1118 for information on opening hours and whale shows.

Admission to the **Museum of Anthropology** is free on Tuesdays. For further information, call 228-5087 or write to them at 6393 N.W. Marine Dr., Vancouver, B.C., V6T 1A7.

Sea Wing Sailing School and Yacht Charters, 1815 Mast Tower Rd., Granville Island, Vancouver, B.C., V6H 3X7 (669-0840) and **Cooper Sailing Centre**, 1620 Duranleau St., Granville Island, Vancouver, B.C., V6H 3S4 (687-4110) are two of several companies offering sailing lessons and boat charters from Granville Island. Contact **Ecomarine Ocean Kayak Centre**, 1668 Duranleau St., Granville Island, Vancouver, B.C., V6H 3S4 (689-7575) for information on kayak lessons and rentals.

For the latest in windsurfing, contact **Surf City**, 420 West 1st Ave., Vancouver, B.C., V5Y 3S9 (872-8585).

For information about fishing licences, where to find promising catches and what lures to use, call the federal department of Fisheries and Oceans at 666-0383 or 666-2268.

Contact **Pacific Sunset Nature Tours**, 305-4559 Imperial St., Burnaby, B.C., V5J 1B7 (437-3150) for information on trips from Vancouver to the Stein Valley, Widgeon Creek, Stave Lake and the Joffre Lakes. Jack Christie's *Day Trips from Vancouver* presents some interesting possibilities for short jaunts in the region, as does Anne Tempelman-Kluit's *Green Spaces of Vancouver*.

NORTH AND WEST VANCOUVER

Lynn Headwaters Regional Park and Lynn Canyon

A short hike in North Vancouver's Lynn Headwaters Regional Park, mere minutes from downtown Vancouver, should convince even the most skeptical traveller how well provided the city is with adventuring opportunities.

A rugged mountain park, situated between the Capilano and Seymour watersheds, Lynn Headwaters offers wilderness day hikes for experienced outdoorspeople as well as developed trails for families and less experienced hikers. The Lynn Loop Trail and the Headwaters Trail are the most popular routes.

To reach the park from Vancouver, cross either the Second Narrows Bridge or the Lions Gate Bridge and then follow the Trans-Canada Highway to Lynn Valley Road, which leads to the park entrance.

One of the largest remaining specimens of western red cedar in the Lower Mainland can be seen within the park. This tree, 55 m (180 ft.) tall, is estimated to be more than 600 years old. Both the *Hiking Guide to the Big Trees of Southwestern British Columbia* and *Exploring Lynn Canyon and Lynn Headwaters Park* are useful guides to the park. This semiwilderness on Vancouver's doorstep is bear country, so exercise caution.

The free suspension bridge across Lynn Canyon, 80 m (262 ft.) above Lynn Creek, while not as dramatic as Capilano Suspension Bridge and Park, mentioned later in this chapter, is still worth a visit. It is well signposted once you take the Lynn Valley Road exit off the highway.

Seymour Demonstration Forest

A 5600-ha (13,837-a.) portion of the Seymour Valley in North Vancouver was opened to the public in 1987 as a demonstration forest and regional park. The management forester and staff on the site show visitors how proper protection and management of resources within a forested watershed are crucial to maintaining water quality.   The forest is open daily from dawn to dusk and on Sundays free guided tours on an interpretive trail are offered. Also on Sundays, the 11-km (7-mi.) road to the Seymour Dam is closed to vehicles, allowing cyclists a traffic-free ride to the dam and nearby salmon hatchery. To get there from downtown Vancouver, cross the Second Narrows Bridge, take the third exit (Lillooet Road), head north past Capilano College, then through a cemetery and onto a signposted gravel road. Phone the Demonstration Forest at 432-6286 for more information.

Mount Seymour Provincial Park and Recreation Area

Another year-round recreation area on Vancouver's doorstep, Mount Seymour Park lies a 30-minute drive from downtown; after crossing the Second Narrows Bridge, take the Mount Seymour Parkway exit off Highway 1, then turn up Mount Seymour Road.

The north shore mountains, the legacy of intense volcanic activity over 100 million years ago, consist of forested slopes with an understory of berry bushes. The first road through Mount Seymour's yellow cedars was built in the 1950s. Now, the access roads lead to downhill ski facilities, including two chair lifts and four rope tows, as well as a ski school and cross-country trails.

The park office at the entrance to Seymour provides a good brochure delineating the park's many hiking trails. One major hike is the Baden-Powell Centennial Trail, a 42-km (26-mi.) trail stretching from Deep Cove, on Indian Arm, across the north shore through Cypress Provincial Park and over to Horseshoe Bay at the southern entrance to Howe Sound. This trail divides the north shore mountains into a dozen readily accessible sections.

Another rewarding hike is the one to Mount Seymour. Of the mountain's three peaks, the third and highest provides the best reward—360° views. The 8-km (5-mi.) return trip takes about four hours. A good family hike is the Goldie Lake Interpretive Trail.

Call Mount Seymour Park at 929-1291 for information on individual camping and Golden Ears Park at 463-3513 for details about group camping on Mount Seymour.

Winter cross-country ski trails include Goldie Lake Loop, Flower Lake Loop and Hidden Lake Loop.

Capilano Suspension Bridge and Park

Seventy m (23.3 ft.) above the Capilano River swings the Capilano Suspension Bridge. The bridge leads to year-round nature trails and in summer you can watch totem-pole carvers at work. We like to take out-of-town friends there following a browse around the Capilano Salmon Hatchery. Take Lions Gate Bridge to Marine Drive, turn up Capilano Road and continue to number 3735 on your left.

Capilano Salmon Hatchery

The first fish farm in the province, the hatchery is particularly interesting to visit between July and October when adult coho and Chinook jump up ladders en route to the spawning area. It's fun to pack a picnic, inspect the salmon, then cross the Capilano River for some forest hiking and a peek at Cleveland Dam, Vancouver's main drinking water supply. Entrance to the dam is beyond the suspension bridge at 4500 Capilano Road.

You might want to hike the whole Capilano Canyon along the Capilano Pacific Trail, which follows the west side of the river from Cleveland Dam down to Ambleside Beach near the river's mouth. It's an easy 7.5 km (4.6 mi.). You can park at the Cleveland Dam, then at the end of your hike take a No. 239 bus back up Capilano Road. The hike takes you past the fish hatchery and provides really lovely glimpses of the canyon, with its huge trees and lush ferns.

Whitewater kayakers enjoy the challenge of the fast water running through the canyon. Races are often held here in the summer months.

Grouse Mountain

Grouse Mountain opened for skiing in 1937, and today its short downhill runs, lit up at night, are a beacon to visitors. Skiers are whisked to the alpine area in the Skyride, a Swiss-built ski gondola.

Hikers who want to do Grouse should check into the guest services booth at the bottom of the skyride to pick up trail maps and get further information about conditions.

One possibility is to go up the mountain under the skyride. Spring hikers here can spot darting rufous hummingbirds and hear the courtship cacophony of mating grouse mingling with the traffic noise of downtown commuters.

Another popular hike leads past Grouse to Goat Mountain, from which you get good views of the Lions, the twin peaks which are the highest and most visible on North Vancouver's skyline. Known to the Capilano people as the chief's daughters, or sisters, who keep watch over the peace and "brotherhood" of the Pacific Coast, the mountains are, in the words of poet Pauline Johnson, continually "wrapped in the suns, the snows, and the stars of all the seasons."

Cypress Provincial Park

A drive up to the Cypress lookout, just 8 km (5 mi.) north of West Vancouver on Highway 1, is virtually imperative for every traveller to Vancouver and with good reason, since the views of the city below, the Strait of Georgia, Vancouver Island and distant Mount Baker are superlative.

In summer, spring and fall, Cypress is a hiker's world full of berries in season and interesting side trips to such locations as Yew Lake. Strong day-hikers or backpackers can tackle the Howe Sound Crest Trail, a 30-km (19-mi.) loop that starts in Cypress Park and runs past the Lions to Porteau Cove Provincial Park on Howe Sound.

In winter, Cypress is something of a mecca for nordic skiers, who can enjoy lit trails in the Hollyburn Ridge area of the park on snowy evenings. A large number of trails interconnect within a relatively small area. There are more than 26 km (16 mi.) of groomed tracks, and back-country skiers can also make their way to the top of Hollyburn Mountain for great views of the city below. Hollyburn Lodge, on Hollyburn Mountain, is an institution, summer or winter. When the lodge first opened in 1927, overnight accommodation cost fifty cents. Visitors, who hiked up from Marine Drive in West Vancouver, slept in their own sleeping bags on a bed of cedar boughs and matting. Nordic skiers left their skis at the lodge all winter, proprietor Fred Burfield charging them ten cents a week for ski care. The atmosphere at the lodge today is still very laid-back.

For information about Cypress Park, call 922-0825 (winter) or 926-6007 (summer). Call Hollyburn Ridge Cross Country Ski Area at 922-0825 for nordic skiing information.

Lighthouse Park

A 25-minute drive from the downtown core, Lighthouse Park in West Vancouver is a popular diving, walking and rock-climbing area for Vancouverites. Take the Lions Gate Bridge and proceed west along Marine Drive through Park Royal and Ambleside shopping areas. The park is well signposted. Many of the Lower Mainland's 30,000 divers come here to poke in the kelp, spotting white, red, green and blue sea anemones and a thousand different kinds of fluorescent nudibranches. Walkers looking for tide pools can find brittle starfish and pale blue sail-by-the-winds which disintegrate on touch.

GREATER VANCOUVER

Buntzen Lake

A mere 30-minute drive from Vancouver, this beautiful lake has sandy beaches at its south end, hiking and cycling trails, fishing and picnic tables. Buntzen used to be a popular swimming area but high coliform counts in recent years have deterred bathers. It gets very busy in summer but is a lovely place to hike any time of year.

To get to Buntzen Lake, follow the main road, Highway 7A, out of Vancouver through Port Moody to Ioco Road. At this intersection, turn left and follow the green Greater Vancouver Regional District signs for Belcarra Park. Before reaching the park, take the well-marked right turn to Anmore and Buntzen Lake.

Indian Arm

Indian Arm extends north of Vancouver from the community of Deep Cove, situated at the arm's junction with Burrard Inlet. Indian Arm Provincial Marine Park snakes up the southeast side of the arm, which contains attractions for canoeists, kayakers and scuba divers.

Popular paddles include trips around Port Moody, Bedwell-Belcarra Bay and Jug Island, all accessible via the Barnet Highway (Highway 7A) which heads east out of Vancouver through Port Moody to Ioco Road. The Port Moody paddle is a treat for bird watchers, but be cautious of ocean swells and powerboats. The same is true of the Bedwell Bay-Belcarra Bay route, which takes in Jug and Raccoon islands in Indian Arm.

SUNSHINE COAST

The lower-levels road through West Vancouver and past Lighthouse Park ends in the community of Horseshoe Bay, departure point for ferries to Nanaimo on Vancouver Island, and to one of our favourite spots in the province—the Sunshine Coast.

In this section we take you 130 km (80 mi.) up the Sunshine Coast from the first ferry terminus at Langdale to the northern town of Lund. The trip involves two ferry crossings, so do allow yourself plenty of time to explore.

As its name implies, the Sunshine Coast enjoys a consistently mild climate, receiving 2400 hours of sunshine a year and only 94 cm (37 in.) of rain. The coastline is characterized by deep inlets and fiords interspersed with long, sandy beaches. Its sheltered location protects it from harsh ocean winds, creating ideal conditions for the many fish farms located along the coast. The resident population (which swells by 25 per cent in summertime) consists of numerous writers, craftspeople, loggers and fisherpeople.

For centuries this was Coast Salish country, and seashell middens at numerous sites and pictographs in many areas along the coast bear witness to long years of habitation.

It's possible to make a day trip to the Sunshine Coast, but many travellers stay on longer. The lures are sport fishing, sunshine, scenery, beaches, wilderness camping, hiking, canoeing and prime kayaking, all within easy reach of Vancouver.

The Sunshine Coast can be reached from the Lower Mainland via a 40-minute ferry ride from Horseshoe Bay to Langdale. The price of your ferry ticket includes two ferry crossings; you may either return to your original starting point or continue and take the next ferry (from Earl's Cove to Saltery Bay) at no extra cost. For ferry schedules, call B.C. Ferries at 685-1021

(Vancouver) or 886-2242 (Langdale). Maverick Coach Lines operates a twice-daily bus service from downtown Vancouver; call them at 255-1171 (Vancouver) or 886-7742 (Langdale) for schedules. Tyee Air runs a 20-minute flight from Vancouver Harbour to Sechelt. Contact them at 689-8651 (Vancouver) or 885-2214 (Sechelt).

From Horseshoe Bay the B.C. ferry crosses Howe Sound, passing between Bowen and Gambier islands. En route you may spot sport fisherpeople clustered around the legendary Hole in the Wall fishing spot just below Highway 99.

Accommodation on the Sunshine Coast covers the range from provincial campsites to many cozy bed-and-breakfast homes. (Check *Accommodations* for listings.)

If you plan on doing any hiking on the Sunshine Coast, pick up copies of *103 Hikes in Southwestern British Columbia* and *109 Walks in the Lower Mainland. Sunshine* and *Salt Air   A Recreation Guide to the Sunshine Coast* is another useful reference. Sailors will want to be equipped with Bill Wolferstan's *Cruising Guide to British Columbia, Vol. III*, which covers the Sunshine Coast, Fraser Estuary and Vancouver to Jervis Inlet.

The Sunshine Coast is also ideal for cycle trips since roads are quiet and not too hilly. Simon Priest and Kimberley Klint's book *Bicycling Southwestern British Columbia and the Sunshine Coast* provides details.

Gibsons

From the Langdale ferry terminal a short drive leads up the coast to Gibsons. The rugged scenery dissolves into a gentler landscape; colours become more subtle and the atmosphere tranquil.

En route to Gibsons, you might want to walk the 240 m (800 ft.) up Soames Hill to enjoy a panoramic view of Howe Sound and Gibsons' harbour. Follow Marine Drive from the ferry terminal. Halfway to Gibsons a white, yellow and blue sign on your right hand side leads to a gravel parking area.

In Gibsons itself, visitors can stroll along the floats at the government wharf, a favorite location for "The Beachcombers," the CBC television network's most popular series ever. (Although the last episode was shot last year, reruns of the show continue to be seen around the world.) In the evening, a stroll along the lit shoreline at the harbour captures the relaxed atmosphere of this place. The Elphinstone Pioneer Museum at Gibsons features local history displays and a very large shell collection.

From Gibsons, Highway 101 leads 12 km (7 mi.) west to Roberts Creek Provincial Park, a small 25-vehicle campsite with a pebble beach—a gem of a campground for frazzled parents keen to take the family for a weekend's camping within an hour of the big city.

Mount Steele

It comes as a surprise to many Lower Mainland nordic skiers that the Sunshine Coast, in particular the area east of the Sechelt Peninsula and north of Gibsons, is a prime destination, given good snow conditions.

On the "Provincial Parks of the Lower Mainland" map, you'll find the area sandwiched between Gray Creek to the north and Chapman Creek to the south. Beautifully constructed cabins exist at Edwards Lake, McNair Lake and Batchelor Lake, just 3 of the 10 lakes in the region, and at Mount Steele. The route into the area includes 6.5 km (4 mi.) of gentle logging road and a further 4.8 km (3 mi.) of trail to the Edwards Lake cabin. The cabins are connected by over 20 km (12 mi.) of trails, including one to the summit of Mount Steele. Use of the cabins is on a first-come, first-served basis.

Maps of the area with descriptions of road access from Sechelt are available from the B.C. Forest Service at 1975 Field Rd., Sechelt, B.C., V0N 3A0 (885-5174).

Sechelt

Situated on the isthmus that marks the start of the Sechelt Peninsula, this town is the main service centre for the surrounding area. In true seaside tradition, the smell of fish and chips wafts over the place and, away from the main mall, the dress and hardware shops seem to be caught in a time warp. Take time to drop down to see the totem poles on the Sechelt Indian Band property. You don't need permission to go onto the land, and if you travel up the coast during the summer months you might well see war canoe racers taking their crafts up to races hosted by the Sechelt band.

Accommodation here ranges from bed-and-breakfasts with tennis (the Wakefield Inn, just north of town) to the 86-vehicle campsites of Porpoise Bay, a sheltered beachside provincial park on the eastern shore of Sechelt Inlet. This is a family favourite due to the size of the banana slugs in June and to the salmon run programs in the fall. Paddlers use the park as a base for exploring the many marine parks in the area.

Porpoise Bay Park is one of the two best access points (Tuwanek, farther north up the east side of the Sechelt Inlet, is the other) to the Sechelt Inlets Marine Recreation Area, 8 recreation sites covering 155 ha (383 a.). Very popular with kayakers and canoeists, this calm, three-fingered inland sea encompasses 480 km (298 mi.) of shoreline and has an average July temperature of 18° C (64° F). A 54-km (34-mi.) circuit taking in Nine Mile Point, Kunechin Point, Tzoonie Narrows, Skaiakos Point and Piper Point makes an interesting 3- to 4-day trip. Harbour seals and bald eagles abound in the area.

A comprehensive breakdown of kayaking here is given in John Ince and

Hedi Kottner's *Sea Kayaking Canada's West Coast*. As they point out, there is much to see and appreciate in this patch of water, including helicopter logging operations, the immense cliffs of Tzoonie Narrows and delicious oysters at Storm Bay. Mountain goats can sometimes be seen treading the narrow mountain ledges high above Narrows Inlet.

Sechelt Inlet and the inlets reaching northeast from it, Salmon and Narrows, are becoming increasingly well known for diving. In the Lambs Island vicinity lurk giant wolf eels and lingcod weighing up to 18 kg (44 lb.). In Sechelt Narrows, you might also spot golfball-sized lithoid crabs with their blue-spotted pincers. These crabs live in pits bored by sea urchins and in other tight spots.

Another attraction of the area are the 160-year-old pictographs at the entrance to Salmon Inlet.

Pender Harbour

Pender Harbour, 63 km (39 mi.) from the Langdale ferry terminal, includes the communities of Madeira Park, Garden Bay and Irvines Landing. Diving in the area is good, with the best visibility occurring in winter, although the water remains relatively clear year-round due to cool summer temperatures.

Ruby and Sakinaw lakes, located between Madeira Park and Earls Cove and easily accessible from Highway 101, are noted for trout fishing in season. Ruby Lake Resort, R. R. #1, Madeira Park, B.C., V0N 2H0 (883-2269), with its stately swans and paddleboats, is typical of the family-oriented accommodation in the region.

Princess Louisa Inlet

Jervis Inlet, which empties into Malaspina Strait in the Pender Harbour area, reaches from the Sunshine Coast into the heart of the Coast Mountains. Apart from being prime kayaking territory—Area Six of *Sea Kayaking Canada's West Coast* details trips in the inlet—Jervis' main claim to fame is its offshoot, Princess Louisa Inlet.

If you plan to explore Princess Louisa Inlet by kayak, allow at least 4 days; a week is probably best. The best launch site is at Irvines Landing in Pender Harbour. En route up the inlet, paddlers, sailors and pleasure-boat cruisers are treated to quintessential Pacific Northwest scenery: towering mountains in the distance, craggy cliffs, evergreen trees and countless waterfalls, combined with a wealth of sea mammals and sea birds.

The Ministry of Parks puts out a delightful brochure telling the legend of Princess Louisa Inlet, considered by many to be the jewel of the coastal inlets.

Named Suivoolot, meaning "sunny and warm," by the Coast Salish, the inlet exudes a mystical quality that complements its imposing setting. Almost completely enclosed, it runs for 8 km (5 mi.), hedged by 1000-m (3280-ft.) cliffs, and is 800 m (1 mi.) wide at its widest point.

From mid-June on, more than 60 waterfalls drop down the sheer cliffs. One of the most spectacular is Chatterbox Falls, a 40-m (120-ft.) plume at the head of the inlet. Water in the inlet can be as warm as 20° C (68° F) in summer. The land at the head of the inlet was given to the province in 1953 by James F. "Mac" Macdonald, who bought the property in 1927 with money earned from striking it rich in Nevada. After many years of hosting visiting boaters, Mac wanted to ensure the preservation of one of the most beautiful spots in the world.

Probably the most apt sentiments ever written about Princess Louisa Inlet are recorded by Maggie Paquet in her *Parks of British Columbia and the Yukon*. She quotes from Erle Stanley Gardner's tale *Log of a Landlubber*: "There is no use describing that inlet. Perhaps an atheist could view it and remain an atheist, but I doubt it."

From June to the end of September, Sunshine Coast Tours and Charters (886-8341 in Sechelt) runs triweekly day trips up to Princess Louisa Inlet, complete with picnic lunch, a stop at the falls, a viewing of Indian pictographs, a run through Malibu rapids and sightings of seals and eagles.

Skookumchuck Narrows

One of the highlights of the Sechelt Peninsula, whether you travel up the inlet by boat or take Highway 101 from Sechelt to the northern village of Egmont, is the Skookumchuck Narrows (Skookumchuck is Chinook for "strong water"). The west coast's largest salt-water rapids occur off North Point on the outgoing tide and off Roland Point on the incoming tide. On a 3-m (10-ft.) tide, 750 billion l (200 billion gal.) of water churn through the shallow narrow channel.

A one-hour hike to Roland Point leads from the parking lot in the village of Egmont. Tall second-growth timber, swordtail ferns and well-maintained boardwalks make this a typical B.C. hike. Fisherpeople (and bald eagles!) wait for the ebb in the kelp beds below North Point.

The best time to visit Skookumchuck is on the rising tide: the more metres of change in the tide, the better the show. On a .6-m (2-ft.) low tide and a 4.6-m (15-ft.) high tide, the earth seems to shake! Be sure to pick up a monthly timetable from the Tourist Information Bureau in Sechelt.

The rapids are at their peak during December and early June. Whirlpools up to 18 m (60 ft.) across and 2.4 m (8 ft.) high are not uncommon, so it is imperative that boaters carry a tide book, know how to use it and go through the narrows only at slack tide. At low tide, the bays reveal a colourful display of sea life, with giant barnacles, colonies of sea urchins, sea anemones and mollusks. The action of the currents causes these creatures to grow to extravagant sizes.

There is primitive camping within the Skookumchuck Narrows Provincial Park—and the sweetest-smelling biffies we encountered during our research.

Powell River

The major industrial hub of the Sunshine Coast, Powell River, is a 45-minute ferry ride across Jervis Inlet from Earl's Cove, at the top of the Sechelt Peninsula, to Saltery Bay. (Ferries also connect Powell River with Comox on Vancouver Island, allowing a scenic circle trip from Vancouver.) Home to one of the world's largest pulp and paper mill complexes, the town offers all the amenities of a modern logging town and is also the hub of a wide variety of recreational opportunities.

Fishing is excellent at Coho Point, just off the northernmost tip of Texada Island, south of Powell River. Between Texada and Harwood islands, Rebeccas Reef offers good fishing. Closer to the mainland, fishing for large Chinooks can be surprisingly productive around the "hulks," a group of concrete ships used to form a breakwater for the pulp mill.

Powell River is officially proclaimed the scuba diving capital of Canada, with more than 100 dives mapped by local diving experts. Charters, rentals and air are available locally as are guides and detailed information on dive sites. You should also refer to the Pacific Coast diving bible, *141 Dives in the Protected Waters of Washington and British Columbia* by Betty Pratt-Johnson, for specific information.

Several sunken ships ranging from 6 m (20 ft.) to 45 m (150 ft.) in length lie within diving range of Powell River. One example is the 26-m (87-ft.) tug, the *Shamrock*, which sank off Vivian Island; divers still bring up brass items and other memorabilia from the vessel. Rare red coral thrives in the area, as do huge, shy octopuses and wolf eels which pose no threat to divers. Huge lingcod, up to 1.8 m (6 ft.) long, make their home in the shipwrecks or in dark caves created by boulders. Saltery Bay, where the ferry docks, has its own mermaid—the first underwater statue in Canada.

The **Powell Forest Canoe Route** is a well-used lake paddling circuit set into the coastal mountains behind Powell River. Its accessibility to the Lower Mainland is an attraction for family paddlers but it does run through logging country—indeed, it was loggers who first built the portages—so your peace may occasionally be shattered by the revving of logging trucks.

The route, which covers 10 lakes, provides views of coastal rain forest and can be canoed in its entirety or in sections. Twenty forest service recreation sites and camping areas in the vicinity make accommodation a cinch. Fishing for kokanee, cutthroat trout and rainbow trout is good. Detailed information, including a map, is available from the Powell River Forest Service office, and we recommend paddlers check with the office for up-to-date conditions before embarking on the trip. The route is best travelled between April and November, as the higher lakes are frozen during the winter months and roads become inaccessible.

The recommended starting point for those travelling the whole distance is Lois Lake, south of Powell River. To reach the lake, canoeists should take the MacMillan Bloedel Branch 41 logging road just south of the Eagle River Bridge, about 2 km (1.3 mi.) south of Lang Bay. Signs along the road direct you to the Lois Lake departure point. Canoeists can paddle up the lake, then portage to Horseshoe Lake over a scenic trail alongside Horseshoe River.

From there, the route leads through Nanton Lake, Ireland Lake, Dodd Lake, Windsor Lake, Goat Lake and Powell Lake, with several portages along the way. Scenery ranges from deciduous-tree-covered lowlands to rugged mountain peaks surrounded by fiordlike lakes.

The Powell River area also boasts some good hiking terrain. One popular hike is the Willingdon Beach Nature Trail, which winds along the ocean between Westview and the town of Powell River. For detailed information on hiking in the area, you might want to consult *Sunshine and Salt Air, A Recreation Guide to the Sunshine Coast*.

Texada Island, accessible by ferry 10 times daily from Powell River, is dotted with campsites. Shelter Point Regional Park, on the southwest coast of the island, 24 km (15 mi.) from the ferry landing, is one of the quieter spots. Here, hiking trails wind through first-growth forests; oysters and clams can be collected on the beaches for dinner and salmon can be caught offshore. Once the mining centre of the Pacific Northwest, Texada is rumoured to have had at one time the only opera house north of San Francisco, or so the locals claim! No trace of the opera house remains.

Useful Information

Contact **Dive BC**, 5824 Ash St., Powell River, B.C., V8A 4R4 (483-9740) for local diving information.

Detailed information on the Powell Forest Canoe Route, including a map, is available from the Forest Service Office, Powell River District, 7077 Duncan St., Powell River, B.C., V8A 1W1 (485-2554).

B.C. Ferries operates the service between Powell River and Blubber Bay on Texada Island, as well as the ferry service to Comox on Vancouver Island. Call them at 669-1211 for information on ferry schedules and fares.

Lund

Twenty-three km (14 mi.) north of Powell River, Highway 101 ends right at the water in the village of Lund, a tiny community that dates back to 1899, when the Thulin brothers came to settle and named the place for their Swedish hometown. The hotel they built, the Breakwater Inn, still dominates the Lund waterfront today, providing accommodation for paddlers and boaters en route to Desolation Sound and Savary Island, Hernando Island and the Copeland Islands. (For information, call 483-3187.) Lund also provides a base for scuba divers and salmon fishers.

Savary Island

Almost 200 years ago, Captain George Vancouver described Savary Island in his log as a "beauty such as we have seldom enjoyed." Situated 6 km (4 mi.) west of Lund and accessible only by boat or water taxi, Savary is known as B.C.'s south sea island for its mild climate and sandy beaches. Call the Lund Water Taxi (483-9749) to book the 12-minute ride to the island.

Eight km (5 mi.) long and crescent-shaped, Savary Island sits in warm waters where tides from northern Vancouver Island mingle with tides from the south; ocean temperatures are generally in the 22° C (72° F) range. Since there are no campsites here, accommodation takes the form of cabin rental or bed-and-breakfasts. Juanita Chase owns one of the few trucks on Savary and knows of places for rent; contact her at 483-4314. Food is available at the world-famous Mad Hatter (483-4312).

Copeland Islands

The Copeland Islands lie north of Powell River, just outside Desolation Sound Marine Park. Popular with canoeists, these mossy islands feature primitive campsites. Paddlers can launch at Lund, on the exposed west side of the Malaspina Peninsula, if the weather is calm, when it's windy, put-in is at protected Okeover Inlet. A free map entitled "Coastal Marine Parks of British Columbia," available from local tourist information offices, shows the islands in detail.

Desolation Sound and Beyond

Lund and Campbell River (on the east coast of Vancouver Island) are the main launching points for boats going to Desolation Sound Provincial Marine Park and Recreation Area, 32 km (20 mi.) north of Powell River. The largest of the coastal marine parks in British Columbia, Desolation Sound offers protected warm waters backed by views of the Coast Mountains. At the

Sailing in Howe Sound. *Photo by Mary Simpson*

peak of the summer season, as many as 300 boaters can be scattered around the park, meaning that June and September are the optimum times to be there.

The Indian pictographs, shoreline lakes and stunning views along the 64 km (40 mi.) of park coastline make this a superb kayaking and sailing area. When Captain George Vancouver explored these waters in 1792, he found them forlorn and fishless. Modern anglers seldom get skunked, however, as salmon fishing is good in the sound's warm waters; oysters are also readily available.

Bill Wolferstan's *Cruising Guide to British Columbia, Vol. II: Desolation Sound to Discovery* provides details on good anchorages in the park, including Prideaux Haven, Tenedos Bay and Grace Harbour.

Kayakers travelling to the sound should allow at least 4-5 days for the paddle. Launch at Lund or at Okeover Arm Park, 10 km (6 mi.) south of Lund. Once you're in the sound, any one of the dozen tiny islands is suitable for camping; do be sure to have a good stock of fresh water on board, though. *Sea Kayaking Canada's West Coast* gives detailed descriptions of the area.

If you really want to escape the summer crowds on the central coast, you might want to consider a sail north from Desolation Sound to Port Hardy or even Prince Rupert. The Discovery Islands, north of Desolation Sound, and the Blackfish Archipelago, even farther north, offer many islands for exploring and good opportunities for viewing wildlife, in particular killer whales or "blackfish."

Useful Information

Bare-boat or skippered sailboat charters to Desolation Sound can be arranged either in Vancouver or in Comox through such companies as **Seawing Sailing School & Yacht Charters**, 1815 Mast Tower Rd., Granville Island, Vancouver, B.C., V6H 3X7 (669-0840); **Cooper Boating Centre**, 1620 Duranleau St., Granville Island, Vancouver, B.C., V6H 3S4 (687-4110), and **Desolation Sound Yacht Charters**, 201-1797 Comox Ave., Comox, B.C., V9N 4A1 (339-4914 or 339-7222).

Kayak trips are run by **Pacific Rim Paddling**, Box 1840, Station E, Victoria, B.C., V8W 3C6 (384-6103) and by **Coast Mountain Expeditions**, Box 25, Surge Narrows, B.C., V0P 1W0 (286-2064). Coast Mountain Expeditions also offers a heli-hiking trip in the Coast Mountains around Toba Inlet.

Queen Charlotte Strait

Travelling northwest from Desolation Sound, boaters enter first Johnstone Strait, then Queen Charlotte Strait, which rims the northeastern portion of Vancouver Island.

Nearly 20 km (12 mi.) wide at its narrowest point, the shallow Queen Charlotte Strait contains resident marine life that is considered to be among the richest on the west coast of North America. Divers in the area can expect to see vast fields of pink and white gorgonian coral, a relatively recently discovered species. Basket stars, furry brown sea spiders and yellow sponges all grow on top of each other in this rich marine soup.

HOWE SOUND/SQUAMISH

Horseshoe Bay, the departure point for Nanaimo on Vancouver Island and Langdale on the Sunshine Coast, is also the departure point for ferry trips to Bowen Island, which has long enjoyed a tradition of entertaining day visitors from the mainland. From the flapper era until the outbreak of World War II, Union Steamships operated six extensive picnic grounds, where up to 2000 people could be seated under cover, near the ferry dock at Snug Cove.

Today, a fine hike on thickly wooded Bowen Island is to the top of Mount Gardner for panoramic views of Howe Sound. Two major valleys lead out from Snug Cove, dividing Bowen into three mountain masses, of which Gardner is the highest. Don't bother to take your car across to Bowen Island (a 20-minute crossing) for this hike. The beginning of the 6-hour, 16-km (10-mi.) round trip can be easily reached via Government Road from the ferry dock.

Sailors can enjoy good, usually sheltered, sailing in Howe Sound except when a Squamish (a strong wind from the north blowing directly down the sound) is causing whitecaps. Sheltered anchorages exist in the bays on the south end of Gambier Island, north of Bowen. There are other small nooks and crannies around nearby Keats Island. Fishing for salmon and a wide variety of rockfish and bottomfish can be arranged on an hourly basis from Sewell's Landing at Horseshoe Bay. (Our favourite skipper is Jean Miller, whose boat, *The Happy Hooker*, is seldom jinxed!)

A very popular camping site along the sound is located just off Highway 99, which leads north from Horseshoe Bay to Whistler. Porteau Cove Provincial Park, 8.5 km (5 mi.) south of the interesting old mining community of Britannia Beach, offers oceanfront camping, good fishing and highly regarded scuba diving. During the 1989 shooting of the Gene Hackman movie *The Narrow Edge*, a whole train station was built at Porteau Cove and Via Rail trains were trucked in for the railroad sequences.

Britannia Beach, 45 minutes from Vancouver at km 52 (mi. 32) on Highway 99, is a great place to visit for a tour of an old mine and a spot of gold panning— recovery guaranteed—at the B.C. Museum of Mining. The museum is situated at the old Britannia Copper Mine, which, in the 1920s, was one of the world's largest.

A spectacular way to see Howe Sound is by train. You can take the B.C. Rail Dayliner from the North Vancouver depot to the interior town of Squamish or travel on the Royal Hudson Steam Engine. The B.C. Rail train continues north from Squamish to Lillooet, Williams Lake and Prince George. The Royal Hudson trip can be combined with a return cruise back to Coal Harbour in downtown Vancouver via the M. V. *Britannia*, operated by Harbour Ferries.

Useful Information

For schedules and reservations on either the Dayliner or the Royal Hudson trip, contact **B.C. Rail** at 984-5246. **Harbour Ferries** coordinates the combined Royal Hudson and M. V. *Britannia* trip, so contact them at 987-9558 for further information.

Contact the **B.C. Museum of Mining**, Box 188, Britannia Beach, B.C., V0N 1J0 (688-8735 from Vancouver or 896-2233 in Britannia) for opening hours.

Squamish

If you are driving north of Porteau Cove Park on Highway 99, you will pass two small provincial parks just before you get to the town of Squamish. Murrin, 3 km (2 mi.) beyond Britannia Beach, is a popular day outing for casual fishers, family hikers and rock climbers from novice to intermediate. Four km (1.8 mi.) farther along, the spectacular 335-m (1100-ft.) Shannon Falls are the focal point of the provincial park of the same name.

Squamish itself, 60 km (38 mi.) north of Vancouver at the tip of Howe Sound, is dominated by the 2678-m (8786-ft.) Mount Garibaldi and the 652-m (2140-ft.) Stawamus Chief. The great monolith of the Stawamus Chief is named for the profile of a sleeping Squamish Indian, which it resembles in outline. It is second in size only to the Rock of Gibralter as the largest freestanding granite outcropping in the world.

High adventure and urban convenience combine to make the Squamish area one of the premier "free" rock-climbing centres in North America. The Chief alone provides 280 climbing routes, ranging from novice faces to the legendary walls of the Sword, the Split Pillar and Roman Chimneys. The dramatic University Wall climb, ending on Dance Platform, is rated the hardest rock climb in Canada.

Climbs in the surrounding area include the Gullies, the Papoose and Night mare Rock. Four major gullies split the walls of the Chief, and while the north-north and south-south gullies are short climbs and not particularly outstanding, the south and north gullies are impressively deep cuts and more interesting and challenging.

The Papoose is a prominent bluff found directly above the parking lot for the Woodfibre ferry, just off Highway 99. It consists of a number of moderately difficult one-day climbs. Nightmare Rock, situated just north of Murrin Park, is rated moderate to difficult.

For hiking enthusiasts, the Chief has three easy summits: the main, the central and the south. Trailhead for all three is located at the end of a dirt road that runs off the east side of the highway, 2.5 km (1.1 mi.) south of Squamish. Primitive campsites exist just before the base of the Chief and water is available from the nearby creek or the Stawamus River.

Avid windsurfers will already know about the "Squamish Spit," considered by many to offer some of the best windsurfing in Canada. Where the Squamish River ("squamish" means "mother of the wind") flows into Howe Sound the winds blow year-round and the views are breathtaking. You can see the Stawamus Chief, Shannon Falls, snow-capped mountain peaks, Howe Sound and dozens of neon-coloured windsurfing sails. While the waters are cool at the river's mouth, temperatures can get positively Hawaii-like in the sound. About 9000 windsurfers visit "Hood River North," as the spit is known in windsurfing circles, every summer.

The Squamish Windsurfing Society administers the spit and charges a daily fee of $5. You reach the spit by turning left at the McDonald's intersection in Squamish and taking the first right onto Buckley Avenue. Buckley leads across the railway tracks into Government Road. Just past the Squamish Feed Suppliers, turn left onto the first gravel road. From here drive a short distance to a T intersection, turn left, and continue for a further 2 km (1.2 mi.).

Paddlers in the Squamish region can tackle the Squamish River, a day trip from put-in at the Powerhouse, 23 km (14 mi.) north of Cheekeye, to take-out at Brackendale. This trip is recommended for paddlers keen to obtain river experience, since most hazards can be easily seen and avoided.

Ski-plane glacier tours of the Squamish area operate daily from May 1 to November 30.

Horseback riders can explore the area with Cheekeye Stables, located 7 km (4.3 mi.) north of Squamish off Highway 99. Half-day rides lead to riverside watering holes and viewpoints; on overnight trips, riders follow the Squamish River to the white sand beaches of River Bend, complete with distant views of the Tantalus glacier shield.

Useful Information

Call **Glacier Air Tours** at 898-9016 for more information on their glacier sightseeing tours.

Contact **Cheekeye Stables**, Box 312, Brackendale, B.C., V0N 3G0 (898-3432) for information about their horseback trips.

For more information on climbing, hiking and canoeing in the area, contact the Squamish Travel Infocentre, 37950 Cleveland Ave., Squamish, B.C., V0N 3G0 (892-9244).

Lake Lovely Water

This newly established recreation area, 88 km (55 mi.) north of Vancouver, is a 1300-ha (3212-a.) patch of scenic wilderness popular with climbers. The route to the lake is poorly signed. Travel north of Squamish on Highway 99 towards Whistler, take the turnoff to Paradise Valley and cross the bridge over the Cheakamus River. Two km (1.3 mi.) past the bridge, a gravel road branches off to the left. Follow this road for 1.7 km (1 mi.) to the Squamish River, where there is a water gauging station. There is room here for about four or five cars to park. From this point, travellers should ask permission to cross the land, which belongs to the Squamish Indian Band. For a fee, band members may assist hikers to cross the Squamish River. Otherwise, you will definitely need your own canoe or kayak.

The hiking trail starts on the west side of the river by the federal government cable car (which is used only to monitor river levels and is not suitable for crossing). The Federation of Mountain Clubs (FMC) have been responsible for most of the trail construction. The trail starts off level but soon becomes a steep climb, so it is definitely not for the unfit. The elevation gain is 1050-1200 m (3500-4000 ft.).

Lake Lovely Water offers fishing and some spectacular views. The Alpine Club of Canada (ACC) has a cabin on the lake; non-members interested in staying here should contact ACC. So far the area is undeveloped, but BC Parks plans to provide pit toilets and camp pads at a future date.

Vancouver Helicopters and Whistler Air Service both offer charter flights into the Lake Lovely Water area. Whistler Air will also fly in your canoe if you're going on a fishing trip.

Useful Information

Contact **Vancouver Helicopters** (683-4354) or **Whistler Air Service** (932-6615) for information about charter flights in the Squamish area.

For information on the ACC cabin, contact the **Alpine Club of Canada**, Box 1026, Banff, Alberta, T0L 0C0 (403-762-4481).

Contact the Squamish Indian Band, Box 86131, North Vancouver, B.C., V7L 4J5 (985-7711) to obtain permission to cross their land.

WHISTLER AREA

Continuing along Highway 99 from Squamish, we head north to Whistler and beyond to the prime potato-growing country of the Pemberton Valley. There have been a number of improvements made to Highway 99 in recent years, so this route is no longer the death-defying trip it used to be. But there are still many twists and turns, so take plenty of Gravol if you are prone to car sickness, then sit back and enjoy the stunning mountain views en route. If you plan on doing any hiking in the area you might want to arm yourself with the books *103 Hikes in Southwestern British Columbia* and *Hiking in Garibaldi Park.*

Garibaldi Park

Once known to only a few Vancouver outdoorspeople, Garibaldi now rates as B.C.'s most used wilderness park, attracting 80,000 visitors a year to its alpine meadows, remote lakes and mountain peaks. Its 195,083 ha (480,000 a.) of mainly volcanic peaks centre around Mount Garibaldi, a 2678-m (8787-ft.) peak named after Guiseppe Garibaldi, the 19th-century Italian patriot, soldier and statesman.

The park's southern boundary, which runs roughly parallel to the town of Squamish, abuts Golden Ears Park. The village of Whistler is situated just off Garibaldi's northwestern boundary, which is wedged between Lillooet Lake and the start of the fertile Pemberton Valley. Garibaldi's main attractions are its 196 walk-in wilderness campsites. Just 122 km (77 mi.) north of Vancouver by road and 64 km (40 mi.) by air, it is good hiking and fishing country, and suitable for exploration with children aged eight and over.

The three main areas of the park that cater to visitors—Diamond Head, Black Tusk and Cheakamus Lake—all lie in the central western portion.

Skiing near Elfin Lakes, Diamond Head. *Photo by Lloyd Twaites*

The Diamond Head area includes Mount Garibaldi, Diamond Head, the Opal Cone and Mamquam Lake. In summer, delicate pink and white heather blossoms carpet the area and Opal Cone is particularly rich in alpine flowers. Access to the Diamond Head parking lot is via a 16-km (10-mi.) logging road signed "Garibaldi (Diamond Head)," just past the Mamquam River bridge 4 km (2.5 mi.) north of Squamish.

One of the most popular day trips in the Diamond Head area is the 7-hour, 23-km (14.5-mi.) trip from the parking lot to the Elfin Lakes shelter. The cabin can accommodate 36 but can be quite busy in summer, so be prepared to camp in the nearby meadows, which are most brilliant from late July through August. From Elfin Lakes you can make other trips to the Gargoyles (eroded rock formations), Opal Cone and Mamquam Lake.

Diamond Head is also popular with nordic skiers, especially since it takes only 1½ driving hours from Vancouver to reach trailhead. Good snow conditions, beautiful telemark slopes and breathtaking scenery are guaranteed. From the end of October through May, an average of 20 m (66 ft.) of snow falls on the Diamond Head area.

Day ski trips include the run to the day shelter at Red Heather Ridge. The 4-hour ski to Elfin Lakes can be complemented by a trip along the Saddle, a pass between the Gargoyles and Columnar Peak. The winter route to the Elfin Lakes hut is well marked and avoids the avalanche-prone summer hiking route, but overnight skiers should be prepared to snow camp if necessary.

The most challenging trip in the area, known as the Garibaldi Neve Traverse, links Diamond Head with Black Tusk and is considered one of the classic ski tours in the B.C. Coast Range. Since good weather is essential for this trip (it runs for 50-70 km/31-44 mi., depending on your route), skiers will usually stay overnight in the Elfin Lakes shelter before making the one-day run to a hut at Sphinx Bay on Garibaldi Lake. It is necessary to travel roped for some sections of this run. Including side trips, the traverse can stretch into a week of strenuous, challenging skiing. Always check the mountain weather forecast (276-6112 in Vancouver) before skiing the area, and take along maps, skins, shovels and avalanche transceivers.

Black Tusk and Garibaldi Lake form the centre of Garibaldi Park. Within a small radius and easily accessible are a large number of outstanding attractions, including Panorama Ridge, Helm Glacier and the Barrier, as well as Lesser Garibaldi and Barrier lakes. In summer, large alpine meadows blossom into carpets of wildflowers. Hikers can move between many points of interest and mountaineers will find challenging peaks.

To get a taste of the area, you can make a day hike to Garibaldi Lake, a 17.5-km (11-mi.) round trip that takes about 6 hours. This glacier-blue lake is reached from a trailhead 37 km (23 mi.) north of Squamish on Highway 99; a sign 2 km (1.2 mi.) after the Garibaldi train station points right to the Black Tusk Recreation Area parking lot. Overnight camping is allowed at Garibaldi Lake or the Taylor Creek Campground, both popular summer weekend spots. Park headquarters are located at the west end of Garibaldi Lake.

Summer is the best time to hike up to the top of Black Tusk, accessible from the Taylor Creek Campground. The high point of this volcanic plug is 2315 m (7600 ft.), and the last few hundred metres of the ascent are made via a chimney; negotiate very carefully, particularly if other climbers are ahead of you dislodging loose rocks. Handholds are required and the use of a rope is advisable for beginners. Once you reach the top, you are rewarded with a breathtaking vista of the park.

A less travelled but interesting alternative approach to the Black Tusk area is via the Helm Creek Trail. Go in a group, since it will take at least two or three people to operate the cable car that crosses the Cheakamus River. The well-graded trail gives access to the area northeast of the Tusk: Cinder Cone, Helm Glacier, Empetrum Peak and Helm Lake. To reach the trailhead, follow the Cheakamus Lake Road, which runs east of Highway 99 just before you get to Whistler.

Contact the Visitor Services Coordinator, BC Parks, Garibaldi/Sunshine Coast District, Brackendale, B.C., V0N 1H0 (898-3678) for information and brochures on Garibaldi Park.

Whistler-Blackcomb

The past decade has seen an explosion of activity in the Whistler-Blackcomb region. Tucked into the base of Whistler and Blackcomb mountains, European-style Whistler Village is the hub of this year-round resort. In winter, the downhill skiing facilities on Whistler and Blackcomb rate in the top ten in North America, catering to a local and international clientele. In summer, adventurers radiate out from Whistler Village to hike, mountain bike, water ski, windsurf, kayak, raft and climb mountains.

The whole complex is about a 90-minute drive from Vancouver along the scenic Sea-to-Sky Highway (Highway 99), which winds along the fiord-like Howe Sound coastline. Maverick Coach Lines runs three trips daily to Whistler. The 2½-hour B.C. Rail trip from the North Vancouver station also offers great views.

Accommodation in Whistler runs the gamut from luxury hotels to modest bed-and-breakfasts. Meals range from French cuisine of the three-caviar-mousse variety to hearty west-coast fare. There is a fine variety of shops, but expect things to be a touch pricey.

While downhill is the name of the game during the winter at Whistler, a wide range of opportunities also exists for cross-country skiing in and around the area.

The Lost Lake circuit, considered one of the best by competing nordic skiers, offers 16 km (10 mi.) of expertly groomed and tracked trails for everyone from beginner to expert. The ticket booth is a quick ski from Whistler Village, just off Bridge Meadows along Fitzsimmons Creek, and there's a warming hut at Lost Lake itself. Qualified nordic instructors will introduce skiers to the new "skate" stroke, or help them polish up their technique on the traditional "kick and glide" method.

North of Whistler Village, 16 Mile Creek, though also popular with snowmobilers, is ideal for cross-country skiing. One route leads to the Showh Lakes, the other to a stand of very large, ancient western red cedar.

South of Whistler, the Cheakamus Lake Road ski route leads into Garibaldi Park. For a longer day or overnight trip, head east and follow Callaghan Lake Road to a number of mountain lakes. Nordic ski equipment can be rented at a number of locations in the village, and information on trails and snow conditions is also readily available.

Skiing in the area continues all through the summer. Blackcomb is the only mountain in North America to offer public summer glacier skiing. At Horstman Glacier on Blackcomb you will find prime spring snow conditions and comfortable temperatures.

Meanwhile, over on Whistler Mountain, the Dave Murray Summer Ski Camp offers top-level coaching plus many other activities for youngsters, including windsurfing, tennis, golf and swimming. Kids arrive from all over

Wedgemount Lake and Glacier. *Photo by Lloyd Twaites*

North America for these seven one-week clinics. They are usually sold out by mid-March, so book early.

Five lakes dot the Whistler valley, offering tons of opportunities in spring, summer and fall for fishing, swimming, windsurfing, canoeing, kayaking, sailing, water-skiing or just plain lazing around.

Alta Lake, one of the largest, is ideal for swimming, sailing, windsurfing and canoeing. The three public beaches are at Lakeside, Wayside and Rainbow. Alpha Lake offers a swimming beach and canoe rentals, while Lost Lake, a short walk from Whistler Village along Lost Lake Trail, has a large public beach and picnic area. Green Lake, the largest in the valley, is the only lake where motorboating is allowed. We find it a bit cold for swimming, but it's a popular water-ski and canoeing venue. All the lakes are accessible via the Valley Trail network that winds through Whistler.

Paddlers who want to travel the lakes and rivers around Whistler can either rent canoes and kayaks or join organized tours. River rafters can head down the Cheakamus, Squamish or Elaho rivers in season, from roughly mid-May to mid-September.

Trout fishers may want to contact Green River Fishing Guides; they run tours to alpine lakes, providing transportation, gear and boats. Four-wheel drive and fly-in fishing excursions are also available.

Whistler is a super place for mountain biking because of easy access to both alpine trails and lower-level back roads which are good for touring. The Whistler Gondola transports bikers and machines to the top of the mountain in 18 minutes. While biking is off-limits on the ski runs, a crisscrossing network of supply roads on the mountain provides a variety of routes back down to the village. Several outfits in Whistler Village offer guided bike tours.

Horseback riders can go out on one-hour trail rides or tie in with the overnight horseback camping trips offered by Layton Bryson Outfitting and Trail Riding.

Day hikers can take the chair lift up Whistler or Blackcomb mountains and then head down. One of the most rewarding hikes from the top of Whistler is the trail along the minor summits called the Musical Bumps (Oboe, Flute and Piccolo) to Singing Pass; you return via the Singing Pass Trail to Whistler Village. If you want to stay overnight in the Singing Pass area, hike up the other side of the pass to the ridge or to Russet Lake, where the Russet Lake Cabin accommodates 8 people.

Another strenuous but spectacular hike in the Whistler area is the trail to Wedgemount Lake, where Wedgemount Glacier tumbles into the lake. The cabin here is open to the public but it may be full on busy summer weekends, so be prepared to camp. The views on this 12-km (7.5-mi.) round trip are great, and the glacier can be approached from the left side of the lake. Access to Wedgemount (the Wedge) is via Highway 99, about 15 km (9.25 mi.) beyond the Whistler gondola terminal and just north of Green Lake. The turnoff to the right is marked and leads across the B.C. Rail tracks to a parking lot.

Whistler Air Services will fly hikers and skiers to remote areas like Stein Lake, the starting point for an 8-day downhill trek to Lytton through the Stein River Valley.

If you want to get into the mountains but don't want to ski or hike, you might consider whirling up for a heli-hike or heli-picnic. An area we particularly recommend is the Rainbow Mountain area.

Useful Information

For information on accommodation at Whistler, contact either the **Whistler Resort Association**, Box 1400, Whistler, B.C., V0N 1B0 (932-4222 or U.S. toll free 1-800-634-9622) or the Whistler Travel Infocentre, Box 181, Whistler, B.C., V0N 1B0 (932-5528), located on Highway 99 by the Whistler Mountain Gondola parking lot.

For more information on outdoor activities in the Whistler area, contact the Whistler Activity Centre in Whistler (932-2394).

For information on bus schedules, call **Maverick Coach Lines** in Vancouver at 255-1171. Contact **B.C. Rail** at 984-5246 to get train schedules.

Layton Bryson Outfitting and Trail Riding, Box 644, Pemberton, B.C., V0N 2L0 (932-6623) offers horseback trips in the area.

Bike tours are led by guides from **Jim McConkey's Sports Shop**, Box 67, Whistler, B.C., V0N 1B0 (932-2391) and **Whistler Backroads (Mountain Bike Adventures)**, Box 643, Whistler, B.C., V0N 1B0 (932-3111). Contact **Sea to Sky Raft Tours**, Box 509, Squamish, B.C., V0N 3G0 (898-2337) or **Whistler River Adventures**, Box 202, Whistler, B.C., V0N 1B0 (932-3532) for information on raft trips. **Whistler Canoe Guides**, Box 151, Whistler, B.C., V0N 1B0 (932-1984) offers a 1½-hour trip down the River of Golden Dreams. **Whistler Kayak Adventures**, Box 834, Whistler, B.C., V0N 1B0 (932-6615) sells kayaks as well as offering rentals, tours and instruction.

Contacts for heli-hiking trips include **Canadian Helicopters**, based in Vancouver, at 1-800-663-1161, and **Whistler Air Services** at 932-6615.

Pemberton Valley/Mount Currie

North of Whistler, the road and the railway tracks wind a further 35 km (28 mi.) to the town of Pemberton. From here, you can continue on the main road to Birkenhead Lake Provincial Park via the Mount Currie Indian Reserve or head northwest to Gold Bridge and Lillooet through the Hurley Pass.

In the 1960s, some Vancouver cars sported stickers saying, "I drove the Hurley Pass," a feat that still deserves recognition today. The Hurley follows the Lillooet River, then climbs over the Cadwallader Range of the Coast Mountains to Gold Bridge, a 2-hour trip from Pemberton that covers 80 km (50 mi.). While it is much improved since the early days, the gravel road is still filled with potholes and loose rocks and is open only in the summer. But the views of fields of blue lupins, backed by rugged blue mountains, make up for the lack of blacktop.

The Hurley, also known as the Railroad Pass Road, leads into an area popular for fishing, horseback riding, dude ranches and old mine sites, all within a 4-hour drive of Vancouver.

As you are heading out of Pemberton on the Hurley Road, watch out for signs giving directions to the relatively new trailhead for Tenquille Lake. This lovely alpine lake, set amid colourful meadows, makes a good fishing destination and the surrounding ridges offer many additional hiking opportunities. The hike to the lake from the trailhead takes about 2-3 hours.

Hot-springs buffs will want to visit Meager Creek, site of the largest springs in B.C. The creek flows into the Lillooet River 64 km (40 mi.) northwest of Pemberton; a logging road follows the river to the creek's mouth, passing close to the springs. One spring, dammed for bathing, flows all winter, making this a fun cross-country skier's destination. Water temperature hovers at 38° C (100° F).

If you take the right fork at the T junction in Pemberton instead of the left fork, which leads to the Hurley Pass, you will end up at the village of Mount Currie.

Turn right at the church to get to the Duffey Lake Road, which provides access to the legendary Joffre Lakes hike. (Part of the Duffey Lake Road is subject to a native land claim. Local residents sometimes raise tolls on the road, which was blocked for most of the summer in 1990.) The trailhead for this spectacular glacier hike past three lakes is at a parking spot 23 km (14.5 mi.) beyond Mount Currie and 1 km (.5 mi.) beyond the bridge over Joffre Creek. From the parking area, it is an 11-km (7-mi.) hike to Upper Joffre Lake; allow at least 6 hours for the round trip. In early summer chunks of ice the size of railroad boxcars calve regularly from the Matier Glacier into Joffre Lake and the sound echoes like thunder through the valley. By August and September the trail is usually clear of snow. One warning: mosquitoes can be a real pain at Joffre Lakes, so go prepared.

A third interesting hike in the Pemberton area is the trip from Lizzie Lake along Lizzie Creek to the alpine area that stretches over to the Stein Divide. Access is from the Lillooet Lake Road, south of Mount Currie. Another fine hike off the Duffey Lake Road follows Blowdown Creek to Blowdown Pass, affording glimpses of the scenic Stein Valley. Consult *103 Hikes in Southwestern British Columbia* for details on these and other hikes in the region.

Another way of exploring the Pemberton Valley area is on horseback to the alpine, with opportunities for gold panning and lake trout fishing. Contact Adventures on Horseback, Box 372, Pemberton, B.C., V0N 2L0 (894-6155 or 894-6968) for more information on organized trips.

FRASER ESTUARY/FRASER VALLEY

From Whistler we take Highway 99 back into Vancouver and then south of the city, across the mighty Fraser River, where it empties into the Pacific Ocean via a variety of arms. The varied landscape of the Fraser delta provides many opportunities for outdoor recreation such as bicycling, boating, bird watching, fishing and hiking.

The many dikes along the arms of the Fraser provide excellent bicycle paths and are ideal for year-round walks. Canoeists can paddle around various islands in the river where it widens to enter the sea. Routes around Barnston Island, McMillan Island, Wood Island and Shady Island are itemized in *Canoe Routes British Columbia* (check libraries and used bookstores for this valuable out-of-print title).

Another major attraction of the estuary is the George C. Reifel Migratory Bird Sanctuary on Westham Island. Signposted and located just beyond the village of Ladner, the first exit after the George Massey tunnel south of Vancouver on Highway 99, the wild-fowl refuge is networked with dike paths, making for a pleasant 2-3 hour walk.

Birders from as far away as Britain come to spot some of the over 230 species seen in the sanctuary, which is a major wintering area for many thousands of migratory birds. Snow geese come in the fall from Wrangel Island, Siberia. Their arrival is celebrated with a snow goose festival in November. Other birds seen here include Canada geese, mallards, pintails, teals and technicolour wood ducks. For the largest variety of birds, visit Reifel between October and March. Ducklings and goslings emerge in May and June. In summer, this is a great place for a picnic and stroll, although the bird life is not so prolific.

The city of Vancouver is conveniently close to the Fraser Valley, a rich, alluvial agricultural belt that provides summer produce and year-round dairy products. Known as the raspberry capital of the world, it is also famous for its strawberries and corn. Many farmers allow people to pick their own fruit and vegetables during summer; check the classified section of the *Vancouver Sun* for listings. To reach the lush countryside of the valley, take the Trans-Canada Highway east out of Vancouver over the Port Mann bridge.

Several different communities in the valley, including Mennonites and Sikhs, hold summer festivals, so it's well worth checking at tourist information centres to pick up information on these.

The Fraser Valley offers numerous hiking opportunities that are particularly good in the spring and fall when the higher elevations are snow-covered. Apart from the Trans-Canada Highway, most roads in the valley are not heavily travelled and make ideal bicycle routes, since they are mostly flat with some rolling hills. *Bicyling Southwestern British Columbia and the Sunshine Coast* has excellent maps and descriptions of various routes, each rated according to terrain and traffic as suitable for beginner, intermediate or advanced cyclists. One of the most pleasant and unusual ways to view the valley and get your bearings is to head up in a hot air balloon on a champagne flight.

Useful Information

Contact the **Reifel Bird Sanctuary**, 5191 Robertson Rd., Delta, B.C., V4K 3N2 (946-6980) for information on their programs and opening hours.

For more information on balloon flights, contact **Fantasy Balloon Charters**, Suite 7, 1465 West 14th Ave., Vancouver, B.C., V6H 1R4 (736-1974).

109 Walks in British Columbia's Lower Mainland and *103 Hikes in Southwestern British Columbia* detail many hikes in the Fraser Estuary and Fraser Valley area.

NORTH OF THE FRASER

Pitt Lake

Pitt Lake, 57 km (35 mi.) east of Vancouver, is a rewarding place for birders to paddle. The Pitt River begins in Garibaldi Provincial Park, near Whistler, then flows south into this narrow lake valley in the Coast Mountains. Terrain around Pitt Lake is typically lush coastal forest.

To reach Pitt Lake from Vancouver, take the Lougheed Highway (Highway 7) east to Pitt River Bridge, turn east onto Dewdney Trunk Road and continue along to the put-in at the lake outlet. Check libraries and used bookstores for copies of *Canoe Routes British Columbia*, which has detailed descriptions of Pitt Lake and the Pitt Polder route. (Polders are pieces of low-lying land reclaimed from underwater.) Since the Pitt Lake/River system is affected by ocean tides, shoreline levels and currents vary considerably. The lake itself is subject to severe winds. Nice canoeing side trips lead down Widgeon Creek or along the polders. The polders also make for good winter, spring and fall hiking, and you'll see plenty of shore birds, ducks and raptors.

Golden Ears Park

On the eastern rim of Pitt Lake lies Golden Ears Park, 48 km (30 mi.) east of Vancouver on Highway 7. This park takes its imaginative name from the twin peaks of T'Lagunna Mountain, which glisten like gold when the rays of the setting sun strike their snow-encrusted heights. Local lore maintains that the colouring of the peaks was a signal to native people of the area that salmon migration times were approaching.

The northern boundary of this 55,594-ha (137,370-a.) park forms the southern boundary of Garibaldi Park, close to Whistler Mountain. Alouette Lake, along Golden Ears' southern edge, is the focal recreation point for most visitors.

Prior to being heavily cleared in the early days of railway logging in B.C. (much evidence of which remains), the Alouette Lake area provided hunting and fishing grounds for the Interior Salish and Coast Salish Indians. Today, this park contains 300 campsites at Alouette and Gold Creek campgrounds, various locations for back-country camping, 930 m (3000 ft.) of developed beach and extensive hiking, walking and horse trails. Western hemlock, western red cedar and Douglas fir provide lush forest cover. Park interpreters work from April to October.

Strong hikers might want to tackle the overnight round trip to the north ear of Golden Ears, which involves crossing a permanent snowfield. The trail is described in *103 Hikes in Southwestern British Columbia*. A less strenuous family hike is the one-hour, 2.7-km (1.7-mi.) Lower Falls Trail from the Gold Creek parking lot, which leads to some of the best scenery in the park.

A one-day paddle will take canoeists up the 18 km (11 mi.) of Alouette Lake, which can be dangerous because of cold water, winds, power boats and snags. Paddlers keen on a longer expedition close to Vancouver can take the 2-4 days necessary to complete the Alouette-Stave Lake circuit.

As Wright states in *Canoe Routes of British Columbia*, "This trip is not for the faint hearted." Check his book for a detailed description of the 80-km (50-mi.) paddle. (Now out of print, this title can often be found in libraries or used bookstores.)

Horseback riding in Golden Ears Provincial Park can be organized through commercial stables in Maple Ridge. On a day ride in summer, horses travel up to Alouette Lake, where they are hitched while riders swim in the lake before going home. The riding season lasts from April to the end of October, and reservations are recommended.

Useful Information

Contact the Visitor Services Coordinator, Golden Ears Park, Maple Ridge, B.C., V2X 7G3 (463-3513) to get maps and brochures.

For more information on horseback riding, contact **Golden Ears Riding Stable**, 23103-136th St., Maple Ridge, B.C., V2X 7E7 (463-8761).

Jack Christie's *Day Trips from Vancouver* describes a trip to the park.

Mission to Harrison Mills

East of Golden Ears, Highway 7 leads to Mission, 71 km (44 mi.) from Vancouver. A terrific outing we made in this area is a day trip by kayak and raft down the Chehalis River, which empties into Harrison River. Ask in Mission for directions to the logging road that accesses the Chehalis, then enjoy your paddle past boulders resembling Henry Moore sculptures and keep an eye out for lone prospectors at the riverside.

Continuing east from Mission, you arrive at the town of Harrison Mills, starting point for the 22-km (14-mi.) drive up the Morris Valley Road to Hemlock Valley Ski and Recreation Area. While Hemlock is primarily a downhill ski area, some cross-country touring and lessons are available. For information and a report on snow conditions at Hemlock, call them at 797-4411.

A rough road running for 15 km (9 mi.) northeast of Harrison Mills takes travellers to a salmon spawning area at Weaver Creek. Chum and sockeye salmon spawn in three creeks here during October and November. Displays put together by Fisheries and Oceans explain the process. In winter, bald eagles can be viewed feeding voraciously in the Weaver Creek area. Contact the local Travel Infocentre, 24033 Lougheed Highway, Mission, B.C., V2V 5X8 (826-6914) for more information and exact dates of the spawning runs.

Harrison Hot Springs

To get to the town of Harrison Hot Springs, continue travelling east on Highway 7 to Agassiz, then follow Highway 9 north. The two hot springs that percolate from the gravel on the shore of Harrison Lake make this one of the most popular resort areas in southwestern B.C.

The hot springs were "discovered" in 1859 by paddlers who capsized in winter and found themselves in warm water. During gold-rush days, miners were transported by sternwheeler to Port Douglas at the north end of Harrison Lake and then via Lillooet Lake and the Douglas Trail to the Cariboo gold fields. This route was finally abandoned when the Royal Engineers built the Cariboo Wagon Road through the Fraser Canyon in the mid-1860s.

The town of Harrison Hot Springs contains the famous Harrison Hotel as well as other kinds of accommodation. In the large pool open to the public, water from both springs is blended and cooled to a pleasant 39° C (102° F). Visitors find that soaking brings relief from various ailments and some people claim to benefit by drinking water from the hot springs.

Sailing and canoeing are the major activities on Harrison Lake. The entire lake is a 120-km (75-mi.) round trip, but shorter round trips can be made to Long Island (55 km/35 mi.) or to Echo Island (32 km/20 mi.). As storms and sudden high winds can barrel down Harrison Lake at any time, paddlers should stay close to shore.

The Harrison Hot Springs area is also thought by some to be home to the Sasquatch, a giant apelike creature whose name comes from the Coast Salish word for "wild men" or "hairy men." In some cases, huge footprints have been found and photographed or cast. While the scientific community remains skeptical about the existence of the Sasquatch, there have been numerous reports of a creature 2-3 m (8-9 ft.) tall and covered completely with dark or fair hair being sighted in woods or at road crossings. If you're lucky enough to spot one, don't be afraid—Sasquatch are not considered to be dangerous!

Jack Christie in his *Day Trips from Vancouver* points out that another spring percolates from the ground at the head of Clear Creek on the east side of Harrison Lake, about 56 km (36 mi.) north of Harrison Hot Springs. Visitors here enjoy the hot spring in an Olympic-sized swimming pool built by a woman prospector in the mid-1950s. Black bears are a common sight at the spring, and there are a number of scenic hikes in the vicinity.

Sasquatch Provincial Park, also on the east side of the lake, is a popular spot for fishing. The park, which now offers a new trail around Hicks Lake and an amphitheatre at Deer Lake, is ideal for family camping. Park interpreters can offer suggestions on how to get the most out of your stay.

Useful Information

Contact the Harrison Hot Springs Travel Infocentre, Highway 9, Harrison Hot Springs, B.C., V0M 1K0 (496-3425) for information on the area.

For information on accommodation at the **Harrison Hot Springs Hotel**, contact them at Harrison Hot Springs, B.C., V0M 1K0 (521-8888).

Both *109 Walks in British Columbia's Lower Mainland* and *103 Hikes in Southwestern British Columbia* describe hikes in the Harrison Lake area.

SOUTH OF THE FRASER

Head east on the Trans-Canada Highway (Highway 1) out of Vancouver, then cross the Fraser River on the Port Mann Bridge, and you will find yourself south of the river on the 154-km (96-mi.) route between Vancouver and Hope. Initially, the road sweeps past the Fraser Valley communities of Langley, Aldergrove and Abbotsford Clearbrook, the outer limits of the commuter belt for Vancouver.

Cultus Lake Provincial Park

The quickest way to reach Cultus Lake Provincial Park is to take the Yarrow exit off the highway (this is also an alternate route to Chilliwack Lake and the Chilliwack River). Travel 20 minutes to the turnoff to Cultus Lake Road; a further 13 km (8 mi.) leads to this small (656-ha/1620-a.) lake park, which despite its size contains 300 campsites.

Park fees are collected from April to Thanksgiving. We really enjoy the lake during off-season when the fishing improves as the water-skiing boats diminish; still, it's a lot of fun in summer when hikers, horseback riders, picnickers and fisherpeople fan out from the four separate campgrounds. During the peak months of July and August it can get a bit raucous with ghetto-blasting campers but the 24-hour security patrols try to keep a lid on things. For information on the park, contact BC Parks, Box 10, Cultus Lake, B.C., V0X 1H0 (858-6792).

Chilliwack River and Chilliwack Lake

Ninety-six km (60 mi.) east of Vancouver lies the Chilliwack River. Take the Sardis South exit off the freeway to Vedder bridge, from which signs will direct you to the Chilliwack River campground. The river can be paddled in one day and is suitable for kayaks or closed canoes. The put-in is east of Chilliwack Lake at Foley Creek. The Chilliwack is a very popular river with rafters, too, and both Hyak Wilderness Adventures, 1975 Maple St., Vancouver, B.C., V6J 3S9 (734-8622) and Reo Rafting Adventures, 390-1199 West Pender, Vancouver, B.C., V6E 2R1 (684-4438) run trips here.

The road to the campground continues on to Chilliwack Lake, which lies in the Skagit Range of the Coast Mountains. This is a great lake for a paddle—you can spend anywhere from 2 hours to a full day on the water. There are also several good hikes in the area, Lindeman Lake, Mount Ford and Radium Lake among them. Refer to *109 Walks in British Columbia's Lower Mainland* and *103 Hikes in Southwestern British Columbia* for trail descriptions. *Day Trips from Vancouver* describes a trip to the area.

Skagit Valley

Continuing east towards Hope along Highway 1, you will come to Bridal Falls, a spectacular spot for a picnic and small hike.

Just before you get to Hope, you can take the Silver Skagit Road south from the Trans-Canada Highway to the Skagit Valley Provincial Recreation Area, adjacent to the western boundary of Manning Park. A 35-km (22-mi.) gravel road leads to the entrance of the recreation area; from there, the road continues a further 26 km (16 mi.) to Ross Lake, which extends south across the border into Washington State.

The scenic Skagit River harbours good fishing holes and is a fine paddling route for canoeists who have some intermediate experience. The 26 Mile Bridge is the usual put-in spot, and it is also trailhead for trails to the Rhododendron Flats on the Hope-Princeton Highway, an excellent destination in late June when the rhododendrons are flowering. Silvertip Provincial Campground is located on Silver Skagit Road at km 41/mile 26 of Highway 1. At km 45 (mile 28), take time at Whitworth Ranch and Meadow to enjoy views of distant Mounts Hozameen and Shawatum. Km 55 (mile 35) marks the trailhead for a 16-km (10-mi.) hike one-way to Galene Lakes.

Naturalists can expect to spot some of the 200 bird species that have been identified in the valley, and wildlife viewing is prime. You might see deer, black bears, river otters, Roosevelt elks, mountain goats and even the occasional rubber boa.

Useful Information

For information on the Skagit Valley, contact the Hope Travel Infocentre, 919 Water Ave., Hope, B.C., V0X 1L0 (869-2021).

109 Walks in British Columbia's Lower Mainland and *103 Hikes in Southwestern British Columbia* include several hikes in the Skagit Valley area. *Day Trips from Vancouver* describes a trip into the valley.

Hope

This town of 4000, 160 km (100 mi.) from Vancouver, sits at the entrance to the Fraser River Canyon, surrounded by the Coast Mountains. Murphy Shewchuk's book *Coquihalla Country* is an excellent guide to the area north and east of town.

Fort Hope was established by the Hudson's Bay Company in 1848-49, and a town grew up here during the 1858 gold rush, which was followed by a small silver boom in 1873. The town's museum, with its large collection of mining artifacts, is well worth a visit.

In recent years, Hope has served as the location for such movies as *First Blood* and *Shoot to Kill*, a bonanza for locals keen to appear on screen with the likes of Sylvester Stallone, Sydney Poitier and Tom Berenger.

Railway buffs will already know of the existence of the Kettle Valley Railway which, until 1959, linked the coast with the Kootenay mining region in the southeastern interior of the province. A major feature along the line were the Othello-Quintette Tunnels, one of the *First Blood* crew's favourite locations. To get to the tunnels from the Hope Infocentre in downtown Hope, take Wallace (the main street) to 6th Avenue and turn right. Turn left on Kawkawa Lake Road, crossing the Coquihalla River Bridge and railway tracks. At the first intersection take the right branch, Othello Road, and continue until you see a sign to the right leading to the Coquihalla Canyon Recreation Area. A short tree-shaded walk leads you down from the recreation area to massive, dark tunnels. Take a flashlight.

Most people who want to canoe or kayak the lower Fraser River put in at Hope and take out 225 km (142 mi.), and about 2-3 days, later at New Westminster. Watch for boils and eddies and make sure you carry enough drinking water, since the water of the Fraser is not drinkable.

Gliding is another popular activity here. The Vancouver Soaring Association has operated out of the Hope airport for the past 25 years. Flights lasting 2-3 hours and reaching heights of up to 3000 m (10,000 ft.) are not uncommon for association members. Distance flights have included such destinations as the Okanagan Valley and Wenatchee in eastern Washington State. On weekends and holidays, novices can take introductory "Joy of Silent Flight" trips. For more information, call the Vancouver Soaring Association at 521-5501.

Three main roads radiate out from Hope. Highway 3, also known as the Hope-Princeton Highway, stretches southeast from Hope, passing through popular Manning Park, before bending north to link up with Princeton. Highway 1, the Trans-Canada, follows the Fraser River to Cache Creek before branching west to the Rockies via Kamloops and Salmon Arm. Finally, Highway 5, the Coquihalla, leads northeast from Hope to the trout-rich ranching country around Merritt, before merging once again with Highway 1 at Kamloops.

The Hope-Princeton Highway

A popular route to B.C.'s southern Okanagan valley is the Hope-Princeton Highway (a section of Highway 3). The road travels through the Nicolum River valley, part of which is still covered to a depth of 5 m (16 ft.) with 45 million cubic m (60 million cubic yd.) of mud and debris from the Hope Slide. The slide was triggered by a minor earthquake on January 9, 1965; a huge section of Johnson's Peak swept down the mountain, engulfed Beaver Lake and continued up the opposite side of the valley. The destroyed section of highway was rebuilt over the slide. It is worth stopping at the view point constructed on the site to read about the disaster and see the still bare slopes of the mountain.

Manning Park

When the Hope-Princeton Highway was officially opened to the public in 1949, Lower Mainland dwellers gained paved access to Manning Provincial Park, one of the province's most popular and varied retreats.

Less than 3 hours east of Vancouver and a mere hour east of Hope on Highway 3, Manning is popular with families, hikers and canoeists for its 4 campgrounds, self-guided nature trails and easy access to the alpine meadows with their spectacular flower show between July and mid-August.

Covering 71,400 ha (17,643 a.), Manning Park is located in the Cascade Mountains of southwestern B.C. The rugged forest-covered mountains are drained by two major rivers that rise within the park: the Skagit, which flows west and south to the Pacific Ocean, and the Similkameen, which, turning east, enters the Okanagan River, a major tributary of the Columbia River.

The park administration centre, midway between Hope and Princeton, does an excellent job of providing brochures, maps and information on wildflowers and interpretive trails.

Campgrounds are located at Hampton, Mule Deer, Coldspring and Lightning Lake, and wilderness camping is permitted in designated areas (check with park administration). You can also stay at the Manning Park Resort, which includes a 41-room lodge, 4 chalet triplexes (some with cooking facilities) and 15 family cabins. The resort is a favourite with nordic skiers.

Manning is justifiably well known for its hiking. In all, hikers can choose from a repertoire of 276 km (166 mi.) of trails.

One of the major hikes is the Skyline Trail, which crosses the Cascade Divide between the Skagit and Similkameen valleys just north of the U.S. border. The main part of the trail traces the ridge north of Lightning Lake's meltwater canyon. The trail descends to the east end of Lightning Lake, from which it is an hour's walk to Manning Park Lodge.

The Skyline Trail can be hiked in one long day, but we recommend at least one overnight camp en route. Mid-June is the earliest time advisable; by then, rhododendrons are blooming in the Skagit Valley and early yellow glacier lilies appear on the south slopes of Skyline Ridge as the snow melts.

In 1967, the Skyline Trail became part of the Centennial Trail running from Simon Fraser University in Burnaby through to Cathedral Provincial Park. The Manning-Cathedral portion of the trail runs some 80 km (50 mi.) from the Monument 83 signpost on Highway 3 to Quiniscoe Lake in Cathedral Park. Trailhead lies 4 km (2.5 mi.) east of the Manning Park Resort. Take plenty of rain gear and allow at least a week for the hike, which takes in camping spots at the 2100-m (7000-ft.) mark.

Another popular hike in Manning is the Heather Trail, which starts from Blackwall Peak, 750 m (2500 ft.) up a switchback road from the highway. The full 21-km (13-mi.) hike to Nicomen Lake requires 10-12 hours to complete, but there are two wilderness campsites located en route. Most hikers choose to day-hike only part of the trail, going as far as the Three Brothers area.

July and August are the times to hike the Heather Trail, since the area is renowned for its beautiful wildflower meadows. At this elevation, the avalanche lilies and western anenomes are the first flowers to arrive after spring melt. Their whites and pinks then give way to the reds, blues, mauves and greens of lupine, phlox, paintbrush and betony. During late July and early August over 100 species of flowers combine in the Manning collage, and excellent interpreters work in the area during these two summer months.

Rhododendron Flats, 32 km (20 mi.) west of Manning Park Resort, is another good destination for flower buffs; June is best for this hike. The pinkish-red rhodos here, some up to 6 m (19 ft.) tall, bloom in the wild and, with the Pacific dogwood and the trillium, are protected in B.C. by a special act of legislation. Rhododendrons also grow in the Skagit Valley immediately southwest of the flats.

Fall hikers in Manning invariably opt to do the Frosty Mountain Loop, a full-day, 24-km (15-mi.) hike starting from the Lightning Lake day use area. Frosty Mountain, at 2400 m (7872 ft.), is the highest peak in Manning and views of the North Cascades from here are superb. Just before the summit, the trail passes through a beautiful alpine larch grove, where deciduous needles turn a deep gold before dropping sometime in late September. From here it is a short (45-minute) scramble to the summit of Frosty.

Experienced wilderness hikers up for a major trek may want to travel the Pacific Crest Trail, which begins east of the park headquarters on Highway 3 and extends nearly 4000 km (2350 mi.) along the mountain ranges of the west coast from the Canadian to the Mexican border. Allow about 6 months for this hike which, as Maggie Paquet points out in her *Parks of British Columbia and the Yukon*, crosses 24 national forests, 7 national parks and 19 major canyons, passes 1000 lakes and ascends 57 mountain passes! Declared a National Scenic Trail by the United States in 1968, the Pacific Crest Trail has supply posts separated by hikes of several days' duration and is subject to vast fluctuations in weather patterns.

Several hundred kilometres of horse trails crisscross Manning. You can bring in your own horses or rent them through the Manning Park Corral, the stables affiliated with Manning Park Resort.

Cross-country skiing is the other activity that draws people to Manning Park. From mid-November to April, nordic skiers flock to Manning's honey-comb of trails, some as short as 4 km (2.5 mi.), others as long as 46 km (29 mi.). Over 30 km (18 mi.) of trails are track-set; others follow hiking trails and involve some trail breaking.

Beginners might start with the 5-km (3-mi.) Little Muddy Trail, which is ideal for families, then graduate to the Cambie Loop. The 46-km (29-mi.) return Loop to Monument 83 presents a challenge for the most advanced cross-country skier.

Daily, regular service from Vancouver into the park by Greyhound bus is available; if you decide to take your car, be sure that it is equipped with snow tires in winter.

Other winter activities in the vicinity of Manning Park Resort include alpine skiing, snowshoeing and ice skating.

Useful Information

Contact the Visitor Services Coordinator, BC Parks, Fraser Valley District, Box 10, Cultus Lake, B.C., V0X 1H0 (858-7161) for a copy of the park brochure and other publications about Manning Park, or stop by the Visitor Centre located at park headquarters just east of Manning Park Resort.

For information on accommodation at the **Manning Park Resort**, contact them at Manning Park, B.C., V0X 1R0 (840-8822).

Horseback riding can be arranged by calling the **Manning Park Corral** at 840-8844. **Stoney Mountain Wilderness Adventures**, Box 1766, Clearwater, B.C., V0E 1N0 (674-2774) offers one-week horse-packing trips in Manning Park and the Cascade Mountains.

Several Lower Mainland companies run ski trips to Manning, including **Benno's Adventure Tours**, 1958 West 4th Ave., Vancouver, B.C., V6J 1M5 (738-5105) and **Sigge's Sport Villa**, 2077 West 4th Ave., Vancouver, B.C., V6J 1N3 (731-8818 or 731-3326).

103 Hikes in Southwestern British Columbia has detailed descriptions of a number of trails in the park.

THE TRANS-CANADA HIGHWAY:
Hope to Cache Creek

The Trans-Canada Highway (Highway 1) follows the middle portion of the mighty Fraser River, which stretches the 193 km (120 mi.) between Hope and Cache Creek. The region was originally home to the Thompson people, named for the explorer who "discovered" them. The Thompson now prefer to call themselves Ntlakapamux. Where the Thompson River enters the Fraser River at Lytton, it passes through Upper Stalo Indian territory, rich salmon-fishing country where for centuries native people harvested the Fraser's waters with dip-nets, spears, traps and harpoons.

In 1808, Simon Fraser became the first white explorer to travel the length of this river, which was later named for him. In 1858-59, the lower Fraser River became the scene of a small gold rush, particularly around Yale. Roads were built and settlers moved in to farm, mine and log. The railway brought more settlement and today all these activities continue, coupled with an active adventuring trade.

As you approach Lytton, you are in a rain shadow. From Lytton to Cache Creek you are in real Zane Grey country, dry ranchland where patches of green irrigation mark the benchlands, elsewhere the tumbleweed tumbles and the wind whistles through brown mountains. Lytton is often the hottest place in Canada in summer, with temperatures that soar well into the 30° C (100° F) range.

Adventuring possibilities include great rafting, fishing and hiking.

Yale

Continue 30 km (20 mi.) north of Hope on Highway 1 to get to Yale. Gold once made Yale the largest town in North America west of Chicago and north of San Francisco, and in the late 1850s it was the terminus of one of the largest sternwheeler operations on the west coast.

The banks of the Fraser have been the site of many a small gold rush, and recreational panners and others can still find "colours" (traces of gold). However, these will never equal Yale's biggest strike, which occurred in the summer of 1858 at Hill's Bar, just downstream. From June to September that year about three tons of gold were taken from the bar, worth about $20 million at today's rates.

Novice panners can get a black plastic pan (good for showing up the gold) from the local hardware store. You will also need a shovel or garden trowel for digging the gravel. Pill bottles or film containers make ideal canisters for your loot. A good gold-panning spot exists just outside of town on the Fraser gravel bars. Turn right at the church and go downhill to Front Street. From here, it's an easy walk down to the river.

If you want to make a weekend of gold panning, you can base yourself at Emory Creek Provincial Park, 20 km (11 mi.) south of Yale. It has good camping sites and it's an easy walk down to the banks of the Fraser. Try washing out some of the river moss that grows on the rocks. At high water, the moss acts as a riffle, trapping gold particles.

First Brigade Trail

Hikers who enjoy a bit of history might want to do the 13-km (8-mi.) round-trip hike over part of the First Brigade Trail, the route established by the Hudson's Bay Company in 1848 to move horses from Fort Yale to Kamloops and on into the Cariboo.

Heading north on Highway 1, you will pass the Alexandra Bridge Provincial Park picnic site, located just outside of Spuzzum. About 300 m (1000 ft.) north of Alexandra Lodge, on the river side of the road, is a cleared area where you can leave your car. The First Brigade Trail, which climbs 122 m (400 ft.) to an elevation of 900 m (2952 ft.), begins almost directly across the road alongside a small stream. The trail zigzags at first as it rises in a mostly easterly direction, then it crosses a rock slide, passes by a high bluff with views of the river and surrounding peaks, and reaches a small lake. As you stop here to take a breather, imagine doing the trail with a herd of 200 horses!

Hells Gate

Many of the long-established rafting companies in the Fraser Canyon are based in Boston Bar, 42 km (26 mi.) north of Yale. An average one-day excursion (run from May to the end of August) takes customers in motorized rafts downriver from Boston Bar to Yale. Tour operators provide a running commentary on the mining history of the area.

The first set of rapids, at Scuzzy Rock, are a prelude to China Bar and to Hells Gate, where the Fraser River churns through a narrow, glacially carved 34-m (99-ft.) gorge. On seeing the gorge in 1808, explorer Simon Fraser thought that it resembled "the gates of hell."

You can also arrive at Hells Gate by car. An aerial tramway crosses this aptly named section of the Fraser Canyon, giving a view of the ladders that assist 2 million salmon a year to climb to their spawning grounds. The Airtram, open daily from April to November, descends 153 m (502 ft.) across the Fraser River in 3 minutes. The salmon chowder, a rich, thick concoction served in the Salmon House Restaurant, is worth the day trip from Vancouver.

Useful Information

For raft trips on the Fraser River, contact **Kumsheen Raft Adventures**, 287 Main St., Lytton, B.C., V0K 1Z0 (455-2296 or toll free 1-800-663-6667) or **Frontier River Adventures** at 929-7612 (Vancouver) or 867-9244 (Boston Bar).

Nahatlatch Lakes

To reach the Nahatlatch Lakes chain, an easy paddle and a popular camping and fishing spot, drive over the Cog Harrington Bridge at Boston Bar to North Bend on the west side of the Fraser River. Follow Chaumox Road north through town for 10 km (6 mi.) to the Ray Washtock Bridge, which crosses the Nahatlatch River, and continue along the main road to the lakes. Campsites exist on all four lakes in the chain, which are connected by short streams. You might see deer and bears here, and you'll be able to fish for rainbow and Dolly Varden trout and steelhead.

The Nahatlatch River, a 20-km (12-mi.) maelstrom of white water, is popular for rafting. Reo Rafting Adventures runs trips that include an overnight stop at their private campsite; contact them at 390-1199 West Pender St., Vancouver, B.C., V6E 2R1 (684-4438).

Day Trips from Vancouver describes a trip to this area.

Lytton

Lytton, located at the junction of the Fraser and Thompson rivers, is a popular base for adventurers. Lytton was formerly the site of the Thompson Indian village of Camchin on Thilkumcheen, meaning "great forks," and native culture is enjoying a strong revival in this section of the province. Recently, public interest has focussed on the movement to secure the nearby Stein Valley River as an unlogged watershed.

Most raft trips on the Thompson River start from Spences Bridge (just north of Lytton), spend one night at a campsite on the riverbank and take-out at the junction with the Fraser. This trip includes such thrills as the legendary rapids of the Frog, the Devil's Kitchen and the Jaws of Death.

Useful Information

Contact **Kumsheen Raft Adventures**, 287 Main St., Lytton, B.C., V0K 1Z0 (455-2296 or toll free 1-800-663-6667), **Clearwater Expeditions**, 613 Bissette Rd., Kamloops, B.C., V2B 6L3 (579-8360), **Hyak Wilderness Adventures**, 1975 Maple St., Vancouver, B.C., V6J 3S9 (734-8622) and **Reo Rafting Adventures**, 390-1199 West Pender, Vancouver, B.C., V6E 2R1 (684-4438) for information on paddle or motorized raft trips on the Thompson.

The Stein River Valley

One of the most interesting destinations in the province, readily accessible from the Lower Mainland, is the Stein River Valley. Located on the eastern margin of the Coast and Cascade mountains, the Stein has for centuries been a place of major spiritual significance for the aboriginal people in the area.

Prior to the arrival of European explorers, native people trapped martens, ermines, minks, lynx and river beavers in the valley. A quick flurry of gold mining in the last century preceded more recent commercial interest in the easily accessible lumber of the valley floor. At press time, concerted work by native people and environmental groups to ensure that the Stein River Valley is preserved has resulted in a temporary moratorium on the start of any logging activity.

Just over 3 hours' drive from Vancouver, the 109,000-ha (269,342-a.) Stein River watershed is the last unlogged complete watershed in B.C. within 160 km (100 mi.) of a heavily populated area. Elevations range from 210 m (700 ft.), where the river empties into the Fraser, to 2925 m (9750 ft.) at the summit of Skihist Mountain. The watershed includes three small glacier systems, four major lakes and about 520 sq. km (200 sq. mi.) of alpine meadow.

The Stein River starts as a trickle on the eastern slopes of Tundra Mountain, travels through Tundra Lake, cascades 240 m (800 ft.) in a series of waterfalls, travels through high meadows and then drops rapidly to the 1020-m (3400-ft.) level into Stein Lake. At the lake's eastern end, the river drops 6 m (20 ft.) to forested valley floors for the last 64 km (40 mi.) to the Fraser.

A trail linking Lytton to Pemberton and the coast contains three pictograph sites and one petroglyph. Sacred to the Lytton Indians, the Stein continues to enthrall the modern-day hiker.

To reach the Stein River mouth, cross the Fraser at Lytton via the free reaction ferry (a boat that utilizes the river's current to propel itself), which operates daily from 5:30 A.M. to 9:50 P.M. The ferry holds two cars. Head north on the West Side Road for 5 km (3 mi.), then turn left opposite the house marked "Site 5." Turn left again at the T junction past an abandoned log cabin. Here the road crosses an Indian reserve and, as this is private land, it would be courteous to ask permission before proceeding. The track crosses Van Winkle Flats and goes under a hydro line to the parking area.

The 58-km (36-mi.) Stein Heritage Trail leads from the sandy benchland of Van Winkle Flats up to Stein Lake. Initially, the trail passes through the lower canyon where the Stein thunders through a narrow gorge hedged by the Devil's Staircase.

After the canyon, a gentler hike meanders through the valley bottom to Earl's Creek. Eddie Earl, after whom the creek is named, located his prospecting cabin here before heading off to fight in World War I. After he was killed, his sister opened the trunk of belongings he had left behind to find it stuffed with gold nuggets, presumed to have come out of the creek.

Fifteen minutes past Earl's Creek, the trail becomes a narrow passage between raging river and crumbling granite outcrop. An orange stain of ochre reveals a pictograph on the granite canvas.

At km 11.6 (mile 7), a hand-operated cable car transports the hiker over to the north shore. Tall black cottonwoods give their name to Cottonwood Creek, which runs into the Stein from the north, 28 km (18 mi.) from trailhead. From here, the traveller moves through more isolated territory to Scudamore Creek, where the second cable crossing is strung between two huge Douglas firs. Where Scudamore Creek enters the Stein at Raven Flats, the Stein River Valley narrows to a steep 1220-m (4000-ft.) gorge, where the trail climbs steeply onto the portion of the valley known as the Upper Canyon and then leads to the alpine areas above heavily wooded Stein Lake at 1035 m (3395 ft.).

Two other hiking access points, both from Pemberton—via Lizzie Creek on the Lillooet Lake Road and Blowdown Creek on the Duffey Lake Road—are often used by those with only a weekend to spend in the valley. Both lead to most of the Stein's half-dozen tributaries. These routes are detailed in *103 Hikes in Southwestern British Columbia.*

Highland Helicopters, operating out of Agassiz, offers flights into the Stein Valley, with pickup by mini-van at the end of the hike. The 15-minute helicopter ride is ideal for families wanting to hike the 37 km (23 mi.) from the Cottonwood Creek campsite to the mini-van pick-up point. We strongly advise that if you take the 3-day hike with children, you strike camp early in the morning to capitalize on their dawn energies!

Vegetation in the Stein ranges from stands of ponderosa pine to meadows of purple penstemons and golden asters. In places, stands of giant cottonwood and birch lead into forests of Douglas fir or dark cedar-spruce, redolent with the perfume of false Solomon's-seal. While both black and grizzly bears inhabit the watershed, hiker sightings are usually limited to bear scat or the occasional rear view of a bear harrumphing off into the bushes.

The Ntlakapamux and Lillooet Indians have proposed the creation of a Stein Tribal Heritage Park which would include a cultural centre and museum coupled with traditional lodges, campsites and river tours. With each passing year, the Voices for the Wilderness Festival held in August does more to raise the profile of the Stein Valley.

Useful Information

For more information on efforts to preserve the Stein Valley watershed, contact the **Western Canada Wilderness Committee**, 20 Water St., Vancouver, B.C., V6B 1A4 (669-9453).

Five Seasons Adventure Tours, 3201 Kingsway, Vancouver, B.C., V5R 5K3 (435-5444) and **Pacific Sunset Nature Tours**, 305-4559 Imperial St., Burnaby, B.C., V5J 1B7 (437-3150) offer hiking trips into the Stein. Contact **Highland Helicopters**, 1685 Tranmer Road, Agassiz, B.C., V0M 1A0 (796-9610) for information on flights into the valley.

The excellent *Stein: The Way of the River* by Michael M'Gonigle and Wendy Wickwire is a useful reference book on the area.

Cache Creek

From Lytton, the Trans-Canada Highway runs parallel to the Thompson River through Spences Bridge to Cache Creek, at the junction of Highways 1 and 97. Cache Creek provides an oasis of motels in what is primarily arid ranching country, and a base for exploring north to the Cariboo.

It's not unusual to spot bluebirds sitting on the fenceposts just outside town in summer. Rockhounds can watch jade being cut and polished at the Cariboo Jade Shoppe at 1093 Todd Road.

Lillooet

Highway 12 follows the Fraser River for 69 km (43 mi.) northwest from Lytton to Lillooet, a place where you can still register your gold-mining claims. Lillooet was an important town during the 1850s gold rush, and you can find out about its fascinating history by visiting the local museum. B.C. Rail offers a one-day return trip to Lillooet from Vancouver. The views along the route are spectacular; from Lillooet, the railway climbs 610 m (2000 ft.) above the Fraser Canyon before heading into Cariboo country.

Today, about 3000 Lillooet Indians, an Interior Salish tribe, inhabit this arid area in and around Mount Currie, Anderson Lake, Seton Lake and Pavilion. Originally fisherpeople and hunters, the Lillooet people were seminomadic during the food-harvesting periods. Men hunted and fished, women cooked berries and gathered roots (using antlers as diggers). Although the culture of the Interior Salish was not as ceremonially ritualistic as those on the coast, the pivotal religious theme remained the deep and personal relationship between an individual and his or her own "guardian spirit." At puberty boys and girls went to the mountains to train by sweatbathing, running and purging themselves with medicine to receive the "power," in the form of a guardian spirit. The Lillooet wove intricate cedar-root pack baskets and did pictographs (rock paintings) and petroglyphs (rock carvings).

THE COQUIHALLA HIGHWAY

The Coquihalla Highway was opened in 1986 as a faster, more direct route between Hope, Merritt and Kamloops. The 115 km (71 mi.) of the new Highway 5 are scenically splendid. The road climbs to the 1240-m (4068-ft.) summit of Coquihalla Pass, descends to run along the Coldwater River, rises again on the Coldwater's eastern valley slope to Merritt, then continues up the Nicola and Clapperton Creek valleys to join Highway 1 just west of Kamloops. The toll for travelling this route, payable at the toll booths near the summit, is $10 for cars and recreational vehicles. There are no facilities other than scenic rest stops en route, so make sure you gas up in Hope or Merritt.

In October 1990, the Okanagan Connector opened, linking Merritt with Highway 97 at Westbank in the Okanagan valley. This extension cuts the driving time between Vancouver and the Okanagan Valley to under 4 hours.

Murphy Shewchuk's book *Coquihalla Country* provides an excellent overview of the area.

Okanagan-Similkameen

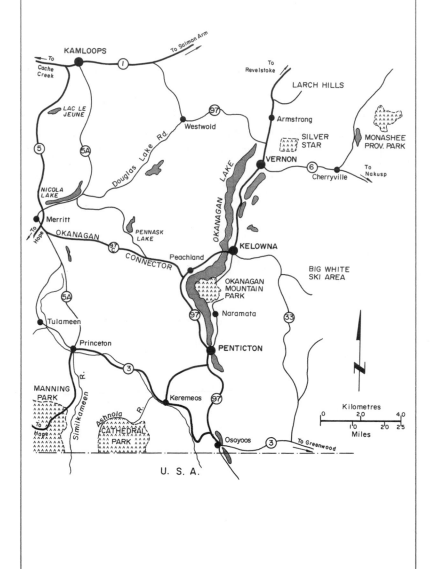

CHAPTER 4

Okanagan-Similkameen

Containing the only true desert in Canada (complete with rattlesnakes), 12 wineries, 22 golf courses and some major parks, the Okanagan Valley, in particular the 3 major centres of Vernon, Kelowna and Penticton, is a popular recreation area for visitors from all over Canada and the United States.

To reach the Okanagan from Vancouver, follow Highway 1 east to Hope, where it continues north and then east, past Cache Creek and Kamloops, to Monte Creek. From there, Highway 97 heads southeast to Vernon in the northern part of the Okanagan Valley. An alternative route from Hope is Highway 5 (the Coquihalla Highway) to Merritt and from there the Okanagan Connector (Highway 97C), which leads to Westbank, near Kelowna, in the central Okanagan. A third route from Hope is Highway 3, which runs through Manning Park and Princeton to Keremeos. At Keremeos, Highway 3A branches off to Penticton, while Highway 3 continues on to Osoyoos, located in the southern Okanagan Valley near the B.C./U.S. border. Highway 97 leads north from Washington State through the valley.

The Okanagan Valley is a broad, irregular depression near the east side of the Interior Plateau in southern B.C. It stretches 160 km (100 mi.) from Osoyoos in the south to Armstrong in the north, and boasts 2000 hours of sunshine annually. At its widest point, the valley extends for 19 km (12 mi.).

Okanagan Lake, the valley's main body of water, is rapidly becoming famous for its friendly sea serpent creature, the Ogopogo, which reputedly lives on the bottom of the lake. Native people first alerted the early European settlers to the creature's existence. They described a fast-swimming lake monster called N'ha-a-tik that lived in a cave at Squally Point, near the town of Kelowna. Animals were regularly thrown overboard from canoes to placate the monster. The shy Ogopogo has become quite a celebrity in recent years as sightings increase and several people claim to have captured it on video and film. When spotted, the monster apparently breaks the water, creating a massive rolling wave action similar to the pattern made by a surfacing submarine. TV crews from Japan, England and the United States have all attempted to get footage of the creature.

Initially the Okanagan Salish made extensive use of the area, enjoying the mild climate which provided ample berries and regular annual salmon runs. In the early 1800s, the North West and Pacific Fur companies began competing for control of the profitable fur trade in the Columbia River area. Rival explorers David Thompson and David Stuart established inland posts to barter with native people for furs before the Hudson's Bay Company consolidated its 35-year hold on the lucrative trade.

In 1859, Father Charles Pandosy, a French Oblate priest, established a mission in the Kelowna area. He successfully introduced apple trees to the district and subsequently fruit orchards were cultivated extensively.

Today, tourism and agriculture form the lynchpins of the Okanagan economy. Warm lakes provide a focal point in summer, and regular, albeit not heavy, snowfalls draw both alpine and nordic skiers in colder weather.

Because Okanagan produce is so tasty, many people time their trips to the area to coincide with the harvest dates of their favourite fruits. Approximate dates in season are: cherries—late June to early July; apricots—mid-July to mid-August; peaches—late July to early September; pears—mid-August to mid-September; apples—August to end of September; prunes—September and grapes—September.

The route we take through the Okanagan-Similkameen region begins at the town of Princeton. From there, we continue east on Highway 3 to the southern Okanagan desert town of Osoyoos, then cover the valley in a south-north direction to Armstrong, just south of Salmon Arm.

A useful reference guide to the area is *Backroads Explorer Vol. 2: Similkameen and south Okanagan* by Murphy Shewchuk.

PRINCETON

The red ochre culled from the Tulameen River was used in face painting by the native peoples in the Princeton area. Today, copper from the rich Newmont Mines nearby is important to this town of over 2000 people, which lies 134 km (83 mi.) east of Hope on Highway 3.

At least 30 good trout lakes lie within an 80-km (50-mi.) radius of Princeton. For travellers interested in native culture, staff at the Princeton Museum can provide directions to the pictographs on the Dewdney Trail southeast of town. Canoeists may want to make the 2- to 4-day trip down the Similkameen River to the U.S. border, taking out at a river crossing approximately 20 km (12 mi.) downstream from Keremeos. South of the border, the river continues for 22 km (14 mi.) to Oroville, Washington, where it flows into the Okanogan. Canoeists on the Similkameen should exercise caution because of fluctuating water levels.

For an interesting side trip from Princeton, take the Whipsaw Creek Road, which leaves Highway 3 at the Whipsaw bridge on a sharp bend about 13 km (8 mi.) south of Princeton. This road to the head of the Hope Trail affords good views, but watch out constantly for logging trucks. Hikers can follow the Hope

Trail up Whipsaw Creek to Hope Pass at 1838 m (5975 ft.), then down the Skaist River to Highway 3 near Rhododendron Flats.

Beyond the Hope Trail signpost, the gravel road winds up Kettle Mountain and across the alpine meadows of Granite Mountain. Hellebore and western anemone stretch across the windswept ridge, and you will find tasty dwarf huckleberries and wild strawberries here in season.

Fans of back-roads travel will want to head north to explore the roads linking Princeton and Merritt. These back roads lie east of Highway 5A and pass by the remains of the many gold and coal mines that studded the Tulameen River, a stream rising in the Cascades and travelling 64.4 km (49 mi.) north in a big loop to merge with the Similkameen at Princeton.

Late in the last century, prankster cowboys from the Allison Ranch near Princeton started rumours of a bonanza at nearby Granite Creek, a joke that backfired on them in 1885 when gold was struck and 2000 souls flooded into Granite Creek to stake their claims. The town of Granite City soon became the "gunslingingest, wildest and drunkenest" mining camp in the province, boasting 22 saloons. When the creek's supplies of gold and platinum were completely exhausted, wild gooseberry and red currant bushes soon reclaimed the area.

The mine at Coalmont continued to deliver coal in quantity, despite really dangerous mining conditions; uncontrollable water seepage caused combustion in scattered pockets and seams of coal. On August 13, 1930 (Black Wednesday), an explosion ripped through the Number Four mine, trapping and killing the 45 men inside. Their deaths marked the beginning of the end for Coalmont, and the shafts, tunnels and adits were finally sealed in 1940.

The town of Tulameen sits between the eastern bank of the Tulameen River and the southern end of Otter Lake. Home to miners during the coal boom, Tulameen had long been a place of congregation for the Salish people, who fished, hunted and gathered wild fruit and vegetables in the fertile Otter Creek valley.

Tulameen was also one of the stops on the old Brigade Trail from Hope to Kamloops. For 50 years, the brigade trails were the routes of trade and commerce in the interior of the province. From the early 1800s to the 1860s, they were used extensively by the Hudson's Bay Company, with groups of up to 50 men and 400 horses travelling the route to move furs and trade goods. Axe blazes more than a century old still mark the Hope-Tulameen Trail through the North Cascades. A portion of this historic route was recently designated as a Heritage Trail and plans are underway for its restoration.

Useful Information
Information about the canoe trip on the Similkameen River can be found in *Canoe Routes British Columbia*, now unfortunately out of print, so you'll have to look for a copy in libraries or used bookstores.

The Best of B.C.'s Hiking Trails contains a good description of the Hope Pass hike and *Backroads Explorer Vol. 2: Similkameen and south Okanagan* is a useful guide for the road up Whipsaw Creek and the back roads to Granite City, Coalmont and Tulameen.

KEREMEOS

About halfway between Princeton and Osoyoos on Highway 3, the fruit-growing centre of Keremeos lays claim to being the Fruit Stand Capital of Canada since it enjoys one of the longest growing seasons in the province.

A popular (but hot) hike north of town is the 3-hour walk into Keremeos Columns Provincial Park. Bring plenty of water for this traverse of sagebrush country and the steep climb to view the volcanic monuments of slowly cooled lava that loom out of the surrounding fir forest. The 20-ha (49-a.) park is accessible only by crossing private property, so ask for permission at the house at the end of the road.

ASHNOLA MOUNTAINS CONSERVATION RESERVE

The Ashnola River Road, just southwest of Keremeos, leads to several Forest Service campsites and provides good access to the northern Cascade Mountains and to Cathedral Provincial Park.

The road passes through the Ashnola Mountains Conservation Reserve, which lies mainly east of Cathedral Park but includes the 2293-m (7523-ft.) Crater Mountain. The reserve supports Canada's largest herd of California bighorn sheep (approximately 400). They are monitored by naturalists from Sheep Cabin, located in the middle of the reserve at the top of the south slope of Flatiron Mountain.

A 5½-hour loop hike leads up to Sheep Cabin via the Corkscrew Creek Trail and returns on the Webster Creek Trail. Trailhead for this and the Centennial Trail into Cathedral Park is at the mouth of Ewart Creek. To reach the creek, turn south from Highway 3 just west of Keremeos onto the Ashnola River Road. Cross the Similkameen River on one of B.C.'s last covered bridges and continue to the Ashnola River, where the road turns south into the mountains. Take a left fork approximately 16 km (10 mi.) from the highway and cross the river onto a narrow dirt road. The driveable road ends at a ford near the mouth of Ewart Creek.

Traffic on the Ewart Creek Trail not heading for Cathedral Park is usually destined for Joe Lake, which lies almost on the divide between Ewart Creek and the Similkameen Valley. The Joe Lake route is signposted and many hikers choose to base themselves here for hiking in the high country, particularly south along the divide towards Harry Lake and Snowy Mountain. The hike to Joe Lake can also be done as a crossover to the Lower Similkameen south of the village of Cawston.

Useful Information

Backroads Explorer Vol. 2: Similkameen and south Okanagan by Murphy Shewchuk is a useful reference book about the area. Forest Service Recreation maps of the area can be obtained from Ministry of Forests, Kamloops Region, 515 Columbia St., Kamloops, B.C., V2C 2T7 (828-4137).

CATHEDRAL PROVINCIAL PARK

One of the most beautiful spots in B.C., Cathedral Provincial Park is increasingly popular with urbanites who make the trip here for long weekends of camping and hiking. It takes about 5 hours to drive to Keremeos from Vancouver, via the Trans-Canada Highway and Highway 3. From Keremeos, travel south about 25 km (16 mi.) on the gravel Ashnola River Road to the Cathedral Lakes Resort parking lot.

Located high in the Cascade Mountains, the park is named after the 2800-m (9184-ft.) peak of Cathedral Mountain, so carved and eroded that it resembles a ruined abbey. The 32 km (20 mi.) of hiking trails that lead to wilderness camping areas radiate out mainly from Lake Quiniscoe, one of the 5 large lakes that dot this 33,000 ha (81,544 a.) wilderness, whose southern border is the 49th parallel. The hikes are manageable for people at most levels of fitness and lead to spectacular views.

Prime hiking in Cathedral Park lasts from July to October, and many hikers base themselves at the Cathedral Lakes Resort at Lake Quiniscoe, which accommodates forty guests. For a fee, the lodge will provide four-wheel drive transport into the park for non-guests keen to explore Lake Quiniscoe, Ladyslipper, Scout, Pyramid, Glacier, Goat and Haystack lakes and Lake of the Woods. Well-defined and marked trails are described in detail in a brochure distributed by the park warden who lives in a cabin next to the lodge.

One of the highlights of Cathedral Park is the wildlife, which includes bighorn sheep, porcupines (who love the subalpine and feast on the bark of lodgepole pines), black bears, mule deer, mountain goats and Columbia ground squirrels.

The park's extraordinary topography was used in the film *Clan of the Cave Bear*. Geologists are fascinated by Stone City, a huge quartzite formation eroded by wind or glaciers over the ages into flat rounded shapes resembling

Near the Giant Cleft, Cathedral Park. *Photo by Lloyd Twaites*

hamburgers. Other destinations include the symmetrical columns of Devil's Woodpile, formed by quick-cooling lava, and the 2.5-m (8-ft.) wide split of the Giant Cleft, which allows a stupendous view of the valley floor far below.

The Cathedral Rim hike, through a series of switchbacks, takes walkers past the major geological features of the park and along the banks of lovely aquamarine Ladyslipper Lake. In summer, more than 200 species of flowers bloom in the park.

Mid-September is a superb time to hike Cathedral Park. The golden mountainsides of alpine larch, a variety found only in a small area of the Rockies and in Cathedral and Manning parks, are a stunning complement to the deep-blue lakes.

Useful Information

Contact the Visitor Services Coordinator, BC Parks, Okanagan District, Box 399, Summerland, B.C., V0H 1Z0 (494-0321) for a copy of the park brochure and map, or pick one up from the Cathedral Park warden.

For information on accommodation at the **Cathedral Lakes Resort**, contact them at R. R. #1, Cawston, B.C., V0X 1C0 (499-5848). Rates include jeep rides and all meals. The resort jeep will also transport campers for a small fee but reservations should be made in advance.

OSOYOOS

The Spanish-theme town of Osoyoos, 4 km (2.5 mi.) north of the Canada-U.S. border at the junction of Highways 3 and 97, lies in the heart of B.C.'s warmest region, just north of the only authentic desert in Canada. The architecture of homes and shops here is predominantly Spanish to complement the climate. While in Osoyoos you might want to take a tour of the Fernandes Banana Farm, the only banana farm in Canada. It's so hot here in summer that the bananas are grown in greenhouses!

Most deserts are huge and sprawling. By comparison, the Pocket Desert, as it is known, is easily accessible and explorable. Just travel 2.5 km (1.5 mi.) south of town on Highway 3 to the sign for the Inkaneep campsite on 45th Street. Turn left and you will soon arrive at a campground run by the Osoyoos Indian Band. The band can give you permission to travel into the desert from this end.

The desert is the traditional home of the Inkaneep (Okanagan for "bottom end") Indians, 12,000 ha (29,652 a.) of it lying within their reserve. A little-known gem, the area receives only 20 cm (8 in.) of rain a year and can be as hot as 44° C (111° F) in the summer. The region features a large population of timid northern Pacific rattlesnakes, greasewood and sage thickets, pictographs on granite boulders and the remains of kekuli (underground) cave dwellings. Greasewood is so named for the way it crackles when it burns.

The desert supports the largest concentration of birds of prey in Canada, and other bird species in the area include bright turquoise lazuli buntings, orange northern orioles, red-winged kestrels and turkey vultures. The sage thrasher is found only in the Okanagan-Similkameen.

The pocket desert is home to many unusual creatures. Several species of tiger beetles, scarabs, butterflies and praying mantises are found nowhere else in the province. Western skinks, little lizards with blue tails, lounge on the rocks. Extraordinary kangaroo rats feed on the bunch grass. With enormous feet and a tail three times as long as its body, the kangaroo rat is 65 per cent water—but never takes a drink. External fur-lined pockets in its cheeks store grass and cacti seeds from which it extracts moisture. Another peculiar resident is the Great Basin spadefoot toad, which uses the "spades" on its hind legs to dig itself into the ground during hot days.

The best time to venture out into the desert is at night when the cool makes the coyotes howl. The Indians called the coyote "God's dog"; its name derives from the Spanish adaptation of an Aztec word, *coyolxauhqui*, for the goddess of the moon who howls at night.

Riding stables adjacent to the Inkaneep campground take tours out into the desert during summer months. Hikers might find April or May the best time to visit because the antelope bushes flower then, as do the prickly pear cacti, and the area's many birds are courting.

Cycling along the old Kettle Valley Railway. *Photo by Lloyd Twaites*

THE KETTLE VALLEY RAILWAY

Nostalgia for the days of steam-driven locomotives has kept interest alive in one of the province's most historic railway lines, the Kettle Valley Railway, which operated for 40 years. From 1916 until economics and weather closed it down permanently in 1964, the Kettle Valley Railway took 23 hours to travel a route east from Vancouver through Hope, Princeton, Penticton, Rock Creek and Midway to Nelson. Another 5 hours took it into Medicine Hat, Alberta.

Today, travellers in the west Kettle Valley can still explore the sections of this track that linked the Kootenays with Vancouver via the Coquihalla Canyon. *Exploring the Kettle Valley Railway* makes interesting reading and is a useful reference guide.

You can see sections of the Kettle Valley Railway by travelling east of Osoyoos on Highway 3 and then heading due north on Highway 33, which links up with Kelowna in the heart of the Okanagan Valley. The road follows the West Kettle River, where sections of track are very obvious. Former stations to look out for are Beaverdell and McCulloch. Just north of the summit of this road, a paved side road joins Highway 33 from the east; this is the access road to Big White, one of the Okanagan Valley's finest ski resorts.

VASEUX LAKE PROVINCIAL PARK

From Osoyoos, Highway 97 heads 35 km (22 mi.) north to Vaseux Lake, one of the most interesting of the many lakes in the Okanagan Valley from both a paddler's and a naturalist's point of view.

The lake and surrounding area form part of a wildlife and bird sanctuary. As you paddle this placid lake, you may spot trumpeter swans (in the spring and fall), geese, coots, great horned owls and canyon wrens. Lakeside trails lead to small blinds with good lookouts. Both hikers and paddlers might spot the California bighorn sheep often seen on bluffs by the highway and now protected in the wildlife reserve. Campers can make use of the nine sites at the campground.

PENTICTON

From Vaseux Lake Park, Highway 97 continues 20 km (12 mi.) north to Penticton, whose superb climate and location caused the Okanagan Indians to call it Pen-tak-ton—"a place to stay forever." Native people made it their headquarters for procuring fish and berries in the summer and hunting game in the winter. Subsequent settlers in the area included Thomas Ellis, who ran a cattle empire.

Today, this thriving town of 24,000 people is the second largest urban centre in the Okanagan-Similkameen and is the region's major destination.

One of Penticton's main attractions is the sternwheeler S. S. *Sicamous*, which plied Okanagan Lake for over 20 years and was commonly known as "the Great White Swan." During the summer, tours of the sternwheeler are available.

Skiers and other winter recreation buffs will want to visit the Apex Mountain Provincial Recreation Area, 32 km (20 mi.) southwest of Penticton off Highway 97. Apex's privately owned ski area offers 36 downhill runs, groomed cross-country trails and food facilities. A cross-country ski trail system is maintained in the nearby Nickel Plate Forest Service area. Two intermediate trails centre on the Mount Riordan and Beaconsfield Mountain areas.

Summer hiking on Apex Mountain takes walkers into the wildflowers of the subalpine, with superb views of Manning and Cathedral parks to the south and west.

Between Penticton and Vernon, various wineries are located close to Highway 97. Most of them offer wine tours during the summer months and the Okanagan Wine Festival is held at the end of September each year.

Useful Information

Contact the Penticton Travel Infocentre, Jubilee Pavilion, 185 Lakeshore Dr., Penticton, B.C., V2A 1B7 (492-4103) for general information about activities in and around Penticton.

For information on accommodation and activities at **Apex Alpine**, contact them at Box 488, Penticton, B.C., V2A 6K9 (292-8221 or toll free 1-800-663-1900).

KELOWNA

Kelowna (the Okanagan word for "female grizzly bear") lies 60 km (37 mi.) north of Penticton on the eastern shore of Okanagan Lake. A medium-sized town, with a population of 63,000, its beaches have been a major attraction from fur-trading times to the present. Kelowna is a well-planned combination of residential and business areas, with an industrial district situated to the north. The floating bridge, which takes Highway 97 across the lake from the west bank to the east, was dedicated by Princess Margaret in 1958. It replaced an inadequate ferry service.

Regattas, music, theatre and ballet thrive in Kelowna, which is also a popular base for the alpine resort of Big White, located 55 km (34 mi.) east of town along Highway 33/Black Mountain Road. Some 25 km (15 mi.) of cross-country trails cater to the nordic skier, and, just past the Big White turnoff on Highway 33, the McCulloch Lake area offers more nordic skiing on groomed trails.

A second, equally popular spot is the Telemark Ski Area, 22 km (13 mi.) south of Kelowna on Highway 97 at Westbank. A large system of Forest Service trails here are marked and groomed by the Telemark Ski Club.

More cross-country skiing is available in the Postill Lake area just north of Kelowna. Take Highway 97 north, turn east at the north end of the airport and then follow signs for 19 km (12 mi.) to Postill Lake, one of 8 lakes located in this Okanagan Provincial Forest. The 1500-m (5000-ft.) elevation makes for light, powdery snow, and over 100 km (63 mi.) of trails, including a biathlon route, converge on Postill Lodge; two major sets, sometimes known as the Grizzly Hills Trails, centre around Postill and Beaver lakes. Postill Lake Lodge offers year-round accommodation and is very reasonably priced; the lodge also operates a number of self-contained cabins.

During spring thaw, the trout start biting and fly-fishing for rainbow or speckled trout is prime on any of the lakes in the region. At South Lake, a 15-minute walk from Postill Lake Lodge, rowboats are available and canoes can be portaged in.

Kelowna provides easy access to a scenic 13-km (8-mi.) stretch of the abandoned Kettle Valley Railway known as Myra Canyon. There are 16 trestle bridges to cross along the route (don't look down if you're afraid of heights!) and it's an ideal trip for a spring or fall hike. It's great on a mountain bike, too, if you don't mind the bumps crossing the bridges. To get there, head east from town on McCulloch Road for about 10 km (6 mi.) and then turn right on Myra Forest Service Road. Follow this road for 8 km (5 mi.) until it intersects the old railway grade.

Useful Information

Contact the Kelowna Travel Infocentre, 544 Harvey Ave., Kelowna, B.C., V1Y 6C9 (861-1515) for general information about Kelowna.

To find out about accommodation at **Postill Lake Lodge**, contact them at Box 854, Kelowna, B.C., V1Y 7P5 (860-1655). For information on accommodation and activities at **Big White**, contact them at Box 2039, Kelowna, B.C., V1X 4K5 (765-3101 or toll free 1-800-663-4151).

Richard Wright's book *British Columbia Cross Country Ski Routes* gives detailed information about routes in the Kelowna area. Unfortunately, this title is out of print, so you'll have to check libraries or used bookstores for a copy.

OKANAGAN MOUNTAIN PARK

Okanagan Mountain Park offers 24 km (15 mi.) of hiking and riding trails through a northern desertlike wilderness region. To get there, drive 17 km (11 mi.) south from Kelowna via Pandosy Street, then down the east side of Okanagan Lake along Lakeshore Road until you arrive at a parking lot for the park. This is rattler country, so be sure to wear sensible footwear (and try to resist turning over stones!).

The major hike in Okanagan Mountain Park is to Wild Horse Canyon, a rather short, deep and isolated canyon where it is thought that native people trapped wild horses, then considered to be pests, in the late 1890s. Around this time Tom Ellis, who had ranched most of the land from Naramata south to the border, opened a cattle trail just west of the rim of Wild Horse Canyon to reach markets at Okanagan Mission. Trailhead parking is now provided at both the northeast and southeast corners of Okanagan Mountain Park. From both corners connecting trails lead through the park.

The northern access trail to Wild Horse Canyon starts opposite the parking lot; it zigzags up through ponderosa parkland, then passes through dry grassland lined with boulders that leads into the entrance of Big Canyon. As you make the hour's hike through the canyon you will see narrow swamps and beaver ponds. At the south end of the canyon, dampness gives way to a desert flat covered in sagebrush, bitterroot, cactus and ponderosa pine. It will take you about 5 hours to reach this point, and the south trailhead lies another 4½ hours ahead.

To reach the southern trailhead, drive 21 km (13 mi.) north of Penticton on the Naramata road to Chute Lake, then take the right fork along Gemmill Lake Road to the parking lot.

VERNON

From Kelowna, Highway 97 continues 47 km (28 mi.) north to Vernon, situated near 3 lakes—Okanagan, Kalamalka and Swan—at the point where 5 valleys meet. A tourist and agricultural centre, Vernon is home to 20,000 people, and is one of our favourite bases for adventuring in the province. We have great memories of winter hang-gliding competitions at Vernon in the late seventies, when hang-gliders threw themselves off local hills to land in fields of snow. And we have a very soft spot for Kalamalka Lake, one of the most beautiful in the province close to a large urban centre.

At the turn of the century, mining fever peaked in the Aberdeen (now Silver Star) Mountain region about 22 km (14 mi.) outside town, and about 25 claims were staked. Today, Silver Star is a year-round recreational area. In winter, the 32 downhill runs over a 485-m (1600-ft.) vertical drop are popular with family skiers from all over the province. Hot tubs, fine dining and night skiing are further attractions.

Nordic skiers used the Silver Star area long before the downhillers, and marked and groomed cross-country routes cover about 80 km (50 mi.) of terrain beginning at the parking lot just off the Silver Star Road. Sovereign Lake, Woodland Bell, Mystery and Black Prince, all named after original mining claims, are the major trails. The resort hosts a popular marathon race in January.

In summer, Silver Star is prime hiking terrain. Hikers can use the chairlift to get up to the mountain's alpine meadows.

Useful Information

Contact the Vernon Travel Infocentre, 3700-33rd St., Vernon, B.C., V1T 5T6 (545-0771) for general information about Vernon and activities in the area.

For information on accommodation and activities at **Silver Star**, contact them at Box 7000, Vernon, B.C., V1T 8X5 (542-0224 or toll free 1-800-663-4431).

A local book, *Hiking Trails enjoyed by the Vernon Outdoor Club*, has good trail descriptions of hikes in the area. The book can be obtained from local sporting goods stores or by writing to the Vernon Outdoor Club, Box 1241, Vernon, B.C., V1T 6N6.

MONASHEE PARK

Vernon is the nearest main centre to Monashee Provincial Park, a wilderness park very popular with advanced hikers. Covering 7513 ha (18,565 a.) in the south-central Monashee Mountains, Monashee (the Gaelic word for peace) is an area of solitude, marked by ever-changing weather patterns and traversed by caribou.

To reach the park, follow Highway 6 east for about 75 km (47 mi.) from Vernon to Cherryville. At a clearly marked junction on the east side of Cherryville, you turn north onto Sugar Lake Road, a gravel logging road that runs alongside Sugar Lake. Follow the road for 60 km (38 mi.) to the Spectrum Falls parking lot just outside the Monashee Park boundaries. The climb from here to the park is about 12 km (7 mi.) of stiff hiking, leading to 24 km (15 mi.) of hiking trails and 10 wilderness campsites. This is a pack-out-what-you pack-in area; hikers are usually very conscientious but aircraft travellers in the region are notorious litterbugs.

The 5-hour hike from the parking lot to the first campsite at Spectrum Lake provides a taste of Monashee hiking terrain, which is characterized by a series of switchbacks. Early on in this hike, you pass through a cedar grove lining the north and south banks of Spectrum Creek, a lovely, shady cathedral of trees sheltering diverse ferns, wildflowers and mosses.

Trout fishing is the main reason many hikers visit Spectrum Lake, which lies in a bowl on the northwest flank of Mount Fosthall, at 2679 m (8787 ft.) the highest peak in the park.

From Spectrum, a further 13 km (8 mi.) along a series of extremely steep switchbacks lead to Peters Lake. The steepest part of this hike is between Spectrum Lake and Little Peters Lake; don't despair and turn back at Belly Up Canyon, as some backpackers do, since you are well over halfway to your destination. The rest of the trail is an easy stroll through wonderful alpine meadows. Many hikers set up a base at the Peters Lake campsite and make day hikes to the Fawn Lakes, a cluster of lakes set in alpine meadow about 250 m (820 ft.) above. A hike northeast from Peters Lake leads to the park boundary and the Valley of the Moon, a round trip that takes a full day. Mountaineers who want to scale Mount Fosthall also usually start from Peters Lake; from Fosthall's peak you can see the tops of the Valhalla Range to the south and Silver Star to the southwest. An easier (4- to 5-hour) climb is up Slate

Mountain, and in the snows of July you can glissade down the mountainside in 20 minutes. Glissading (sliding down snowfields) is a favourite pastime of grizzly bears in these parts, too!

We recommend a mid-September hike in Monashee, since frost has killed the biting bugs by then and red and yellow fall colours predominate. Incidentally, so far Monashee Park bears remain wild and are not panhandlers, so bring your bells or noisemakers to use as deterrents.

For further information about the park, contact the Visitor Services Coordinator, BC Parks, Box 399, Summerland, B.C., V0H 1Z0 (494-0321).

ARMSTRONG

From Vernon, Highway 97A winds north through the community of Armstrong, which services the rich Spallumcheen farming area of the Okanagan. Cheese lovers might want to drop by the Armstrong Cheese Factory, located two blocks north of the museum on Pleasant Valley Road, to watch production of one of Canada's finest cheddars, a cheese that can trace its origins back to 1655 in Britain. The factory is open to the public during regular business hours.

LARCH HILLS CROSS-COUNTRY SKI AREA

To get to Larch Hills, continue north from Armstrong on Highway 97B towards Salmon Arm. Twenty-five km (15 mi.) north of Armstrong, turn east on Grandview Bench Road for 5.5 km (3.5 mi.) and then left onto Edgar Road, for about 3 km (1.9 mi.) until you reach a junction; the left fork from there leads about 3 km to the Larch Hills network of cross-country trails. At an elevation of 1050-1200 m (3500-4000 ft.), Larch Hills' 150 km (95 mi.) of trails through the rolling terrain of Larch Hills Forest enjoy reliable snow conditions from mid-November to mid-March. A beautiful log chalet is situated near the parking lot and there are two warming huts within the trail system.

On the third Saturday in January, skiers compete in the very popular Larch Hills Marathon race as a warmup for the Cariboo Marathon held in early February at 100 Mile House.

The crisscrossing trails, which mainly follow old logging roads, are well signed and a map showing the system in detail is posted at the parking lot. A copy of the trail map is available from the Larch Hills Ski Club, Box 218, Salmon Arm, B.C., V0E 2T0 or from local stores in Salmon Arm.

CHAPTER 5

The Kootenays

From Osoyoos, at the southern tip of the Okanagan, Highway 3 winds east along the Kettle Valley for 120 km (75 mi.) to the town of Grand Forks. The route we follow in this section traces a rough triangle through the Kootenays (named after the area's original inhabitants, the Kutenai people). From Grand Forks we travel on to Trail, then via Salmo to Creston at the southeastern tip of the triangle. Then we head north along the east bank of Kootenay Lake, crossing to the west bank at Balfour to continue north for an exploration of the Arrow Lakes. From there, we travel back down south, through the old mining centres of New Denver and Slocan, to Nelson, the hub of the Kootenays, and on to Castlegar.

The area we know as the Kootenays today consists of fold upon fold of mountains and valleys. It is bound on the west by the Monashee Mountains; the Selkirk Range runs through the middle of the area, and the Purcell Mountains form an eastern hedge between the triangle and the Rocky Mountains. The Arrow Lakes system running from Revelstoke south to Castlegar, and Kootenay Lake to the east, coupled with the Kootenay River, provide the main drainage systems in the region.

The Kootenay climate, influenced by both continental and maritime air, shares traits with most of interior B.C. Winters tend to be cold and dry except at higher elevations, where snowfall can be heavy from mid-November to April. Summers are hot, dry and low on humidity, though at higher elevations the occasional August snow flurry is not uncommon.

Like Cariboo Country to the west and north, the Kootenays are a world unto themselves. Originally, the Interior Salish people occupied much of the land to the west of Kootenay Lake, while the territory of the Kutenai extended east almost to the Rocky Mountains. The Kutenai followed a way of life entirely different from the rest of B.C.'s interior peoples. They had more in common with the Plains Indians of Alberta, dressing and worshipping in similar fashion. Experts suggest that the Kutenai probably migrated from the plains to escape raiding parties of the powerful Blackfoot tribes.

The Kutenai home was a tepee covered with buffalo hide. The people practised the Sun Dance, trapped golden eagles on hilltops and treasured their medicine bundles. Craving buffalo meat, the Kutenai made early summer, fall and even midwinter trips through the Rockies to hunt on the plains. Dogs packed the heavy loads, also bringing home duck and venison from the kill.

The Kootenays

To Revelstoke

Shelter Bay
Galena Bay
23

MONASHEE PROVINCIAL PARK

23

Upper Arrow Lake

Nakusp

31

PURCELL WILDERNESS CONSERVANCY

To Vernon

New Denver
6

Silverton
9A

VALHALLA PROV. PARK

Kaslo

Needles
Fauquier

KOKANEE GLACIER PROV. PARK

Ainsworth Hot Springs

Slocan

Lower Arrow Lake

6

Balfour

Crawford Bay

NELSON

Kootenay Lake

3A

CASTLEGAR

6

Kilometres
0   20   40
10   20 25
Miles

N

Salmo

To Cranbrook

3
Trail

3
Creston

To Osoyoos
3

Rossland

Grand Forks

U. S. A.

Kutenai bows were famous for their drive power, so much so that the Blackfoot Peigan tribe preferred them to flintlocks.

David Thompson began his exploration of the Columbia River system in the early 1880s in connection with the fur trade. The 1864 gold bonanza at Wild Horse Creek was followed by mineral rushes that led to mining in the Riondel area in 1882 for galena (lead-zinc-silver ore), then twenty years later to the establishment of Silver King Mine on Toad Mountain, near the present site of Nelson. Once Europeans began to pursue fur trade and mining interests in the region, the Kutenai people were displaced and their customs rapidly disintegrated.

The Kootenay region has a rich history and it remains a vibrant part of the province, mainly due to enthusiastic residents who wouldn't live anywhere else. Dependent on agriculture and tourism, the area is a haven for many people keen to maintain alternative lifestyles and philosophies. One group who have made the Kootenays home are the Doukhobors. Emigrating from Russia in 1908 to escape religious persecution, they settled on communal farms in valleys around Grand Forks and Castlegar.

Isolated pockets of land in amongst the mountains and waters of the Kootenays house small communities. Revelstoke, situated on the Trans-Canada Highway, provides road access from the north. Highway 6 runs through the middle of the region, and the Crowsnest Highway (Highway 3) runs along the southern edge of the province just 13 km (8 mi.) north of the Washington/Idaho border.

Too wide to bridge and too long to bypass, the Kootenay, Slocan and Arrow lakes are knit together by a network of good highways and a fleet of busy (and free) ferry boats operated by the provincial government. Kootenay Lake, 156 km (97 mi.) long, is the largest inland lake in the province. The chief parks in the region are Valhalla Park, Kokanee Glacier Park and Recreational Area and the Purcell Wilderness Conservancy. An excellent reference map of the area is contained in the BC Parks brochure called "Provincial Parks of the Kootenays." A copy can be obtained from most Travel Infocentres or by writing to the Visitor Services Coordinator, West Kootenay District, BC Parks, R. R. #3, Nelson, B.C., V1L 5P6 (825-4422).

The Kootenays is a great place for adventurers, offering exciting opportunities for cyclists, hikers, skiers, anglers and paddlers. Betty Pratt-Johnson's *Whitewater Trips and Hot Springs, West and East Kootenays, for Kayakers, Canoeists and Rafters*, describes 28 river runs and 12 hot spring locations.

GRAND FORKS TO CRESTON

When you arrive in Grand Forks, be sure to check with the local tourist information office to find out about such events as the River Raft Race held in June and the Sunshine and Borscht Festival held in July. To learn more about the Doukhobor culture, you might want to drop in to the Mountainview Doukhobor Museum on Hardy Mountain Road just outside town (the Travel Infocentre will provide directions).

Twenty-one km (13 mi.) east of Grand Forks on Highway 3 you will reach Christina Lake, which offers well-organized water-skiing, watersliding and swimming facilities, plus oodles of accommodation. Pick up information about the area at the Travel Infocentre in Grand Forks.

Continuing east, you arrive at Rossland, an old gold town which, at the turn of the century, was B.C.'s fourth-largest city, producing half of the province's gold. Modern-day "prospectors" can get a sense of what life was like then by visiting the Le Roi Gold Mine, the only hard-rock gold mine in Canada open to the public. Equipped with hard-hats and ponchos, you can take a guided tour, experiencing what one writer called "the darkly expectant atmosphere of a gold mine." In its time, the Le Roi mine grossed over $30 million, but by 1929 the mine on Red Mountain was exhausted. Visitors to the area can also pan for gold or study geological samples and mining equipment at the Rossland Historical Museum. Contact the museum at 362-7722 for information on mine tours and hours of operation.

In winter, skiers like to visit nearby Red Mountain, where Canada's famous downhiller Nancy Greene made her initial runs. There are a number of places to stay in Rossland, all a far cry from the days when the cheapest accommodation in town was a chair (with a rental fee of $1 per night) at the International Music Hall and Opera House, the site of many a touring vaudeville show, prize fight and opera.

From Rossland it's 8 km (5 mi.) to Trail, where you can complete a tour of the vast Cominco mining plant before winding east to Creston via Salmo, south of Nelson. Contact the Cominco Public Relations office in Trail at 364-4113 to arrange a tour.

CRESTON

Anchoring the southwest corner of the Kootenay triangle, the town of Creston (population 4000) is located about 13 km (8 mi.) north of the B.C./ Idaho border near Highway 3's intersection with Highway 3A.

Overlooking the Kootenay River valley between the Selkirk and Purcell ranges, Creston is situated on a plateau above the Creston Valley, one of the most fertile valleys in the province. This is a prime fruit-growing area, so you might want to keep the following fruit ripening times in mind when planning a visit: early fruits—strawberries July 1-16, raspberries July 20-August 7, cherries July 20-August 7; soft fruits—apricots July 20-August 12, peaches August 1-September 15, plums August 15-September 15. Apples ripen over several months, beginning with transparents around July 25 and ending with Rome Beauties in mid-October. Vegetables start with potatoes in mid-July and end with corn in mid-August.

Creston is also a popular destination for bird watchers, since over 250 species inhabit or visit the Creston valley. The area between Creston and Nelson is home to more than 140 pairs of ospreys, making it one of the largest osprey nesting grounds in the world. At the south end of Kootenay Lake, ospreys build their nests, which can weigh up to 45 kg (100 lb.), high atop trees; some even make homes for themselves on the Canadian Pacific Railway bridge.

The 6880-ha (17,000-a.) Creston Valley Wildlife Management Area abutting the southern end of Kootenay Lake is an excellent bird-viewing area. These marshlands are home to many ducks, swans, geese and other species. Naturalists working out of the wildlife centre, open between May and October, lead hikes, marsh crawls and canoe trips that zero in on these and other regional creatures like turtles, calliope hummingbirds and moose. During July and August, Summit Creek Campground, less than a km (.6 mi) from Creston, provides a good base for exploring this wetlands waterfowl conservancy area, which is funded by Ducks Unlimited and the provincial and federal governments.

A relaxed 1- to 3-day canoe trip will take paddlers down Creston valley, putting in at the Canada-U.S. border on Highway 21 and canoeing downriver north towards Kootenay Lake. Take-out is on the east side of Kootenay Lake along Highway 3. The trip passes through excellent viewing areas for wild fowl.

During summer months houseboats can be rented on Kootenay Lake. Year-round fishing for rainbow trout, Dolly Varden trout and lingcod is possible here, with prime months for trophy fishing being November through February. Rainbow trout of up to 9 kg (20 lb.) have been caught in the fall. Kokanee salmon can be caught from May through August.

Automobile travellers usually opt for the scenic drive on Highway 3A along Kootenay Lake, an 80-km (50-mi.) stretch of superb vistas. The route takes in Black Bear Park with its 10 ha (25 a.) of hiking trails and picnic sites.

From Kootenay Bay on the east side of the lake to Balfour on the west side, travellers (and cars) can enjoy the longest free ferry ride in North America: a 45-minute trip featuring scenic shoreline and rugged mountain views.

During January and February, folks snowshoe and cross-country ski in the Creston area, capitalizing on the abundant trails.

Useful Information
Contact the **Creston Wildlife Management Centre** at Box 640, Creston, B.C., V0B 1G0 (428-3259) for information on their activities.

Contact the Kootenay Country Tourist Association, 610 Railway St., Nelson, B.C., V1L 1H4 (352-6033) for current information on houseboat rentals, fishing and other activities.

The Kootenay Lake ferries and the ferries from Galena Bay to Shelter Bay run approximately every hour. The Fauquier-to-Needles ferry runs every half-hour. Schedules are subject to change, so phone 354-6521 for up-to-date information.

Tanna Patterson-Z's book *Exploring the Creston Valley* is a useful guide to the region.

AINSWORTH HOT SPRINGS

After you have arrived by ferry at Balfour, Highway 31 leads a further 16 km (10 mi.) north to Ainsworth, a small friendly town of about 100 people overlooking Kootenay Lake and the Purcell Mountains.

A mining boom hit Ainsworth in the late 1800s when galena was discovered in nearby Metal Mountain. At the turn of the century fire virtually destroyed the town. Today, Ainsworth's lodges and one motel cater to a clientele keen to take the waters.

The potency of the hot springs that are Ainsworth's main attraction first came to light about two centuries ago when local native people noticed deer bathing their wounds in water flowing from a cave. Tribal members subsequently soaked in the hot waters and found them to have healing powers, probably due to high mineral content.

The Ainsworth hot springs are unique among the province's 95 documented hot springs in that their waters are heated by molten rock boiling up from the earth's core, technically known as an intrusive spur. (The remainder of B.C.'s hot springs are created by surface moisture seeping underground through rock faults and cracks. Deep underground the water heats up, minerals dissolve and then the water returns to the surface via the same route, cooling slightly in the process.)

Located a mere 45 m (150 ft.) from the Mermaid Lodge and Motel, the natural hot springs pool and cave is open year-round. Folks soak and relax indoors in the 29-45° C (85-114° F) waters or explore the horseshoe cave.

About 15 m (50 ft.) long and 1 m (40 in.) deep, the lit cave reveals walls coated many colours from mineral deposits and algae: white (calcium), yellow (sulphur), green (copper or algae), black (volcanic deposits or algae). Ambient temperature in the cave is 40-45° C (105-114° F), and a hose at the cave entrance provides a cooling shower.

An outdoor pool, with a capacity of 150, is slightly cooler (32-35° C/90-95° F). Snapdragons, sweet peas, geraniums, roses and other flowers grow alongside until the winter snows set in.

Other outings in the vicinity include Cody Caves Provincial Park. Located on the eastern slopes of the Selkirk Mountains, the park can be reached via a narrow forest road that begins at a small gravel pit about 3 km (2 mi.) north of Ainsworth on Highway 31. The 15-km (9-mi.) road is passable from June through October in most high-clearance vehicles and the route is well marked. The network of explorable underground passages, actually forming one vast cave, stretches over 800 m (1000 ft.). Limestone beds laid down about 600 million years ago were subsequently thrust upward by mountain-building forces that occurred around 170 million years ago. The resulting cracks and joints were then exposed to water, which, percolating down through the rock, dissolved the limestone and, over the years, enlarged the cracks and joints to form the complex system of caves.

An excellent brochure produced by the Ministry of Parks has a map of the various chambers and explains such caving terms as moon milk, stalagmites, soda straws, bacon strips and draperies. Henry Cody, a silver prospector who discovered the cave at the end of the 19th century, thought that the cave's inner chambers were walled with gold ore, but the coating turned out to be calcite formations.

Be sure to bring three sources of light when exploring caves: you'll need two flashlights as well as matches and candles. Dress warmly, and wear a hard-hat and rubber-soled boots. Never cave alone and don't touch cave formations since the oil in human skin prevents calcite deposits forming at the point of contact.

Tours through the cave are available for a reasonable fee from the park concessionaire who is in attendance at the parking lot from 10:00 A.M. to 5:00 P.M. daily throughout the summer. Coveralls, hard hats and lights are provided. Bookings for groups can also be arranged. In winter, nordic enthusiasts ski up to the caves from Ainsworth.

Useful Information

Contact **Ainsworth Hot Springs Resort** at Box 1268, Ainsworth Hot Springs, B.C., V0G 1A0 (229-4212) for information on opening hours.

For information about Cody Caves Park, contact the Visitor Services Coordinator, BC Parks, West Kootenay District, R. R. #3, Nelson, B.C., V1L 5P6 (825-4421).

KASLO

North of Ainsworth at the junction of Highway 31 and Highway 31A lies the town of Kaslo. Kaslo's location on the shores of Kootenay Lake between the Selkirks and the Purcells has caused it to be dubbed "the Switzerland of the Americas."

Once a mining centre and the fifth largest city in B.C., Kaslo today has a population of 950; even at that, it is still the largest community along Highway 31.

The S. S. *Moyie*, the last of the sternwheelers to ply the waters of Kootenay Lake, is now beached on Front Street in Kaslo. Its final voyage was on April 27, 1957. The ship now houses the Kaslo Travel Infocentre and the local museum, where you can easily spend a few hours exploring the mining past of the area.   Fishing, swimming, hiking and hang-gliding are popular pastimes here. There are also many ghost towns in the region. For some really good ghost-town atmosphere, head west from Kaslo along Highway 31A to Sandon. Now deserted, Sandon was once a thriving mining city, boasting B.C.'s second hydroelectric plant, 2 major railways, 3 newspapers, 24 hotels (each with a saloon), an opera house and a brewery. Its museum is open daily from 9:00 A.M. to 6:00 P.M. July through September.

PURCELL WILDERNESS CONSERVANCY AREA

North of Kaslo and east of upper Kootenay Lake and the southern tip of Duncan Lake lies the massive (131,000-ha / 323,705-a.) Purcell Wilderness Conservancy Area, a spectacular section of the rugged and wild Purcell Mountains that divide the East and West Kootenays.

The historic Earl Grey Pass Trail crosses the northern portion of the conservancy, connecting Argenta, on the east side of Kootenay Lake, with Toby Creek, west of Invermere. This 61-km (38-mi.) trail is quite rugged, so it's not suitable for novices. All hikers should get the latest update on trail conditions from the district parks office before setting out.

Other routes from Argenta to the Purcell Wilderness Conservancy are the Kootenay Joe Trail and the Fry Creek Trail. You will need a good map of the area to get all the creeks straight. The two trails can be hiked together in a loop, which takes a good 8 to 9 hours.

The Kootenay Joe Trail ascends to 1341 m (4400 ft.) at Kootenay Joe Pass and takes a minimum of 3 hours to hike. To reach the trailhead, you will either have to get to the mouth of Fry Creek by boat or travel in by road via Highway 31 to Cooper Creek at the head of Kootenay Lake. From Cooper Creek, a gravel road leads east and south to the communities of Argenta and Johnson's Landing, on the east shores of the lake. The distance from Cooper Creek to trailhead, at the end of the road just south of Johnson's Landing, is 17.6 km (11 mi.). Along the way, raspberries and blue elderberries are plentiful in season. Near the pass, a Forest Service picnic table with a view of Kootenay Lake is a good place to stop for lunch.

For a circular trip, descend from the pass and cross Seven Mile Creek and Carney Creek to reach the Fry Creek Trail back to Kootenay Lake. The trail passes through a canyon where recent rock blasting has widened the trail ledge, a real improvement since hikers would not survive a fall into the fast creek waters.

The Fry Creek Trail can be hiked on its own, starting from the same trailhead as that for the Kootenay Joe Trail. The trail heads south, crossing Kootenay Joe Creek, and then turns up Fry Creek about 35 minues from the trailhead.

Useful Information

Information about the Purcell Wilderness Conservancy Area can be obtained from the Visitor Services Coordinator, BC Parks, West Kootenay District, R. R. #3, Nelson, B.C., V1L 5P6 (825-4421).

THE ARROW LAKES

The Arrow Lakes area makes a lovely destination. A bit off the beaten track, it shows some of the best of B.C.—protected inland waters, perfect for paddling or fishing, studded with interesting little communities. Highway 31 runs along the northern section of Kootenay Lake, then follows the Lardeau River to Galena Bay, on the east side of Upper Arrow Lake. To get to the Arrow Lakes region, follow Highway 23 south from Galena Bay. It hugs the eastern shores of Upper Arrow Lake until it reaches the town of Nakusp (population 2500).

You can also reach the Arrow Lakes by coming in from Vernon, 192 km (120 mi.) to the west in the Okanagan. Use Highway 6, which crosses the Arrow Lakes from Needles to Fauquier via a free ferry.

The Forest Service has two excellent maps of recreation sites in the Upper and Lower Arrow Lakes area. Copies can be obtained from the Ministry of Forests, 518 Lake St., Nelson, B.C., V1L 4C6 (354-6286). Contact the Nakusp Travel Infocentre, Box 387, Nakusp, B.C., V0G 1R0 (265-4234) for further information about the Arrow Lakes region.

NAKUSP

Originally established during the mining boom in the Slocan Valley at the turn of the century, Nakusp was also an important stopping point for sternwheelers on the Arrow Lakes until the 1950s. The Nakusp Museum and Archives, open May through September, provide an interesting glimpse into the areas's past as a thriving mining region.

Nakusp is now known primarily for its hot springs. Half a dozen natural springs lie in the immediate vicinity, including the Nakusp Hot Springs, 13 km (8 mi.) north of the village centre. Waters in the mineral pool here reach 44° C (112° F); the pool used for swimming is more temperate at 39° C (105° F). Both pools are outdoors and are open year-round. Inside the lounge of the main building, a concession sells snacks and beverages and rents swim suits. The hot springs at nearby Halcyon, St. Leon, Halfway River and Octopus Creek are undeveloped, but worth looking for if you want a secluded soak.

Anglers use Nakusp as a base from which to fish the surrounding rivers and lakes for trophy-sized rainbow trout, Dolly Varden, kokanee salmon and whitefish. There are four campgrounds in the area—Nakusp Hot Springs (30 sites), Summit Lake (42 sites), Nakusp Village (25 sites) and Royal Coachman (50 serviced sites).

In winter, Nakusp is a base for heli-skiing in the Selkirk and Monashee ranges.

Useful Information
Contact **Nakusp Hot Springs Resort**, Nakusp, B.C., V0G 1R0 (mobile phone 352-4033) for further information.

Contact **Kootenay Helicopter Skiing Ltd.**, Box 717, Nakusp, B.C., V0G 1R0 (265-3121) to find out about heli-skiing in the Nakusp area.

NEW DENVER

The town of New Denver (population 700), 56 km (35 mi.) southeast of Nakusp on Highway 6, services the hiking, fishing, boating and skiing needs of visitors to the area.

From December through April, Valhalla Mountain Touring takes small groups of back-country skiers into the nearby Valhalla Range for a week's touring through endless powder. The company's base camp, an hour and a half's trip up a logging road by snow cat, features a refurbished mining cabin. Evening menu highlights include salmon pie, avocado mousse and a dish called "Eggplant Faceplant." Each morning, the snow cat transports skiers, along with 2 guides, to the bottom of one of 4 ski basins for a day of ski touring or telemarking. Other activities include moonlight skiing, belly dancing and ski jumping off the outhouse roof.

Just south of New Denver on Slocan Lake, Silverton Resort offers fully equipped log cabins that provide a base for hiking to Idaho Peak, which overlooks the Valhallas, the New Denver glacier and the Kokanee glacier.

Useful Information

For more information on **Valhalla Mountain Touring**, contact them at Box 254, New Denver, B.C., V0G 1S0 (358-7714). Contact **Silverton Resort**, Box 107, Silverton, B.C., V0G 2B0 (358-7157) for information on accommodation.

VALHALLA PARK

Both New Denver and Slocan, 34 km (21 mi.) to the south, are good kick-off points for Valhalla Park. A decade-long struggle by hundreds of people to preserve these 500 sq. km (193 sq. mi.) of wilderness ended successfully when the provincial government created the park in the spring of 1983.

The Valhallas are named for the hall of immortality where souls of Norse heroes went after they were killed in battle. Most of the eastern slope of the range lies within the park, bordered on the west by the 30 km (19 mi.) rock and sand shoreline of Slocan Lake. Gladsheim, at 2827 m (9423 ft.) the highest peak in the park, thrusts up from the Mulvey Basin, due east of Asgard peak.

In Viking mythology, Asgard is the domain of the gods above the clouds and Gladsheim their "joyous home" throne room. Midgard Peak, to the southeast, is the earth or "middle kingdom." Mount Bor, on the extreme western boundary of Valhalla, is named after the ancestral deity, while Hela Peak, to the north just beyond Devil's Couch, is the home of the "underworld." Mountain High Recreation offers skiing and hiking in the Valhalla Mountains. Different kinds of accommodation are available at their McKean Lakes Lodge, situated at 2070 m (6900 ft.). Some of the mountains of the Mulvey Basin, such as Mount Dag and Little Dag, enjoy an international reputation in expert mountaineering circles.

To enter Valhalla, Viking heroes first had to die gloriously in battle. They were then cremated on a drifting boat; their spirits, guided by Valkyries, were received into Valhalla for eternity by the god Odin. Appropriately enough, access to Valhalla Park is mainly by boat.

Day-trippers head out from the centres of New Denver, Silverton or Slocan to fish, hike or study lakeside native pictographs. Canoeing on Slocan Lake is also popular. Since Valhalla Park stretches for 28 km (17 mi.) along the lake's western edge, taking in 20 secluded beaches, a canoeing tour from beach to beach makes for an easy 3- to 5-day family vacation.

Several good hikes exist in Valhalla Park. From New Denver, boaters can head across Slocan Lake to Wee Sandy Creek; a 6-hour, 11-km (7-mi.) hike of the same name begins 1.2 km (.75 mi.) to the south. The trail follows the creek up through a forested canyon to Wee Sandy Lake, a good spot to fish for fat trout and to see the mountain goats that live on the surrounding bluffs.

Sharp Creek Trail begins on the west shore of Slocan Lake immediately north of Sharp Creek and follows the creek to the ruins of an old cabin at 1920 m (6299 ft.). Allow 6 hours for this 8-km (5-mi.) hike, which ends at the New Denver glacier.

Nemo Creek Trail, which runs south along the lake and begins 50 m (160 ft.) north of Nemo Creek, is a favourite with day hikers. It take 4 hours to do this 7-km (4.3-mi.) trail along the creek passing Nemo Falls, the "rock castles" of large glacial erratics and an old trapper's cabin along the way before the trail peters out.

Fishers and wilderness campers tend to head for the Beatrice Lake Trail. It will take you about 6 hours to complete this 12.5-km (7.8-mi.) hike, which starts just south of Evans Creek and connects with the shoreline trail to Slocan leading up from the south. Beatrice Lake is filled with large rainbow trout, as is Evans Lake, a further hike over a steep ridge.

The only two land routes into Valhalla Park are from Slocan. One follows a 6.4-km (4-mi.) trail up Gwillim Creek canyon. The other leads to the Mulvey Basin (and all those Norse peaks) via the Drinnon Pass/Gwillim Lakes Trail in the western section of the park. The pass, running just above wildflower and hummingbird meadows, is only 3.2 km. (2 mi.) from the trailhead at the end of the Hoder Creek logging road.

The parks board recommends that wilderness hikers not travel in the Mulvey Creek drainage area leading from the basin because of a poor to nonexistent trail and a large population of grizzly bears. The ridges around the basin provide opportunities for advanced hikers wishing to traverse the western boundary/height of land of the park.

Anyone who plans to do extensive hiking in the Valhallas should get up-to-the-minute trail information from the parks division in Nelson.

Useful Information

For trail information, contact the Visitor Services Coordinator, BC Parks, West Kootenay District, R. R. #3, Nelson, B.C., V1L 5P6 (825-4421).

The Valhalla Wilderness Society, Box 224, New Denver, B.C., V0G 1S0, offers a detailed trail guide of the park for a small fee.

For information on mountain tours, contact **Mountain High Recreation,** Box 128, Slocan, B.C., V0G 2C0 (355-2518 or 266-7790).

Canoe rentals and boat shuttles are available in New Denver and Silverton. Helicopter service is provided from Nelson and Castlegar. Contact the Travel Infocentre in Nelson for the names and addresses of operators.

SLOCAN

Experts disagree on the origin of the name of this village of 300 people located 33 km (20 mi.) south of New Denver. Some think it comes from the Shushwap Indian word *slok-ken*, meaning "frogs," while others think it derives from *slokam*, "to catch salmon." Still others conjecture that it is taken from *schlocan* or *sloghan*, the Okanagan Indian word meaning to pierce or strike on the head (when harpooning salmon).

In any case, this once booming mining town of the 1890s, which had a population of 6000 at its height, is now the smallest incorporated city in the world and serves as a good base for exploration of the surrounding area.

Paddlers can take a day to travel the Slocan River, putting in at Slocan and taking out at the highway crossing where the river flows into the Kootenay River.

Cyclists can join one of the Kootenay Mountain Bike Tours. Beginning in Nelson, the Slocan Valley tour takes 3 days and 2 nights to cover the 96 km (60 mi.). Lemon Creek Lodge and Campground, southwest of Slocan, is one of the stops along the route. The rustic lodge offers comfortable accommodation and excellent home cooking. A popular year-round base for adventurers, it sleeps 30 and has an authentic Finnish sauna. The campground is a pleasant grassy area with shower facilities. The lodge offers a variety of guided tours depending on the season: canoeing on Slocan Lake, hikes into Six Mile Lakes, canoe and hiking combos or ski tours into the Valhallas and Kootenay Glacier Park, and a Heritage Hot Springs tour.

Useful Information

To find out about cycling tours in the region, call **Kootenay Mountain Bike Tours** at 354-4371 or write to them at Box 867, Nelson, B.C., V1L 6A5.

Lemon Creek Lodge can be reached at Box 68, Slocan, B.C., V0G 2C0 (355-2403) for information on accommodation and guided tours.

NELSON

Nelson, the hub of the Kootenays, is beautifully situated on the west arm of Kootenay Lake at the junction of Highways 6 and 3A. Locals claim that, among its population of 8000, Nelson can count more artists and craftspeople per capita than any other city in Canada.

The "Queen City of the Kootenays" was once the rest-and-relaxation town for tired miners and a busy port for the sternwheelers that connected rail lines divided by water. Recently, it has become a prime film location, appearing in motion pictures like *Housekeeping* and Steve Martin's *Roxanne*.

The icy waters of Kootenay Lake and the nearby Selkirk Mountains make Nelson a popular base for alpine fishing, mountain climbing, hiking and backpacking.

In the city itself, you can walk back into Victorian times by going on a Heritage Walking Tour that takes in more than 350 buildings of historical interest. The Nelson Museum, open every afternoon in the summer and afternoons except Sundays in winter, has exhibits devoted to the city's gold and silver rush days, as well as some documenting Doukhobor culture and the Interior Salish and Lower Kootenay groups who originally lived in the area. Pick up a brochure describing the tour at the Travel Infocentre, 225 Hall St., Nelson, B.C., V1L 5X4 (352-3433).

KOKANEE GLACIER PARK

One of the oldest and most scenic parks in the province, Kokanee Glacier Park is a 25,600-ha (63,258-a.) mountain wilderness wedged in the Slocan Range of the Selkirk Mountains directly north of Nelson, west of Ainsworth Hot Springs and east of Slocan.

There are two main access roads into the park. The most popular leads off Highway 3A 20 km (12.5 m.) northeast of Nelson to the Gibson Lake parking lot. The second major route is from Highway 31A, just north of Kaslo. A 24-km (15-mi.) gravel road, adjacent to Keen Creek, leads to the Joker Millsite. There are also routes into the park from Ainsworth Hot Springs, Slocan, Balfour and Silverton.

Established as a park in 1922, Kokanee (Okanagan for "little salmon," referring to the landlocked sockeye of the area), is riddled with mining trails built during the great mining boom of the Silver Slocan period. It is these trails, well-maintained by the parks division, that make hiking and skiing in Kokanee rewarding; otherwise, the park is virtually undeveloped.

Named for the glacier on the slopes of Kokanee Peak (2774 m/9098 ft.), Kokanee Park contains at least 30 lakes within its boundaries, most lying at elevations ranging from 1700-2100 m (5576-6880 ft.). Turquoise-blue in colour, many are artificially stocked with Yellowstone cutthroat trout. The terrain of Kokanee is rugged; it includes the Sawtooth Range to the north and many other peaks, half of them above the 2100-m (6880-ft.) mark.

Hiking in Kokanee Park is prime during the three snow-free months—July, August and September—but freak snowstorms can occur even then. The well-known Gibson Lake–Slocan Chief Cabin Trail is a 10-km (6-mi.) hike of moderate difficulty that traverses Kokanee Pass and passes by Kokanee and Kaslo lakes; it takes about 4 hours to complete.

Built in 1886 by the Smuggler Mining Company to house their employees, the Slocan Chief Cabin is available year-round as a public shelter, housing a maximum of 20 people per night. Over the summer, accommodation is available on a first-come, first-served basis, but the cabin, in the midst of some of the best ski-touring in B.C., has become so popular with back-country skiers that a lottery has been established to determine who can sleep at the Slocan Chief during the winter months. The parks branch in Nelson starts accepting letters on September 15. Reservation requests should include the group leader's name, address and phone number, the number of people in your group (a maximum of 12) and the preferred dates (Saturday to Saturday) with two alternatives. Cut-off date is October 14. The parks board then begins to draw parties until all dates are filled.

The best way to get to the cabin in winter is via the Gibson Lake Road. Skiers in the area should be able to recognize avalanche hazard signs and know how to take the necessary precautions. To avoid the long ski-in on unplowed road, adventurers can also be flown in from Nelson by Canadian Helicopters.

A good summer hike in the park is the 5-km (3-mi.) journey from Joker Millsite to the Slocan Chief Cabin. Hikers keen for less travelled trails can head in from Slocan on the Lemon Creek to Sapphire Lakes route or come in on the Enterprise Creek/Enterprise Pass route from Silverton to the west.

Backpacking anglers come into the park for the Yellowstone cutthroat, which responds well to fly. The Yellowstone is generally olive green; it is liberally dotted with black spots and sports a distinctive red slash at its throat. In Kokanee Lake, which has the largest population (and the biggest fish), the trout can be up to 33 cm (13 in.) long.

What visitors to this craggy country usually remember best are the smell of wild heather, the flower-filled meadows, the whistles of the many hoary marmots, and the occasional glimpse of the deer, bears, blue and Franklin grouse and golden eagles that live here.

Useful Information

Contact the Visitor Services Coordinator, BC Parks, West Kootenay District, R. R. #3, Nelson, B.C., V1L 5P6 (825-4421) for a brochure containing a map of the park and other information and to make reservations for the Slocan Chief Cabin in winter.

Canadian Helicopters in Nelson (352-5411) can fly skiers or hikers into the park.

Bob Harris's book *The Best of B.C.'s Hiking Trails* describes several of the trails in Kokanee Glacier Park.

CASTLEGAR

Forty-three km (27 mi.) west of Nelson on Highway 3A lies Castle-gar. Known variously as the crossroads of the Kootenays and the gateway to the Arrow Lakes, Castlegar is one of the major transportation hubs of the region. Four highways lead into this city of 6000, which is situated in an elbow of the Columbia River where the foamy Kootenay River tumbles out of the mountains.

Castlegar's distinctive Doukhobor culture, which includes marvellous Russian fare such as borscht, is reason enough to visit this community. The Doukhobors, descendants of communalist pacifists who escaped persecution in czarist Russia at the turn of the century, settled first in Saskatchewan and later in the timbered valleys of the West Kootenays. For a glimpse of their early lives in the Castlegar area, you might want to visit the Doukhobor Historic Village across from the Castlegar airport. Here you can sample some of their delicious traditionally vegetarian fare.

A good time to visit Castlegar is in early June, when Doukhobor choirs from all over Canada gather to celebrate their music and traditions. The early Doukhobors memorized as many as 150 psalms and hymns; today their accomplished singers know 50 psalms and hymns, and music continues to play a central role in their community. Nearby Brilliant usually hosts this harmonious festival. Contact the Castlegar Travel Infocentre, 1995-6th Ave., Castlegar, B.C., V1N 4B7 (365-6313) for more information.

CHAPTER 6

B.C. Rockies

The area we define as the B.C. Rockies extends from Revelstoke east to the Alberta border and south to the 49th parallel separating B.C. from Idaho and Montana. Between Revelstoke and the Rocky Mountains lie the Monashee, Selkirk and Purcell ranges.

As mountains go, the Rockies are a relatively young range. Created about 100 million years ago, the mountains surged up from under the earth's surface as a result of collision damage between the major subterranean plates. The Purcell Mountains are much older. Bounded by the Rocky Mountain Trench on the east, the Purcells originated about 1500 million years ago, when the only form of life on earth was algae. The Rockies are, for the main, just that, bare rocky mountains, while the Purcell Range is steep and tree-covered. The two ranges became neighbours during the dinosaur era.

Major drainage in the area is provided by the 1900-km (1180-mi.) Columbia River, which rises in Columbia Lake north of Canal Flats and pours into the Pacific Ocean at Astoria, Oregon. The Columbia Valley is surrounded by 4 national parks. Excellent rafting can be found at Golden, where the Columbia is joined by the fast-moving Kicking Horse River. The valley is also a major flyway for migratory birds, many of whom nest in the spring in its sloughs and marshes.

This mountainous terrain was originally inhabited by the Shuswap and Kutenai peoples. The Kutenai made regular hunting forays east out of the Rocky Mountain Trench, using secret mountain passes, to kill buffalo on the Alberta plains. Their hunting and fishing existence was disrupted by European explorers and by subsequent gold booms, such as the 1863 rush that spawned Kootenay communities like Fort Steele. Lead, zinc and silver mines later went into production in Kimberley.

In the late 1800s, Major A. B. Rogers, an engineer with the Canadian Pacific Railway, made several trips through this area with his nephew searching for a pass through the Selkirk Mountains. Adverse weather on these trips often forced the men to bivouac and flog each other with their pack straps to keep warm. They persevered, however, and in 1882 Rogers happened upon the pass through the mountains that now bears his name.

In 1898 the CPR built a railway through the Crowsnest Pass to service the coal reserves of Elk Valley, which today remains the main coal producing region of B.C. As the railway opened the area up to travellers and commerce,

B.C. Rockies

HAMBER PARK

KINBASKET LAKE

ALBERTA

LAKE REVELSTOKE

YOHO NATIONAL PARK

Lake Louise

MT. REVELSTOKE NATIONAL PARK

GLACIER NATIONAL PARK

Golden

KOOTENAY NATIONAL PARK

To Kamloops

REVELSTOKE

Columbia R.

95

MOUNT ASSINIBOINE PROV. PARK

HEIGHT OF THE ROCKIES WILDERNESS AREA

BUGABOO GLACIER PROV. PARK

Radium Hot Springs

ELK LAKES PROV. PARK

Invermere

Fairmont Hot Springs

PURCELL WILDERNESS CONSERVANCY

Canal Flats

Elk River

KOOTENAY LAKE

ST. MARY'S ALPINE PROV. PARK

TOP OF THE WORLD PROV. PARK

Elkford

Kimberley

Sparwood

Cranbrook

Fernie

ALBERTA

Elko

Kilometres

0   40

Miles

0   25

To Salmo

3

Creston   Yahk

U.S.A.

tourism started to play a very important part in the region's development. European visitors found that these mountains reminded them of the Alps, yet were colder and wilder.

The climate in the region varies from range to range and from peak to peak. Broadly speaking, however, it's safe to say that snow can fall on the mountains right through the year but doesn't usually start building up until November. At higher altitudes nights can get cold. Spring occurs in April and May in valley bottoms, May and June at higher elevations. Although the weather is totally unpredictable at any time of year, we have found that September is one of the nicest months to visit this area. Early frosts have killed off some of the biting bugs, the alpine larch are changing colour and, while nights are frosty, days can be gorgeous sunny affairs, under the bluest skies you'll probably ever see.

The range of adventuring possibilities in the B.C. Rockies is magnificent and varied. You can hike, fish, raft, game-watch or just plain sit in your vehicle and drink in the stunning scenery. Naturalists will enjoy the numerous birds, animals and flowers, while skiers and climbers can tackle some of the most challenging terrain in the country.

If you are camping in the area, bring along a stove; during the summer months, there is sometimes a total ban on fires due to the danger of forest fire. Above the tree line bugs tend not to be too bad, but pack some bug repellent just in case. You will burn more quickly at high altitudes, so we recommend sunscreen and sunglasses. And take special precautions with food, hanging it or using bear poles; the bears in the B.C. Rockies are notorious scavengers. Registration is required for all parks in the area and you must obtain back-country permits for overnight treks.

Useful books for any trip into the mountains include *Wildflowers of the Canadian Rockies, The Canadian Rockies Trail Guide* and *Ski Trails in the Canadian Rockies.*

We begin our adventuring in this region by travelling east towards Alberta on the Trans-Canada Highway from Revelstoke, through Mount Revelstoke and Glacier national parks, then on to Golden, from which we explore Hamber Park and Fortress Lake to the north and the famous Yoho National Park, which borders on Banff National Park in Alberta, to the east. From there, we head south along Highway 93, taking in Kootenay National Park and Mount Assiniboine en route to the town of Radium Hot Springs. We visit the ancient Bugaboos, then continue south to Invermere with a side trip east to Height-of-the-Rockies Wilderness Area. Then it's on to Fairmont Hot Springs, Top of the World Provincial Park and Kimberley, the province's highest city. Finally, we visit the Purcell Wilderness Conservancy and St. Mary's Alpine Park before continuing south to the centres of Fort Steele, Cranbrook and Fernie. Our trip concludes at Elk Lakes Provincial Park.

REVELSTOKE

Revelstoke is the start of mountain country if you are travelling in from the west. Located 100 km (63 mi.) northeast of Salmon Arm on the Trans-Canada Highway, the city sits at the north end of Upper Arrow Lake at the junction of the Columbia and Illecillewaet rivers.

Revelstoke is a popular base for exploration of Mount Revelstoke and Glacier national parks. North of town on Highway 23, abundant forests cut with hiking trails lead to high alpine meadows. Three pleasant hikes are Standard Basin, an easy 6-hour, 21-km (13-mi.) round trip within an extensive alpine area; Martha Creek, which takes 5 hours to cover 9 km (5.7 mi.) of alpine and forest adjacent to Martha Creek Provincial Park, and the 22-km (13.9-mi.) LaForme Creek trip, which usually takes 6 hours.

Durrand Glacier Chalet, 30 km (19 mi.) northeast of Revelstoke, makes an excellent base for superb touring and telemark skiing. The chalet, a pine and cedar Swiss-style mountain lodge that accommodates 20 people, sits on a knoll at the 1980-m (6350-ft.) level at the base of the spectacular Durrand Glacier in the northern Selkirk Mountains. It is well placed to capitalize on the record snowfalls—averaging over 1600 cm (630 in.) a year—of the area. Host and guide Ruedi Beglinger offers guided tours of a total of 18 peaks and 33 different ski routes in a 200-sq.-km (77-sq.-mi.) vicinity.

Highlights include the 762 vertical m (2500 ft.) of Tumbledown Mountain. Close to the chalet are runs such as Elevator, Bella Vista, Utopia, No Panic in the Titanic and the Haute Route de la Forêt, spread over 503 m (1650 ft.) of elevation.

Durrand's winter season runs from October to early July; average snow-pack under April sun reaches 6 m (20 ft.). A week-long, hut-to-hut ski tour takes in the hut at Mount Moloch, northeast of Durrand right next to Dismal Glacier, and, weather permitting, can include Mount Fang and Forbidden Glacier.

Summer weekend or midweek hiking tours from Durrand Chalet head into the alpine world between 1830 m (6000 ft.) and 2750 m (9000 ft.), and trips suitable for all ages and abilities are offered. Trails connect 5 mountain lakes and August is the prime time to see alpine flowers. The fresh chalet food is a mix of Swiss and Canadian cuisine. Access to the Durrand Glacier Chalet is by a 15-minute helicopter ride from Revelstoke.

Rainer Glyckherr's Blanket Glacier Chalet, another mountain chalet in the area, is situated 30 km (19 mi.) southwest of Revelstoke. High in the Monashee Mountains, the chalet can only be reached by a 12-minute helicopter flight from Revelstoke. It can accommodate 15 guests and is equipped with wood and oil stoves and a wood-fired sauna. The Blanket Glacier Chalet provides a fine base for ski-touring the area, either independently or on guided trips.

During the summer, the chalet opens for hiking, canoeing, fishing and mountaineering.

East of Revelstoke lie two large reservoirs, Lake Revelstoke and Kinbasket Lake. Created for flood control and hydroelectric power generation, the lakes offer good fishing with some developed hiking trails. B.C. Hydro has published a useful guide to the reservoirs. Highway 23 provides access to three campsites on Lake Revelstoke and one on Kinbasket Lake. Since black and grizzly bears are common to the area, take suitable precautions with your food.

Paddlers who want to canoe the Goldstream, a medium-sized river approximately 93 km (58 mi.) north of Revelstoke on Highway 23, should contact the Ministry of Forests for detailed information. The route covers 18 km (11 mi.) of grade 1 canoeing.

The Revelstoke area enjoyed a small gold rush in the 1860s, and hopes still linger of another one: 800 placer and mineral claims exist today in the region. Monashee Outfitting and Downie R. V. Resorts Ltd. offer gold-panning trips in the streams flowing from the Selkirks and Monashees into Lake Revelstoke. Even if you don't hit paydirt, you will enjoy sightings of deer, moose, mountain goats and caribou. For further information on gold panning, you can contact the Gold Commissioner located in the Revelstoke Courthouse.

A great way to relieve the aches and pains of driving the long distances of the Trans-Canada Highway is to stop off at Canyon Hot Springs, 35 km (22 mi.) east of Revelstoke (and the same distance from Rogers Pass).

CPR workers building the railway at the turn of the century "discovered" these mineral waters in Albert Canyon in the Selkirks and built a timber enclosure to contain them. Today, water is piped from a spring several kilometres down the valley to feed a 56,780-l (15,000-gal.) hot pool and 227,120-l (60,000-gal.) swimming pool. The temperature in the hot pool remains a steady 40° C (104° F) and, in the swimming pool, 26° C (80° F). The 81-ha (200-a) development at the hot springs is well situated for hikers in Glacier and Mount Revelstoke parks and has campsites available from May through August.

Useful Information

The B.C. Hydro publication *Lake Revelstoke and Kinbasket Lake Recreation Guide* is available from the Revelstoke Travel Infocentre (837-5345), located at the junction of the Trans-Canada Highway and Highway 23 North.

Contact **Selkirk Mountain Experience (Durrand Glacier Chalet)**, Box 2998, Revelstoke, B.C., V0E 2S0 (837-2381) or **Blanket Glacier Chalet**, Box 1050, Canmore, Alberta, T0L 0M0 (678-4102) for information on accommodation, helicopter access and hiking or skiing trips.

For details about the Goldstream River Canoe Route, contact the Ministry of Forests, 1761 Big Eddy Rd., Box 470, Revelstoke, B.C., V0E 2S0 (837-7611).

For information on gold panning, contact **Monashee Outfitting**, Box 2958, Revelstoke, B.C., V0E 2S0 (837-3538) and **Downie R.V. Resorts Ltd.**, Box 520, Revelstoke, B.C., V0E 2S0 (radio phone: Revelstoke N426446).

Canyon Hot Springs, Box 2400, Revelstoke, B.C., V0E 2S0 (837-2420) can provide information on the mineral pools and camping.

MOUNT REVELSTOKE NATIONAL PARK

Mount Revelstoke National Park lies in the rugged Selkirk Range of the Columbia Mountains. The southwest part of the park adjoins the municipality of Revelstoke, a handy feature since there are no campsites in the park and several private campgrounds do operate in the vicinity of the city.

The Trans-Canada skirts the southern boundary of the park, giving hikers easy access to the alpine meadows of the Southern Selkirks via the 35 km (22 mi.) of established trails. Driest trail conditions are from mid-July to mid-September. Fine views of sharp peaks and avalanche-scarred valleys are typical in this park.

The excellent alpine hiking here is typified by the Eva Lake Trail, a 12.8-km (8-mi.) round trip. Get your park map from the Parks Canada office at the federal building (post office) in downtown Revelstoke.

Eva Lake Trail is well marked. It takes 2 hours to get from trailhead on Mount Revelstoke to the lake, and wilderness camping is permitted. As you get close to the lake you can inspect the chasm of Coursier Creek and see Mount Begbie. From Eva Lake, a side loop trail leads on to the Jade Lakes. If you time your hike for the first Monday in August, you can join park naturalists on the annual B.C. Day pilgrimage to Eva Lake.

In winter, nordic skiers and snowshoers can ski the 5-km (3-mi.) packed and groomed ski trail at the base of Mount Revelstoke; 2 km (1.3 mi.) are lit for night skiing. Another popular winter route starts 1 km (.6 mi.) from the Trans-Canada Highway and leads up Summit Road. Moist Pacific air releases a mass of winter snow over the Columbias, so exercise avalanche precautions during any winter travel.

Useful Information

For more information about Mount Revelstoke Park, contact the Park Superintendent, Mount Revelstoke National Park, Box 350, Revelstoke, B.C., V0E 2S0 (837-8155). *Glacier Country: A Guide to Mount Revelstoke and Glacier National Park* by John Woods is a useful resource guide.

Avalanche Crest Trail, Glacier National Park. *Photo by Lloyd Twaites*

GLACIER NATIONAL PARK

Of the 5 national parks within B.C.'s boundaries, Glacier, 49 km (30 mi.) east of Revelstoke on the Trans-Canada Highway, has been the site of much human activity over time. And since it contains over 400 glaciers, it is certainly the most glaciated!

At its highest point (1382 m/4534 ft.), the road through Glacier National Park runs through Rogers Pass. Due to the steep terrain and the constant threat of avalanches in the area, road construction was not completed until 1962.

It was the railway that opened up this area to travellers initially. As Maria Tippett and Douglas Cole point out in their book on the art of British Columbia, *From Desolation to Splendour*, the English writers Rupert Brooke and Rudyard Kipling were both awed by the Rockies and Selkirks when they travelled by train through this part of the country in the early 1900s.

Kipling found the landscape here very different from that of the rest of Canada; in his mind, the jade lakes belonged in Tibet, the peaks in parts of the Himalayas. Brooke was struck by the "other-worldly serenity" of the Rockies and Selkirks but also by their desolation. "The pines drooped and sobbed," he wrote; to love the country here was "like embracing a wraith."

These impressions were most definitely influenced by the weather pattern of the Selkirks, where it rains, on average, every third day. Only the Purcells divide the Selkirk Range from the Rockies, and so winds from the coast have plenty of time to gather moisture as they pass over the central interior plateau on their way east.

Modern-day visitors who feel awed by the area's cloud-wreathed peaks and desolate grandeur should take advantage of the more than 140 km (87 mi.) of alpine and forest hiking trails to get a more intimate feel for this park.

Three campgrounds in Glacier National Park, at Loop Brook, Illecillewaet and Mountain Creek, contain 340 campsites between them and provide good kick-off points for hiking within park boundaries. The Alpine Club of Canada operates the Wheeler Hut, located just past the Illecillewaet campground. It is the only ACC hut to which you can drive.

One of the better-known hikes in the area, the 11-km (7-mi.) Avalanche Crest Trail, starts just beyond the Illecillewaet campground and takes approximately 5 hours to complete. It affords some splendid views of the Illecillewaet Glacier and the 3350-m (11,000-ft.) peaks of the Dawson Range. A popular backpacking trip is the Copperstain Trail, which runs for 16 km (10 mi.) from the Beaver River Valley to the open alpine ridges of Bald Mountain. The trail starts from the picnic area 13 km (8 mi.) east of Rogers Pass.

Peaks like the Hermit, Mount Sir Donald, Tupper and the Swiss peaks have earned this corner of B.C. the nickname "the Canadian Alps" in climbing circles in Europe and the U.S.A.

High rainfall in the area makes for a good snowpack in winter, so it is not surprising that ski-touring connoisseurs have started to enjoy some of the opportunities the area offers. Skiers usually base themselves at Glacier Park Lodge, at the summit of Rogers Pass on the Trans-Canada Highway, from which it is a 2-hour climb to recreational skiing at Balu Pass.

Winter wilderness ski touring in Balu is typified by 5-km (3-mi.) nonstop cruises through fresh powder which is, on average, about 13 m (43 ft.) deep. Skiers can head out from the lodge in small parties with certified guides from the Association of Mountain Guides, a good precaution in an area where digging avalanche test pits before doing runs is a vital part of any skiing trip.

During their mandatory registration with the park warden in Glacier Park, travellers are made aware of potential avalanche hazards. Rogers Pass is the site of the world's largest avalanche control program, with up-to-the-minute information on the local snowpack and weather conditions available on a 24-hour basis.

The Rogers Pass Information Centre is located next to Glacier Park Lodge. The centre is open daily and is worth a visit to see the displays on the history of the area and to watch the avalanche control films. Information on trails and park activities is also available.

Another base for winter tourers (whose season can extend from mid-November to the end of May) and for summer hikers (hiking is best between mid-June and early September) is Selkirk Lodge, located on the edge of the vast Albert Icefield, just outside of the Glacier Park boundary. The lodge can be reached by helicopter from Revelstoke and is another point of access to the "champagne powder" of the Selkirks. Week-long ski tours to this lodge, situated at an elevation of 2200 m (7200 ft.), begin and end in Revelstoke every Saturday from February to May. In summer, hiking, glacier walks and mountaineering activities can be undertaken from the lodge. There is a summer access trail from Albert Canyon Hot Springs.

During July, keen rafters take to the mountain waters of the Illecillewaet River. The Tangier River, which originates in the Northern Selkirk Mountains, joins the Illecillewaet at Canyon Hot Springs, causing the Illecillewaet to almost double in size. On its way to the Columbia River at the city of Revelstoke, the Illecillewaet winds through some rain forest, its banks lined with giant red cedar. Several rafting companies based in Revelstoke offer trips down the river.

Useful Information

Information on Glacier National Park can be obtained from the Park Superintendent, Revelstoke and Glacier National Park, Box 350, Revelstoke, B.C., V0E 2S0 (837-5155) or from the Rogers Pass Information Centre at 837-6274.

Contact **Glacier Park Lodge**, Rogers Pass, B.C., V0E 2S0 (837-2126) for information on accommodation and ski tours. Write to **The Alpine Club of Canada**, Box 1026, Banff, Alberta, T0L 0C0 (403-762-4481) for information on memberships and reservations at the Wheeler Hut. For information on winter and summer trips, contact **Selkirk Lodge**, Box 1409, Golden, B.C., V0A 1H0 (344-5016).

Contact **Alpine Rafting Company**, Box 1409, Golden, B.C., V0A 1H0 (344-5016) for trips on the Illecillewaet River.

Ski trips in the park are detailed in the book *British Columbia Cross Country Ski Routes*. (Look for this out of print title in libraries and used bookstores.) *Glacier Country: A Guide to Mount Revelstoke and Glacier National Park* by John Woods is another useful resource.

GOLDEN

Located about 62 km (38 mi.) east of Glacier National Park's eastern boundary, the town of Golden is a handy base for rafters, hikers, cyclists, skiers and fisherpeople because of its central location and its day-trip distance from Yoho, Kootenay, Banff, Glacier and Mount Revelstoke national parks. Golden is in the Mountain Time Zone, which begins 80 km (50 mi.) east of Revelstoke, so be sure to move your watch ahead one hour if you are travelling from the west. Several Golden-based operators offer rafting tours of the Kicking Horse River. Considered one of the most scenic and exciting runs in eastern B.C., the Kicking Horse Canyon is prime white water. A more scenic and less adrenalin-producing run takes rafters along the Blaeberry River just west of Golden. This river winds past panoramic Rocky Mountain scenery and follows part of the route taken by David Thompson on his search for a northern trading route in the early 1800s.

One of the adventures we most enjoyed in the Golden area was the relatively new experience of organized hut-to-hut hiking. Back-country hut ski-touring or hiking is common in Europe but has only recently become popular in Canada. Golden provides one of the best bases in the province for the hut-to-hut experience, summer or winter.

Golden Alpine Holidays guides hikers or skiers between their chalets in the Esplanade Range, a long ridge just north of Glacier National Park that runs parallel to the Rocky Mountain Trench and the Columbia River. The average elevation is 2440 m (8000 ft.) and a tree line at 2133 m (7000 ft.) means that the extensive trail system leading through alpine meadows can be comfortably covered in day hikes from one of Golden Alpine's 3 back-country chalets. The spacious two-storey chalets, each with 6 separate bedrooms upstairs accommodating up to 18 guests, are an easy day hike from each other and are all located close to an alpine lake with panoramic views. Access to any of the chalets is by a scenic 15-minute helicopter ride from Kinbasket Lake just outside Golden.

July and August are the best times for hiking the meadows, which are full of Indian paintbrush, yellow arnica, alpine speedwell and several varieties of saxifrage. The 80 alpine lakes and tarns are backed by views of the Selkirks, the Purcells and the Rockies, and you can enjoy the occasional sight of moose wandering past. After a day of hiking, it's fun to relax at the chalet, enjoying the wood-heated saunas and gourmet meals like ginger chicken and cherries jubilee. And one of the Golden Alpine outhouses has a sweeping panoramic view of snow-capped mountains and flower-filled fields, placing it very high in the loo-with-a-view stakes!

The hut-to-hut experience is also popular with nordic and alpine skiers during the winter months; the chalets are an approximately 4½-hour ski apart.

More than 50 named runs fan out in the vicinity of the chalets. The most challenging, Peak-to-Creek, appeals to strong telemarkers, since it descends over 1200 m (3900 ft.) from the summit of Mount Cupola. Golden Alpine guides offer some telemark coaching to novice cross-county skiers.

Adventure Bound Canada (ABC) Wilderness Adventures runs hut-to-hut ski tours in the high rolling alpine meadows of the Purcell Mountains, beside the headwaters of the Spillimacheen River. Their new Purcell Lodge is a base for some superb cross-country skiing as well as summer hiking trips. Access to the lodge is by helicopter or by an easy hiking trail in summer. In addition to the lodge, unique accommodation is offered in back-country huts fashioned after the Mongolian yurt, a round, portable structure particularly suited to the winter mountain environment and built to withstand extreme snow loads. From either of the two yurts, the ski to the ridge is only a 150- to 300-m (490- to 980-ft.) climb, and the telemark runs are varied so that everyone from beginners to experts can enjoy them. In the evenings, the food served in the lodge or in the wood-heated yurts could well be chicken cacciatore or beef stroganoff.

Selkirk Lodge, west of Golden, provides a base for excellent ski touring or telemarking on the nearby Albert Icefield. The lodge, situated at 2200 m (7200 ft.), has accommodation for 12 guests and access is by helicopter. Guests are always accompanied by one of the lodge's experienced guides who are fully trained in avalanche hazard evaluation and rescue techniques. The summer hiking season is short but spectacular and a photographer's paradise.

North of Golden, up the Blaeberry River, lies the Mistaya Chalet, operated by Mistaya Alpine Tours. The chalet is a spacious two-storey building located beside an emerald-green lake at an elevation of 2042 m (6700 ft.). Accommodation for up to 12 people is provided in 5 bedrooms. Abundant snowfall and a variety of terrain provide excellent skiing opportunities, and alpine flower meadows and scenic ridges offer pleasant hiking in summer. Proximity to the extensive Wapta Icefield makes single- or multi-day traverses of the icefield possible, using the high-altitude hut system of Banff National Park. Avalanche and mountaineering instruction is provided by certified guides from Mistaya.

Beaverfoot Lodge is another year-round retreat catering to visitors interested in nordic touring or in hiking, paddling and horseback riding. To get to the lodge, drive 42 km (26 mi.) east of Golden on the Trans-Canada Highway and then head south on a gravel road for 13 km (8 mi.).

The Beaverfoot River flows past the lodge, which is nestled in the Beaverfoot valley between the Ottertail and Beaverfoot ranges. The main lodge accommodates 24 people, and 3 smaller log cabins in more remote areas allow for summer camping or easy hut-to-hut touring along 60 km (40 mi.) of groomed cross-country trails. Ideal for families as well as individuals, Beaverfoot offers good home-cooked food and a spectacular mountain wilderness location.

Hikers will be interested in making the 5-km (3-mi.) trek from Beaverfoot Lodge to the 38-m (124-ft.) Wapta Falls, which cascade down into the Kicking Horse River in Yoho National Park.

Bird watchers in the Golden area might want to visit Burges and James Gadsden Provincial Park, west of Golden on the Trans-Canada Highway. The sanctuary here includes much of the Moberly Marsh on the north side of the

Columbia River; the land for the park was donated by the pioneering Gadsden family as a haven for nesting and migrating ducks, herons and other waterfowl. The Golden area has also attracted cyclists for many years. An extremely popular mountain route is the Golden Triangle, a scenic 316-km (190-mi.) journey with the towns of Golden, Lake Louise (in Alberta) and Radium Hot Springs at its points. The southern part of the Golden Triangle covers much of Kootenay National Park, well known for its wildlife, and the leg north from Radium Hot Springs to Golden follows the Columbia River Valley between the Purcell and Rocky mountain ranges. Several companies offer cycling tours of the triangle.

Useful Information

For information on raft trips on the Kicking Horse and Blaeberry rivers, contact **Kootenay River Runners**, Box 81, Edgewater, B.C., V0A 1E0 (347-9210); **Glacier Raft Company**, Box 428, Golden, B.C., V0A 1H0 (344-6521) or **Alpine Rafting**, Box 1409, Golden, B.C., V0A 1H0 (344-5016).

Golden Alpine Holidays, Box 1050, Golden, B.C., V0A 1H0 (344-7273 or 348-2361); **Adventure Bound Canada**, Box 811, Golden, B.C., V0A 1H0 (344-2639); **Selkirk Lodge**, Box 1409, Golden, B.C., V0A 1H0 (344-5016) and **Mistaya Alpine Tours**, Box 990, Golden, B.C., V0A 1H0 (344-6689) all offer information on hut-to-hut skiing and hiking trips. Information on helicopter access is provided when you book a trip. **Beaverfoot Lodge** can be reached at Box 1560, Golden, B.C., V0A 1H0 (346-3216 or 346-3205).

Rocky Mountain Cycle Tours, Box 1978, Canmore, Alberta, T0L 0M0 (403-678-6770) specializes in 5-, 6- and 7-day cycle tours of the Rockies. They do the Golden Triangle, a B.C. Lakes tour and a trip through mountain resorts. **Benno's Adventure Holidays**, 1958 West 4th Ave., Vancouver, B.C., V6J 1M5 (738-5105) runs similar trips.

The Chamber of Commerce, Golden, B.C., V0A 1H0 (344-7125) can provide general information about the area.

HAMBER PARK

Hamber Provincial Park, the wildest and most inaccessible park in the B.C. Rockies, lies directly north of Glacier National Park and adjoins Alberta's Jasper National Park.

The vast Clemenceau Icefield abuts the southern tip of Hamber, forming a barrier between the park and Kinbasket Lake. Combined, the Clemenceau and the Columbia Icefield to the east provide the headwaters of the Athabasca River. The cool, glacier-fed waters of Fortress Lake lie 1336 m (4384 ft.) above sea level.

Hamber Park was initially slated to span the distance along the Rockies between Mount Robson National Park to the north and Yoho Park to the south, linking them to create one vast Rocky Mountain park. But commercial pressures caused the boundaries to be restricted to their current limits.

Now inaccessible by road, Hamber can be reached via a difficult 23-km (14-mi.) hike from Sunwapta Falls in Jasper National Park or by a one-hour float-plane flight from Golden, the method most fisherpeople use to get to Fortress Lake.

The Sunwapta Canyon to Fortress Lake Trail (detailed in *The Canadian Rockies Trail Guide*) requires about 8 hours one way, and is definitely a hike only for the experienced and the intrepid. It should only be attempted very late in the summer or in early fall, when water levels are low, because of a treacherous ford en route. Trailhead lies 55 km (34 mi.) south of Jasper on the Icefield Parkway.

Whether you arrive at Fortress Lake by air or on foot, it's hard not to share the feelings of University of Toronto geology professor A. P. Coleman, who wrote of his visit there one July day in 1892: "Suddenly there opened out below us the most marvellous lake imaginable. Our hearts fairly stood still at the sight." Almost totally ringed by mountains and icefields, Fortress Lake's extraordinary turquoise-emerald waters teem with wild stocks of trophy brook trout that can be as big as 3 kg (7 lb.).

The Fortress Lake Wilderness Camp is a summer-only tent camp situated on the gravel delta at the mouth of Chisel Creek. The view from here of the Clemenceau Glacier, surrounded by majestic mountain peaks, is magnificent.

Moose, grizzly bears, black bears and mountain goats range through the park, which combines pockets of dense spruce, hemlock and fir with alpine meadowland.

There is limited hiking from the camp on Fortress Lake up onto the alpine ridges and around the base of Chisel Peak near the glaciers. There are plans to have more routes marked soon, including an 11-km (7-mi.) trail along the lakeshore to be developed in conjunction with BC Parks. Other hiking in the area necessitates bushwhacking.

Useful Information

Some information about Hamber Park can be obtained by contacting the Visitor Services Coordinator, BC Parks, Prince George District, 1011-4th Ave., Prince George, B.C. V2L 3H9 (565-6340).

For information on float-plane flights to Fortress Lake, contact **Amiskwi Air** in Golden at 344-2534.

Write or call **Fortress Lake Wilderness Camp**, Box 26, Field, B.C., V0A 1G0 (343-6386 or 343-6481) to find out about accommodation there.

YOHO NATIONAL PARK

Yoho is a Cree word that translates roughly as "how magnificent," and visitors coming to walk and fish in this national park will soon understand how the region got its name.

The park is a 30-minute drive east of Golden on the Trans-Canada Highway. Along with the neighbouring national parks of Banff, Jasper and Kootenay and the renowned Burgess Shale, Yoho is part of the UNESCO Canadian Rockies World Heritage Site. Bounded by Banff National Park on the east and Kootenay National Park to the south, Yoho lies totally within the boundaries of B.C.

Yoho is a park of glacial lakes and towering mountain peaks. The steep mountains that caused enormous engineering problems for Canada's early railroad builders are responsible for the park's many waterfalls, which are part of the Kicking Horse River drainage basin. The river runs the more than 50 km (31 mi.) west from Wapta Lake to Golden, where it pours into the Columbia River. The portion of the Kicking Horse River within Yoho National Park was recently designated as a Canadian Heritage River, ensuring the long-term conservation of its natural, historic and recreational value.

Stunning waterfalls, 206 species of birds, exotic fossils, prolific wildlife and a 400-km (252-mi.) network of trails make Yoho a superb destination for the hiker. The townsite of Field, located within park boundaries, is the park's administration and main information centre, dispensing trail guides, maps and other resources year-round. The West and East information centres are open from mid-May to mid-October.

The park operates 3 roadside campgrounds during the summer: Kicking Horse, Hoodoos and Chancellor Peak. A walk-in campground lies a short distance from Takakkaw Falls, at 384 m (1260 ft.) the second highest waterfall in B.C. and one of the highest in Canada.

The best time of year to hike the high Rockies is in August and September, since snow can remain in the passes well into July. Strong sunscreens are recommended for protection against the higher altitude rays. Mosquitoes won't bother you above the tree line but take repellent for the forested areas. Nights are cool, so take a three-season sleeping bag if you are planning to camp, as well as a lightweight camping stove, since there is often a total ban on open fires.

One of the most common large mammals seen in Yoho is the elusive mountain goat, which is often mistaken for a mountain sheep. Goats are entirely white in colour and have short, shiny, black horns irrespective of their sex. Mountain sheep are brown with light-coloured rumps; females and young males have short, brown horns while mature males have large, thick, curled horns. If you are goat spotting, remember that they spend most of their time on cliffs and ledges as a safety precaution against their predators, bears and mountain lions. They eat grasses, ferns, mosses and lichens. In winter, a thick coat protects them from the cold while they graze on thin crusts of lichen. One of the best places to see these shy creatures is at the turnoff to the Yoho valley east of Field. Binoculars are a must here. Another favoured grazing spot can be seen from the lower Spiral Tunnels viewpoint near the park's eastern boundary, just past Field. (The tunnels, incidentally, were built by the CPR to ease the railway's climb from the Kicking Horse River valley to the summit of Kicking Horse Pass.)

Soon after you enter the park from the west, you will come to the trailhead to Wapta Falls, a one-hour hike over gentle terrain. Here the Kicking Horse River plunges 30 m (98 ft.) along a 61-m (200-ft.) width of cascade. The name Kicking Horse commemorates the efforts of geologist and naturalist James Hector, a member of the Palliser Expedition formed to search for passes through the Rockies in the mid-1800s. At one point, after Hector and his hungry men (they had only managed to catch two grouse and one trout in six days) forded a river, a horse kicked Hector in the chest and knocked him out for two hours. He remounted when he regained consciousness, and in great pain crossed what he called Kicking Horse Pass to shoot a moose, much to everyone's delight.

If you continue east along the Trans-Canada for another 22 km (13 mi.), you will arrive at the turnoff to Emerald Lake. Most travellers will want to turn here to see the flat-rock Natural Bridge, left behind when the Kicking Horse River wore a hole through the solid bedrock. A concrete walkway allows for safe viewing of this natural phenomenon.

A bit farther along this road lies Emerald Lake, one of the most photographed lakes in the Rockies. Beginning from the picnic area at the lake's edge, a 2-hour trail (5.2 km/3.2 mi.) loops the shoreline. The Emerald Lake Lodge, located right on the water, is renowned internationally for its luxurious accommodation.

The East Information Centre, east of Field, offers information on Takakkaw Falls, which is a 20-minute side trip up the Yoho Valley Road. For people interested in natural features resulting from glacial action, Takakkaw is an excellent example of hanging valley falls.

There are many day or overnight hikes in Yoho starting from the Takakkaw Falls parking lot. Trails double as nordic routes in winter, but beware of the extensive avalanche areas in the region, especially beyond the switchbacks.

You can take a full day or longer to hike and explore the new Yoho Iceline Trail along the western slope of the Yoho valley. Compared by some to the experience of hiking in the foothills of the Himalayas, since it winds over moraines and by turquoise tarns with constant views of mountains and glaciers, this trail is an ideal introduction to the Rockies. One particularly spectacular view is the sweep of Emerald Glacier below the rugged east face of the Vice-President. Hikers will also enjoy the beautiful vista of the Wapta Icefield, one of the largest icefields in the Rockies. Beginning above the Whiskey Jack Youth Hostel near the Takakkaw Falls parking lot, the trail makes a nice 18-km (11-mi.) loop above the tree line, travelling halfway down to Celeste Lake, around Laughing Falls and returning via the Yoho Valley Trail. There is a back-country campsite 11 km (6.8 mi.) along the Iceline in Little Yoho Valley. The Stanley Mitchell Hut, run by the Alpine Club of Canada, is also located here. Strong hikers can make a side trip from the campsite to the top of Twin Falls and over Whaleback Mountain for stunning views of glaciers.

Less ambitious hikers can walk the Yoho valley to Point Lace Falls or Laughing Falls in an afternoon by following the Yoho Glacier Trail, which ends 8.5 km (5.3 mi.) from the parking lot.

The area around Lake O'Hara is also very popular for hiking. Originally "discovered" by CPR surveyor J. J. McArthur, the region owes its name to his friend, Lieutenant-Colonel Robert O'Hara. O'Hara was so impressed that he returned many times to explore its lakes and mountains. Similarly impressed, the Alpine Club of Canada has hosted many annual camps in the alpine meadows near the lake. The club cabin, now called the Elizabeth Parker Hut, still exists and is the most heavily used noncommercial back-country facility in the mountain parks.

In 1926, the CPR, to encourage mountain travel, built a lodge on the shores of the lake. Since then, the Lake O'Hara Lodge has established a reputation as a splendid back-country destination, particularly in winter. The lodge contains a sauna, a picture gallery and a gourmet kitchen from which emerge such delicacies as prawns with Pernod and braised duck with cherry sauce to complement the many varieties of wine available from the cellar. But the lodge's prime attraction is the surrounding scenery—a ring of mountains 3000 m (9800 ft.) high that encircle the lake's blue waters. During summer, guests can stay either in the lodge or in small cabins on the lakeshore. In winter, accommodation is in the lodge only. Summer or winter, reservations are mandatory and should be made far in advance.

Access to the lake starts from a parking lot 11 km (7 mi.) west of Lake Louise, Alberta, on Highway 1A. From here, you can either hike the fire access road or follow the Cataract Brook Trail, a less direct but more interesting route. Another option is to reserve a place on the bus that regularly takes guests to and from the lodge. At the time of writing, a daily quota system is in place for day visitors using the bus in order to preserve the fragile natural environment and the back-country hiking experience in the area. To avoid disappointment, phone or write ahead to the park information centre to reserve space on the bus.

Reservations are also required for campsites at the lake and will ensure you a seat on the bus. You can book up to 2 months in advance, by phone or mail, through the park information office, and reservations must then be confirmed in person at the East Information Centre, where maps and the latest trail information are available. Like the other parks in the Rockies, this is bear country, so remember to hang your food from the bear poles erected at most backcountry camping sites.

A large network of trails radiates out from the lake, leading to a series of sparkling alpine lakes and flower-covered meadows and surrounded by such spectacular snow-capped peaks as Odaray Mountain, Mount Schaffer and Wiwaxy Peaks. After spending several days exploring the trails in the vicinity of the lake, ambitious hikers can continue on the Great Divide Trail through McArthur and Goodsir passes to connect up with the Rockwall Highline Trail described in the Kootenay National Park section of this chapter.

Skiing is also popular in the Lake O'Hara area. A day trip up the fire access road makes an enjoyable ski. Even better, an overnight stay at the Elizabeth Parker Hut or the Lake O'Hara Lodge will allow you to make additional trips around the lake or through the meadows and plateaus of the area.

A superb day trip for advanced skiers is the Lake O'Hara to Moraine Lake traverse, via Opabin and Wenkchemna passes. To save time, it is advisable to ski the fire road the afternoon before the trip and stay at either the lodge or the Elizabeth Parker Hut. The long, arduous trip is best done in the spring; even then, it can easily take 10 hours to complete. Check with the park wardens at the information centre in Field before leaving, as this is definitely avalanche terrain. Skiers should be equipped with avalanche transceivers and have a knowledge of avalanche rescue techniques.

Yoho National Park is also home to one of the most important fossil sites in the world, the Burgess Shale, located high above the tree line 5 km (3 mi.) west of Field. Named a UNESCO World Heritage Site in 1980, the 530-million-year-old site is less than a city block long but contains the remains of an ancient sea. More varieties of life are preserved in fantastic detail here than exist in all of our modern oceans.

It is not just the wealth of fossils (over 100 species of previously unknown soft-bodied animals) that makes the Burgess Shale so exciting, but their perfect state of preservation. Most measure only an inch or two in length, but strange species like a 7-13 cm (3-5 in.) predatory worm that fed on small mollusks can also be seen. One tiny cigar-shaped creature possesses 5 eyes and an elephant's trunk. Of the 140 species of animals identified in this Cambrian grave, some 85 per cent are distantly related to contemporary animals.

While the actual site of the Burgess Shale is closed to the public, Parks Canada puts out an excellent pamphlet on the fossils and offers guided interpretation trips to an exposed area of the Burgess Shale formation on nearby Mount Stephen.

A good book is Stephen Jay Gould's *Wonderful Life: The Burgess Shale and the Nature of History*, which tells the story of how the Burgess Shale came to be and how the fossilized creatures found here fit into the scheme of evolution.

Useful Information

Park maps and information are available from the Park Superintendent, Yoho National Park, Box 99, Field, B.C., V0A 1G0 (343-6324) or from the East or West information centres, located on the highway just inside the park boundaries, from mid-May to mid-October. To make reservations for the Lake O'Hara bus or campsites, call 343-6433.

For information about accommodation at **Lake O'Hara Lodge**, contact them in summer at Box 55, Lake Louise, Alberta, T0L 1E0 (604-343-6418) or in winter at Box 1677, Banff, Alberta, T0L 0C0 (403-762-2118).

Since the Whiskey Jack Youth Hostel is only open in summer and is very busy, reservations are recommended. Contact the Canadian Hostelling Association, Box 1358, Banff, Alberta, T0L 1C0 (403-762-4122).

KOOTENAY NATIONAL PARK

Abutting the southeast portion of Yoho National Park and a good chunk of the western boundary of Banff National Park, Kootenay National Park descends in a boot shape. Highway 93, which joins the Trans-Canada Highway at Castle Mountain, outside Banff, Alberta, runs down the spine of the park to Radium Hot Springs, situated at the park's southwestern toe.

Highway 93 takes hikers close to trailhead for the more than 200 km (125 mi.) of trails in this 140,600-ha (347,426-a.) park. There are three vehicle/tent campgrounds: Redstreak, McLeod Meadows and Marble Canyon.

Overnight trips within Kootenay require a park-use permit, obtainable from the park information centres up to 24 hours in advance of your trip; this applies year-round, as snowshoeing and nordic skiing trips have become more popular in recent years. As in other national parks, camping in Kootenay is restricted to designated campsites only, most of which operate on a quota system. During the popular summer months, it is advisable to reserve accommodation at these sites early to avoid disappointment. Mail reservations are accepted.

Kootenay contains within its boundaries the valleys of the Vermilion and Kootenay rivers and encompasses part of the Main and Western ranges of the Rocky Mountains. The juxtaposition of mountain ranges and wide, open valleys makes for superlative hiking conditions. A range of climatic conditions (it is hotter and drier in the south near Radium Hot Springs) makes for a broad variety of plant species, from blue-bunch wheat grass to white rhododendrons. Over 150 species of birds inhabit Kootenay Park, as well as a wide range of mammals, including plenty of bears, mule deer and Rocky Mountain bighorn sheep.

One of the best-known hikes here is the Rockwall Highline Trail, a 3- or 4-day backpack along the base of the Kootenay Wall between Helmet Falls and Floe Lake. The Kootenay Wall is a 500-m (1640-ft.) escarpment along the eastern face of the Vermilion Range of the Rockies. Most hikers travel the 53-km (32-mi.) trail from north to south, keeping the snowy side of the peaks in view. The hike starts on Highway 93 at the Paint Pots, natural ochre beds which native Kutenai people used as pigment and in trade, and culminates in a view of Floe Lake, at the foot of the wall just beyond Numa Pass. Reservations for wilderness campsites must be made at the Marble Canyon Information Office before you head out. Greater Heights Mountain Adventures offers guided trips along this trail.

For those wanting a longer trip, this hike can be started at Lake O'Hara; follow the Continental Divide over McArthur and Goodsir passes to meet the Rockwall Highline Trail at Helmet Creek. If you are really ambitious, you can cross the highway at the Floe Lake parking lot and continue along the Ball Pass Trail into Banff National Park, passing through the scenic Egypt Lakes area. From there, the trail goes through Simpson Pass, past Sunshine Ski Village to Citadel Pass, and into Mount Assiniboine Provincial Park. Exit to civilization at the Spray Lakes Reservoir west of Canmore, Alberta, by way of either Assiniboine Pass or Wonder Pass. This excellent alpine hike covers quite a distance; from Lake O'Hara to the Floe Lake parking lot is 72 km (45 mi.), and it is another 64 km (40 mi.) to Spray Lakes from there. This route forms part of the (as yet informal) long-distance Great Divide Trail. Once again, remember that you are in bear country and use the bear poles at most of the back-country campsites to hang packs and food.

Another popular Kootenay hike is the day trip to the Stanley Glacier. A well-graded trail runs for 4.4 km (2.8 mi.) from the parking lot on Highway 93 into a basin of jumbled boulders in the shadow of the active glacier. This is also a favourite ski trail in winter. Other nordic ski trails in the area are the Simpson River Trail (16 km/10 mi. return) and Hector Gorge (11 km/7 mi. return).

The Kootenay and Vermilion rivers offer some exciting rafting opportunities as well as a chance to see wildlife.

Useful Information

Park information and wilderness campsite reservations can be obtained from the Park Superintendent, Kootenay National Park, Box 220, Radium Hot Springs, B.C., V0A 1M0 (347-9615) or from the Information Centres at Marble Canyon or West Gate, which are open from June to early September.

Detailed descriptions of the hikes in Kootenay Park can be found in *The Canadian Rockies Trail Guide* by Brian Patton. *British Columbia Cross Coun-*

Campground at Magog Lake, Mount Assiniboine Park. *Photo by Mary Simpson*

try Ski Routes by Richard and Rochelle Wright details some ski trips in the park. It's out of print, so look for it in libraries and used bookstores.

Greater Heights Mountain Adventures, Box 2147, Banff, Alberta, T0L 0C0 (613-232-6275) offers guided trips along the Rockwall Highline Trail. **Adventure Canada**, 1159 West Broadway, Vancouver, B.C., V6H 1G1 (736-7447) offers combined hiking and rafting trips in Kootenay Park.

Contact **Glacier Raft Company** at Box 428, Golden, B.C., V0A 1H0 or call 344-6521 in Golden or 347-9218 in Radium for information on their Kootenay River raft trips.

MOUNT ASSINIBOINE PARK

Tucked into the instep of Kootenay National Park, Mount Assiniboine Park is often mistakenly thought to be in Alberta. In fact, the eastern boundary of this roughly triangular, 38,600-ha (95,380-a.) park is the B.C./Alberta border.

The slightly tilted Matterhorn-shaped peak that dominates this park is of course the 3618-m (11,867-ft.) Mount Assiniboine, first scaled in 1901. No point in the park lies below 1500 m (4900 ft.). For centuries, the Assiniboine Indians successfully hunted the Rocky Mountain elk, mule deer, moose, mountain goats and bighorn sheep that still abound in the area.

Lakes stud the southeast corner of the park; the biggest, Lake Magog, lies at the foot of Assiniboine Peak. The park's 60 km (38 mi.) of trails are well utilized year-round, since hiking and skiing are the main ways to get into the park (helicopter travel is the other). Highway 93, through Kootenay National Park, and Highway 1, through Banff National Park, provide the closest road access to Assiniboine.

One of the most popular ways of travelling into the park in summer is by hiking across the meadows backing onto the Sunshine Village near Banff, Alberta. The trail leads from the Sunshine gondola to Lake Magog via Quartzridge, Citadel Pass, Golden Valley and Valley of the Rocks; it's a good 7 hour hike covering 27 km (17 mi.).

Other popular hiking routes to Lake Magog are the Spray Lakes Reservoir route, which begins west of Canmore, Alberta, and leads into the park via Assiniboine or Wonder passes, and the Simpson River route, which begins on Highway 93, just south of the Vermilion River bridge.

In winter, the route from Sunshine Village should be tackled only by experienced and well-equipped ski tourers because of the avalanche dangers at Citadel Pass and the confusing, undulating terrain of the Valley of the Rocks. If you do travel in on this route, be sure to read the daily avalanche hazard bulletins posted at the Sunshine ski area. The 28-km (17.6-mi.) ski-in via Assiniboine Pass is the best and safest way to reach the gem of this park, the 60-year-old Mount Assiniboine Lodge.

Built by the Canadian Pacific Railway in 1928, the lodge sits at an elevation of 2170 m (7118 ft.), making it the highest lodge of its kind in Canada. It offers accommodation for 22 people in its main lodge and cabins, which are located in a picturesque setting overlooking Lake Magog. The lodge caters to wilderness hikers and ski tourers with a combination of European-style hospitality and outdoor expertise. Gourmet food and soft beds are a fine way to end days of hiking in the alpine or telemark touring with host Sepp Renner, a certified mountain guide who spent 14 years as a helicopter skiing guide.

The main camping area in Mount Assiniboine Park is situated on the west side of Lake Magog. A group camping area with space for up to 25 people, at nearby O'Brien Meadows, is available by reservation from the East Kootenay parks office. Camping is also permitted at the north end of Og Lake. The Naiset Cabins, 4 alpine shelters on the east side of Lake Magog, are another popular destination. From December 1 to May 31, these cabins are available by reservation. Climbing shelters also exist in the Assiniboine Bowl (the R. C. Hind Hut) and at Surprise Creek, Mitchell River and Police Meadows.

Assiniboine offers excellent and varied hiking; be sure to consult *The Canadian Rockies Trail Guide* for detailed information. Helicopter access into the park is available from Banff or Canmore on specific days of the week. Winter skiing conditions are usually perfect in the park's fine, light, powdery Rocky Mountain snow. Helicopter access is recommended but those who wish to ski in should follow the routes and advice in *Ski Trails in the Canadian Rockies*. Winter camping in Mount Assiniboine Park is becoming more and more popular with hearty adventurers.

Useful Information

Information on the park and reservations for the campground and Naiset Cabins can be obtained from the Visitor Services Coordinator, BC Parks, East Kootenay District, Box 118, Wasa, B.C., V0B 2K0 (422-3212).

For information or reservations at **Assiniboine Lodge**, write to Box 1527, Canmore, Alberta, T0L 0M0 or call 403-678-2883.

Information on helicopter flights can be obtained from **Canadian Helicopters** in Canmore at 403-762-4082.

Five Seasons, 3201 Kingsway, Vancouver, B.C., V5R 5K3 (435-5444); **Greater Heights Mountain Adventures**, Box 2147, Banff, Alberta, T0L 0C0 (613-232-6275), and **Adventure Canada**, 1159 West Broadway, Vancouver, B.C. V6H 1G1 (736-7447) offer guided hiking trips into Assiniboine.

Pioneer on Skis by Erling Strom tells the story of the early days of Assiniboine Lodge. In another interesting book, entitled *Lizzie Rummel, Baroness of the Canadian Rockies*, Ruth Oltmann describes the role this interesting woman played in establishing and managing back-country lodges in this region of the province.

RADIUM HOT SPRINGS

The town of Radium Hot Springs (pop. 300) lies 105 km (65 mi.) south of Golden at the junction of Highways 95 and 93.

The hot springs that give the town its name are accessible to the public at the Radium Aquacourt, located east of town and just inside the boundary of Kootenay National Park. The hot pool is kept at 40° C (103° F), and the cool pool at 27° C (80° F). Principal salts found in the springs include calcium sulphate, magnesium sulphate (Epsom salt), sodium sulphate (Glauber's salt) and calcium bicarbonate. The hot pool is particularly popular in winter after a day of skiing—your hair is frozen in the chilly air while the rest of your body relaxes in the hot water. For some interesting information about these springs, pick up the Parks Canada brochure entitled "Nipika: A Story of Radium Hot Springs" from the park information centre.

The Radium Hot Springs Lodge, across the road from the Aquacourt, provides a convenient base for alpine skiers at nearby Panorama Mountain, and heli-skiing operators will take downhillers into the Bugaboo Range from here.

Some fine Rockies hiking is available in the Diana Lake–Pinnacle Creek area northwest of Radium off Highway 95. The privately owned Diana Lake Cabin can be booked by individuals or groups; it sleeps 12 and has both an airtight heater and a wood stove. The cabin is an 8-km (5-mi.) hike from the end of the Pinnacle Creek Road. It can also be reached by helicopter from Canmore or Radium Hot Springs.

Pinnacle Meadows is at the centre of some of the best wilderness hiking in the western Rockies. These high alpine meadows harbour many species of plants, some of which take 15-20 years to flower and have adapted to the specific climatic conditions here in order to survive. Cushion plants like moss campion grow long taproots for anchorage in the shallow soil. Other plants, such as saxifrage and stonecrop, hug the ground and produce waxy or leathery leaves to avoid being dried out by the wind. Anemones have a furry coating on leaves and stems to trap heat; young plants are red, containing their own inbuilt PABA sunscreen to protect sensitive tissues from sunburn.

Another popular spot for hikers, cyclists, paddlers, fisherpeople and skiers is Taliesin Guest House, three quarters of an hour north of Radium on Highway 95. The guest house is situated on the forested benchlands overlooking the Columbia River Valley, a major migration flyway for birds. Guest bedrooms face onto either the Septet Range near the Bugaboos or majestic Tower Peak.

Using Taliesin as a base, hikers and climbers can go into the Bugaboos, Yoho National Park or Kootenay National Park. Nordic skiers skim along the edge of the Columbia River Valley or follow old logging trails in the hills around the guest house.

Canoeists can meander down the Columbia or try the more difficult waters of Toby Creek, the Kootenay River or sections of the Kicking Horse River. Two companies currently offer raft trips on the Kootenay River and through the remote White River Canyon. The White River joins the Kootenay River near Kootenay National Park after flowing north from the Continental Divide near Top of the World Park.

Just north of Radium (take Highway 93 to Settlers Road, then travel to Mile 9) is the Nipika Touring Centre. Nipika's 20 km (12.6 mi.) of nordic loop trails near the confluence of the Cross and Kootenay rivers lead into Kootenay National Park.

Useful Information

For information on the hot springs and the surrounding areas, call the Radium Hot Springs Information Office at 327-9331.

To make accommodation reservations, contact **Radium Hot Springs Lodge**, Box 70, Radium Hot Springs, B.C., V0A 1M0 (347-9622) or the

Taliesin Guest House, Box 101, Parson, B.C., V0A 1L0 (348-2247). For information on the **Diana Lake Cabin** at Pinnacle Meadows, write to Box 2397, Banff, Alberta, T0L 0C0 or call 403-762-4396.

Glacier Raft Company, Box 428, Golden, B.C., V0A 1H0 (call 344-6521 in Golden or 347-9218 in Radium) and **Kootenay River Runners,** Box 81, Edgewater, B.C., V0A 1E0 (347-9210) offer trips on the White and Kootenay rivers.

For information about the **Nipika Touring Centre,** contact them at Box 903, Invermere, B.C., V0A 1K0 (342-3130).

THE BUGABOOS

Bugaboo Glacier Provincial Park and Alpine Recreation Area, to the west of Radium Hot Springs, lies at the northern part of the Purcell Mountains and contains the range's largest icefields.

Long a favourite with many of North America's 200,000 mountain climbers, the Bugaboo Mountains were formed some 70 million years ago when molten rock welled up to create massive intrusions within the old metamorphic rocks of the Purcells. Subsequent weathering by water and glacial ice removed much of the weak overlying rock, revealing the solid granite masses and chiselling them into the spectacular spires now known collectively as the Bugaboos.

It was climbers like the legendary Austrian guide Conrad Kain (1883-1934) who first alerted North Americans to the recreational possibilities of the Bugaboos. The name is thought to have come from an early Scottish prospector who declared the area a "bugaboo" on account of its loneliness. And solitude is what most hikers and climbers in this 25,000 ha (61,775 a.) of wilderness will find.

Access is along a good gravel road, open late spring through late fall, leading from Brisco, 27 km (17 mi.) north of Radium Hot Springs on Highway 95, to a public parking lot just outside the park boundary. Visitors should not use the private parking lot belonging to Bugaboo Lodge unless permission has been received. Thundering logging trucks mean you should exercise caution at all times on the road.

From the parking lot, a steep 5-km (3-mi.) trail follows the lateral moraine of the Bugaboo Glacier to the Boulder Camp and the Conrad Kain Hut, which provides accommodation for 50 people. The hut is maintained by the parks division and a fee is charged for its use. However, visitors should not assume that there will be room in the hut and should be equipped with all the necessary equipment for wilderness camping. Another hut, the Malloy Igloo, accommodates a maximum of 6 people. Many climbers start out from the Conrad Kain

Hut to climb North Hauser Tower, Pigeon Spire and Bugaboo Spire. The 13-km (8-mi.) route from the hut to the Malloy Igloo, located on Malloy Glacier, is recommended only for roped parties, as several glaciers have to be crossed along the way.

From the Bugaboo Lodge parking lot, a major, quite underutilized trail leads to the azure waters of Cobalt Lake (also known as Blue Lake on some maps) at the northern limit of the Bugaboos. One of the great views on this hike is from the ridge that divides the Bugaboo and Vowell creek drainages and lies entirely above the tree line at 2400 m. The Septet Range covers the eastern skyline and the Bugaboo and Vowell peaks rise up in the south and west. A faint trail continues north along the open ridge for 16 km (10 mi.). Cobalt Lake, cradled between Northpost, Brenta and Cobalt lake spires, is an easy hike down from the ridge across alpine meadows. From the lake, it's a 2-hour hike to the shoulder of Northpost Spire. Another route, involving some glacier travel, leads to the Conrad Kain Hut. The Cobalt Lake area is quite a popular destination for heli-hikers.

The Bugaboo Lodge, operated by Canadian Mountain Holidays, offers accommodation as well as heli-hiking and heli-skiing trips.

Useful Information

For more information on the Bugaboos, get the brochure available from the Visitor Services Coordinator, BC Parks, East Kootenay District, Box 118, Wasa, B.C., V0B 2K0 (422-3212).

Canadian Mountain Holidays runs the Bugaboo Lodge and offers heli-hiking and heli-ski trips into the area. Contact them at Box 1660, Banff, Alberta, T0L 0C0 (403-762-4531).

INVERMERE

A small town of almost 2000 people on the shores of Windermere Lake, 16 km (10 mi.) south of Radium Hot Springs, Invermere is the regional service centre of the Upper Columbia Valley. Explorer David Thompson first visited here in 1807, establishing Kootenae House, a fur-trading post close to the mouth of Toby Creek. From here, he set out to map the vast wilderness between the Rockies and the mouth of the Columbia River.

Today, Invermere caters to summer visitors. It is very popular with Albertans since it is only 3½ hours from Calgary by car. The town's Windermere Valley Pioneer Museum's main log building was once the Lake Windermere Station at Athalmer, a small town a short distance away. When a freight train was derailed and plowed through the station one day in 1975, the CPR considered the building to be irreparable and sold it to the Windermere District

Historical Society for a dollar. A federal government grant was obtained to cover the costs of hauling the station building up the hill to Invermere and restoring it. Among the museum's artifacts are a Shuswap Indian dugout canoe, a copy of David Thompson's journal, of which only 500 copies were made before the plates were destroyed, and many mementoes of early stern-wheeler days and pioneer times.

Windermere Lake is a good spot for sailing and paddling, while Athalmer Beach Provincial Park, on the lake's shores, is a popular base for campers and sail boarders. Panorama Resort, about 17.5 km (11 mi.) west of downtown Invermere, is a year-round focal point, offering hotel and condominium accommodation as well as opportunities for alpine and nordic skiing and summer hiking—Panorama Mountain is crisscrossed with 25 km (16 mi.) of looped, groomed trails. Call the resort at 342-6941 for information. Keep in mind that the weather in the Purcells can be very fickle, so you should always take a day pack with extra warm clothes, even in mild weather.

HEIGHT OF THE ROCKIES WILDERNESS AREA

As a result of the 12-year struggle by the Palliser Wilderness Society to preserve this area for recreation and wildlife, the Height of the Rockies was established as B.C.'s first Provincial Forest Wilderness Area in August 1987.

The Height of the Rockies covers 73,000 ha (180,038 a.) east of Invermere. A wildlife-rich wilderness of alpine lakes, it is home to an estimated 1800 mountain goats, 100 grizzly bears, 2000 deer and 2000 elk. It encompasses 15 peaks more than 3000 m (9800 ft.) high, making much of the area above the tree line. It is currently administered by the provincial forests ministry from its Invermere district office.

Four trailheads, which can be reached by gravel road in summer, provide access to the Height of the Rockies area. They are situated at Forsyth Creek in the southeast, at both the middle and north forks of the White River, and at the end of the Palliser River Road (an extension of Settlers Road, 14 km/9 mi. north of Radium Hot Springs on Highway 93). Other access is via alpine pass trails leading from Banff National Park and Peter Lougheed Provincial Park in Alberta, or the Elks Lake Provincial Park and Recreation Area on the B.C./Alberta border south of Banff National Park.

Palliser River Guides and Outfitters have run horse-pack trips in this area for many years. Their trips provide opportunities for hiking and fishing as well as trail rides through spectacular scenery. Contact them at Box 238, Radium Hot Springs, B.C., V0A 1M0 (347-9274).

Plans to further develop trails and campsites in the wilderness area are currently under review by the Ministry of Forests. Call the district office in Invermere (342-4200) for information.

FAIRMONT HOT SPRINGS

The resort centre of Fairmont Hot Springs, 24 km (15 mi.) south of Invermere on Highway 93/95, caters in winter to skiers and in summer to hikers and paddlers. At both times of the year, visitors can benefit from the curative powers of the 35-45° C (95-115° F) waters of the resort's 1000-sq.-m (10,000-sq.-ft.) pool, which is open to the public. The Kutenai Indians were the first to use the odourless and sulphurless Fairmont waters for medicinal purposes.

A meandering 3- to 5-day paddle along the headwaters of the Columbia River in this area is popular with families and experts alike. Put-in is on Columbia Lake or where Highway 93/95 crosses the river just near the hot springs and take-out is 235 km (146 mi.) later at Donald Station, north of Golden on the Trans-Canada Highway. Birders on this route can expect to spot ospreys, eagles, ducks and great blue herons. Flat gravel sandbars, suitable for camping, occur frequently, and anglers can catch a variety of trout and sometimes sturgeon.

Another pleasant canoe route in this area is a 2- to 3-day trip along the Kootenay River from Canal Flats, south of Fairmont Hot Springs, to Fort Steele, the site of the North-West Mounted Police post established by Major Sam Steele in 1887. The Kootenay River trip passes through scenic wilderness unsurpassed anywhere in the province; wildlife is abundant and there are few hazards along the way.

Two rafting races are held annually on the Kootenay River. The first, part of the Kimberley Beer Festival, is held in July and runs from Canal Flats to Fort Steele. The second coincides with the Sam Steele celebrations at Cranbrook in August and goes from Bummer's Flats to Fort Steele.

Useful Information

Information on hiking and skiing trails, as well as Forest Service campsites, is contained in the Forest Service Recreation Sites brochure for the Invermere district. A copy can be obtained from the Ministry of Forests, Nelson Region, 518 Lake St., Nelson, B.C., V1L 4C6 (354-6286).

Contact the Kimberley Travel Infocentre, Box 63, Kimberley, B.C., V1A 2Y5 (427-3666) for information on raft races and other activities in the area.

WHITESWAN LAKE, TOP OF THE WORLD AND PREMIER LAKE PROVINCIAL PARKS

South of Canal Flats, north of Cranbrook and Kimberley, and east of the Columbia River lie three parks in an alpine region of spectacular beauty representative of the best of the Rocky Mountain region of B.C. Good gravel roads branch east off Highway 93/95 just south of Canal Flats, leading to Whiteswan Lake, Top of the World and Premier Lake.

In both winter and summer, the natural hot springs beside the Lussier River provide welcome respite for nordic skiers and hikers in Whiteswan. Whiteswan Lake is a major destination for rainbow trout fishing; only fly fishing is allowed at Alces Lake. At Alces—the Latin word for "moose"—visitors can observe the many Shiras moose, a subspecies whose range is confined to this corner of B.C.

The jewel in this three-park crown is undoubtedly Top of the World Park, legendary among both hikers and fisherpeople. Back-country camping, hiking, fishing, ski-touring and mountaineering provide the main adventuring opportunities here, and many people use the Fish Lake Cabin as a base. Most of the park is at or above 1800 m (5900 ft.) and Mount Morro, at 2912 m (9551 ft.), dominates the park. The area was once the traditional home of the Kutenai Indians. As many archaeological sites show, the Kutenai mined chert, a highly valuable glossy grey rock they used for making fine weapons and tools and traded south to Montana and east to Alberta.

The 6-km (4-mi.) hike from the parking area to Fish Lake is a good one for families. Advanced hikers branch out from Fish Lake to Coyote Creek Campsite, Summer Pass, Wildhorse Ridge, Sparkle Lake and Alpine Viewpoint. Fish Lake itself is remarkably clear and cold (10° C/50° F). It is subject to sudden squalls, so anglers who use rafts to get out onto the lake should be sure to wear life-jackets. The Fish Lake Cabin, accommodating 20-25 people, is available for overnight use on a first-come, first-served basis, with firewood and stove supplied. A small fee is charged for its use. Anglers keen to fish the lake for its plentiful cutthroat and Dolly Varden trout must ensure they possess a valid B.C. fishing licence before they enter the park. Horses are permitted in the park on the Fish Lake, Coyote Creek and Galbraith Creek trails only.

Other attractions of Top of the World Park include an almost constant kaleidoscope of summer flowers, occasional sightings of large mammals such as Rocky Mountain bighorn sheep and mountain goats, and good birding. The biggest pests are porcupines, who will chew on boots or fishing tackle if you leave them lying around.

Premier Lake Provincial Park, the final park in this trio, is accessible via a 15-km (9-mi.) gravel road that heads east from Highway 93/95 just north of Skookumchuck. The 4 lakes in this forested, 662-ha (1635-a.) park offer great fishing and are linked by hiking trails. In winter, Premier is a major range for deer, elk and bighorn sheep, who graze here at the base of the sawlike Hughes Range.

More information on Whiteswan Lake, Top of the World and Premier Lake parks can be obtained from the Visitor Services Coordinator, BC Parks, East Kootenay Division, Box 118, Wasa Lake, B.C., V0B 2K0 (422-3212).

KIMBERLEY

The highest city in Canada at 1117 m (3663 ft.), the mining community of Kimberley is situated 100 km (62 mi.) south of Fairmont Hot Springs. Kimberley, which looks like a Bavarian alpine village, is a fun place to visit, and in winter it's a good base for downhill and back-country skiing in the Purcell Mountains. The Purcell Range here in the southeastern part of the province doesn't get the cold, wet slush that sometimes falls on the Coast Mountains, or the extreme temperatures that you can encounter in the Rockies, so it is ideal for back-country touring.

Most back-country operators provide telemark instruction as well as an introduction to the use of skins for ski-touring. Skins, two long, thin, synthetic strips with a sticky side that attaches to the bottom of the ski and a furry side that provides traction for uphill climbs, are essential equipment for mountain touring.

Useful Information

The Forest Service Recreation Sites map of southeastern B.C. is a good general reference guide to back roads, trails and campsites in the area. A copy can be obtained from the Ministry of Forests, Nelson Region, 518 Lake St., Nelson, B.C., V1L 4C6 (354-6286).

Ptarmigan Tours offers several week-long hut-to-hut ski tours in the southern Purcells. Contact them at Box 11, Kimberley, B.C., V1A 2Y5 (422-3270).

PURCELL WILDERNESS CONSERVANCY AREA/ST. MARY'S ALPINE PROVINCIAL PARK

We cover the Purcell Wilderness Conservancy in our chapter on the Kootenays because of the access from Argenta on the northeast side of Kootenay Lake. But access to the area is also possible from several points between Invermere and Kimberley, the most developed being the Toby Creek Trail to Earl Grey Pass. Historically, this is an interesting route to take into the wilderness, since Earl Grey's summer cabin still stands on Toby Creek, 3 km (1.9 mi.) from the eastern end of the trail. Grey, a Governor General of Canada and sponsor of football's famous Grey Cup, was one of the first proponents of recreational use for this patch of wilderness.

Many of the trails were built and used prior to the 1930s and only remnants remain. Trails above timber line are usually easy to follow but access trails through forested valleys are often overgrown. The B.C. Forestry Service has tried to open up some trails but the hiker should be prepared for strenuous travel and some bushwhacking.

Attached to the Purcell Wilderness Conservancy's southern boundary are the 9000 ha (22,240 a.) of St. Mary's Alpine Provincial Park. High in the Southern Purcells, the park is characterized by steep and rocky alpine terrain ideal for summer hiking, wilderness camping and winter ski-touring.

Because of recent mining exploration near the boundary of the park, access to St. Mary's is no longer the arduous bushwhack of days gone by. St. Mary's Lake Road, approximately 45 km (28 mi.) long, leads into the park from Kimberley. The road is rough, so a four-wheel-drive vehicle is advised.

Because of its location, the park has few visitors. Hikers who do venture into St. Mary's often choose fall, when the larch is turning a brilliant gold, for their visit. There's lots to explore here: 29 lakes and tarns, 7 creeks and many high waterfalls and cataracts.

The northern part of the park, which lies entirely above the tree line, is the most spectacular. Two attractive and accessible lakes, Totem and Price, are definitely worth a visit.

Ski-tourers can make a south-north traverse of the park. Starting from some steep slopes east of Mount Manson, you ski across a necklace of alpine lakes to Lyali Lake before heading to Bleak Lake; this is followed by a run along the west ridge of the park's highest peak, Mount St. Mary, and then a descent into Wesley Creek, where most skiers will want to make a detour to the Dewar Hot Springs. These springs are so hot that a permanently rigged hose siphons cold water from a nearby creek to make the water temperature tolerable for humans.

Ptarmigan Tours has several huts in the Purcells just outside the park boundary and has run hut-to-hut skiing expeditions in this area for over a decade. Week-long tours lead through glacial cirques (steep-sided basins), powder bowls, high passes and treed alpine valleys. Sound instruction in nordic skiing techniques and avalanche safety are mainstays of the trips. Most tours start and finish at the main Ptarmigan Lodge, complete with a sauna and such hearty fare as elk stroganoff and roast chicken. Tours, offered from mid-December to the end of March, include helicopter transportation, meals, accommodation and avalanche transceivers.

Useful Information

To find out more about the Purcell Wilderness Conservancy or St. Mary's Alpine Provincial Park, including detailed access and trail information, contact the Visitor Services Coordinator, BC Parks, East Kootenay District, Box 118, Wasa, B.C., V0B 2K0 (422-3212).

For information on the expeditions run by **Ptarmigan Tours**, contact them at Box 11, Kimberley, B.C., V1A 2Y5 (422-3270).

The Earl Grey Trail is described in Bob Harris's *The Best of B.C. Hiking Trails*.

FORT STEELE PROVINCIAL HERITAGE PARK

The heritage village of Fort Steele has undergone four major phases in its history. Situated on a bend in the Kootenay River about 98 km (61 mi.) south of Fairmont Hot Springs on Highway 93/95, it is now a major summer tourist destination, a heritage site representative of an East Kootenay turn-of-the-century village. In days gone by, it was the site of the Kootenay River ferry crossing on the Dewdney Trail from Hope to Wild Horse Creek, a short distance away.

Rich placer diggings of gold in Wild Horse Creek fuelled the first gold rush here in 1864. By the late 1880s disputes had arisen with the local Kutenai people, who objected to the fencing of their land. As a result, Samuel B. Steele and a detachment of 75 North-West Mounted Police rode in from Alberta to build the first NWMP post in British Columbia. A subsequent major silver-lead boom led to more prosperity for Fort Steele, but its importance was totally eclipsed in 1898 when the B.C. Southern Railway chose Cranbrook as its divisional point. After a ghost-town phase in the early part of the century, Fort Steele was gradually restored by the provincial government, so today's visitors can explore the approximately 50 buildings, watch a show at the excellent Wild Horse Theatre, see a printing press in action and generally be reminded of Fort Steele's former glories.

Fort Steele is also a base for side trips to Wasa Lake Provincial Park, with its excellent beaches and good fishing; Kikomun Creek Provincial Park, another good fishing spot just west of Elko, and the Kootenay Trout Hatchery.

Contact the Visitor Services Coordinator, BC Parks, Fort Steele, B.C., V0B 1N0 (489-3351) for further information about the heritage park and surrounding area.

CRANBROOK

With a population of over 16,500 people and a history that stretches back to its incarnation as the Kutenai village of A'Qkisga'ktlect, Cranbrook, 16 km (10 mi.) south of Fort Steele, is the major city in the southern B.C. Rockies and has the only commercial airport in the region.

Situated in the Rocky Mountain Trench, the city's economic bases are forestry, mining, ranching, transportation and tourism. It claims more sunshine hours than any other community in the province!

Within a 50-mile radius of Cranbrook over 100 lakes provide paddling and fishing opportunities. A 500,000-year-old tilobite bed exists just a few miles east of the city. And the town itself is proud of its heritage; its downtown is full of large, imposing homes and buildings from past eras.

FERNIE

The town of Fernie, picturesquely situated in the Elk River Valley on the Crowsnest Highway (Highway 3) east of Cranbrook, provides a jumping-off point for quite a few adventure activities.

There's good sailing, fishing and paddling on nearby Lake Koocanusa, and white-water rafting day trips on the Elk and Bull rivers provide opportunities for hoodoo and wildlife viewing. (Hoodoos are weird-looking pillar formations that result from water erosion.) The Fernie Snow Valley Resort, 14 km (7 mi.) west of town, is a year-round base for outdoor activities.

South of Fernie, on Lake Koocanusa, lies 560-ha (1384-a.) Kikomun Creek Provincial Park. The painted turtles here are a major attraction. Kids particularly love watching these creatures. The turtles were erroneously thought to hibernate in winter, but are in fact up and about year-round.

Kikomun is a good cycling park, since a network of paved roads links small, warm-water lakes. Fishing for smallmouth bass is good in these lakes and visitors can also view spawning channels, badgers, turkey vultures and heron rookeries nearby.

At the foot of the rugged Lizard Mountain range, 10 km (6 mi.) west of Fernie, Island Lake sits close to tree line at an elevation of 1370 m (4494 ft.) and is surrounded by giant cedars. Island Lake Lodge, a log building that accommodates 24 people, is an ideal spot from which to do some hiking or back-country skiing. Over 15 km (10 mi.) of nordic trails branch out from the lodge and the opportunities for alpine ski-touring in the snow-filled bowls surrounding Island Lake are limitless. The snow conditions are often better here than on the eastern slopes of the Rockies. Access to the lodge is by road in summer and by snow cat in winter.

Paddling possibilities in the Fernie area include the 5-day trip down Elk River from its headwaters north of Elkford to Elko, on Highway 3 south of Fernie. The Elk was named "Stag River" by David Thompson for the large number of elk or wapiti that could be seen along the valley, and wildlife viewing is still good. Paddlers should have some experience and should watch for log jams and sweepers.

Useful Information

The Fernie Travel Infocentre, Box 747, Rotary Park, Highway 3, Fernie, B.C., V0B 1M0 (423-6868) can provide information on parks and activities in the area.

Contact **Island Lake Mountain Tours**, Box 580, Fernie, B.C., V0B 1M0 (423-3700) for more information on accommodation and skiing and hiking tours.

ELK LAKES PROVINCIAL PARK

Directly north of Fernie on Highways 3 and 43 lies Elk Lakes Park, a hike-in wilderness camping park in the Front Ranges of the Rocky Mountains. Its lake waters, although too cold for swimming, are good for fishing, and its mountains and glaciers offer good alpine hiking and challenging mountain climbing. Wildlife, though not abundant, can still be observed. To get to the park, turn north off Highway 3 at Sparwood onto Highway 43. The first 30 km (19 mi.) to the town of Elkford are paved but the road changes to gravel and gets progressively rougher as it heads north. Check in Elkford for current conditions.

Contact the Visitor Services Coordinator, BC Parks, East Kootenay District, Box 118, Wasa, B.C., V0B 2K0 (422-3212) for further information on access and trails.

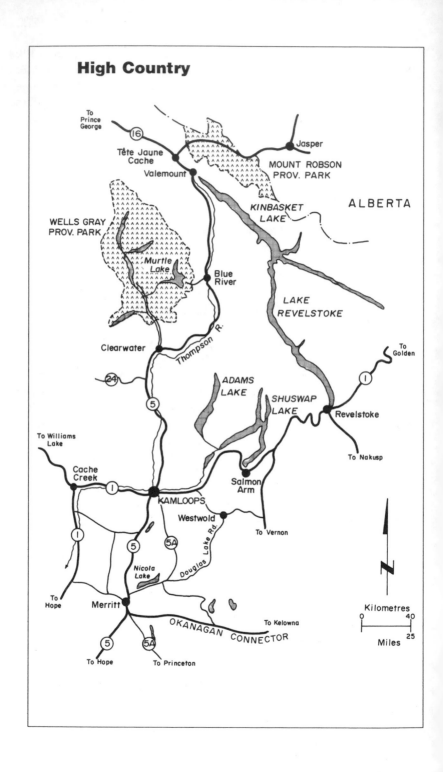

High Country

To Prince George

16

Tête Jaune Cache

Valemount

Jasper

MOUNT ROBSON PROV. PARK

KINBASKET LAKE

ALBERTA

WELLS GRAY PROV. PARK

Murtle Lake

Blue River

LAKE REVELSTOKE

Clearwater

Thompson R.

24

5

ADAMS LAKE

SHUSWAP LAKE

To Golden

1

Revelstoke

To Williams Lake

Cache Creek

1

To Nakusp

KAMLOOPS

Salmon Arm

Westwold

Douglas Lake Rd.

To Vernon

To Hope

1

5

5A

Nicola Lake

To Kelowna

Merritt

OKANAGAN CONNECTOR

5

5A

To Hope

To Princeton

Kilometres
0   40

25
Miles

CHAPTER 7

High Country

B.C.'s high country sweeps in a great arc north and east of the town of Merritt to include the Nicola River valley and the upland country of the Douglas Plateau, part of the vast Thompson Plateau, which separates the Coast Mountain range in the west from the Monashee Mountains in the east.

As its name implies, this is high plateau country, much of it 2000 m (6440 ft.) above sea level. Rivers that drain the region include the Nicola River, which rises in the Douglas Plateau and joins the Thompson River at Spences Bridge. The mighty Fraser River begins as a trickle in Mount Robson Park, while the Clearwater River rises in Wells Gray Provincial Park. The terrain runs the gamut from pine-forested lake country to natural bunch-grass ranchland, the site of legendary spreads like the Douglas Lake Cattle Ranch. The Cariboo Mountains slice through Wells Gray Park, while on the slopes of Mount Robson adventurers can glimpse the sort of dense, first growth forest commonly seen in the coastal wetlands.

High country weather is as varied as its topography. Winters are cold, with temperatures seldom climbing above the freezing mark, and there is lots of snow at higher elevations. The Coquihalla Valley, for example, is noted for its annual snowfall, which can make travel on the Coquihalla Highway during winter a bit of a white-knuckle affair! Spring usually arrives in the region during April and May, covering hillsides with wildflowers. Summers are hot, with temperatures rising in places like the Nicola Valley to the 40° C (104° F) mark. July, August and September, the most popular months for visiting, are often punctuated with spectacular thunderstorms.

The Interior Salish and Athapaskan peoples called this territory home, hunting and travelling through mountain passes. In parts of the high country they spent winters living in kekulis (pit-houses). You can still see depressions in the ground from these kekulis in Monck Park on the north shore of Nicola Lake, near Merritt.

European fur traders began to arrive in the area in the early part of the 19th century. The Hudson's Bay Company's 400-strong horse brigades ranged the Nicola Valley and North Cascade mountain passes. Ranchers moved in in the latter part of the century, helped by the 1880s construction of the Canadian Pacific Railway, which distributed their beef across the country.

Today, the Nicola Valley is still prime cattle country, and forestry also plays a major part in the region's economy.

For paddlers, this high country is one of the most rewarding areas in the province. Anglers flock to the many out-of-the-way lakes that dot this plateau terrain, while Wells Gray and Mount Robson parks present superb hiking and horse-packing opportunities. In touring B.C.'s high country, we start at Merritt, continue up Highway 5 (the Coquihalla) to Kamloops and then head east on Highway 1 to Salmon Arm and the Shuswap Lake area. We also follow Highway 5 (the Yellowhead) north from Kamloops into the interior, stopping at Clearwater, Blue River, Wells Gray Provincial Park and Tête Jaune Cache before ending up at Mount Robson Provincial Park on the B.C./Alberta border.

MERRITT

The town of Merritt (pop. 6000) services the surrounding ranching country and the 150 lakes of the Nicola Valley, which are visited by anglers in search of rainbow and cutthroat trout, kokanee salmon and Dolly Varden char. The completion of the Coquihalla Highway has made the Nicola Valley, now only a half-day's drive northeast of Vancouver and an hour south of Kamloops, quite popular with travellers, but it is still possible to find isolated fishing lakes and stretches of wide-open ranchland off the beaten track.

One of the best reference books on the area is *Coquihalla Country* by Murphy Shewchuk. Another useful resource is the Forest Service Recreation Sites map published by the Ministry of Forests. Write to the Ministry of Forests, Kamloops Region, 515 Columbia St., Kamloops, B.C., V2C 2T7 (828-4137) for a copy.

KANE VALLEY

The Kane Valley, south of Merritt, is a good cross-country skiing area. Developed cooperatively by local groups and the Ministry of Forests, it features dry, powdery, shallow snow covering old stock trails and abandoned logging roads, making it a favourite haunt for skiers of all abilities. To get there, follow Highway 5A south of Merritt for 18 km (11 mi.), then head west on the Kane Valley Road. A map of the 40 km (25 mi.) of trails is available at the parking lot.

Two loops cater to beginner-intermediate level skiers: Menzies' Loop, a 3-hour, 15-km (9-mi.) return loop through open country west of the Kane Valley Road, and Mathew's Loop, a 5-km (3-mi.) run on which moose and deer can often be seen. The 5-km (3-mi.) Robinson's Loop is a good trail for intermediate skiers.

Corbett Lake Country Inn, farther south on Highway 5A, is set in the foot-hills of the Cascade Mountains and makes a nice base for people skiing the Kane Valley in winter or fishing Corbett and Courtney lakes in summer. It serves excellent meals and offers cabin or lodge accommodation. Contact them at Box 327, Merritt, B.C., V0K 2B0 (378-4334) for information.

KENTUCKY AND ALLEYNE LAKES

Continuing south on Highway 5A, travellers will reach the Nicola Valley–Kentucky/Alleyne Provincial Recreation Area. Bates Road, 5.3 km (3.3 mi.) south of the village of Aspen Grove, provides access to this area well known to fisherpeople.

The walk around Alleyne Lake, situated where dry grasslands give way to slightly wetter pine and fir forest, is a 2-hour marsh ramble replete with nesting birds in season and other aquatic creatures. May and June are the time to visit Quilchena Falls, a day-long round trip of about 15 km (9 mi.) starting from the ponds at the junction of Kentucky and Alleyne lakes.

The Kentucky Bluey Lakes loop trail, which takes 3-4 hours to complete, is the hike to make for wildflowers, ponderosa pine, Douglas fir and saskatoon berries.

NICOLA LAKE

Historically, the area around Nicola Lake, 30 km (18 mi.) northeast of Merritt on Highway 5, is ranching country. The Nicola Ranch, a 6000-ha (14,826-a.) spread near Merritt that includes the former Nicola townsite, is one of the main ranches. In 1989, a Taiwanese firm bought the ranch with an eye to tourism development.

The Nicola Ranch was started in 1918, a decade after the establishment of the Quilchena Hotel, a good adventuring base for the area. This historic hotel, located on Highway 5A, 23 km (13 mi.) north of Merritt, is open between mid-April and mid-October and offers accommodation, horseback riding and golf.

Bird watchers find the Nicola Lake area rewarding. Cyclists may want to take advantage of one of the organized tours of the valley. Starting from Hope, the route runs along the Coquihalla Highway to Merritt and then via Highway 5A to Kamloops. The trip generally takes 2-3 days and cyclists stay at the Quilchena Hotel en route.

Useful Information

For information on accommodation and activities, contact the **Quilchena Hotel**, Quilchena, B.C., V0E 2R0 (378-2611).

Cycling tours of the area are organized by **Benno's Adventure Tours**, 1958 West 4th Ave., Vancouver, B.C., V6J 1M5 (738-5105).

DOUGLAS LAKE

From Quilchena, you might want to make the 80-km (50-mi.) drive northeast on the Douglas Lake Road to Westwold on Highway 97. This 2-hour drive will take you through the vast Douglas Lake Ranch country, one of our favourite parts of the province.

The plateau lakes along the way, such as Chapperon and Salmon, are home to feisty fish, and for centuries provided food and camping areas for the Okanagan Indians.

Drive up the Hamilton Mountain Road for sweeping views of Douglas Lake. Hikes in this area are prime in May and June, when the wildflowers are in full bloom, and in late September and early October, when the fall colours are at their most spectacular.

PENNASK LAKE

You can also head southeast from Quilchena on the 93-km (58-mi.) gravel Pennask Lake Road, which links Quilchena with Peachland in the Okanagan Valley.

Fisherpeople have long used this road (open only in the summer) across the Douglas Plateau to reach some of the finest rainbow trout lakes in the province. Nine lakes lie in the immediate vicinity of the Paradise Lake Road, which branches southward off the Pennask Lake Road near the 28-km (17-mi.) signpost. A resort on the northwest corner of Paradise Lake and a Forest Service campsite on nearby Island Lake are good bases from which to explore the trails leading to a further 8 lakes. Consult your Forest Service map for directions.

Since Pennask Lake rainbow trout are considered genetically superior in terms of fighting ability, Pennask Lake is the principal source of rainbow trout eggs for the provincial restocking program. The lake was once the site of an exclusive fly-fishing club owned by James D. Dole of Hawaiian pineapple fame, and Queen Elizabeth and Prince Philip spent a happy three days here during their 1959 Canadian tour.

Other excellent fishing is available at Peter, Hope, Glimpse, Roche and

Chataway lakes. Check local regulations for fly-fishing restrictions.

The Merritt Travel Infocentre, located at the exit from the Coquihalla Highway, can provide up-to-date information on local fishing spots.

HIGHLAND PLATEAU

Sixty kilometres (37 mi.) northwest of Merritt lies the town of Logan Lake. The scenic drive leads up out of desert country, descending into the ancient volcanic crater of the Highland valley. The valley, rich in copper, is also a splendid mother lode of fishing lakes.

Tunkwa Lake—home of legendary 3-kg (6.6-lb.) trout—can be reached by a gravel road 40 km (25 mi.) north of Logan Lake. From this road, another leads up the north face of Mount Savona, a source of green and cream-coloured opalite and a popular destination for rockhounds. East of Logan Lake is Paska Lake, another good fishing and canoeing area with an excellent open-area campsite created by the Forest Service.

LAC LE JEUNE

An easy 4-hour drive from Vancouver via the Coquihalla Highway, Lac Le Jeune Provincial Park lies 70 km (43 mi.) north of Merritt and is a favourite destination for anglers fishing for rainbow trout. One hundred and forty-four campsites cater to travellers who can also enjoy the 146 m (160 yd.) of developed beach. Lac Le Jeune is a typical B.C. high-country lake, where the morning mists rising off the waters give a real feeling of solitude.

In winter, the adjacent acreage of the Lac Le Jeune Resort is a prime cross-country skiing area. The 56 km (35 mi.) of trails in this rolling ranch country are signed, groomed and graded for different skill levels. Lac Le Jeune is well known in nordic circles for its various marathons and races; it contains 5-km (3.1-mi.) and 10-km (6.2-mi.) racing circuits and a biathlon course. The lodge on the site can accommodate 60 people and there are also several lakeside cabins for rent. Contact the resort at Box 3215, Kamloops, B.C., V2C 6B8 (372-2722).

KAMLOOPS

At the end of the Coquihalla Highway, 88 km (55 mi.) northeast of Merritt, the city of Kamloops, incorporated in 1893, is the oldest city in the province. Home to over 60,000 people, it is the second largest city in B.C.'s interior (Prince George is the largest). Kamloops is the hub of B.C.'s cattle industry and is developing rapidly as an important mining centre. Its setting at the confluence of the North and South Thompson rivers, within fishing distance of over 200 lakes, makes it a popular adventuring base.

The Shuswap Indians called this place *Kahm-o-loops*, meaning "the meeting of the waters," and early traders from the Pacific Fur Company and the North West Company (taken over by the Hudson's Bay Company in 1821) bartered leaves of tobacco for beaver pelts with the local native people. (Five leaves of tobacco were traded for one beaver skin; twenty prime pelts would secure one yard of white cotton.) Fort Kamloops became the centre for the Inland Empire fur trade. A thousand horses were based here, and pack trains of up to 300 animals travelled across the province to collect furs from remote forts for transport down the Columbia River on Hudson's Bay Company boats. The Cariboo gold rush of the mid-1860s mainly bypassed Kamloops, but its fortune was cemented by the laying of the CPR tracks through town in 1885.

History buffs might enjoy an amble through the Kamloops Museum, open year-round, which features 2 floors of excellent exhibits dealing with native culture and fur-trade history.

The section of the South Thompson River between Chase (50 km/32 mi. east of Kamloops) and Kamloops is an easy and popular 1-2 day trip for canoeists, who can make the run in either direction. The river here passes through the interior dry belt, so expect to see clay hoodoos, the remains of some Salish semisubterranean homes (kekulis) and a certain amount of bird life. The Trans-Canada Highway runs parallel to the river for most of the way. Clearwater Expeditions offers rafting trips on the Thompson. Contact them at 613 Bissette Rd., Kamloops, B.C., V2B 6L3 (579-8360).

Many of the lakes within easy driving distance of Kamloops are stocked with Kamloops trout (a variety of rainbow trout), eastern brook trout and kokanee (a landlocked form of sockeye salmon). Anglers using both flies and spinners can check with the Travel Infocentre in downtown Kamloops to find out where the fish are biting. There are numerous fishing resorts situated on the lakes and offering a variety of facilities.

SHUSWAP LAKE AREA

From Kamloops, the Trans-Canada Highway heads east to Salmon Arm, the largest town (pop. 11,200) in the Shuswap area, situated at the tip of one of Shuswap Lake's four arms. Its setting makes it a natural for bird watching (more than 65 species nest in the area), nordic skiing, canoeing and hiking.

The great Shuswap tribe, who at their peak numbered 5000, gave their name to this area. The hunting and fishing range of these Interior Salish people branched west of the Fraser River, eastward to the Columbia River and from north of McBride to south of Kamloops. Today, residents of the area boat extensively on Shuswap Lake. The town of Sicamous (from the Shuswap word meaning "narrow" or "squeezed in the middle") is a good place to rent fully equipped houseboats. Approximately 1000 km (630 mi.) of shoreline with safe, sandy beaches makes this a good lake to canoe or kayak, and the water is usually fairly calm. The Shuswap Lake Marine Park consists of 14 sites located around the lake, many of them with adjoining campsites.

White-water canoeists and kayakers looking for more of a challenge prefer the nearby Shuswap and Adams rivers. Raft trips down the Adams are run by Interior Whitewater Expeditions.

Useful Information

For maps and information about Shuswap Lake Park, Shuswap Lake Marine Park or the Adams River salmon runs, contact the Visitor Services Coordinator, BC Parks, Thompson River District, 1265 Dalhousie Drive, Kamloops, B.C., V2C 5Z5 (828-4494).

For information on houseboat rentals, contact the **Shuswap Houseboat Operators Association**, Box 962, Kamloops, B.C., V2C 5R3 (372-7770).

Interior Whitewater Expeditions can be contacted at Box 129, Celista, B.C., V0E 1L0 (955-2447) for information on their raft trips.

ADAMS RIVER

Every four years a major sockeye salmon run heads up the Adams River, and these "dominant" runs, as they are known, draw thousands of visitors to the area. (The next will be in 1994.) Although the lower Adams River is only 11 km (7 mi.) in length from its source in Adams Lake to its mouth in Shuswap Lake, it becomes a remarkable sight in the fall when it teems with home-bound crimson-red sockeye salmon heading for their spawning grounds.

The fry emerge in the spring from the eggs laid in the riverbed, then spend a year in Shuswap Lake before starting out for the Pacific. The adult sockeye then spend 3 years travelling the ocean before migrating 485 km (300 mi.) back up the Fraser, Thompson and Adams rivers to spawn.

In October, during the special Salute to the Salmon presented at the Roderick Haig-Brown Conservation Area along the North Shuswap Road, the federal department of Fisheries and Oceans (salmon are a federal matter in Canada since they spend the majority of their lives in the ocean) and the provincial parks people put on displays, show films on the sockeye and point out trails to the various viewpoints.

Time your visit for the afternoon, after all the tour buses have headed out. Check out the excellent home-cooked food sold by the local Lions Club and other community groups. Shuswap Lake Park can accommodate salmon-watchers at its more than 200 campsites. To reach the Adams River and the Roderick Haig-Brown Conservation Area, head west from Salmon Arm on the Trans-Canada Highway to Squilax, then head northeast on paved highway for 3.8 km (2 mi.) to the junction just after the Adams River bridge. Turn right for the salmon viewing area. You can get to Adams Lake by turning left just before you get to the bridge. Contact the Visitor Services Coordinator, BC Parks, Thompson River District, 1265 Dalhousie Dr., Kamloops, B.C., V2C 5Z5 (828-4494) for information on the salmon runs.

TOD MOUNTAIN

Highway 5 (the Yellowhead) leads north from Kamloops to some fine fishing country. If you set up a base in summer in the Heffley Lake area, 31 km (20 mi.) northeast of Kamloops, you can fish, swim and hike to the wildflower-covered summit of nearby Tod Mountain. During winter, ice-fishing and downhill skiing at Tod Mountain are the main adventures. Accommodation on Tod is privately owned, so most skiers stay in Kamloops. Contact the information office at Tod Mountain (578-7222) for more information.

CLEARWATER

The small town of Clearwater, 125 km (78 mi.) north of Kamloops on the Yellowhead Highway (Highway 5), is making a major effort to diversify its mainly forest-based economy. In the heart of the North Thompson River valley, Clearwater capitalizes on its location as the gateway to Wells Gray Provincial Park and on other activities such as hiking and nordic skiing in the immediate vicinity.

Clearwater Expeditions, based in town, arranges rafting trips on the Clearwater River. A day trip on the Clearwater takes rafters through canyons where the current is swift and ospreys frequently soar overhead. The break for lunch usually takes place at an old Indian campground, where woodland caribou once crossed the Clearwater and where the salmon fishing is still excellent. The highlight of the afternoon is a run through Saber Tooth, the most dynamic rapid on the trip—rated a grade 5—and some fine grade 3 rollers also occur before the trip comes to an end.

Paddlers who intend to run the North Thompson River usually put in at the community of Avola, midway between Clearwater and Blue River on High-

Rafting on the Thompson River. *Photo by Lloyd Twaites*

way 5. From here to Clearwater it's a 2-day run for intermediate paddlers. A historical trip that takes in Mad River Canyon (you must portage this) and Porte d'Enfer (Gates of Hell) Canyon, this voyage is not for the squeamish.

Less-experienced canoeists who want to run a section of the Thompson can put in at Clearwater and do the 2-3 day run to Kamloops. The main tricky areas are Fishtrap Canyon and Heffley Rapids. This is a major river, so paddlers should scout anything that looks unusual.

Murphy Shewchuk's *Backroads Explorer, Vol. I: Thompson-Cariboo* is a good reference for travellers in the area.

Useful Information
For information on rafting trips down the Clearwater River, contact **Clearwater Expeditions**, 613 Bissette Rd., Kamloops, B.C., V2B 6L3 (579-8360). Similar trips are also offered by **Interior Whitewater Expeditions**, Box 129, Celista, B.C., V0E 1L0 (955-2447).

WELLS GRAY PROVINCIAL PARK

Commonly known as the Waterfall Park, Wells Gray is recognized as one of the great wilderness parks in North America. Located just north of Clearwater, it is a 1½-hour drive north from Kamloops on Highway 5 (and a 5-hour drive from Vancouver).

The third largest provincial park in B.C., Wells Gray covers 530,000 ha (1,309,645 a.); it is almost the size of Prince Edward Island and is bigger than many of the world's small nations. The park celebrated its 50th anniversary in 1989.

Encompassing the greater part of the Clearwater River watershed in the Cariboo Mountains, Wells Gray is named after Arthur Wellesley (Wells) Gray, provincial minister of lands from 1933 until his death in 1944.

The extremes of climate here make for very cold winters with plenty of snow, which lingers until at least mid-April, and warm summers with frequent thunderstorms (as paddlers on the park's many lakes will know!).

The main access to the park is the 69-km (43-mi.) Clearwater Valley Road which heads north from Highway 5 at Clearwater and leads through the park to Clearwater Lake. From the west, roads run from Bridge Lake and 100 Mile House to Canim Falls and Mahood Lake in the southwest corner of the park. The third option is to travel 24 km (15 mi.) west from Blue River along a gravel road to Murtle Lake on the park's eastern rim.

Wells Gray is a heavily glaciated, formerly extremely volcanic park whose varied topography of mountain peaks and river valleys makes it an ideal habitat for 170 species of birds and 50 species of mammals. The park is home to the largest remaining population of mountain caribou in southern B.C. The wildlife, coupled with the park's serenity (except in hunting season), make it a popular destination for hikers, canoeists, cross-country skiers and anglers. As much of the park is open to hunting during the fall season, travellers should exercise caution and wear bright clothing.

There are some wonderful hikes in the Clearwater valley area. A 4-hour hike leads to the base of Helmcken Falls, at 142 m (466 ft.) Canada's fourth highest falls. This rugged, steep hike is not ideal for kids, but the falls, which are twice as high as Niagara and dramatically noisy, may also be viewed only a few minutes' walk from the parking area at the end of the Helmcken Falls Road. The trailhead for the hike is in the same parking lot.

For optimum summer flower viewing, make the Battle Mountain–Alpine Meadows trek. This hike takes 5 hours to complete, and a further 3 hours if you hike the full 25 km (16 mi.) to the summit of Battle Mountain. The trail starts on the east side of the main access road 6 km (4 mi.) south of the park entrance, then climbs into and traverses Caribou Meadows, running past Mount Philip Trail to the alpine meadows around Fight Lake. The trail continues from the lake up a ridge to Battle Mountain. It is an ideal overnight trip, as there are several interesting side trails to be explored.

The 9 summits of the Trophy Mountains (peaking at 2577 m/8453 ft.) are visible from the Yellowhead Highway. The trail to the mountains is an excellent hike that starts at the end of the 15-km (9-mi.) Trophy Mountain logging road (also signposted as the Bear Creek camp road). You should allow at least 5 hours for ascent to the highest point in the Trophies; however, it is an easy one-hour hike to the Trophy meadows and the lower summit. Lupin and Indian paintbrush cover the mountain meadows above the tree line in summer, and clear mountain streams provide fresh drinking water. This hike could easily be expanded into 3 or more days, allowing time for exploring the summit ridges.

The most comprehensive guidebook to the area is undoubtedly Roland Neave's *Exploring Wells Gray Park*, with its excellent road and trail descriptions. All the hikes in Wells Gray are well documented both in this book and in the comprehensive provincial park map published by the Ministry of Parks.

In summer, exploration of Wells Gray tends to be confined to the southern portion of the park, as there are no access roads to the northern areas. In winter, the area travelled becomes even smaller, centring around the volcanic Murtle Plateau and the broad southern end of the Clearwater valley.

This comparatively small back-country area is becoming more and more popular with ski-tourers because of reliable snows, easy terrain, negligible wind chill and terrific scenery. The Clearwater Valley Road is kept open in winter to the park entrance and for a further 7 km (4 mi.) to the Dawson Falls campground, the only campground open in winter. A graded system of cross-country trails covers 80 km (50 mi.). The best reference book for tourers is Richard Wright's *B.C. Cross Country Ski Routes*; while the book is out of print, libraries and many secondhand bookstores still have copies.

Moose are common in the Green Mountain area, a low but prominent ridge dividing the Clearwater valley, and they are frequently spotted by skiers. The other major lure of nordic skiing at Wells Gray is the frozen falls. At Dawson Falls the sprays congeal into what one writer describes as an "ice mask" 15 m (50 ft.) high by 90 m (300 ft.) wide. There is also "the Bookmark" at Helmcken Falls, a spectacular ice cone that stands taller than a 20-storey building and is broader at its base than a football field. This column of spray, which freezes solid over the winter, can be as high as 305 m (1000 ft.). Allow yourself at least 3 hours to make the easy 14-km (7-mi.) round trip from the parking lot at Dawson Falls campground to Helmcken Falls. Other good routes include the Green Mountain, Majerus Homestead, Pyramid Mountain, McLeod Hill and Clearwater Lake trails.

The highlight of the ski season at Wells Gray is the annual Wells Gray Ski Marathon, held in the middle of February as part of the national loppet series for both racers and recreational skiers.

One of the most enjoyable ways for skiers of every skill level to tackle ski-touring in Wells Gray is to use their chalet system, the most extensive in any B.C. provincial park. The system covers a 40-km (25-mi.) traverse over the Trophy Mountains, over Table Mountain, through Cariboo Meadows and onto Battle Mountain. Two alpine chalets, a log cabin and a fire look-out cabin are strategically located along the way. The closest chalet is only one hour from the trailhead, while the others are spaced at intervals of a day's ski apart. They can be rented with or without guiding or catering services. The full-service package includes accommodation, delicious meals and professional guides, while the basic provides just a chalet with use of the cooking facilities for people who wish to supply their own food and do not require a guide. The chalet operators offer similar options for hikers during the summer.

Helmcken Falls Lodge, located right at the entrance to the park, is a comfortable place to stay. Built in 1948 as a hunting lodge, it was completely renovated in 1981 and today hosts visitors from all over the world. Guests may participate in a variety of organized outings or use the lodge as a base for their own activities. From June through September, programs include hiking trips, wilderness canoeing and backpacking, horseback riding (week-long guided trips), basic mountaineering, glacier travel and fishing.

Stoney Mountain Wilderness Adventures also provides week-long skiing, hiking, climbing, horse-packing and canoeing trips in Wells Gray.

Clearwater, Azure, Mahood and Murtle lakes are the main bodies of water in Wells Gray Park. All are situated in U-shaped valleys carved out by glaciers long ago. Clearwater and Azure are each approximately 26 km (16 mi.) long and connected by a short portage. Campsites dot the shores and, particularly on Clearwater Lake, are sometimes fronted by good beaches. Since Azure Lake lies east-west, watch out for high winds that can cause storms. Clearwater trout are some of the tastiest we've ever eaten; one evening we cooked some just before setting up camp and settling in for an overnight storm complete with spectacular thunder and lightning. The next day the lake looked like a mirror, perfect for an early-morning skinny dip.

Clearwater Lake was created when a lava flow dammed the valley over 7000 years ago. Hikes along the Falls Creek Trail provide excellent views of the flow and the nearby Kostal Lake Trail passes by the extinct Kostal Cone. Clearwater can be reached via a 33-km (20-mi.) gravel road that leads due north from the park entrance at the end of the Clearwater Valley Road. There is no road access to Azure Lake.

The Cariboo Mountain range, which forms a backdrop for Azure and Clearwater lakes, also provides scenic viewing for paddlers on Murtle Lake, which is accessible from Blue River. Murtle lies within the Murtle Lake Nature Conservancy. No boats, cars or planes are allowed in the area, so it is very quiet.

Fishing for feisty Kamloops trout is excellent on this large lake. You might want to take time too to visit tiny Fairy Slipper Island, to view the healthy population of *calypso bulbosa* (fairy slipper orchids).

Mahood Lake, which juts out from the southwest corner of the park, is a popular lake for paddlers and for powerboaters. It is accessible from Bridge Lake.

Useful Information

Park information, including an excellent map, can be obtained from the Visitor Services Coordinator, BC Parks, Thompson River District, 1265 Dalhousie Drive, Kamloops, B.C., V2C 5Z5 (828-4494) or from the Travel Infocentre located at the junction of Highway 5 and Clearwater Valley Road. The infocentre can also provide the latest road, campground and trail information.

For information on accommodation and trips, contact **Helmcken Falls Lodge**, Box 239, Clearwater, B.C., V0E 1N0 (674-3657).

Wells Gray Provincial Park Backcountry Chalets can be reached at Box 188, Clearwater, B.C., V0E 1N0 (587-6326) for information on chalets.

Contact **Stoney Mountain Wilderness Adventures**, Box 1766, R. R. #1, Clearwater, B.C., V0E 1N0 (674-2774) for information on their various wilderness trips. *Exploring Wells Gray Park* and *Nature Wells Gray* are both excellent resource books.

BLUE RIVER

Blue River, a logging and tourist town, increasingly provides services for summer and winter travellers in the area.

Southeast of Blue River, skiers and hikers can base themselves at the Monashee Chalet, located at 1828 m (6000 ft.) in the spectacular Monashee Mountains. Excellent powder skiing in winter and alpine meadows for summer hiking are the prime attractions here. The cabin is fully equipped for preparing your own meals or a cook can be supplied. A 3-km (2-mi.) hiking trail provides access to the cabin in summer. In winter, a snow cat is available for a nominal charge to transport your gear to the cabin. For more information about the Monashee Chalet, contact Interior Alpine Recreation, Box 132, Blue River, B.C., V0E 1J0 or phone 403-477-7706 (Edmonton, Alberta).

VALEMOUNT

The village of Valemount, where the Cariboo, Monashee and Rocky mountains converge, offers a range of facilities for travellers and bills itself as the North Yellowhead Hospitality Centre. Valemount lies 320 km (201 mi.) north of Kamloops on the Yellowhead Highway.

A pamphlet of hiking trails in the area is put out by Valemount village offices and is available in most motels. One of the most popular day hikes (an 8-10 hour round trip) is the Mount Terry Fox Trail in Terry Fox Park. The park and the 2650-m (8695-ft.) mountain peak are named in honour of the one-legged runner who died of cancer during his historic run across Canada. To get to this trail, go 6 km (4 mi.) north of Valemount on Highway 5, turn right at the Terry Fox Trail turnout, travel a further 5 km (3 mi.), then follow the left fork in the road until you get to the gravel pit, trailhead for the hike.

A further 8 km (5 mi.) north is the Jackman Flats cross-country ski area, with over 15 km (9 mi.) of groomed tracks for beginner and intermediate skiers.

Valemount is also the base for Headwaters Outfitting, which offers skiing, hiking or horse-pack trips to their chalet on Dave Henry Creek just outside the western boundary of Mount Robson Park in the Rocky Mountains. The chalet is situated at 1830 m (6000 ft.) in subalpine meadows, with a spectacular view of the surrounding peaks. The chalet and adjacent log cabin can accommodate 14 people. Contact Headwaters Outfitting at Box 818, Valemount, B.C., V0E 2Z0 (566-4718) for more information.

TÊTE JAUNE CACHE

This community is at the terminus of Highway 5, 340 km (211 mi.) northeast of Kamloops. From here, the Yellowhead Highway (now called Highway 16) heads west to Prince George and on to Prince Rupert, then ends 1000 km (620 mi.) later in the Queen Charlotte Islands. East of Tête Jaune Cache, the highway heads to Edmonton, Alberta, via Jasper.

The town is said to be named after a blond-haired trapper (tête jaune is French for "yellowhead") who cached his furs in the area. It is the starting point for an ambitious ski traverse of the Southern Cariboo Mountains, a trip suitable for strong, experienced back-country skiers only. This 2-week trip takes in glaciers galore (Gilmour, South Canoe, Rausch and Mileage), offering plenty of opportunity to practise route-finding skills among the maze of crevasses and icefalls. The highest peak en route is Mount Sir Wilfrid Laurier in the Premier Range (one of a group of rugged, 3500-m (11,483-ft.) peaks bearing the names of different Canadian prime ministers) which makes for an excellent ski ascent. The route also includes more gentle ridge runs, smooth snowfields and ice-bound alpine lakes.

Guided trips of the Cariboo Mountain Traverse are offered by the Schaffers' Nordic Ski Institute, Box 1050, Canmore, Alberta, T0L 0M0. Contact them at 403-678-4102 for more information.

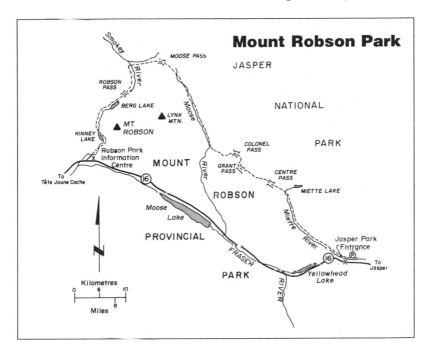

MOUNT ROBSON PARK

One of the oldest parks in the province, Mount Robson celebrated its 75th birthday in 1988. Its dominant peak, Mount Robson, is, at 3954 m (1297 ft.), the highest in the Canadian Rockies, and the park offers excellent hiking and beautiful alpine scenery. Mount Robson's other major claim to fame is that it contains the headwaters of the Fraser River, which rises in the southwest corner of the park as a trickle and empties 1280 km (795 mi.) later into the Pacific Ocean.

The Yellowhead Highway (Highway 16) provides easy access to the park just 20 km (12 mi.) east of the junction of Highways 5 and 16.

From June through September, hikers around Mount Robson can expect to see over 50 species of alpine flowers and many of the 170 species of birds identified here, including the northern hawk owl, the water pipit, the horned lark, the ptarmigan and the fox sparrow. Among the mammals that live here are black and grizzly bears, mule deer, moose, elk and caribou.

Most hikers would agree that the fairly well-travelled routes in and around Berg Lake in the park's northwest corner are the highlights of Mount Robson Park. You need a back-country camping permit for use of the campsites along the Berg Lake Trail and a small fee is charged for each night's use. The permits, together with up-to-date trail information, can be obtained from the

Mount Robson Visitor Centre located at the Mount Robson Viewpoint on Highway 16. The centre is open from May to September.

A popular 2-day hike of approximately 22 km (14 mi.) leads up the Robson River valley from the park's visitor centre through the Valley of a Thousand Falls and past Emperor Falls to Berg Lake at 1628 m (5340 ft.). From the lake, the trail continues through Robson Pass into Jasper National Park in Alberta to link up with a trail system leading to the town site of Jasper.

Mount Robson towers above Berg Lake, the blue ice of Berg Glacier clinging to its northwest face. Since it is one of the few advancing glaciers in the Canadian Rockies, it regularly calves great chunks of ice that float serenely in the lake, adding another dimension to hiking in this area.

Pathways Tours maintains a summer camp at Berg Lake, flying in visitors by helicopter from Jasper for week-long trips into the alpine with resident naturalists. Tours are run from both their Alpine Base Camp and their Berg Lake Base Camp. From the Alpine Base Camp, hikers walk into the alpine meadows, where there's a good chance of spotting mountain goats and caribou. At Berg Lake Camp, walkers can take the trail to the Valley of a Thousand Falls. Many painters and photographers choose the latter option because the scenery at Berg Lake is so spectacular.

Another excellent 7- to 10-day trip circles Mount Robson, crossing 6 passes. Starting up the Miette River, it leads through Centre Miette Pass, Grant Pass and Colonel Pass before descending to the Moose River. The trail then follows the Moose River to Moose Pass and drops down into Calumet Creek; from there, it runs down to the creek's confluence with the Smoky River and then south to Adolphus Lake and Robson Pass. Berg Lake and its more heavily used trails are just ahead. Since this route is not regularly maintained, it requires some route-finding skills and creek fording. We recommend it for experienced hikers only. If you prefer to take a guided trip along this route, one is offered by Five Seasons Adventure Tours.

Ski-tourers in Mount Robson Park have to take into account the possibility of temperatures as low as -34° C (-22° F), but compensation comes in the form of excellent wildlife spotting, with a chance to see moose, coyotes, wolves and great gray owls. Moose Lake and Yellowhead Lake are ideal trails for beginners, while Kinney Lake is for intermediate skiers. The Kinney Lake Trail continues on to Berg Lake but passes through a high-risk avalanche area so travellers should check first with a park warden.

Useful Information
Park information, brochures and maps can be obtained from the Visitor Services Coordinator, BC Parks, Prince George District, 1011 4th Ave., Prince George, B.C., V2L 3H9 (565-6270).

For information on the hiking trips offered by **Pathways Tours**, write to them at 5915 West Boulevard, Vancouver, B.C., V6M 3X1 or call 263-1476 or 1-800-663-3364 (toll free). For information on their guided tours of Mount Robson write or call **Five Seasons Adventure Tours**, 620-1033 Davie St., Vancouver, B.C., V6E 1M7 (682-6022).

Mount Robson Adventure Holidays, Box 146, Valemount, B.C., V0E 2Z0 (566-4351 or 566-4386) runs guided hiking and canoe trips in the park. **Headwaters Outfitting**, Box 818, Valemount, B.C., V0E 2Z0 (566-4718) offers horse-packing trips.

The Canadian Rockies Trail Guide contains detailed descriptions of the trails in Mount Robson Park, especially those in the Berg Lake area.

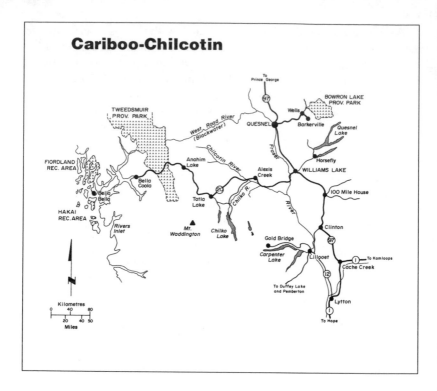

Cariboo-Chilcotin

CHAPTER 8

Cariboo-Chilcotin

The Cariboo-Chilcotin region ranges from Lillooet in the southeast to Prince George in the northeast, west through the southern portion of vast Tweedsmuir Provincial Park and then on right to the coast. Experts differ as to the precise boundaries of the Cariboo, home to some great ranching country and equally fine adventuring possibilities. However, folks generally agree that the Cariboo plateau starts at Kelly Lake, north of Lillooet, extending over the territory we cover to Williams Lake in the north.

The Chilcotin extends from the edge of the Fraser River at Williams Lake to the northern reaches of Tweedsmuir Park and is a plateau covering 38,850 sq. km (15,000 sq. mi.) of grazing land interspersed with forests of pine, spruce and fir. The Coast Mountains form a natural boundary. The word *chilcotin*, from which the area gets its name, can be translated as "ochre river people." According to *British Columbia Place Names*, this does not refer to the colour "but to the mineralized substance (usually red or yellow) which was much prized by the Indians for use as a base for paint or dye."

The Coast Mountains are the first of five major mountain ranges that slice across British Columbia between the Pacific Ocean and the Rockies. They stretch northwest from Vancouver in a 1440-km (907-mi.) arc about 160 km (100 mi.) in width. The Coast Range's best known peaks are those on Vancouver's north shore, specifically Mount Seymour and the Lions.

At the heart of the Coast Range is the massive peak so often visible in the Chilcotin: Mount Waddington, whose twin pinnacles at 4016 m (13,172 ft.) make it the highest mountain in Canada outside of the Yukon. It was named after Alfred Waddington, whose survey crew tried to find a rail route to the coast. British Columbia pioneers Don and Phyllis Munday first spotted Mount Waddington while climbing on Vancouver Island. This started a twelve-summer-long fascination with the mountain and its environs, documented in Don's autobiographical book *The Unknown Mountain* (now out of print, unfortunately). In their summer explorations of the area, the Mundays charted and named many peaks in the Coast Range but it was always Waddington that towered over their endeavours.

Because of its sheer peaks and ridges of granite, Mount Waddington resembles Mount Blanc in France. Hanging glaciers periodically calve on the mountain and people who helicopter in to explore usually touch down on the Teidman Glacier, at about 1980 m (6494 ft.), before bivouacing far away from the paths of avalanches and rock slides. The Nordic Ski Institute runs ski-mountaineering trips to the area, which is also climbed by experienced mountaineers in the summer.

For centuries the Lillooet and the Shuswap—Interior Salish peoples—and the Chilcotin and the Carrier—Athapaskan or Dene peoples—inhabited this vast region. Leading a seminomadic existence, they lived from May to September in villages on the banks of a river or lake, where the fish were in good supply. In winter, the Lillooet and the Shuswap moved to pit houses located on the plateau, usually along a river.

The Athapaskan people acted as packers, carriers and guides for the first immigrant miners to their territory, selling the miners dried berry flat-cakes and dried salmon and teaching them the medicinal properties of various plant species. The native peoples were horrified at the lack of respect the white immigrants showed for what they killed to eat.

For centuries the Athapaskan people had secured a constant food supply by respecting the spirits of the fish they ate and the bears they killed. Their treatment of bears profoundly illustrates the philosophical schism between the aboriginal world and that of the immigrant. As writer Robin Skelton points out in his book *They Call It the Cariboo*, "When a bear was killed the Dene spoke to it as if it were a close relation, offered it a pipe of tobacco, and apologized formally and frequently for having killed it. The bear's skull was always placed in a tree or in the fork of a tent pole as a mark of respect and to propitiate its spirit."

In the 1820s, Hudson's Bay Company explorers moved through the Bridge Creek area (now 100 Mile House) looking for a fur-trade route leading from Kamloops to the coast. Forty years later the lives of the Athapaskan people were changed forever by the Cariboo gold rush.

From 1858, when prospectors started streaming into the area, until the peak of the rush in 1862, the Cariboo bristled with hopefuls headed for the mother lode. They came in via a variety of routes until the Royal Engineers surveyed and built the Cariboo Wagon Road. Since the contractors were paid by the mile, they marked each mile with a post. At various intervals, log houses built for the construction crews became rest places for the stage coaches that followed. Communities sprang up at these mile houses where prospectors fed and watered their horses and enjoyed a spot of well-deserved rest and recreation.

Today, the mile houses cater to visitors much as they did to the needs of gold-rushers. Starting at Mile 0, the town of Lillooet (where you can still register a valid claim at the mines office), the route passes through 70 Mile House and 100 Mile House and ends at Barkerville, once the largest town west of Chicago and north of San Francisco. From the time of the gold rush onwards, European immigration continued, with mining, logging and ranching taking place in the area.

Because of the Cariboo's elevation, winters are cold and crisp while summers are pleasantly hot, cooling off at night. Cariboo snowfalls can be heavy. The Chilcotin's climate is similar, with areas around the mountain ranges exhibiting their own microclimates.

The economy centres on logging, mining, ranching and fishing off the coast. Adventurers can expect to find some great horse-packing and hiking here, as well as fine waterways and nature viewing.

To reach the Cariboo by car from Vancouver, take the Trans-Canada Highway to Cache Creek, then head north on Highway 97 to Clinton and onwards. An alternative route is to leave the Trans-Canada at Lytton, heading north on Highway 12 to Lillooet and from there continuing along Highway 97 through the Cariboo.

For our money, the most pleasant way of getting to the Cariboo is to take the scenic B.C. Rail trip from North Vancouver to Williams Lake, and on to the central B.C. city of Prince George. Rated one of the top 10 scenic trips in the world (and we wager that the food in Cariboo Class rivals that on the Orient Express!), the train climbs out of Lillooet to 610 m (2000 ft.) above the Fraser River. On one trip we made, our co-passengers, a group of grannies and grandpas from Long Island and some daredevil paragliders from Chamonix, France, were silenced by the spectacular views of the Fraser Canyon as our train hustled down to Lillooet.

North of Lillooet the clear blue waters of Bridge River flow into the muddy eddies of the Fraser. Look carefully down on the bluffs at water's edge to see the salmon-drying racks at this historic meeting place and fishing spot for the Lillooet Indians. At Pavilion, the train tracks bend once, allowing a final view of the arid canyon before climbing into the rolling ranchland of the Cariboo. Pavilion (the French word for "flag") is so named because it was the tradition of the native people of this area to mark graves with a series of streamers. By the time you reach Kelly Lake, the landscape has evolved into typical Cariboo grazing country. Fat cattle, meadows interspersed with lakes, stands of fir and carpets of summer wildflowers characterize the region. For more information on this B.C. Rail trip, call them in Vancouver at 984-5246.

One of the most comprehensive publications on adventuring in the Cariboo is the *Cariboo-Chilcotin-Coast Travel Guide* put out annually by the Cariboo Tourist Association. We highly recommend that you write them for a copy or pick one up at any regional tourist infocentre during your trip. The address is Cariboo Tourist Association, Box 4900, 190 Yorston Ave., Williams Lake, B.C., V2G 2V8 (392-2226 or toll free 1-800-663-5885).

The route we follow to explore the Cariboo-Chilcotin area extends from Cache Creek west to Lillooet, then north to Clinton. From Clinton, Highway 97 (the Cariboo Highway) leads us north through 100 Mile House and on to Williams Lake.

From Williams Lake we branch west on the Freedom Highway right through to Bella Coola on the coast, taking in the southern portion of Tweedsmuir Park. We then return to Williams Lake to explore the country east and north of town around Quesnel, Barkerville and the Bowron Lakes.

CACHE CREEK TO LILLOOET

From Cache Creek, Highway 97 proceeds northwest to Clinton. En route to Clinton, Highway 12 branches off due west to link Cache Creek, via Pavilion, with Lillooet. Between Cache Creek and Pavilion the road passes through Marble Canyon Provincial Park, a sentimental favourite of ours. Dominated by limestone cliffs overlooking Crown and Turquoise lakes, this tiny oasis lies in the middle of arid country: we particularly like its waterfall and nearby "Teapot," a novel rock formation.

At Pavilion the road bends south to Lillooet, Mile 0 on the old Cariboo Highway and the gateway to some fine adventuring terrain.

WEST OF LILLOOET

Nordic skiers visiting the Lillooet area can make the 2-hour drive to Tyax Mountain Lake Lodge, the largest log structure in the Pacific Northwest. Situated on Tyaughton Lake ("Lake of the Jumping Fish"), Tyax is surrounded by nordic trails that also crisscross the lake. Heli-skiers can head up to the light powder of the Spearhead and Schulap mountains, while ice anglers have a wide choice of lakes. Summers at Tyax consist of fishing on Tyaughton Lake, horseback riding, hiking and gold-panning. A highlight is the 4-day trail ride to alpine meadows.

Spruce Lake Tours also offers back-country ski-touring adventures here, using a network of comfortable log cabins. Pearson Pond Cabin, west of Tyaughton Lake, forms base camp for trips into the 1890-m (6300-ft.) country of the southern Chilcotin. Trips are tailored to individual groups and ski guides know the territory well. SLT rents cabins to responsible groups during off-peak periods and in summer.

In summer, hikers can head into Taylor Basin, just north of the old Chilcotin Trail between Tyaughton and Spruce lakes. This high country leads to spectacular alpine meadows above the timber line.

Trailhead access is via a 90-km (56-mi.) drive up Bridge River from its mouth, then right up Tyaughton Lake Road to the mouth of North Cinnabar Creek. A 2- or 3-day backpacking trip into the Basin, with a campover near the Lucky Strike mine, gives you plenty of time to make a rewarding loop into Eldorado Basin and back. Another trip from Lucky Strike leads up to the 2355-

m (7730-ft.) peak of Bonanza Pass. This hike, together with some local history, is detailed in Bob Harris's book *The Best of B.C.'s Hiking Trails*.

More great hikes can be found in the Spruce Lake/Warner Pass area, where the Coast Mountains meet the Chilcotin Range less than 250 km (158 mi.) from Vancouver. It's easy to get to and teeming with wildlife. Elk, ruffed grouse and the occasional herd of bighorn sheep are common inhabitants, and avalanche lilies, arnica and lupine carpet the meadows.

To reach Warner Pass you can either hire a float plane in Squamish to make the one-hour trip to Spruce Lake, or travel in by road over the Hurley Pass to clear, trout-stocked Gun Lake, 10 miles from Tyax Lodge. From Gun Lake it is about 40 km (25 mi.) to the pass. Hikers travel along a horse trail that meanders by a series of lovely lakes as it climbs towards Warner Pass at 2380 m (7806 ft.). From the pass you have a grand view of the Warner ridge and the Taseko River Valley. The trail then descends into the valley and continues northwest to Taseko Lake, about 25 km (15 mi.) from Warner Pass. A rough, gravel road running from the lake connects with the main highway to Williams Lake.

Most hikers will prefer to head north from the pass on a circular route past Elbow Mountain and along the Tyaughton valley to the west of Relay Mountain. Below Castle Peak, the route heads south, back to Spruce Lake, where you can rendezvous with a float plane or begin the longer hike back to Gun Lake. (Speaking of float planes, we could tell you a story about some friends of ours who, having previously arranged for a helicopter beer drop during their hike, flagged down the wrong helicopter—but we don't want to embarrass them!) The Forest Service publishes an excellent brochure on the Spruce Lakes Trails area.

Gun Lake Resort runs large, reasonably priced housekeeping cabins complete with oil lamps and wood-burning stoves. Campsites are available on the lakeshore.

Old trails and mining roads lead to Yalakom country, northeast of Tyax. Epitomizing the crisp, clean solitude of the open range, this area encompasses Poison Mountain, Buck Mountain, China Head Mountain, Nine Mile Ridge, South French Bark Creek, Churn Creek, Tyaughton Creek, Yalakom River and the Camelsfoot Range. If you are planning a trip to this area, you might want to look out for a copy of Richard Wright's *Backroads Guide: Volume I—Bridge River Country*.

Useful Information

For information on accommodation and organized activities, contact **Tyax Mountain Lake Resort**, Tyaughton Lake Road, Gold Bridge, B.C., V0K 1P0 (238-2221) or **Gun Lake Resort**, General Delivery, Gold Bridge, B.C., V0K 1P0 (238-2326).

Contact **Spruce Lake Tours**, 2375 West 35th Ave., Vancouver, B.C., V6M 1J7 (263-2118) for information on their back-country ski tours or cabin rentals.

To get the Forest Service brochure on the Spruce Lakes Trails area, write to their Vancouver office at 4595 Canada Way, Burnaby, B.C., V5G 4L9 (660-7608).

CLINTON

To reach Clinton, travel 40 km (25 mi.) north of Cache Creek on Highway 97. The town makes a good base for adventurers interested in dude ranching or nordic skiing.

Though we haven't made a practice of listing dude ranches in this guide, we do mention a couple in this section since riding is so much a part of the Cariboo experience. Modern-day riders are limited to horses, but during the gold rush 23 two-humped Bactrian camels were imported from Asia to act as pack animals. They proved less than suitable, however; their pungent odour frightened mules and horses, their soft feet were torn by the rocky, mountainous roads, and they ate the miners' socks! Eventually the camels were turned loose.

Forty km (25 mi.) northwest of Clinton in Big Bar Lake country, Circle H Mountain Lodge, located at 1500 m (5000 ft.) in the mountains of the southern Cariboo, offers pleasant family accommodation in an 18-person-capacity lodge. Pick-up can be arranged from the B.C. Rail station at Clinton. Some of the activities organized by the lodge, which has a pool and sauna for guests, include daily summer rides led by resident wranglers to alpine meadows, fishing on Big Bar Lake for rainbow trout and canoeing at Kelly Lake. For more information, contact Circle H Mountain Lodge, Jesmond, Box 7, Clinton, B.C., V0K 1K0 (459-2565).

Nordic skiers returning to the coast after the 100 Mile House Cariboo Ski Marathon in February often stop off in Clinton for the 12-km (7-mi.) minimarathon at Big Bar Provincial Park. (Contact the Clinton Chamber of Commerce to get exact dates.) We like to stop off for chili after the race at the Clinton Motor Lodge, which also does a mean hamburger for the casual traveller. We love the lounge, which is decorated in quarried stones and crammed with old snowshoes and other memorabilia of pioneering days.

70 MILE HOUSE

Summer travellers who want a taste of ranching life can travel 10 km (6 mi.) east off the Cariboo Highway at 70 Mile House to Green Lake. At the

Flying U Ranch here a combination of unlimited horseback riding, ranch-style food and canoe rentals lets visitors enjoy the best of the Cariboo. Contact the ranch at Box 69, 70 Mile House, B.C., V0K 2K0 (456-7717). Green Lake, with its groves of aspen and lodgepole pine, is a lovely camping or picnicking spot.

BRIDGE LAKE AREA

Continuing along the Cariboo Highway north of 70 Mile House, you can branch east on Highway 24 to Lone Butte, then continue on to the Bridge Lake area, also known as the Interlakes region. Brimming with 50 lakes, many well-stocked with brook and rainbow trout, the area has a variety of accommodation, mostly cabins and campsites around Bridge Lake.

Sheridan Lake is the most consistently productive fishing lake in the region; anglers pull out an average of 12,000 rainbow and 1200 brook trout here each year.

If you want to ride horses, Eagan Lake Ranch, located 9 km (5 mi.) south of Bridge Lake off Highway 24, is a working ranch complete with lakefront family-size log cabins.

Forty-one km (25 mi.) east of Lone Butte off Highway 24 is Nature Hills Resort. The resort hosts a challenging 15-km (9-mi.) Bush-a-thon annually as a warmup event for the Cariboo Ski Marathon. At Nature Hills you can enjoy ice fishing, wildlife spotting on groomed trails or the novelty of a llama-drawn sleigh ride, followed by a meal in the resort's Italian restaurant.

Useful Information
For more information on accommodation and organized activities, contact **Eagan Lake Ranch Resort**, Box 34, Bridge Lake, B.C., V0K 1E0 (593-4343) or **Nature Hills Resort**, Johnstone Road, R. R. #1, Comp 215, Lone Butte, B.C., V0K 1X0 (593-4659).

100 MILE HOUSE

Eighty km (50 mi.) north of Clinton on Highway 97, the town of 100 Mile House makes a great base for a variety of adventures.

The world's longest pair of cross-country skis (5.6 m/18 ft.) are displayed outside the tourist infocentre here; the mixed terrain, blue winter skies and an elevation of about 1500 m (3000 ft.) make the southern Cariboo one of the most versatile nordic skiing spots in western Canada.

The Red Coach Flag Inn, just down the road from the infocentre, acts as headquarters for the famous Cariboo Ski Marathon. Avid nordic skiers from the U.S.A., Australia and England join Canadians for this 50-km (32-mi.) event held annually on the first weekend in February. Usually more than 1000 people compete, ranging in age from 4 (junior loppet contenders) to 70. The best skiers finish in under 2 hours, while stragglers make a day of it. All finishers get an "I did it" pin.

Offering a mix of hills, gullies, frozen lakes, forests and level terrain, the 100 Mile–108 Mile area covers 200 km (126 mi.) of track through light, feathery snows. Skiers can base themselves at the Hills Health and Guest Ranch, the only wilderness spa in North America, just north of 100 Mile House. The resort's pool is a plus and organized horseback riding in the area in summer is very pleasant.

The 108 Resort, on the shores of 108 Lake across Highway 97 from the Hills, caters to summer golfers and boaters and to winter skiers. As you swish past the snake fences along the 6 km (4 mi.) of lit golf course track, take time to glance up for a not infrequent glimpse of the northern lights.

A super trail-riding experience in the area for buckaroos over the age of 8 is the annual Great Cariboo 9-Day Trail Ride, held at the end of July. Starting from the 100 Mile House area, participants cover a different area of the Cariboo each year, riding by day and singing and dancing around the campfire by night. In 1989 folks mustered in Clinton to ride the range of the O.K. Ranch in the Jesmond area and in the Marble Mountains. Horses are provided, but you can bring your own mount if you like. Highly experienced staff consist of a trail boss, guide and wranglers. This ride really is the ultimate way to explore Cariboo back country.

West of 100 Mile House lies the pleasant Cariboo Moose Valley Canoe Route, an ideal outing for the whole family. Moose Valley, a chain of 12 small lakes, is surrounded by forests and marshes. Its gentle waters lend themselves to a 2-day outing. Portages between lakes are relatively short and easy, with the exception of swampy territory between Beaverlodge and Long lakes where you may choose to line your canoe. Miles of groomed trails lead to secluded campsites along the lakeshore, 2 of which have tree houses. There is a unique split-log shelter with a stone fireplace and sleeping bunks on Rainbow Island on Marks Lake. A refurbished log cabin on Maitland Lake operates on a first-come, first-served basis.

Main access to the canoe route is via the Exeter Road, west of 100 Mile House. Follow the road, which begins just opposite the historic Bridge Creek Barn, until you cross the railway tracks at the B.C.R. Exeter Station. The final 28 km (17 mi.) to the main launch at Marks Lake is adequately signposted. Keep your lights on to drive this wide gravel logging road.

The ideal time to visit Moose Valley is during summer (not many mosquitoes) or fall. Abundant wildlife includes mule deer, black bears, moose and sandhill cranes. In June and July expect to see moose calves. Bebb's and

Diamond willow border the marshes. Stands of evergreens include large-diameter Douglas fir, black spruce and aspen.

Keemak Outfitters, based in Forest Grove just east of 100 Mile House, offers a unique winter trip—day or overnight expeditions by dog team. Keemak uses Alaskan malamutes to travel the Cariboo back country on the natural highways formed by frozen lakes and streams. Whether you want to learn to drive your own team or have them carry your load while you ski, taking this trip is like turning back the clock.

Useful Information

Contact the **Red Coach Flag Inn**, Box 760, 100 Mile House, B.C., V0K 2E0 (395-2266) for information on accommodation and the annual ski marathon. For information on their facilities and activities, contact **Hills Health & Guest Ranch**, 108 Ranch, Comp 26, 100 Mile House, B.C., V0K 2E0 (791-5225) and **108 Golf and Country Inn Resort**, R. R. #1, Box 2, 100 Mile House, B.C., V0K 2E0 (791-5211).

More details on the **Great Cariboo Ride** can be obtained from Box 1025, 100 Mile House, B.C., V0K 2E0 (791-6305).

Contact **Keemak Outfitters**, Box 245, Forest Grove, B.C., V0K 1M0 (397-2348) for information on their winter trips with dog teams.

LAC LA HACHE

Twenty-five km (16 mi.) north of 100 Mile House on Highway 97 lies Lac la Hache. Both the town and the lake take their name from an incident in which an unfortunate Hudson's Bay Company mule, loaded up with hatchets, plunged through the lake's ice.

During the second weekend of February, Lac la Hache hosts a 3-day winter carnival. The backbone of the festivities, which include snow golf, ice augering (boring), dog-sled mushing and ice fishing for kokanee, are the World's Largest Outhouse Races. This race, dreamt up to counteract cabin fever induced by long, cold Cariboo winters, involves the dragging of portable biffies along frozen Dixon Bay on Lac la Hache. The RCMP entry, a blue and white outhouse topped with a red light, issues tickets when other outhouses attempt to pass.

Sixteen km (10 mi.) east of Lac la Hache, the new nordic and alpine development at Mount Timothy encompasses 30 km (19 mi.) of nordic trails.

The tourist infocentre at 100 Mile House can provide information on both the February festivities at Lac la Hache and developments at Mount Timothy. Call them at 395-5353.

WILLIAMS LAKE

The gold rush bonanza of the 1860s bypassed the cattle town of Williams Lake, 90 km (56 mi.) north of 100 Mile House. Instead the town's fortunes have depended upon the more reliable bases of stockyards, forestry and agriculture. Today it is well-known for its early July rodeo, the Williams Lake Stampede. Originally an opportunity for Cariboo-Chilcotin residents to get together and blow off steam during the short, relatively quiet period between spring calving and summer haying, the rodeo is now a major item on the cowboy circuit.

The original stampedes took place where the mills now stand. In the Mountain or Suicide Race event (won many times by the horse Grey Eagle), riders would run their horses full tilt down Fox Mountain to the stampede grounds. The Roman racing event required a rider to stand on the backs of a 2-horse team that was galloping down the track.

Patrolling RCMP would put stampede-goers who got out of hand in cattle cars (temporary jailhouses) overnight and then turn them loose in the morning. The mood was easy, fun the priority; even Princess Margaret passed through in 1958 to catch the action! Today, rodeo at the Williams Lake Stampede is still some of the most exciting on the North American cowboy circuit.

For travellers provisioning for outdoor adventures in the Williams Lake area, we would highly recommend a visit to the Overwaitea store in town. No, we don't have shares in the company; it's just one of the best stocked supermarkets we've visited on our travels!

Williams Lake is also a good base for hiking in the Cariboo area. Mid-June to mid-August is prime, with mid-July being the best time for flowers (and bugs too, unfortunately).

A day trip to Mount Tatlow in the Nemaiah Valley west of town leads to 2 good fishing lakes dubbed the "Dolly Lakes" by local hikers since they are full of Dolly Varden trout. If you want the weather to remain clear, don't point at Mount Tatlow—according to native legend, if you point at the mountain it will start to rain.

Another pleasant day hike takes in the Viewland Mountain Forest Service Trail, which affords a view of Quesnel and Horsefly lakes.

The Williams Lake Travel Infocentre at 1148 Broadway, Williams Lake, B.C., V2G 1A2 (392-5025) can provide up-to-date information on the stampede and on hiking trips in the area. The infocentre is located at the junction of Highways 97 and 20.

THE FREEDOM HIGHWAY:
Williams Lake to Bella Coola

The nearly 500-km (315-mi.) Chilcotin Highway (Highway 20), linking Williams Lake with the coastal town of Bella Coola, is the only central interior road to the coast. As such, it has become a major route for travellers with varying outdoor interests.

For many years the Chilcotin region was cut off from the rest of the province because it was not connected by road to the Pacific. Although the road was started in 1888, it was not completed until 1953, when a group of local residents literally bulldozed the final stretch from the town of Anahim Lake to Bella Coola, so frustrated were they at the lack of action on the part of the provincial government. Their action earned the road its popular name—the Freedom Highway.

Highway 20 is paved for 170 km (107 mi.), from Williams Lake to just west of Chilanko Forks, then is gravel-surfaced through to the Bella Coola valley with the exception of paved sections at Nimpo and Anahim lakes.

As you head west from Williams Lake, the first turn-off is Dog Creek Road. Approximately 19 km (12 mi.) south on this road, the Springhouse Trails Ranch offers summer horseback riding and hiking opportunities. Contact the ranch at R. R. #1, Box 2, Springhouse Trails Road, Williams Lake, B.C., V2G 2P1 (392-4780).

The Gang Ranch

A 2-hour drive farther south on the Dog Creek Road leads you to the legendary Gang Ranch, which, with 12,140 deeded ha (30,000 a.) and 388,500 ha (960,000 a.) of Crown land, is one of the largest and oldest ranches in the province.

The Gang was founded in the mid-1800s by ranchers Jerome and Thadeus Harper, who romantics claim were outlaws from the Blue Ridge Mountains of West Virginia. The brothers raised beef cattle on the tall, waving blue-bunch wheat grass of the area to supply meat for hungry miners. Today, cattle range the rolling grasslands stretching as far as the eye can see.

Bordered to the west by Big Creek, to the east by the Fraser River, to the north by the Chilcotin and to the south by Churn Creek, the Gang Ranch, after various changes in ownership, is now titled to a Pennsylvania holding company for Saudi-Arabian interests.

Guests can take advantage of the week-long packages where they live and work with cowboys or take horse-packing trips into the back country. In winter, you can dog-sled in this rolling countryside. For information on vacation packages at the Gang Ranch, write to General Delivery, Gang Ranch, B.C., V0K 1N0 or phone them at 459-7923.

Becher's Prairie

Sheep Creek Bridge, which crosses the Fraser River 23 km (14 mi.) west of Williams Lake, forms the unofficial boundary of Chilcotin country, an area rich in tradition and immortalized in the writing of British Columbia author Paul St. Pierre.

Rock hounds in this area can scout the shores of the Fraser River at low water to collect rhodenite, jasper, thulite and chert.

Naturalists will want to visit Becher's Prairie, a wide patch of natural grassland through which Highway 20 passes on the way to the town of Riske Creek. Named after Fred Becher, who operated a store and post office at Riske Creek, Becher's Prairie is distinguished by the birdhouses mounted on fenceposts along the highway. Mountain bluebirds, chickadees and tree swallows live in these birdhouses, which were initially established for bluebirds to help clear up a grasshopper infestation. Bluebirds, distinctive azure-coloured members of the thrush family, seem to love ranching country: we have also spotted them in profusion along the Trans-Canada Highway in the Cache Creek–Ashcroft area and in the foothills of the Rockies. Curlews, horned larks, killdeers and western meadowlarks also live in the area and make use of the birdhouses.

In summer, this Chilcotin plateau is warm and dry. It is real Zane Grey country, blanketed by sagebrush and rabbitbrush. The many summer wildflowers include brilliantly coloured prickly pear cactus (May-June), Mariposa lilies (June-August) and horsemint (July-August). Douglas fir and lodgepole pine dominate the forests and trembling aspen puts on a lovely yellow display in fall.

As you continue west along Highway 20, look out for depressions called "kekuli holes" in the surrounding land; these were the semisubterranean winter homes of the Chilcotin and Shuswap people in earlier times. Usually about 1.5 m (5 ft.) deep and between 3.6 m and 7.5 m (12 ft. and 25 ft.) in diameter, most of these pit houses were circular. Four to six centre posts provided internal support for peeled log rafters, peeled roofing poles and clay or sod overlay. The houses were entered by way of a notched ladder through an opening that also served as a chimney hole. Although well-insulated, the pit houses were dark and very damp because of poor ventilation.

A more popular type of winter housing for the native people of the region were the above-ground "stick houses." These were rectangular, gabled-roof houses built of peeled and split poles, similar in design to a modern A-frame. The structures were chinked with moss and then covered with a layer of clay and sod for insulation and waterproofing.

The 50-year-old Chilcotin Lodge, near Riske Creek, provides accommodation in this area, and it's possible to do some cross-country skiing around the lodge in winter. You can contact them at General Delivery, Riske Creek, B.C., V0L 1T0 (659-5646).

Farwell Canyon-Hanceville

To really get a sampling of the different landscapes of the Chilcotin, travellers can take the Farwell Canyon–Hanceville drive, which covers just over 220 km (140 mi.) of open range, treed uplands, river terraces and deep river canyons. Leaving Highway 20 at Riske Creek, 47 km (28 mi.) west of Williams Lake, the route leads southwest to Big Creek before looping back to join the highway at Hanceville, making it an approximately 4-hour journey.

South of Riske Creek, the swift Chilcotin River, popular with rafters, has created Farwell Canyon, once the site of a native village. The hoodoos and other water-carved sandstone formations are one of the area's main attractions; keep an eye out for petroglyphs along the riverbanks near Riske Creek. The Chilcotin, which flows east to the Fraser, runs a glacial milky green colour due to the presence of till and is home to rainbow and Dolly Varden trout, steelhead and salmon. The miles of virgin snow on logging roads along the river provide fine cross-country ski routes in winter.

Naturalists travel to this area to view the bands of California bighorn sheep in the Junction Sheep Reserve, a 6700-ha (16,500-a.) patch of turf where the Chilcotin and Fraser rivers meet 25 km (16 mi.) southwest of Williams Lake. You can reach the reserve via a gravel road that heads south from a turnoff approximately 9 km (5 mi.) before Farwell Canyon when travelling from Riske Creek.

Several bands of sheep, totalling 400 members in all, have done well here in comparison to more southerly bands, since there is less competition from humans and cattle in the Chilcotin. In a 1954 cooperative exercise with Oregon State, sheep from the Chilcotin plateau were trapped live and used to restock bighorn ranges in Idaho, North Dakota, Washington and Oregon.

Moose and mule deer winter in the area between Big Creek and Hanceville and are often spotted in March and April. Black bears, coyotes and foxes also roam the region.

White Pelican Provincial Park

The town of Alexis Creek is 118 km (70 mi.) west of Williams Lake on Highway 20. Thirty-four km (21 mi.) to the northeast lies White Pelican Provincial Park, the breeding ground of the endangered *Pelecanus erythrohynchos* or white pelican. You can reach the park via a very rough road through private range land. Public access is prohibited between March 1 and August 31 to protect the nesting birds, and restrictions also apply to airplanes flying over the lake. Check with park officials at the Cariboo District Office, 540 Borland St., Williams Lake, B.C., V2G 1R8 (398-4414) before attempting to visit this area.

Chilanko Marsh

Continuing west on Highway 20 from Alexis Creek, you reach Puntzi Lake. Nearby Puntzi Mountain is often the coldest place in the province during winter, with the mercury dipping well below -40° C (-40° F).

In mid-June, about 600 young, banded Canada geese from the Okanagan are freed into Chilanko Marsh. This project, begun in 1981, is coordinated by Ducks Unlimited. Nesting canvasbacks and shovelers are also found in the marsh, along with many species of migratory waterfowl, shore birds and predators. The marsh lies across from Puntzi Mountain Airstrip, a forestry water-bomber centre.

Taseko and Chilko Lakes

If you turn south off Highway 20 at Hanceville, a 3- to 4-hour drive over about 117 km (74 mi.) of gravel road will take you to Taseko and Chilko lakes. These two lovely lakes, set among the highest peaks of the snow-crusted Coast Mountains, are a popular destination with shutterbugging hikers and paddlers.

At 1171 m (3842 ft.), Chilko is the province's highest major lake. Its bright green waters and the craggy mountain peaks that front it on the west make it a truly unforgettable sight. It is also notorious for its fierce storms.

Summer wildflowers and excellent fishing are major attractions in this chunk of the Chilcotin. In good summer weather it's one of our favourite parts of the province. And although campsites are numerous, the area is large enough for travellers to experience a real sense of isolation.

There are Forest Service campsites at almost every lake here; many have boat launching ramps and hiking trails nearby. All sites are free but camping is restricted to fewer than 14 consecutive days per party. Leave the ghetto blasters at home and pack out your garbage when you leave, including any fish guts, which will attract bears.

This area of the southern Chilcotin offers some interesting boating, varying from placid lake shoreline paddling to rafting on some excellent white water.

Taseko Lake, 30 km (18 mi.) long, is a good 5-day canoe/camping trip with excellent fishing at incoming streams.The lake is subject to high winds, however, so caution is advised.

In calm weather, Chilko Lake can be a scenic 1- to 2-week paddle, but its susceptibility to high winds means paddlers should build the possibility of some non-paddling days into their itinerary. The winds blow least during July and August over this extremely cold, glacier-fed lake. In fall, native people fish for salmon at ancient fishing stands where the Chilko River flows out of the lake. When the sockeye run, over half a million of them can be seen spawning on the gravel beds here.

Canadian River Expeditions offers a great 11-day circle trip that starts with a cruise up the coast from Vancouver to Bute Inlet, followed by a float-plane flight to Chilko Lake for a day's hiking and fishing. Travellers then embark on an exciting raft trip along Chilko Lake into the Chilko, Chilcotin and Fraser rivers. Take-out is at Lillooet, where the train returns rafters to Vancouver. The Chilko, probably the best known of the area's rivers, is a 107-km (67-mi.) run that takes about 3 days to complete. Expert paddlers can put in at Chilko Lake, travel down the Chilko River and take out at Alexis Creek on the Chilcotin River. One writer has called it the finest river trip in Canada. Most paddlers break this varied trip into three sections: from the lake to Lava Canyon, through Lava Canyon, and from the Taseko River junction to the Chilcotin River junction.

The first stretch, from the lake to Lava Canyon, is pleasant paddling in grade 1 and 2 water, but Lava Canyon's daunting 60-m (197-ft.) banks constrict the river and create many sets of grade 5 rapids, so the second section should be attempted only by experienced, strong paddlers in closed canoes or rafts. The final section is a swift run with a few tricky spots and one short portage.

Another good 2- to 3-day paddle is the trip south along the Chilcotin River from its source in Chilcotin Lake until it drops 338 m (1099 ft.) to the Chilko. The volume of water on the upper Chilcotin is so minimal compared to its surge when it joins the Chilko that it's almost like another river. The lower part, below the Chilko, can be done by experienced canoeists but several stretches, including the Chilcotin Canyon, are recommended only for rafters.

Paddling the Chilcotin is particularly appealing because of the variety of land forms and the interesting flora and fauna. Since this semi-arid region is low on rainfall, mosquitoes and other bugs are scarce. Several adventure travel companies run river trips for rafting enthusiasts.

Useful Information

Forestry Service Recreation Site maps, available from the Ministry of Forests, Cariboo Region, 540 Borland St., Williams Lake, B.C., V2G 1R8 (398-4420), are invaluable for road and campsite information.

Contact **Canadian River Expeditions**, Suite 10, 3524 West 16th Ave., Vancouver, B.C., V6R 3C1 (738-4449) for information on their Chilcotin cruise/raft/train trips.

Clearwater Expeditions, 613 Bissette Road, Kamloops, B.C., V2B 6L3 (579-8360) offers trips on the Chilko and Chilcotin rivers and through the Gang Ranch on the Fraser River.

Kumsheen Raft Adventures, 287 Main St., Lytton, B.C., V0K 1Z0 (455-2296 or toll free 1-800-663-6667) and **Hyak Wilderness Adventures**, 1975 Maple St., Vancouver, B.C., V6J 3S9 (734-8622) run raft trips on the Chilko, Chilcotin and Fraser rivers. **Reo Rafting Adventures**, 205-1901 Barclay St.,

Vancouver, B.C., V6G 1L1 (684-4438) organizes similar trips using paddle rafts.

The Yohetta Valley

Chilko Lake lies due south of Highway 20 between the highway communities of Alexis Creek and Chilanko Forks. The surrounding Yohetta wilderness, covering 1500 sq. km (580 sq. mi.) of forests, mountains and lakes, is becoming an increasingly popular destination with European travellers. The Federation of Mountain Clubs of B.C., together with other interested groups, has so far unsuccessfully been lobbying the provincial government to make this area part of the proposed Chilko Lake Provincial Park.

A fine hike here is the Tchaikazan-Yohetta trail, a two-valley loop between Chilko and Taseko lakes. The trail, well used by hikers, hunters and horseback riders, runs west through the Tchaikazan Valley and back through the Yohetta Valley. The two valleys are joined by an established route that goes over Spectrum Pass and past Dorothy Lake.

Spectrum Pass is spectacular, with its creek in a hanging valley that drops through a rock canyon into the big bend of the Tchaikazan River. It is recommended that hikers climb up the far side where there are fewer bears and no side gullies to cross.

The 15 craggy, glacier-covered peaks that surround the head of the Tchaikazan River; whistling marmots; mountain goats; alpine flowers, and the certainty of snow drifts when going over Spectrum Pass are additional attractions on this scenic 2-day backpacking trip.

Several side trips are possible from the trail. One route leads hikers to the head of the Tchaikazan River and the snouts of the converging Monmouth and Tchaikazan glaciers. Another, beginning at Dorothy Lake, yields a view of Chilko Lake by going north or south of the Mount Goddard–Mount Kern massif. The northerly option continues by a rough side-hill trail to Nemaiah Valley.

Adventurers may want to explore the area on horseback with one of the guide-wranglers who work in the region. Week-long tours of the Tchaikazan-Yohetta loop take riders up to the 2250-m (7380-ft.) mark and down again through countryside where moose graze on river willows and grizzly bears browse grassy meadows.

Contact Yohetta Wilderness, Box 69, Duncan, B.C., V9L 3X1 (748-4878) for information on their horse-packing and hiking trips in the Taseko Lake–Yohetta Valley area.

Tatlayoko Lake

The Tatlayoko Valley, 35 km (22 mi.) south of the Highway 20 town of Tatla Lake, is the head of the Bute Inlet watershed. The impressive Mount Waddington looms in the distance. Prevailing winds from the southwest make this area relatively bug-free; Douglas fir, pine and fragrant spruce blanket some slopes and the alpine begins at 1676 m (5500 ft.).

A third-generation pioneer family, the Bracewells, operate Alpine Wilderness Adventures from their Circle X Ranch at the north end of Tatlayoko Lake. Two week-long trips offered in July and August—the Pioneer Trip and the Explorer Trip—are among the best horse-packing trips available in B.C.

The Pioneer Trip ventures up to the top of the 2160-m (7200-ft.) Potato Mountain range. Accommodation is in an alpine log cabin or colourful tepees situated at the 1770-m (5800-ft.) level near Echo Lake. The cabin is heated by stoves airlifted onto Potato Mountain by a Ducks Unlimited helicopter. On your rides out from this alpine camp you will see grizzly pastures where the silvertips have left clear claw marks on the trees, sometimes as high as 3 m (10 ft.) off the ground.

Ice caves formed by water running through packed snow can be explored in the 2100-m (7000-ft.) range. A tangy lemongrass grows in these caves. At these levels, ptarmigans are common.

The Bracewells are well versed in local legends. According to one story, the area was once roamed by outcasts who had been expelled from a Chilcotin settlement because they were suspected of eating a missing baby. Wandering into the Chilcotin plateau, the small group planted wild potatoes so that native people wouldn't hunger again. The woman who planted on Potato Mountain was called Niut, and after her death a nearby peak was named after her; when Niut's peak is hidden in dark clouds, her spirit is said to be angry. Up until fifty years ago, Chilcotin Indians regularly harvested these remote valleys, filling burlap bags with small sweet potatoes.

Grizzlies, black bears, coyotes, mule deer, mountain goats and a comprehensive variety of alpine flowers on Potato Mountain make this prime photo-safari country. In ancient times the Potato Mountain peaks lay at the bottom of the Pacific Ocean, so travellers can see thick outcroppings of marine fossils in amongst the wildflowers.

In winter, Potato Mountain offers 180 sq. km (70 sq. mi.) of mountaintop plateau for nordic and telemark skiing. Skiers starting from the Circle X Ranch can arrange to be dropped off by helicopter to ski the uncharted wilderness of the Coast Mountain range. Interconnecting trails on the ranch itself capitalize on the area's dry powder, moderate climate and abundant wildlife.

Horse-packing near Kleena Kleene. *Photo by Sam Whitehead*

Useful Information

Contact **Alpine Wilderness Adventures** at General Delivery, Tatlayoko Lake, B.C., V0L 1W0 or 1111 Pine St., Kamloops, B.C., V2C 3A7 (372-2338) for information on their horse-packing and skiing trips.

Kleena Kleene Area

Twenty-one km (13 mi.) west of Tatla Lake, the town of Kleena Kleene (Kwakwala dialect for "oolichan grease") provides a point of access to the excellent nordic skiing of the Pantheon Range to the west. Hidden Mountain Tours runs a cozy alpine log cabin as a base from which skiers can enjoy powder slopes and impressive views of Mount Waddington. Visitors can reach the cabin by helicopter or via a 2-day ski-in, with overnight accommodation at another log cabin on a lake. Guide Sam Whitehead is a qualified nordic ski instructor with training in avalanche safety and first aid. All skiers are provided with avalanche transceivers and trained in their use. The Hidden Mountain Tours cabin also makes a grand base for summer alpine hiking.

Chilanko Lodge, on One Eye Lake north of Kleena Kleene, is a comfortable base for fishing, horse-packing, hiking, canoeing, sailing, mountaineering and nordic skiing.

One Eye Outfit offers horse-packing and canoeing trips in the Klinaklini River area south of Kleena Kleene and in the McClinchy River and Charlotte Lake area bordering Tweedsmuir Provincial Park.

Useful Information

Contact **Hidden Mountain Tours**, Kleena Kleene, B.C., V0L 1M0 (476-1155) for information on their skiing and hiking trips to Hidden Mountain and **One Eye Outfit**, Box 4045, Williams Lake, B.C., V2G 2V2 (398-8329) for information on organized horse-packing and canoeing.

Nimpo Lake/Anahim Lake Area

The town of Nimpo Lake, 304 km (182 mi.) west of Williams Lake on Highway 20, is home to many operators who fly avid anglers to distant, isolated lakes. The scenic lake, tucked below Mount Kappan, is the float-plane capital of B.C. Charter flights are available from here or from Anahim Lake, 26 km (16 mi.) farther west, for hikers and paddlers wishing to get to the Mackenzie Heritage Trail (formerly the Grease Trail), the Turner Lake chain in Tweedsmuir Park or other remote spots in the area.

Fly-in fishing resorts are located on the Dean River, the Blackwater River and Eliguk and Moose lakes. The Dean River is internationally famous among anglers for its fighting steelhead.

Anahim Lake, the major settlement of the west Chilcotin, hosts an annual stampede in July. Scheduled flights connect the town with Bella Coola and Williams Lake.

A wilderness river canoe trip starting almost due north of Anahim Lake takes experienced paddlers on a 10-day voyage down the West Road (Blackwater) River, which skirts parts of the Grease Trail. The Blackwater flows in an easterly direction from its headwaters on Far Mountain to the Fraser River approximately 320 km (200 mi.) away. The river moves from the snow-capped peaks of the Coast Mountain range in its upper regions through rolling hills, dormant volcanic cones and forested lake areas. Canoeable for about 240 km (150 mi.) of its length, the Blackwater is best paddled in July and August. Its numerous waterfalls, rapids, chutes and 15-22 portages provide a challenge for avid canoeists and kayakers, but it can quite happily be paddled in parts by less experienced canoeists.

Pools along the river are rich in rainbow trout. Deer, moose, cariboo, foxes, timber wolves, cougars, lynxes, minks, beavers, otters and both black and grizzly bears inhabit the Blackwater watershed. Trumpeter swans winter along the fast-moving ice-free stretches of the river. The colourful wood duck lives in

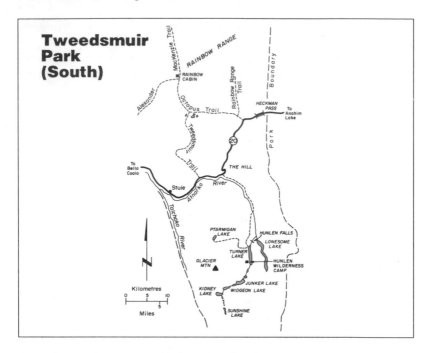

the region, and ospreys and bald eagles fish the river's waters and the three lakes through which it passes.

On Eliguk Lake, recommended for put-in, spectacular fly-fishing can result in catches of 10- to 20-kg (22- to 44-lb.) rainbow trout. Take-out is at the Blackwater road crossing; don't miss it, as the river enters a dangerous, impassable canyon just below.

Rich Hobson's books *Grass Beyond the Mountains, Nothing Too Good for a Cowboy* and *The Rancher Takes a Wife* describe the trials and tribulations of Rich and his friend Pan Phillips as they homesteaded the Blackwater area in the 1930s, establishing first the Home Ranch and then later the Batnuni Ranch. Another popular author, Paul St. Pierre, has written both fiction and nonfiction about this region. *Breaking Smith's Quarter Horse, Smith and Other Events* and *Chilcotin Holiday* capture the pioneering spirit of the Chilcotin and the people who live there.

Information on fishing, river trips and resorts in the area can be obtained from the Travel Infocentre, 1148 Broadway, Williams Lake, B.C., V2G 1A2 (392-5025).

Tweedsmuir Provincial Park (South)

Covering 981,000 ha (2.4 million a.) of wilderness, Tweedsmuir Provincial Park, B.C.'s largest, offers many adventure opportunities for hikers, naturalists, anglers and canoeists.

Bound by the craggy Coast Mountains on its western edge and the more gentle, varicoloured Rainbow Range to the east, this roughly triangular park is so vast that we have broken it into two sections, north and south, for purposes of discussion. Here we will talk about the southern portion; we cover the north in Chapter 9, "North by Northwest." South of Eutsuk Lake, the park encompasses part of the Alexander Mackenzie Heritage Trail and the Turner Lake chain.

Be sure to get a copy of the BC Parks brochure on Tweedsmuir, which does an excellent job of describing the park and its history as well as the adventuring possibilities. Another good way to get a bearing on Tweedsmuir is to contact the people at the Tweedsmuir Wilderness Centre, who have run tours in the park for over a decade.

Tweedsmuir is accessible by both road and air. Highway 20 enters the park via Heckman Pass and descends "the Hill," a section of steep narrow switchbacks over 20 km (13 mi.) down into the valley of the Atnarko River. Chilcotin Stage Lines provides a biweekly bus service between Williams Lake and Bella Coola which will let travellers off at almost any point along the road. Wilderness Airlines provides scheduled air services from Vancouver to Bella Coola, and charter-flight operators will fly passengers from either Bella Coola or Nimpo Lake to the lakes within the park.

The area that is now the park was used for thousands of years by people travelling on foot between the villages of the Nuxalk (Bella Coola) people on the coast and the Chilcotin villages in the interior. The trails established by aboriginal people were later used by explorers and surveyors looking for ways to transport furs and gold to the Pacific. Today, these historic trails form the basis for the park's network of hiking and horse-packing routes.

In the 1930s, park promoter and guide Tommy Walker began developing a system of trails and cabins in the Rainbow Mountains area. A parks branch trail-building program in the seventies added three scenic routes: a trail leading to Rainbow Mountains from Highway 20, a trail that climbs 260 m (853 ft.) to Hunlen Falls and Turner Lake, and a side trail to the alpine terrain of Glacier Mountain.

The Rainbow Mountains are actually a large dome of eroded lava and fragmented rock, renowned for their colourful, bare slopes of ashes and clinkers in shades of red, orange and yellow. The trail starts just west of Heckman Pass on Highway 20 at the Rainbow Range trailhead and provides the shortest (8 km/5 mi.) route to the alpine areas. From there, experienced backpackers can explore almost unlimited terrain. An excellent 2- to 3-day circular route via the Octopus Lake Trail is described in Bob Harris's *The Best of B.C.'s Hiking Trails*.

The trail to Hunlen Falls starts 6 km (4 mi.) east of park headquarters. It follows an old tote road for 13 km (8 mi.), then climbs 600 m (1968 ft.) in 78 switchbacks to a wilderness campsite at the north end of Turner Lake. A trail from the campsite leads across a footbridge to a viewpoint of the falls. The one-way trip is 19 km (10 mi.) and generally takes 8-10 hours.

From the Turner Lake campsite, a side trail leads 12 km (7 mi.) to Ptarmigan Lake, a splendid alpine area on Glacier Mountain.

Many short hikes start near Stuie, situated in the Atnarko River valley about a mile from the confluence of the Atnarko and Talchako rivers, which combine to form the Bella Coola River. A good place to use as a base here is the Tweedsmuir Lodge, which looks across the valley to the towering peaks of the Coast Range. Guides are available through the lodge for hikes into the Rainbow Mountain Nature Conservancy Area, along the Alexander Mackenzie Trail, and to Lonesome Lake, Turner Lake and Hunlen Falls.

The trails from Stuie lead to views of the Atnarko River, original-growth Douglas fir forests, waterfalls, alpine meadows and kettle ponds. ("Kettle pond" is the term applied to potholes formed by whirling stones in a stream under a glacier, which were dubbed "giant's kettles." Kettle ponds can also be circular hollows in a stretch of glaciated sands, gravels and clays caused by the presence of a great detached block of ice which eventually melted.)

An interesting 2-hour hike in the area is the Burnt Bridge Creek portion of the Mackenzie Trail, which runs along the park's western boundary. Following directions provided in the parks brochure entitled "Bella Coola Valley," you can descend as Alexander Mackenzie did through alder and cedar to the Burnt Bridge Creek and along the canyon bottom to the Bella Coola River. The river, which runs white due to silt from the glacier-fed Talchako, was said by Mackenzie to be the colour of ass's milk.

The best time for hiking in Tweedsmuir is from mid-July to mid-September. You'll need insect repellent on most trips and you must exercise extreme caution when hiking in the vicinity of the Atnarko River during the fall salmon run when grizzly and black bears practise their own brand of fishing. Remember that Tweedsmuir is a wilderness park; hikers should have appropriate clothing and equipment for wilderness travel.

Tweedsmuir Lodge, serviced by twice-daily Wilderness Airlines flights from Vancouver, is also popular with people interested in fishing in the area. There is excellent fishing within 270 m (300 yd.) of the lodge.

Two main runs of that glamour fish, the steelhead, occur in the Bella Coola–Atnarko system. The spring run lasts from March to May, when the fish come in to spawn; in the fall, the run lasts from October through November and usually includes larger fish (some up to 9 kg/20 lb.). The Chinook salmon run from mid-May to July, while coho come into the rivers from September to November. Trout and char can be caught year-round on the Atnarko.

Commercial horse-packing in southern Tweedsmuir is the exclusive terrain of the Dorsey family of Anahim Lake, who have guided in the Chilcotin for three generations. Throughout July and August, rides of a week to 10 days' duration take horse-packers through the colourful volcanic peaks of the Rainbow Range, along the Mackenzie Trail from Gatcho Lake to Bella Coola and into the alpine territory of the Itcha/Ulgatcho Mountains.

The **Turner Lake Chain**, sometimes known as the Hunlen Lakes, is a string of 7 lakes lying in a broad valley on the western edge of the Chilcotin plateau in southern Tweedsmuir Park. The lakes in the chain offer true wilderness paddling, easy portages and good campsites, as well as excellent fishing. Linked by Hunlen Creek, they are located 1100 m (3600 ft.) above the Atnarko Valley, into which the creek ultimately cascades over 260-m (853-ft.) Hunlen Falls.

Travellers can fly in by float plane to the Hunlen Wilderness Camp on Turner Lake or to one of the other lakes from the town of Nimpo Lake. It takes 20 minutes to fly from Nimpo Lake to Turner Lake. It is also possible to hike in to the Turner Lake Chain.

The entire chain is ideal for wilderness canoe travel. Where the connecting streams between the lakes are navigable, they are cleared of sweepers by the parks staff; where they are too rocky, short bypass trails have been built. The paddling is almost entirely on flat water and none of the 6 portages takes longer than 20 minutes. The 5 parks branch campgrounds along the lake chain are equipped with steel-ring fireplaces, outhouses and tenting areas. All of the campgrounds and trails are clearly marked with signposts, and the longer portages have resting poles for the canoes.

In the 1950s, Ralph Edwards, the legendary pioneer of Lonesome Lake in the Atnarko Valley, brought two pairs of spawning cutthroat trout up from his homestead and released them into Turner Lake. The trout have multiplied and spread up and down the lake chain, attracting a large population of loons to the lake system and making a paddle of the area particularly rewarding for anglers.

Each lake has its own character. Cutthroat Lake, as the name implies, is a good place to wet a line. You can often spot moose browsing on wild horsetail tips in the shallows of Vista Lake. Junker Lake has a beautiful beach and excellent campsite. Surrounding the lakes are the knife-edged spires of Glacier Mountain to the northwest, the snow-covered Talchako and Ape mountains to the southwest and the rounded Walker's Dome to the southeast.

Many travellers here choose to make their base at the Hunlen Wilderness Camp run by John Edwards, Ralph's son. Located at the inlet end of Turner Lake, the camp has several housekeeping cabins and a fleet of canoes available for rent. Hikers can prearrange to have canoes left for them at the parks campground (near the falls at the lake's outlet) or to be met by the camp's work boat. For those who fly in, the float plane will drop you off at the beach in front of the camp. A trip to the camp is worth it just for a taste of John's fresh-baked bread and cinnamon buns!

The hiking in the Turner Lake Chain is a terrific bonus and there are many day hikes that can be done from the Hunlen camp. One day-long round trip from the parks campground leads up above the timber line to Ptarmigan Lake, the largest lake in the Glacier Mountain group. From early July until late August the flowers in this area are something to see, and the view is magnificent. Another all-day round-trip hike from Edwards's wilderness camp descends to his father's homestead on Lonesome Lake. Invaluable reading matter for those who do this trip is *Ralph Edwards of Lonesome Lake*, which chronicles the efforts of Edwards and his daughter Trudy Turner in helping to save the trumpeter swans from extinction.

Edwards also recommends a short (1-2 hour) hike beginning at Kidney Lake, the last lake in the chain; the route climbs 240 m (800 ft.) to Sunshine Lake for spectacular views of open alpine areas and 3000-m (10,000-ft.) peaks sculpted with hanging glaciers.

In the heart of Tweedsmuir Park lie the Tanya Lakes. The people of the Ulkatcho nation have started trekking back to these lakes in late July, as their ancestors did for thousands of years, to catch and dry the big Chinook salmon that run up Takia Creek from the Dean River. Located on the old Grease Trail trading route, the Tanya Lakes were the last stopover for native traders before they descended from the interior plateau into the coastal valleys. Dotting the jackpine ridges that line Tanya meadows are the remains of several smokehouses. Today, the Ulkatcho hold an annual fall gathering here, spearing the salmon with gaffs made from the tines of old hay forks or from nails, then boning the fish and smoking them.

Useful Information

Contact the Visitor Services Coordinator, BC Parks, Cariboo District, 540 Borland St., Williams Lake, B.C., V2G 1R8 (398-4414) for park maps and brochures.

Hummingbird Nature Tours, 31-22374 Lougheed Highway, Maple Ridge, B.C., V2X 2T5 (467-9219) offers week-long backpacking trips into the Rainbow Mountains.

Tweedsmuir Wilderness Centre, Box 10, Bella Coola, B.C., V0T 1C0 (no phone) runs backpacking trips in the park as well as lodge-based day trips. Contact **Tweedsmuir Lodge**, Bella Coola, B.C., V0T 1C0 (982-2402) for information on accommodation and guides for hiking trips into the park.

Contact **David Dorsey Jr., Guide and Outfitter**, Box 3066, Anahim Lake, B.C., V0L 1C0 (742-3251) for more information on horse-packing trips.

Information on the Turner Lake Chain can be obtained from **Hunlen Wilderness Camp**, Box 308, Bella Coola, B.C., V0T 1C0 (no phone) or through **Tweedsmuir Travel**, Box 780, Bella Coola, B.C., V0T 1C0 (982-2434).

Wilderness Airlines (689-2588 in Vancouver, 982-2225 in Bella Coola or 1-800-452-2291 toll free) and **Dean River Air Services** (742-3303 in Nimpo Lake) provide charter float-plane services to the various lakes of the park region.

Contact **Chilcotin Stage Lines** (392-4283 in Williams Lake) for up-to-date bus schedules and fare information.

Bob Harris's book *The Best of B.C.'s Hiking Trails* contains information and trail descriptions of hikes in the Rainbow Mountains and the Hunlen Falls/ Turner Lake area of Tweedsmuir Park.

The Alexander Mackenzie Heritage Trail (The Grease Trail)

Although only part of the 420-km (264-mi.) Mackenzie Trail or "Grease Trail" crosses Tweedsmuir Park, we will discuss the trail in its entirety here.

The trail is named after Alexander Mackenzie, who in 1793 became the first European to cross the North American continent, preceding the Lewis and Clark expedition by more than twelve years. Native guides led Mackenzie and his nine companions on the last stages of his journey to the Pacific, reaching tidewater on what is now named the North Bentinck Inlet.

The trail crosses west-central B.C. from the mouth of the West Road (Blackwater) River between Prince George and Quesnel to Dean Channel, northwest of Bella Coola. The entire trail can be hiked by an experienced backpacker in just under 3 weeks. Hikers with limited time can complete shorter sections by making use of float-plane services. Passing through a variety of biogeoclimatic zones, the trail is on its way to becoming one of the big North American hikes, both because of its historical importance and because of the varied flora and fauna to be found along the route.

The name "Grease Trail" recognizes that the original trail was a trade route along which the coastal Indians traded oolichan grease from processed fish for moose and beaver hides and obsidian with tribal people in the interior. Oolichan grease was a major source of Vitamin D in the diet of native peoples in B.C.; it was also used for medicinal purposes and to enhance food flavours in much the same way as modern cooks use butter. Oolichan grease was a prized gift and was used in many ceremonies.

It's best to tackle the Mackenzie Trail in late summer or early fall, after clouds of mosquitoes and blackflies have disappeared from its low swampy stretches. The rivers will be easier to ford at this time of year and most of the late snow will have melted in the high mountain passes. The trail can be hiked both ways, but most people walk from east to west, following in Mackenzie's footsteps.

Before reaching Tweedsmuir, the trail skirts the Blackwater River, running through relatively flat terrain with several stream crossings (take your hiking staff!). The rugged part of the trail starts on the upper Blackwater between Chinee Falls and the park boundary. Along this section some hikers opt to fly out at Eliguk or Gatcho lakes; others prefer to fly in to these lakes just to hike the 80-km (50-mi.) Tweedsmuir Park section of the trail. Because of the numerous lakes in the upper Blackwater region, float planes can land in many places here, so you can really customize your trip. However, you should allow a few days leeway in case bad weather prevents flying.

Backpackers who like alpine terrain will enjoy the Rainbow Mountains (also known as "the mountains that bleed"), through which the Mackenzie Trail passes. West of the Tweedsmuir Park boundary, the trail leads through typical west-coast rain forests filled with tall red and yellow cedars, mountain hemlocks, massive Douglas firs, sword and deer ferns and a wide variety of berry bushes.

The final few kilometres of Mackenzie's epic journey must be made by boat from Bella Coola to Mackenzie Rock in the Dean Channel, where the explorer inscribed succinctly in grease on a rock, "Alexander Mackenzie, from Canada, by land, 22nd July 1793."

The Alexander Mackenzie Trail was declared a Provincial Heritage Site in July 1988 and work continues on signs and interpretation notes. The Trail Association is working to establish a Sea-to-Sea Heritage Route that follows the route of the voyageurs from Lachine, Quebec, to Fort Chipewyan, then hooks up with Mackenzie's trail across Alberta and B.C. to Sir Alexander Mackenzie Provincial Park in Dean Channel, west of Bella Coola on the Pacific Ocean.

Useful Information

An excellent guidebook, *In the Steps of Alexander Mackenzie*, contains 25 detailed fold-out maps as well as excerpts from the intrepid Scot's journal. It can be obtained in Vancouver from outdoor stores like **Mountain Equipment Co-op** and **Taiga**, or from **The Alexander Mackenzie Trail Association**, Box 425, Kelowna, B.C., V1Y 7P1.

Hummingbird Nature Tours, 31-22374 Lougheed Highway, Maple Ridge, B.C., V2X 2T5 (467-9219) offers guided backpacking trips in Tweedsmuir along the Mackenzie Trail.

Wilderness Airlines (689-2588 in Vancouver, 982-2225 in Bella Coola or 1-800-452-2291 toll free) and **Dean River Air Services** (742-3303 in Nimpo Lake) provide charter float-plane services to the various lakes of the region.

Bella Coola Valley

The Bella Coola Valley is home to the native people of the Coast Salish Nuxalk nation. According to local mythology, the valley is also considered to be the home of the mythical thunderbird, its bowl-shaped walls and encircling peaks forming the nest of the mighty, eagle-like bird.

Alexander Mackenzie was the first white man to descend into the Bella Coola Valley, in 1793, and the Hudson's Bay Company post established here in 1869 existed for thirteen years. In 1894 Reverend Christian Saugstad and a group of fellow Norwegians moved here from their first North American settlements in Minnesota and the Dakotas. As many as 1000 descendants of the original 90 settlers now live in the Bella Coola Valley, whose fiord-like North Bentinck Arm undoubtedly reminded them of the ocean fiords of Norway. This remote valley first became vehicle-accessible on the completion of the Freedom Road (Highway 20) in 1952.

Hagensborg, 28 km (17 mi.) beyond the west entrance to Tweedsmuir, still reflects its Norwegian heritage. It is also the site of the Bella Coola airport, where travellers can get connector flights to Vancouver and the Chilcotin.

The Snootli Creek Fish Hatchery is located 4 km (2.5 mi.) west of town. Guided tours allow visitors to view the Chinook, chum, coho and steelhead stocks raised for release in the nearby Bella Coola and Atnarko river systems.

About 10 km (6 mi.) out of Hagensborg are the Thorsen Creek petroglyphs, one of the few sites in the province where large stylized Polynesian-looking rock carvings can be seen. Ask at the Bella Coola information centre for directions to the site, which lies above a beautiful creek.

Situated at road's end, Bella Coola is 480 km (298 mi.) from Williams Lake. The settlement is located near the mouth of the Bella Coola River, 100 km (63 mi.) from the open sea and the island village of Bella Bella. There is no longer a ferry service to and from here but charter boats and daily flights connect Bella Coola with Vancouver, the Chilcotin and nearby coastal communities. For adventurers, Bella Coola is a kick-off point for the Inside Passage and central coast.

History buffs can take a charter boat or short flight to Sir Alexander Mackenzie Provincial Park, situated on the north shore of Dean Channel west of Bella Coola. Paddlers may choose to canoe the fast-flowing Bella Coola River, down which Mackenzie travelled with his aboriginal guides at the end of his transcontinental journey.

South of town lies Rivers Inlet, a famous destination for sports fisherpeople since a world-record tyee, weighing 36 kg (80 lb.), was caught here. Excellent fishing videos of this area are obtainable from White Knight Video, 1849 Welch, North Vancouver, B.C., V7P 1B7 (986-9311).

Useful Information

The Bella Coola Travel Infocentre, Box 670, Bella Coola, B.C., V0T 1C0 can provide information on boat charters and fishing lodges.

Contact **Wilderness Airlines** (689-2588 in Vancouver, 982-2225 in Bella Coola or 1-800-452-2291 toll free) for information on scheduled and charter flights to and from Bella Coola.

Hakai and Fiordland Recreation Areas

Ocean kayakers keen to duplicate the Broken Island experience of the west coast of Vancouver Island are increasingly drawn to the two relatively new marine parks accessible by chartered boat or float plane from Bella Coola. The Hakai Recreation Area is located midway between Bella Bella and the northern Vancouver Island community of Port Hardy. A terrain of protected inner islands and exposed outer islands, it is ten times larger, more remote and varied than the Broken Islands and requires a 1- to 3-week expedition to do it justice.

Hakai covers 124,000 ha (306,407 a.) of islands, wide channels and narrow inlets with a variety of sea life and the justifiably famous salmon-fishing grounds of Hakai Passage. Sandy beaches on the western perimeter of Hakai are easily accessible and provide good campsites. Since the area is so remote, kayakers should be experienced ocean paddlers, proficient in navigation and rescue techniques. The area is also accessible by chartered boat or float plane from Port Hardy. The Inside Passage ferry route from Port Hardy to Prince Rupert and Alaska follows the eastern edge of the Hakai Recreation Area.

To the north lies the 91,000-ha (224,863-a.) Fiordland Recreation Area, which includes Mussel and Kynoch inlets at the northern end of Mathieson Channel. The surrounding rugged kilometre-high coastal mountains and cascading waterfalls are typical of the spectacular scenery of this area. There are several beaches and river estuaries suitable for camping in both inlets.

Useful Information
Contact the Visitor Services Coordinator, BC Parks, Northern Region, 1011 4th Ave., Prince George, B.C., V2L 3H9 (565-6270) for further information on these recreation areas.

Klahanie Kayaking Adventures, 1295 Johnston St., Vancouver, B.C., V6H 3R9 (682-4250) offers guided kayaking trips of 5, 8 or 11 days in the Hakai area.

Ince and Kottner's book *Sea Kayaking Canada's West Coast* provides an excellent description of both Hakai and Fiordland.

EAST OF WILLIAMS LAKE

While the Freedom Highway provides plenty of adventuring opportunities west of Williams Lake, the terrain east of town is also rich in exploring possibilities. Paddlers are particularly drawn to Quesnel Lake, whose long wishbone-shaped waters point farther east towards Wells Gray Park. In all, the lake's myriad arms and bays provide 800 km (500 mi.) of paddling shoreline, backed by mountain peaks reaching 2400 m (8000 ft.) in spots. At 667 m (2224 ft.) it is the deepest lake in the province and prone to unpredictable weather shifts. Large (13- to 18-kg/30- to 40-lb.) lake trout and 6-kg (15-lb.) rainbow trout swim in its cool waters.

A paved road from 150 Mile House, 12 km (7 mi.) east of Williams Lake, leads to Likely, at the western end of Quesnel Lake, from which boaters pass through the turbulent Narrows to Cedar Point, a tree-lined park. As you proceed up the west arm of the lake, the sandy beaches of Hazeltine Creek are located to starboard.

The lake's many islands include Cariboo Island, located approximately 19 km (12 mi.) from the Narrows, Twain Islands, situated on the lee side of Cariboo, and the Beehive Islands. Horsefly Bay, at the entrance to Hobson Arm, is the site of a major salmon migration each fall.

On the north arm of Quesnel Lake, Grain Creek, Long Creek, Goose Point, Bowling Point, Roaring River and Wasko Bay are all spots with campsites, sandy beaches and protected moorage. Mitchell River, at the end of the arm, is a prime nesting and rearing site for Canada geese, and you can spot osprey and eagle nests in several locations. Wildlife includes black and grizzly bears, minks, wolverines, coyotes and caribou.

Terrain along the lake's east arm is completely different. Because of the many sheer cliffs, there are few protected moorages. Mountain goats inhabit the cliffs, and Little Niagara Falls is a fine place to stand on a hot day for an impromptu shower.

The Quesnel River flows west out of Quesnel Lake starting at Likely, and, along with the Cariboo River, provides some varied kayaking and rafting.

The Quesnel River Hatchery is situated at the point where the Quesnel River flows out of the lake, close to Likely. Completed in 1982, the hatchery produces approximately 3.2 million Chinook fry a year for the McGregor, Bowron, Willow, Slim, Blackwater, Nasko, Chilcotin, Chico, Cariboo, Quesnel, Horsefly and McKinley river systems, plus about 30,000 coho fry for the McKinley Creek watershed.

Rearing time at the hatchery starts with the spawning season in about mid-August, when crews head out to remote locations to gill-net and fence-trap "ripe" females for their eggs and male fish for their milt (sperm). Eggs and milt are collected as soon as possible after the fish are caught.

Females are killed by a sharp blow to the head, hung by their tails, bled and carefully cleaned before their eggs are removed and placed immediately in portable ice chests. The male salmon deposits milt when it is held by one person while another strokes its underbelly. The milt is placed in coolers.

As newly fertilized eggs are very sensitive to movement, the eggs and milt are flown daily to the hatchery by helicopter, and fertilization then takes place in stable incubation trays. Clean well water flushes continually through the fertilized eggs for 30 days until they are "eyed" (a black eye appears). Next they are "shocked"—dropped from a height of about 60 cm (24 in.) into 5 cm (2 in.) of water in the bottom of a bucket—to identify unfertilized eggs, which turn white and are then removed by hand with tweezers. If left in the incubation tray, unfertilized eggs provide a breeding ground for fungus that smothers live eggs. Each batch is kept separate during the hatching and rearing process so they can be returned to the exact spot where their parents were found. After 60 days the alevins hatch; tiny food sacs attached to their bellies provide sustenance until they "button up" (finish absorbing their food sacs) at about 3 months of age in mid-November to December.

The fry, as they are now called, are then moved outdoors to rearing tanks, then rearing channels where they are fed Oregon moist pellets, a fish by-product pepped up with vitamins and nutrients. Water flow is constantly monitored to ensure adequate oxygen supply. Nets across the ponds deter birds of prey and a round-the-clock watch is kept for winter storms, which can play havoc with the generator that monitors and pumps the water supply through the channels.

In April, the fry are transported in tank trucks to a spot near their release site; from there, helicopters, equipped with large hanging buckets, airlift the fish to the river where they are released under the cover of night. Most of the Chinook will spend at least a year in fresh water before migrating to the Pacific Ocean, where they remain for 2 to 3 years before coming home to spawn.

You can make your own way through the hatchery by following the signs or arrange a tour by contacting the manager. Hatchery hours are from 8:00 A.M. to 4:00 P.M. every day.

Likely, 93 km (58 mi.) east of Williams Lake, hosts a well-attended Logger Sports Day held annually during the first week in July. Men and women contestants compete in over 20 different events derived from traditional jobs such as choker setting, hand bucking and pole climbing. The Molly Hogan event requires the competitor to take a length of wire cable and bare-handedly splice the ends together to form a circle; this skill is used by loggers to join cables or attach line to equipment.

Likely, named after prospector John A. "Plato" Likely, is one of the few remaining gold rush settlements. Nearby Horsefly was the site of the first Cariboo gold rush in 1859. Both places can be visited as part of a circle day trip on the 210-km (130-mi.) Gold Rush Trail that starts from Williams Lake. Take along a gold pan and try your luck.

A shorter route cuts across the scenic ranching valley along Beaver Creek, which was the site of a strange shooting in gold rush days—one of the camels used as pack animals during that time was shot in Beaver Valley by a prospector who mistook it for a giant grizzly!

The hike to Eureka Bowl, at the end of a mining road past Horsefly, leads to a lovely waterfall and the site of an old gold mine where core samples can sometimes be found lying around. Yanks Peak, near Likely, is another popular spot for hikers.

Nordic skiers can explore the Corner Lake Trails near Horsefly, which offer 13.5 km (8.5 mi.) of beginner and intermediate skiing.

Canoeing is possible on the 3 lakes in the Beaver Valley and on the Horsefly River and Horsefly Lake. All 3 areas are home to a variety of wildlife. Since a canoe or kayak makes possible a quiet approach to moose, bears, beavers and other animals, be sure to keep a respectable distance. Moose, particularly when with their young or feeling threatened territorially, have been known to charge paddlers.

An easy weekend trip within 50 km (31 mi.) of Williams Lake, the Beaver Valley route is accessible if you travel east on the Likely Road. The only real hazard in this 3-lake chain (Beaver, George and McCauley) is occasional shallow water.

The Horsefly River is a 90-km (56-mi.) drive southeast of Williams Lake. Put-in is at Squaw Flats, 10 km (6 mi.) downriver from Horsefly, and take-out is at Mitchell Bay on Quesnel Lake. A fairly flat river, the Horsefly does contain some sweepers and log jams.

Horsefly Lake, 100 km (63 mi.) northeast of Williams Lake, makes a good 2- to 3-day paddle, but beware of sudden high winds. A provincial campsite at the west end of the lake and a Forest Service campsite at Suey Bay on the east end are comfortable bases from which to photograph and fish

More experienced paddlers might want to travel the Quesnel River route, a 3-day paddle with casual riverside camping available. Rafters and kayakers usually put in at Likely, where the river flows out of the lake, but it is also possible for canoeists to put in at Quesnel Forks; take-out for everyone is at the town of Quesnel, 104 km (65 mi.) downstream, where the Quesnel River meets the Fraser.

The fast-flowing Quesnel River travels through Bullion Camp, where Dancing Bill Latham struck it rich in 1859. Beyond Bullion is a rock-clogged canyon known as Devil's Eyebrow by locals. The confluence of the Quesnel and the lumber-laden Cariboo River at Quesnel Forks makes for big water volume and the Big Canyon section (just before Quesnel) is recommended only for rafters.

The Cariboo River is wilder than the Quesnel and is better suited to expert paddlers. The river rises in the Cariboo Mountains and passes through the southern part of Bowron Lake Park. It is recommended that paddlers drive from Quesnel to Bowron Lake Park and canoe the last portion of the Bowron Lake circuit in reverse, through Bowron Lake to Unna Lake where the Cariboo River heads south out of the park. Its banks are rife with moose, black bears, grizzly bears and a wide variety of raptors (birds of prey). The 4- to 5-day trip takes in an obligatory portage at Cariboo Falls, a short distance downstream from Unna Lake. Logs are dumped into the river downstream of Cariboo Lake, and these, combined with eddies and fast sections, are hazards that paddlers must watch for as the route passes through Sellar Creek, Spanish Creek, Murderer's Gulch and Quesnel Forks. One place to take out is at Quesnel Forks, but the trip can also be continued on the Quesnel River to Quesnel. The route is described in detail in Richard Thomas Wright's *The Bowron Lakes—A Year Round Guide.*

Motorists keen to explore Cariboo back-country byways should be sure to pick up the comprehensive pamphlets describing the Quesnel area circle tours from the tourist infocentre in Quesnel.

One of the most enjoyable of these tours is the Maeford Lake/Cunningham Pass route linking Likely and Barkerville, a 140-km (88-mi.) stretch of road through true back country. After crossing the Cariboo River just south of Keithley Creek, the tour follows the Maeford Forestry Road into wilderness high country, past Maeford and Ghost lakes, up over Cunningham Pass and on to Barkerville. Travellers should check with the Forest Service field office in Likely for up-to-date road information.

Useful Information

The Forest Service Recreation Sites map, an invaluable guide to the back roads and camping sites of the area, can be obtained from the Ministry of Forests, Cariboo District, 540 Borland St., Williams Lake, B.C., V2G 1R8 (398-4414). The Forest Service field office in Likely (740-2230) has up-to-date information on road conditions.

Contact the **Quesnel River Hatchery** at 790-2266 to arrange for a tour.

The Tourist Information Centre, 703 Carson Ave., Quesnel, B.C., V2J 2B6 (992-8716) can provide brochures on the scenic circle tours and attractions in the area. The Cariboo Tourist Association, Box 4900, Williams Lake, B.C., V2G 2V8 (392-2226) has similar information.

QUESNEL TO BARKERVILLE

Quesnel, located 120 km (75 mi.) north of Williams Lake on Highway 97, served as a jumping-off point for miners heading into the Cariboo gold fields in the mid-1800s. Today, this town of 8000 provides services for visitors en route to Barkerville and the Bowron Lakes.

Visitors usually stop off at Cottonwood House Provincial Historic Park, 35 km (21 mi.) east of Quesnel on Highway 26. Archival photos pay tribute to Cottonwood's original incarnation as a well-provisioned roadhouse for prospectors.

Wells, 45 km (28 mi.) past Cottonwood House Park, sprang up in the 1930s and was a major gold mining centre until the sixties. Today it retains the clapboard look of an earlier era, complete with board sidewalks and colourful false-fronted stores. Nordic skiers come to Wells to ski nearby areas like Mount Murray, Bald Mountain and the bowl at the head of Williams Creek.

BARKERVILLE

In summer, visitors are invariably drawn to Barkerville, 9 km (6 mi.) past Wells on Highway 26. Barkerville figures largely in Cariboo gold rush lore; it was founded in 1862 when prospectors hurried to the banks of Williams Creek after Billy Barker, an English prospector, and his cronies hit pay dirt in a creek channel. Over $1000 worth of gold was brought up in 48 hours. The town grew up around this rich area.

In its heyday, Barkerville was as sophisticated as a boomtown could be, and boasted of being the largest town in North America west of Chicago and north of San Francisco. A fire demolished the town in 1868 and its rebuilding resulted in a façade of order, presided over by the dreaded Judge Begbie. Although often called the "hanging judge," he actually sentenced only two men to the scaffold. He did not, however, take crime lightly and his stiff sentences deterred many potential outlaws and thieves. He was almost solely responsible for the preservation of law and order in the Cariboo gold fields during those years. Richard Wright's excellent book *Discover Barkerville* describes in detail the history of the area and its personalities.

Today, Barkerville is a provincial park with 40 reconstructed buildings and living history programs that run all summer, making it an ideal family holiday destination. Many visitors come up via B.C. Rail from Vancouver and stay in nearby Wells or Quesnel. If you plan to visit the area without a vehicle, be sure to organize transportation to Barkerville well in advance of your arrival, as last-minute arrangements can be expensive.

Contemporary visitors can eat in late-1800s style restaurants, pan for gold and watch excellent theatre productions that recreate the gold rush days. Save time for a brief visit to the Barkerville cemetery; packed with the gravestones of young prospectors, it is a poignant reminder of what proved for many to be a futile search for the mother lode.

Barkerville Provincial Park has 3 campgrounds, several picnic areas and marked hiking trails. In winter, it is a popular cross-country skiing area, with a trail going through the main street to the restored courthouse at Richfield.

Contact the Visitor Services Coordinator, BC Parks, Barkerville, B.C., V0K 1B0 (994-3332) for park brochures and information.

BOWRON LAKE PROVINCIAL PARK

Between Wells and Barkerville, a side road heads 40 km (22 mi.) north to Bowron Lake Provincial Park. Like many other British Columbia parks, Bowron Lake owes its existence, at least in part, to the dedication of conservationists—in this case, Frank Kibbee and Thomas and Eleanor McCabe.

In the area at different times, both Kibbee and the McCabes carried out studies of the extensive bird and animal life of the region, ultimately persuading the provincial government to classify the land as a game reserve in 1926. It was reclassified as a park in 1961. The park is named after John Bowron, a gold-rush pioneer who settled in the area and eventually became Gold Commissioner of nearby Barkerville.

Deep in the heart of the Cariboo Mountains west of the Rockies, the park's sloping, rectangular chain of 6 major lakes (and several smaller ones) is the most documented canoe circuit in North America, with good reason. Within the space of a week (ideally 10 days, to allow for unexpected weather), paddlers can canoe this circuit of lakes which range in size from not much larger than a pond to 38 km (24 mi.) in length. Paddlers can indulge their voyageur instincts on this 116-km (72-mi.) route, in many ways a quintessentially Canadian experience. Glacier-streaked mountains rising to 2100 m (6888 ft.) are reflected in dark-blue waters; moose browse in the shallow marshes at lake edge or swim to distant islands; grizzly bears come down to the Bowron River in fall to feast on spawning sockeye salmon. This safari fills paddlers with a special kind of peace that permeates your mind and can last for months. Not surprisingly, the many summer paddlers include outdoor enthusiasts from Europe, the United States and other parts of Canada who fly to Quesnel, then head east to the end of the road in the Bowron Lake Park.

The circuit can be paddled independently (the size of any one group is restricted to 6 people) or with an organized group like Pathways Tours (the only tour company who have their own campsites on the chain). Basically, age is no limit to the Bowron chain, particularly if you go with an organized group. Pathways organizes one special family tour a year when children over 12 are accepted. Adults in their seventies often join the Pathways trips, too. The joy of going with a group like Pathways is that everything is taken care of: provisioning, equipment and coaching in paddling techniques.

While a basic level of fitness is a prerequisite for the trip, portages (of which there are 6) can be made a lot easier by using two-wheeled canoe carts that you pull along over the land.

Bowron Lake Lodge and Becker's Lodge on Bowron Lake rent a variety of canoes, camping gear and equipment for paddlers and also provide cabins for voyageurs on the outward and return legs of the journey. Many a fond memory of completing the circuit revolves around the hot showers and crackling fires in a lodge at the end of the trip.

Paddlers planning on fishing for trout and landlocked kokanee salmon during the trip can get fishing licences at either lodge. Some of the sweet-tasting trout of this area have a firm pink flesh that is unique to fish living in cold, clear glacial waters. No hunting is allowed in the park, and consequently a great variety of wildlife may be spotted. Moose, for instance, are often seen on Kibbee, Unna, Babcock and Spectacle lakes as well as on the Bowron River. Grizzlies can be observed grazing in the avalanche chutes along Isaac Lake, while mountain goats frequent the upper reaches of Mount Kaza above Lanezi Lake.

Carefully consider the type of canoe and other equipment you will take on this circuit, since you should plan on 4 to 6 hours of paddling for 7 days. Light paddles and comfortable life jackets are a must, and good rain gear and a waterproof tent with no-see-um netting are also important. Synthetic sleeping bags are preferable as they dry quickly. All gear should be double-bagged in plastic to ensure that it stays dry.

When provisioning for the trip, light, varied and nutritious should be the key words (remember the portages). Bring high-energy food like pancake mixes, rice, pasta, pita bread, cheese and fruit, and plenty of trail mix for snacking during the paddles. All tins must be burned and then carried out.

Since bears love bacon, don't bring it. Bowron bear stories abound: the ones we like entail cheeky black bears carting off provisions when packs are set down at portages. All the wilderness campsites, shelters and portages around the circuit are equipped with bear caches which should be used at all times. These platforms, suspended between two trees whose lower trunks are sheathed in metal, are accessible by ladder. As an added deterrent to bears, don't bring in perfumes or scented items.

Wood is provided at most campsites for cooking and campfires but you will need an axe to split the wood blocks. And since the park does lie partially in the coastal rain belt, the wood can be wet, so it is best to bring along a small camping stove. You should also bring toilet paper, since outhouses are not stocked.

Water should be boiled for at least one minute or otherwise treated before drinking or brushing teeth to prevent giardiasis. Another option is a small, portable filter such as the Swiss-made Katadyn product.

All paddlers must register and pay a fee, in cash or traveller's cheques only, at the Nature House, situated at the beginning of the first portage where your journey begins. There is a government campsite adjacent to the Nature House.

The circuit can be travelled at any time between June and the end of October. The lakes freeze over in December and are usually ice-free by mid-May. June is the best time for bird watching or wildlife viewing, and distant peaks are still covered in enough snow to make for some spectacular photo op- portunities. July and August are the busiest months on the Bowron circuit. By mid-September the bugs have gone and lovely fall colours arrive.

Three waves of bugs fly in from June to early fall: mosquitoes, no-see-ums and blackflies, which roll in from July to the end of August. However, if you bring plenty of repellent (types with 95 per cent Deet as the active ingredient work well) and mosquito coils for further protection, a summer paddle is worth it for the warm, sunny skies and cloudless, star-streaked nights.

As this canoe circuit becomes more popular (over 3000 people canoe the chain each summer), timing is of the essence. Most people set out on Saturday or Sunday, so try to time your start for midweek to avoid the crowds.

We recommend early-morning paddling because of calmer waters and cooler weather. Wildlife viewing is often better then, too. If you establish your campsites early, this will leave time for side trips to scenic spots and for fish- ing, bathing and other recreation. Watch for birds in the photogenic Indian- point slough.

Excellent descriptive information on the Bowron Lake circuit is available in the parks branch brochure and in Richard Thomas Wright's book, *The Bowron Lakes—A Year Round Guide*, so we provide just a brief overview here.

The clockwise circuit starts with the hardest portage, a 2.4-km (1.5-mi.) trek over an often slippery, muddy trail from the campground to Kibbee beaver dam. A 2-km (1.3-mi.) portage leads from the end of Kibbee Lake to Indian- point Lake.

A short portage (less than 1 km/.6 mi.) leads to Isaac Lake, at 32 km (20 mi.) the longest one in the chain. Most canoeists choose to paddle close to shore. Five banks of ridges, peaks and ranges complete with avalanche chutes front Isaac Lake. Depending on the weather, your journey here can be a sun- drenched drift under an improvised sail or a squint-eyed paddle against choppy waves. Experienced paddlers may canoe the river chute out of Isaac Lake but there is a portage for those who prefer not to risk a dunking.

The 5.2-km (3.3-mi.) stretch of the Cariboo River between McLeary and Lanezi lakes is a tricky part of the trip. The river is a notorious obstacle course of dead heads and sweepers, so the bow paddler must keep a careful and constant watch.

The country around Lanezi Lake is not prime for camping, so take the inside perimeter of the lake and follow the marked route through the shallows to Sandy and Unna lakes, checking the opaque waters for shallows and dead heads. A short hike starting on the southwest shore of Unna Lake leads to the roaring waters of the 24-m (80-ft.) Cariboo Falls.

Next you will travel shallow Babcock Creek; you will probably want to walk midchannel here, lining your canoe and taking care not to damage the beaver dams as you cross them. The creek leads into the Spectacle Lakes, which are good for fishing and swimming, and where loons can be relied upon to provide a haunting evening concert. During the last leg of your trip you will pass through the Bowron River marshes, good moose-spotting country and an excellent place to watch beavers at work. A final 7 km (4.4 mi.) down Bowron Lake takes you back to the campsite at the beginning of the circuit.

Paddlers who do not wish to cover the entire loop can travel counterclockwise from the outset, canoeing Bowron Lake as far as the head of Spectacle Lakes, an easy journey with no portages, and then returning the same way.

Not quite so placid as the lakes—in fact, rife with log jams, rapids, boulder fields and other hazards—the Bowron River, which flows out of the lake chain to the Fraser, presents the expert paddler with an extremely varied 3- to 5-day trip. It's the sort of river where you're better off with a guide who knows the area, as its route along the west side of the Cariboo Mountains and then across the Fraser Plateau makes it unpredictable. There is fine wildlife and bird viewing along the way, however. Wright's *The Bowron Lakes—A Year Round Guide* gives a detailed description of this river.

In winter, experienced cross-country skiers can ski the Bowron Lake circuit between January and mid-March. The suggested route runs counterclockwise, starting with Bowron Lake. The parks branch in Barkerville can provide additional information on the route.

As the full trip can take 5 to 7 days, depending upon snow conditions, an ideal way to tour is with dog sleds. Wolverine Mountain Guide Outfitters offer winter dog-sled trips in the park and surrounding areas. The dog teams can pack the gear for 4 to 6 people, so that skiers have to carry only a day pack.

Useful Information
A very useful park map and brochure can be obtained from the Visitor Services Coordinator, BC Parks, Cariboo District, 540 Borland St., Williams Lake, B.C., V2G 1R8 (398-4414). Waterproof maps can be obtained from MAPS BC, Surveys and Mapping Branch, Parliament Buildings, Victoria, B.C., V8V 1X5 (387-1441).

Becker's Lodge, Box 129, Wells, B.C., V0K 2R0 (492-2390 or radio phone N69 8552) and Bowron Lake Lodge, 672 Walkem St., Quesnel, B.C., V2J 2J7 (992-2733 or radio phone N69 7937) both provide accommodation, canoe and equipment rentals and fishing licences.

Pathways Tours, c/o 5915 West Boulevard, Vancouver, B.C., V6M 3X1 (263-1476 or toll free 1-800-663-3364) provide excellent guided trips through the Bowron Lake circuit for paddlers age 12 and up and have their own campsites. **Stoney Mountain Wilderness Adventures**, Box 1766, R. R. #1, Clearwater, B.C., V0E 1N0 (674-2774) offers guided canoe or ski trips in the park. **Wolverine Mountain Outfitters**, Box 25, Wells, B.C., V0K 2R0 (radio phone H42 4307) runs horse-packing trips into the mountains northeast of the park as well as canoe trips in the park. Wolverine's ski-trip package can include a dog-sled team if you want one.

The Bowron Lakes—A Year Round Guide by Richard Thomas Wright provides excellent historical information about the area as well as detailed descriptions of canoe routes and winter activities such as nordic skiing.

CHAPTER 9

North by Northwest

Travel north in any part of the world and you usually enter another dimension, somewhere unique, often inaccessible—and northern British Columbia is no exception. Its appeal lies in its sense of exclusivity and its rugged remoteness. Home to few, explored only by the hardy, it is tough country. In the opinion of its adventurers, however, it is more than worth the effort.

This rectangular area is bound along its southern border by the Yellowhead Highway, which leads from the central city of Prince George to Prince Rupert on the coast. The North shares most of its western boundary with Alaska, except for a slice of the Pacific between Prince Rupert and the Portland Canal, a stretch of shoreline that includes the Khutzeymateen Valley (famous for its grizzly-bear population). The northern boundary runs along the 60th parallel with the Yukon. On the east, the region is fenced by the Rocky Mountain Trench.

The Stewart-Cassiar Highway runs north through this area; to the west the brilliant red, yellow, white and purple lava flows of Mount Edziza Park gleam under an azure sky, and on the east rise the Spatsizi Plateau and the headwaters of the Stikine River. *Spatsizi* is the Tahltan Indian word for "red goat," a reference to the all-over tint the goats get from rolling in the dust of a red sandstone formation high up in the mountains.

Four mountain ranges—the Coast, Skeena, Cassiar and Omineca—slice across the North, and in between lie vast plateaus and some of the province's largest lakes (Atlin, Ootsa and Whitesail). In the extreme northwest of B.C. sits the St. Elias Range, which contains the largest glaciers and icefields in the province.

Winters are cold in the North, summers hot. Until recently the town of Stewart held the world record for annual snowfall. In summer, as you venture into the Lakes District off the Yellowhead Highway, bugs can be tiresome, so pack plenty of repellent.

Home for centuries to the native Tsimshian, Tlingit and Tahltan peoples, the North provided ample resources for survival and trade. The Coast Tsimshian and coastal Tlingit controlled the important oolichan oil trade, while the Tahltan (an Athapaskan, or Dene, people) collected obsidian in the interior to make cutting tools that were then traded with other tribes from Alaska to the Queen Charlotte Islands.

To this land came the young Scottish explorer Alexander Mackenzie in

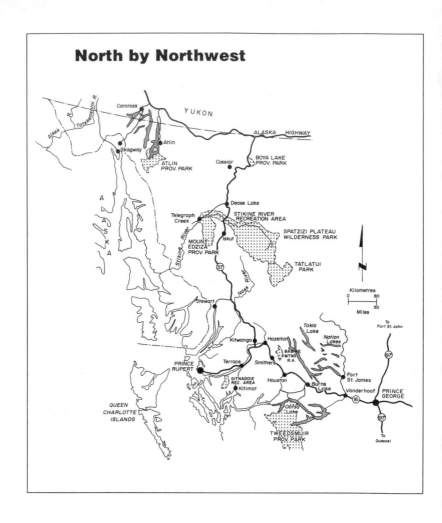

North by Northwest

1793, four years after the harrowing expedition that took him to the North rather than his aim, the Pacific. Establishing fur routes for the North West Company, Mackenzie's voyageurs headed down the Fraser River, bartering with resident native people, before forging west along the now-restored Alexander Mackenzie (Grease) Trail (a trading route used to transport oolichan), until they reached the Pacific at Bella Coola. From 1806 onwards, explorer Simon Fraser established Hudson's Bay Company forts like the beautifully restored one on the edge of Stuart Lake at Fort St. James.

Almost a century after initial European exploration, gold rush fever hit the Klondike region. The rush lasted from 1896 to 1899, peaking in 1898 when 40,000 prospectors poured into the Dawson City gold fields via the infamous Chilkoot Pass near Skagway, Alaska.

Today, mining still forms a lynchpin of the northern economy. The recent Eskay Creek gold findings, south of the Iskut River and north of Stewart, confirm the appropriateness of the nickname given to this portion of B.C. by geologists: the Golden Triangle. Molybdenum is also mined at Endako, near Fraser Lake, while Alcan operates a massive smelter out of Kitimat. Forestry is also very important to the area.

The region's main attraction for visitors is its vast wilderness. The Tatshenshini and Stikine offer some memorable river expeditions; Spatsizi and Mount Edziza are prime hiking and horse-packing territory, while the Lakes District west of Prince George is considered to contain world-class angling waters.

Moose, Osborn caribou, stone sheep, black bears and grizzly bears range the North both within and outside established park boundaries. Herds of caribou move across the Spatsizi Plateau. Eagles and raptors proliferate in the North, particularly on the coast, where good salmon pickings are guaranteed!

Few roads cross the North, so access to some key areas is limited. But this is prime bush-pilot country where it is not unusual to see canoes, kayaks and other outdoor gear being loaded onto light airplanes.

For the northern portion of our book, we travel along the Yellowhead Highway from Prince George to Prince Rupert. En route, the road goes through Vanderhoof, the true epicentre of B.C. From Prince Rupert, we backtrack along the Yellowhead to Kitwanga and then take the Stewart-Cassiar Highway (Highway 37) north through a technicolour landscape. Highway 37 meets the Alaska Highway at Watson Lake, just across the B.C./Yukon border. From there, we travel west to Whitehorse and then south to Atlin, the legendary Chilkoot Trail and the great Tatshenshini-Alsek watershed.

PRINCE GEORGE

The city of Prince George (pop. 66,612) lies at the junction of Highway 97 and the Yellowhead Highway (Highway 16). It is the northern terminus of the B.C. Railway line from Vancouver and a stop on the Canadian National Railway freight line, which runs east-west and terminates in the major port of Prince Rupert.

The third largest city in the province (after Vancouver and Victoria), Prince George has been called the Western White Spruce Capital of the World (quite a mouthful!) due to the fact that it is a megacentre for pulp production. Perhaps more appropriately for adventurers, it is also known as the City of the Hale and Hearty.

Situated at the confluence of the Nechako River, which flows down from the northwest, and the Fraser River, which flows in from the Rockies in the southeast, Prince George is an ideal base for canoeists, hikers, nordic skiers and anglers.

Originally named Fort George by Simon Fraser, who established a North West Company trading post on the site in 1807, Prince George celebrates its native ancestry at the Fort George Park (site of an Indian burial ground) and the Fort George Regional Museum, which pays tribute to the Carrier Indians of the region.

Blessed with 116 parks, Prince George is definitely an outdoors city. At the Forest for the World Park on Cranbrook Hill, visitors can learn about forest management techniques and plant tree seedlings as part of the "Leave Your Roots in Prince George" program.

Winter is no deterrent to outdoor enthusiasts in this part of the world. Many B.C. libraries (and incidentally, the beautiful Prince George Library, full of natural light, is our favourite in the province) and used bookstores have copies of Richard Wright's out-of-print *B.C. Cross Country Ski Routes*, an excellent guide to the area. It gives comprehensive details of the almost 60 km (38 mi.) of trail systems at the Sons of Norway Lodge and the Hickory Wing Ski Club, both in the Tabor Mountain Recreational Reserve 15 km (9 mi.) east of Prince George. Many of the trails are located in an old burn area where a fire raged out of control for twenty-two days. Nearby Tabor Mountain Ski Resort offers ski rentals, downhill facilities and a day lodge.

In both winter and summer, wildlife lovers can head about 9.5 km (6 mi.) east of Tabor Mountain Ski Resort to a raised platform just a 5-minute walk from a pull-out on the north side of the highway. Moose range the length of the Yellowhead Highway, so be patient and you might well spot one of these browsers.

Hikers and nordic skiers who head farther east on the Yellowhead Highway will arrive at Raven Lake–Grizzly Den Recreation Area, a marvellous patch of alpine country reserved exclusively for hikers and cross-country skiers, located about 86 km (54 mi.) east of Prince George. Parking lots for both Grizzly Den and Raven Lake can be found down the Hungary Creek Forest Road.

The U-shaped main system of about 15 km (9 mi.) of trails and public cabins make exploration of the 1328-h (3281-a.) Grizzly Den area a pleasure. The lovely champagne air of high altitude (an average of 1737 m/5700 ft.), coupled with summer meadows full of anemones, columbines, lady's slipper, red heather, moss campion and blue violets, more than compensates for brisk early morning and late evening temperatures.

The Grizzly Den Trail, which climbs 610 m (2000 ft.), takes seasoned hikers to a rudimentary cabin in 2 to 3 hours. Two trails branch off from there: Tumuch Trail heads 8 km (5 mi.) south into an adjoining valley to connect with a logging road, while the other trail runs the 5 km (3 mi.) to a cabin on the shores of rainbow-trout-filled Raven Lake. Both the Grizzly Den and the Raven Lake cabins sleep 20 and are open to the public year-round at no charge. The Grizzly Den cabin even boasts an oil heater.

The Grizzly Den Trail from Hungary Creek is suitable for beginning nordic skiers. A more interesting and challenging route takes advanced ski tourers along Tumuch Lake Road to the south end of Raven Lake Wilderness Preserve, over Tumuch Mountain, through Olga's Pass and then down to Grizzly Den Cabin. It's a strenuous trip but, weather permitting, is rich in views and sightings of the northern lights.

Trails are maintained year-round, and an honour system compels hikers to leave the cabins as tidy as they found them.

North Rockies Ski Tours of Prince George offers 4-, 5- and 7-day guided back-country ski tours to the northern Rockies using their mountain lodge as a base.

Useful Information

The maps of the Forest Service Recreation Sites for Prince George East and Prince George West are useful reference guides for the area. Copies can be obtained from the Ministry of Forests, Prince George Region, 1011-4th Ave., Prince George, B.C., V2L 3H9 (565-6193).

Trail maps of the Raven Lake–Grizzly Den Recreation Area are available from the Ministry of Forests, Prince George District, 2000 South Ospika, Prince George, B.C., V2N 4W5 (565-7100).

Further information on the area can be obtained from either **Caledonia Ramblers**, Box 26, Station A, Prince George, B.C., V2L 4R9 or the **Sons of Norway Ski Touring Club**, Box 245, Station A, Prince George, B.C., V2L 4S1.

Contact **Northern Rockies Ski Tours**, 1960 Garden Drive, Prince George, B.C., V2M 2V8 (564-7814) for more information on the trips they offer.

VANDERHOOF

Thirty-eight km (61 mi.) west of Prince George on the Yellowhead Highway lies the town of Vanderhoof, which can legitimately claim to be the most central community in B.C. A cairn 5 km (3 mi.) east of town marks the geographical heart of the province.

Now a centre for ranchers and loggers, Vanderhoof was named after Herbert Vanderhoof, a publicist from Chicago who was hired in the early 1900s by the Canadian government to lure settlers to western Canada. Ranchers came in droves from Oregon, attracted by large and cheap acreages, but Vanderhoof's elaborate plans for the development of the town site, including the building of a writers' retreat on the banks of the Nechako, never materialized. A later resident of the region, Rich Hobson, wrote three classic stories about the growth of this part of B.C.: *Grass Beyond the Mountains, Nothing Too Good for a Cowboy* and *The Rancher Takes a Wife*. River Ranch, established by Hobson in the 1930s, lies just south of Vanderhoof on the road to Kenny Dam.

The Vanderhoof Bird Sanctuary, spread along 5 km (3 mi.) of the Nechako River, is something of a mecca for birders in spring and fall, when 50,000 birds pass through on their voyages north or south.

One of the optimum ways to view the huge northern migration of Canada geese in April is to paddle down the Nechako River. The first put-in is at km 96 (mi. 60) south on the Kenny Dam Road at the base of 18-m (60-ft.) high Cheslatta Falls. The second put-in is 16 km (10 mi.) downstream at a Forest Service campsite near the River Ranch. The trip to the confluence of the Nechako and Stuart rivers can take from 3 to 5 days and passes through some splendid ranching country, with good game viewing and fishing for rainbow and Dolly Varden.

History buffs and accomplished paddlers can follow in Simon Fraser's footsteps by canoeing the Stuart-Nechako rivers from Stuart Lake (Carrier Lake in Fraser's day) to Prince George, a 3- to 6-day trip. The route through the Nechako Plateau is prime for spotting wildlife, including moose and mule deer on the banks and copious bird life on the river.

An interesting side trip north from Vanderhoof on Highway 27 is Fort St. James, an old Hudson's Bay fort established by Simon Fraser in 1806 on the edge of Stuart Lake. The present buildings, including a storehouse and salmon cache, date from the turn of the century and have been painstakingly restored and preserved largely by volunteers since the mid-1960s. The result is very impressive and entirely authentic, particularly the furnishings in the factor's house.

To get a feel for the countryside surrounding Fort St. James you can hike for a leisurely 4 hours to the top of Mount Pope northwest of town, at 1472 m (4858 ft.) the highest point in this area. From the top there's a wonderful view towards Takla Lake and the Nation Lakes, and west to Babine Lake.

Wilderness paddlers have the option of canoeing the Nation Lake Chain, a one-week voyage ideal for families. This 4-lake chain, connected by the

Nation River, is a 140-km (88-mi.) paddle one way. To get to put-in at Chuchi Lake, continue north from Fort St. James for 120 km (75 mi.) along a gravel road. From Chuchi, paddlers travel west through Tchentlo Lake, Indata Lake and finally Tsayta Lake. Sheltered coves, sandy beaches and lots of fish make for good camping, fishing and wildlife viewing (moose, bears and wolves).

Since these lakes form a chain, an alternative to paddling the return trip is to take advantage of a power-boat ferry service back to your point of departure. Paddlers can also fly in from Fort St. James to Tsayta Lake, paddle downstream to Chuchi Lake and then fly out. Since there is not much traffic on the road leading from Chuchi to Highway 27, hitchhiking can be tricky.

One hundred and sixty km (99.5 mi.) northwest of Fort St. James along a gravel road lies Takla Lake, an even more remote but perfectly paddleable lake. The lake's other attractions include houseboat rentals and British Columbia's most isolated pub, the Takla Rainbow Lodge. You can paddle down to Fort St. James from Takla Lake by heading south through the Driftwood Valley, down the Middle River to Trembleur Lake and on to Stuart Lake via Tachie River.

Useful Information

Excellent B.C. Forest Service Recreation Site maps of the Stuart Lake and Nation-Takla areas are available from the Ministry of Forests, Prince George Region, 1011-4th Ave., Prince George, B.C., V2L 3H9 (565-6193).

B.C. Wilderness Outfitters, 7406 Hart Highway, Prince George, B.C., V2K 3B2 (962-6438) can provide canoe rentals, route information and shuttle service for paddlers. For information on canoeing trips in the Nation Lake chain, contact **Northern Sun Tours**, Box 2522, Smithers, B.C., V0J 2N0 (847-4419).

LAKES DISTRICT/TWEEDSMUIR PARK

If you continue west from Vanderhoof on the Yellowhead Highway you will first reach the town of Fraser Lake (dormitory town for Endako's massive molybdenum mine), and then enter B.C.'s own Lakes District, which centres on the community of Burns Lake.

Distinctly more rugged in character than its British counterpart, this Lakes District extends from Ootsa Lake in the south to Babine Lake in the north in a 100-km (62-mi.) radius. The 300 fishing lakes that fill this high country between the Fraser and Skeena river watersheds house rainbow trout weighing up to 7 kg (15 lb.) and char up to 13 kg (30 lb.).

An early tourist brochure about the area claimed the country was ideal for "the robust out-of-doors type" keen to berry-pick, rock-collect and photograph, and this is still true today. Since the area falls in a bit of a rain shadow, receiving less than 50 cm (20 in.) a year, rock hounds at the Eagle Creek site near Burns Lake and shutterbugs hiking or skiing the area can generally expect sunny skies.

Tourist information centres at Burns Lake and Houston provide up-to-the-minute information on the best fishing pools, ski trails, horse-packing and hiking opportunities.

Nordic buffs can head for the well-established Omineca Ski Club, located south of Burns Lake on Highway 35. The club maintains groomed trails, some lit for night skiing. It has produced several provincial champions and often hosts provincial and national ski events.

Rock hounds might want to take the road 6.5 km (4 mi.) west of Burns Lake to the Eagle Creek Agate-Opal Site, one of the few known localities of precious opal in B.C. The public can explore this No Staking Reserve for leaf-green, white and amber agates, common opal, and some of the rare precious opals that have been reported.

The Lakes District also provides access to the northern part of B.C.'s largest park, Tweedsmuir, specifically to the area north of the Dean River, which bisects the park, and south of Ootsa-Whitesail lakes, which crown Tweedsmuir rather like a floppy hat. Considerably larger than Prince Edward Island, Tweedsmuir is divided into the park proper, which comprises 897,000 ha (2,216,500 a.) and the recreation area of 98,000 ha. (240,000 a.).

Lakes, waterways and the Quanchus Mountain range dominate northern Tweedsmuir. Access to the park is by light aircraft or via the Ootsa-Whitesail Lakes (Nechako) Reservoir, which was created in 1952 to provide headwaters for a hydro-electric plant built farther west, at Kemano, to power Alcan's aluminium smelter at Kitimat on the coast.

Prior to the creation of the reservoir, Eutsuk, Ootsa, Whitesail and Tetachuck lakes formed a system of waterways once popular as a circle boat tour. Now the shoreline of the reservoir is a forest of drowned trees and debris that is hazardous to boaters.

You can reach the reservoir from either Burns Lake or Houston. From Burns Lake, it is a 65-km (40-mi.) trip along Highway 35, including a free ferry ride across François Lake, to the settlement of Ootsa Lake on the north shore of the reservoir. The route from Houston is slightly longer (96 km/60 mi.) and leads alongside the Morice River, then past Owen Lake to Wistaria Landing and Wistaria Provincial Park on Ootsa Lake.

Kayakers and canoeists are advised not to travel on the reservoir, as strong winds often gust through these lakes. Instead, transportation by motorboat to Chikamin Portage between Whitesail and Eutsuk lakes can be arranged. At the portage, a two-person team runs a manually operated railway that winches all boats across a 350-m (1148-ft.) stretch of land between the reservoir and Eutsuk Lake. More than 800 boats make use of this well-maintained facility each year.

There are wilderness campsites around the lake and several trails branch out to smaller lakes and alpine tundra in the both the Chikamin and the Quanchus mountain ranges. Backpackers using routes around Mount Wells and Tweedsmuir Peak may encounter woodland caribou herds. Another trail follows Musclow Creek to the trout-filled waters of Musclow Lake.

Many people like to explore the Quanchus Mountains on horseback. The Burns Lake and Houston tourist information centres can supply up-to-date information on guide-outfitters.

When planning a trip to Tweedsmuir, keep in mind that it is a wilderness park. As the park brochure rather severely states, "Outdoor recreation opportunities are almost unlimited, but those who are not prepared to be completely self-sufficient or who do not wish to employ a professional guide should not contemplate a visit."

Kayakers and canoeists will also enjoy travelling the Nanika-Kidprice Canoe Route just west of the park. This route links 5 lakes and is very scenic with abundant wildlife. The return trip from Lamprey Lake to Nanika Falls takes 3 to 4 days. Two of the lakes, Lamprey and Anzac, offer good fishing.

Useful Information

For further information and brochures on Tweedsmuir Park, contact the Visitor Services Coordinator, BC Parks, Skeena District, Bag 5000, 3726 Alfred St., Smithers, B.C., V0J 2N0 (847-7320).

An extremely useful Recreation Sites map of the Lakes District area can be obtained from the Ministry of Forests, who also publish a Forest Service Recreation brochure of the Nanika-Kidprice Canoe Route. Contact them at 3726 Alfred St., Smithers, B.C., V0J 2N0 (847-7425).

For information on canoeing trips in the Nanika Lake chain, contact **Northern Sun Tours**, Box 2522, Smithers, B.C., V0J 2N0 (847-4419).

For general information on the area, including guide-outfitters or boat transportation to the Chikamin Portage, contact the Chamber of Commerce, Box 339, Burns Lake, B.C. V0J 1E0.

THE BULKLEY VALLEY

From Burns Lake Highway 16 continues to Smithers, the centre of the Bulkley Valley. Three main groups of adventurers frequent the Bulkley Valley area—skiers, fisherpeople and paddlers. The area is famous for the size of its fish (luring such anglers as Bob Hope) and the large range of skiing trails and rivers. There are also excellent opportunities for hiking and camping in such areas as Ethel Wilson Provincial Memorial Park near Babine Lake, north of the Yellowhead Highway.

The park is named after the British Columbia writer who died in 1980 and is best known for her novel *Swamp Angel*, which tells the tale of a woman who escapes from a bad marriage and travels to a remote lake in northern British Columbia.

Smithers itself (pop. 4778) is dominated by nearby 1676-m (5500-ft.) Hudson Bay Mountain, which offers downhill and nordic skiing facilities. Downtown, the atmosphere is quasi-German, with Bavarian architecture and red-brick sidewalks.

Because the Bulkley Valley saw a great deal of mining exploration in the thirties, the area still bristles with roads that make good cross-country trails. A super way for nordic skiers to explore the area is to contact the Bulkley Valley Cross-Country Ski Club, as they offer group trips with a leader as well as slide shows, clinics and potluck dinners. A long season, which can start as early as mid-November and last until the end of April, makes for fairly reliable snow conditions for downhillers as well.

A nice varied day trip on the mountain is the Toboggan Creek Trail, a 19-km (12-mi.) return trip for experienced skiers with a 700-m (2296-ft.) vertical rise. To reach the trail, head west from Smithers and turn left at the Lake Kathlyn Road, drive 2.4 km (1.5 mi.) and then take a left fork onto Glacier Gulch Road, which climbs another 2.4 km (1.5 mi.), crosses a hydro line and leads to a small road heading right. Park here, then follow the trail northwest along the base of the mountain to Toboggan Creek and up the Toboggan Valley.

Another popular nordic trail in the Hudson Bay Mountain area leads to McDonnell Lake, a 40-km (25-mi.) circuit.

The Babine Mountains Recreational Area, about 15 km (9 mi.) east of Smithers off the Yellowhead Highway, provides extensive opportunities for nordic skiers, who usually have a monopoly on trails since snowmobilers tend to confine themselves to their own recreation sites on Dome and Onion mountains.

An appealing day outing for those with young children is the route to Sunny Point (7 km/4.4 mi.), while the 26-km (16-mi.) circuit into Silver King Basin is for the more energetic. Other good nordic trails in the Babine area include Cronin Mountain, McCabe Trail (29 km/18 mi. round trip) and Harvey Mountain Trail (22 km/14 mi. round trip), all catalogued in Einar Blix's book *Trails to the Timberline*.

Possibly the longest and certainly most scenic nordic trip in the Bulkley Valley is through the Telkwa Pass. To reach trailhead at Telkwa, travel 11 km (7 mi.) east of Smithers on the Yellowhead. This trip takes planning, since skiers should arrange for friends to meet them at Clore River, 80 km (50 mi.) from Pine Creek on the Telkwa side. In parts of the avalanche-prone pass, ice walls and vertical rock reach high into the sky, giving skiers the feeling of being in an icebox.

The Babine Mountains Recreation Area is also prime for hiking, and wilderness camping is popular here even though there are no facilities. Consult *Trails to the Timberline* for good trail descriptions. Another pleasant way to explore the Bulkley Valley is by canoe. The 80-km (50-mi.) stretch along the Bulkley River from Houston to Smithers makes a good day trip. In fall, paddlers can enter the annual Bulkley Valley Fall Fair canoe race which follows the same route. The Bulkley is also popular with salmon and steelhead anglers.

Put-in is at a camping site about 2 km (1.3 mi.) west of Houston. Early on, the river seems small, but this is deceptive; at its confluence with the Morice (named after northern cartographer, priest and historian Father Morice), the Bulkley's waters increase considerably. Stop-off points en route to Smithers include Paddon's General Store at Quick, the site of Hubert, a town that never was, and Tellwa.

Other interesting canoe trips in the area can be made on the Morice, Tolka and Suska rivers, as well as through the Swan Lake Chain.

The Babine River, which runs north and east of Smithers, is considered in angling circles as the world's greatest steelhead river, and it is also a world-class white-water run for rafters and kayakers. One site along the river is known as Grizzly Drop since as many as 15 bears can be spotted at one time during salmon spawning runs. The Babine is a rafting river par excellence and operators usually work from June to September. David Duckett from the California-based rafting company High Adventure Quest says that none of the 30 rivers he has run in western North America can match the Babine.

Fossil hounds and bird watchers will be interested in visiting Driftwood Canyon Provincial Park. The 14-ha (35-a.) fossil bed exposed by Driftwood Creek contains pieces of shale, which, when split, reveal fossils of insects, plants, fish and prehistoric birds. Collecting is allowed, but visitors are advised to dig in the talus slope below the canyon wall, since the wall itself is unstable. If you find a rare fossil, it's best to donate it to the local museum or parks office for study. The park is a 20 km (12-mi.) drive northeast of Smithers along the Babine Lake Road and a gravel road.

Sandhill cranes migrate through this area in the spring and fall. This 1-m (3 ft.) high grey bird is distinguished by red markings on its forehead and face, and makes a distinctive call not unlike the sound of a bellowing bull. Flocks of several hundred sandhills fly over the Yellowhead in season.

Useful Information
An extremely useful Recreation Sites map of the Smithers and Hazelton area can be obtained from the Ministry of Forests, 3726 Alfred St., Smithers, B.C., V0J 2N0 (847-7425). For further information on the area, including the address of the local ski club, contact the Smithers Chamber of Commerce, Box 2389,

'Ksan Village, near Hazelton. *Photo by Lloyd Twaites*

Smithers, B.C., V0J 2N0 (847-9854).

For information on their 1- to 5-day canoeing trips of the lakes and rivers in the area, contact **Northern Sun Tours**, Box 2522, Smithers, B.C., V0J 2N0 (847-4419). **Action River Expeditions**, 5389 SE Marine Drive, Burnaby, B.C., V5J 3G7 (437-6679) offers 4- to 6-day rafting trips on the Babine/Skeena rivers. **Canadian River Expeditions**, Suite 10, 3524 West 16th Ave., Vancouver, B.C., V6R 3C1 (738-4449) offers raft trips from the headwaters of the Skeena to Hazelton. **Interior Whitewater Expeditions**, Celista, B.C., V0E 1L0 (955-2447) offers 4-day raft trips on the Babine River.

SKEENA RIVER COUNTRY

Between Smithers and Terrace the Yellowhead travels an inverted horseshoe route. Sixty-eight km (42 mi.) northwest of Smithers lies the town of New Hazelton and 6 km (4 mi.) northwest of that is the tiny community of Hazelton, the nerve centre for the Gitksan people in the area and the junction of the Skeena and Bulkley rivers.

Hazelton is the home of the 'Ksan Indian Village Museum, built near the site of an ancient native community to preserve and share some of the Gitksan way of life. Backed by the Roche Deboule mountain range and shaded by sweet-smelling cottonwoods, 'Ksan has become a key destination for visitors interested in this vibrant culture.

Construction of 'Ksan (which means "between the banks" in Nishga) began in 1968. Four communal houses and a carving house were subsequently opened to the public, with totem poles, mortuary poles, canoes and other items added in the ensuing years. The Frog House of the Distant Past, the Wolf House of the Grandfathers, the Fireweed House of Treasures, the Today House of the Arts and the Carving House of All Times all follow traditional longhouse designs. Guided tours are available during the summer for a nominal fee. At different times of the year visitors can watch salmon being smoked, wood being carved, ancient dances being performed and jewellery being crafted.

Also located on the 'Ksan grounds is the Northwestern National Exhibition Centre and Museum, which displays travelling exhibits of art, culture and natural history. The museum houses a unique collection of Gitksan artifacts. These are the property of hereditary chiefs and many are still used in special ceremonies. Visitors will also want to see the magnificent totem poles in the nearby villages of Kitwanga, Kitwancool, Kisgcgas, Hagwilget, Kispiox and Kitseguec. Kitwancool has the oldest pole in North America.

Kitwanga Fort National Historic Site, at the junction of the Yellowhead and Highway 37, commemorates at Battle Hill ('Ia'awdzep) a Gitwangak victory in which logs were rolled down Battle Hill to crush attackers.

Anglers will know that record steelhead trout are caught in local rivers such as the Kispiox. The Kispiox is, in fact, one of the best paddling rivers in the area. From put-in at Sweetin River, just east of Kispiox, to take-out at Kispiox village bridge, the 2-day paddle takes the canoeist through bear and sandhill crane country and past at least 3 fishing lodges. You can fish from the shores of the Kispiox but fishing from canoes is not permitted.

From Kitwanga, which lies 43.5 km (27 mi.) west of New Hazelton, the Stewart-Cassiar Highway runs north to connect the Yellowhead with the Alaska Highway, a route we cover later in this chapter.

Useful Information

For further information on 'Ksan, write to 'Ksan Indian Village Museum, Box 326, Hazelton, B.C., V0J 1Y0 (842-5544).

For guided tours of the historic Gitwangak village at Battle Hill, contact the Gitwangak Band Council, Box 400, Kitwanga, B.C., V0J 2A0 (849-5591). Tours start from the band office at the junction of Highways 16 and 37.

For information on the canoeing trips along the Kispiox River, contact **Northern Sun Tours**, Box 2522, Smithers, B.C., V0J 2N0 (847-4419).

TERRACE

Famous for its white bears and large fish, the town of Terrace lies at the junction of the Yellowhead Highway and Highway 37, 140 km (87 mi.) east of Prince Rupert. Its largest fish, a 42-kg (93-lb.) spring salmon, was caught just 6 km (4 mi.) from downtown.

Kermodei (also spelled kermode) bears, *Ursus americanus kermodei*, are a subspecies of the black bear, *Ursus americanus*. They are a creamy colour, somewhat darker than the larger white polar bear, and are named for the former director of the B.C. provincial museum, Dr. Francis Kermode, who established them as a subspecies in 1905. Their range is the central coastal area of B.C. and they are often spotted ambling through the forested, mountainous countryside around Terrace.

A port of call for the Skeena River sternwheelers in the early part of this century, Terrace is now a government and distribution centre for the northwest. Forestry forms its economic base.

The Kitsumkalum River, which takes its name from the Tsimshian word meaning "people of the plateau," flows into the Skeena River at Terrace. Kitsumkalum Mountain Provincial Recreation Area, 5 km (3 mi.) west of Terrace down a gravel road off the Yellowhead, offers some good nordic and alpine skiing in winter.

Visitors can also travel 24 km (15 mi.) north of Terrace along a logging road to Kitsumkalum Provincial Park on the west shore of Kitsumkalum Lake, where ancient volcanic action has created red sand beaches. Spawning salmon travel to this deep, cold lake, which lies partially below sea level. Creamy Kermodeis can be spotted here, as well as beavers, moose, porcupines and mountain goats. The mountain goat, *Oreamnos americanus*, whose closest relative is the chamois of the Alps, is really more of a goat-antelope and is often confused with the bighorn sheep of southern B.C. and the Dall sheep of the North. The age of these white goats can be determined by the growth rings that appear annually on their short, hollow, black, block-shaped horns. They frequent the rocky cliffs high above the Skeena River and several areas of the Nass Valley.

The Nass River, which rises in the Skeena mountain range and empties into the Pacific at Portland Inlet between Stewart and Prince Rupert, is another great river of the central coast. The maze of logging roads in the valley north of Kitsumkalum Lake provides access to Lava Lake and the Nass Lava Beds, recently designated as Nisga'a Memorial Lava Bed Park.

The beds, considered the country's youngest lava, were created approximately 250 years ago. Lava Lake was formed when the Tseax lava flow dammed the Tseax River, which drains northward into the Nass. After damming the Tseax River, the lava flow pushed the Nass River out of its channel, shunting the steaming waters up against the north side of the narrow valley and submerging a lake to create the Nass Lava Beds. The total flow covered 38 sq. km (15 sq. mi.).

Nishga legend has it that the lava flow occurred in September when the salmon were returning to spawn and the young men were amusing themselves by torturing the fish with burning pitch. Such cruelty and waste prompted the elders of the village to warn that the spirits would be offended. As the cruelty continued, the beating of a spirit drum was heard and the volcanic cone erupted. Only a few people escaped the hot lava, which set the forests on fire and boiled the water in the Nass and Tseax rivers.

Hikers can travel to the cone and crater over areas of jagged lava. Take care, as it is possible to break through the crust and fall into a hollow. Lava beds are always a fascinating site for studying plants, since flora is starting again from scratch; check in particular the lichens and saxifrage.

While you are in the area, we recommend a visit to the Nishga village of Canyon City, accessible across the Nass via a suspension footbridge. One side of the bridge is attached to slabs of lava flow.

One of the best ways to get to Canyon City is to canoe or kayak the Nass River. The river plays an important role in Nishga life, centring on the tremendous oolichan run which usually happens between the first week in March and the first week in April.

A paddling trip of the Nass (Tlingit for "food depot" or "satisfier of the belly") can take from 3 to 7 days. The trip starts at New Aiyansh, north of Terrace in Nisga'a Memorial Lava Bed Park, and takes the paddler west to Kincolith, at the mouth of Nass Bay. Kincolith is serviced by a twice-weekly B.C. ferry and daily North Coast Air float planes from Prince Rupert. Beware of the ebb tides in Nass Bay, which can become very nasty when a wind blows in from the sea over the shoals. And be prepared to do some winter camping if you plan your paddling trip to coincide with the annual oolichan run. Since the Nass Valley is the ancestral homeland of the Nishga, protocol requires that paddlers convey their paddling plans to the band manager in the settlement of New Aiyansh.

Central to Nishga culture is the annual oolichan (candlefish) harvest. The oolichan is so oily that when held near a fire it will ignite and sputter into flame. For centuries Nishga fish camps have been set up at the mouth of the Nass in the early spring and oolichan oil exchanged with other tribes for seaweed, clams, oysters, herring roe and other food.

Oil production from these slippery, silvery fish is an exacting science. Once netted, the fish are dumped into huge wooden vats on shore. Excavated clay from the riverbed lines the burning pits underneath the oolichan vats. Oil extraction takes 18 hours and a pure, non-fishy-tasting oil is the result. Fish not used for oil production are dried on cedar racks.

Other denizens of the oolichan run include satiated bald eagles, seals, sea lions and masses of seagulls. During the harvest, sea-lion stew is a mainstay for the work force.

Another prime run is south of Terrace at Kitimat. The spring high tides that coincide with the full moon help to push the oolichan, notoriously poor swimmers, up the Kitimat and Kildala rivers to spawn. Their return is always heralded by sightings of large numbers of porpoises. Local Indian bands maintain that the presence of a large Alcan aluminum smelter and a Eurocan pulp mill close to downtown Kitimat have made the oolichan in the Kitimat River taste of sulphur.

Halfway between Terrace and Kitimat on Highway 37 lies Lakelse Provincial Park. *Lakelse* is Tsimshian for "fresh-water mussel," so you can expect to find lots of these in the lake, as well as all five species of Pacific salmon and steelhead trout. The waters warm up to very swimmable temperatures in summer. In winter, watch for a resident group of trumpeter swans on the lake. Once almost extinct, this largest species of North American waterfowl is enjoying a steady resurgence in population.

Another attraction for travellers to Lakelse are the hot springs 7 km (4 mi.) beyond park headquarters. More than 570,000 l (150,000 gal.) of beneficial, mineral-filled waters bubble out of the mountain at over 38° C (100° F) to fill 9 odourless pools, some complete with water slides! A year-round resort here capitalizes on this natural phenomenon.

Useful Information

The Forest Service Recreation Sites map of the Terrace-Nass area is a useful reference guide. A copy can be obtained from Ministry of Forests, 3726 Alfred St., Smithers, B.C., V0J 2N0 (847-7425).

Contact the Gitlakdamix Band Office, New Aiyansh, B.C., V0J 1A0 (633-2215) for permission to paddle the Nass River. Detailed route information for the Nass River trip can be found in *Sea Kayaking Canada's West Coast* by John Ince and Hedi Kottner.

Information and a park brochure on Lakelse Park can be obtained from the Visitor Services Coordinator, BC Parks, Skeena District, Bag 5000, Smithers, B.C., V0J 2N0 (847-7565). Contact **Mount Layton Hotsprings Resort**, Box 550, Terrace, B.C., V8G 4B5 (798-2214) for information on accommodation.

For detailed descriptions of trails in the Terrace area, both *Hiking in the Rainforest* by Shannon Mark and Heather McLean and *Trails to the Timberline* by Einar Blix are invaluable.

PRINCE RUPERT

Prince Rupert bills itself as "the City of Rainbows," a delightfully creative way of acknowledging that it probably receives more rain than any other city in Canada. Despite its distance from Vancouver (1800 km/1100 mi.) by road, many people visit Prince Rupert on their travels. Though the Yellowhead is the only road into town, planes, trains and ferries converge here as it is a major stopping-off point for travellers bound for the North (it's only 50 km/30 mi. south of the Alaska Panhandle) and the Queen Charlottes.

The ferries to the Queen Charlotte Islands are operated by B.C. Ferry Corporation, which also operates the ferries to Port Hardy on northern Vancouver Island. Next door to the B.C. Ferry terminal is the Alaska Marine Highway terminal for ferries running north to towns such as Ketchikan, Wrangell, Juneau and Skagway on the Alaska Panhandle. Reservations are essential on any of these ferries in summer, especially if you have a vehicle. Cabins are available but should be reserved well in advance of your trip. On the Alaska ferry, it's more fun, and cheaper, to grab a lounge chair under the solarium roof and set out your sleeping bag.

Prince Rupert serves as the administrative centre for the Tsimshian people in the area. Thirty per cent of this port city's population is native Indian, and the native presence is strongly evident in the totem-dotted parks and longhouse architecture.

Travellers to Prince Rupert enjoy outings such as the ride in a Swiss gondola to the top of Mount Hays, with its spectacular views 555 m (1850 ft.) above the city.

A popular side trip is the 20-minute drive south of Prince Rupert to Port Edward's North Pacific Cannery Village and Museum, built in 1889. Cedar boardwalks connect mess hall, bunkhouses, stores, offices, net loft and boat hoist to recreate one of the 200 remote canneries that dotted the west coast at the beginning of the century. Four hundred people from varying racial backgrounds caught and processed halibut, herring and salmon here at the mouth of the Skeena, derived from two Tsimshian words meaning "water out of the clouds."

Rain pounds down fairly constantly here on B.C.'s most heavily populated grizzly bear habitat, the Khutzeymateen River Valley, a 15-km (9-mi.) unlogged valley along the river that ultimately flows into Portland Inlet from Khutzeymateen Inlet.

A day's boat trip 50 km (31 mi.) north of Prince Rupert, or a quick ride up in a float plane to an anchored "mother" boat, Khutzeymateen (pronounced koots-a-ma-teen) is Nishga for "a confined space of salmon and bears." Provincial biologists estimate that as many as 50 of the province's 6000 to 8000 grizzlies converge on this 400-sq.-km (154-sq.-mi.) dense rain forest to gorge on salmon (they often eat just the nutritious brains), rub against their favourite trees, dig up verdant skunk cabbage to chomp on the roots and wallow in warm, black mud holes on the estuary flats.

These 400-kg (880-lb.) carnivores are capable of running at 50 kph (31 m.p.h.). From May to October, they range along the estuary meadows near the Khutzeymateen River, the Kateen River and Carm Creek. As denning time approaches, they feast on spawning pink, coho, chum and Chinook salmon, sharing territory with black bears and wolves.

They also share their food-rich area with hordes of bald eagles, which nest in the forest's giant (60-m/146-ft.) Sitka spruces. Although a logging company holds the forest licence for this area, several groups are lobbying the government to set it aside as Canada's first grizzly bear sanctuary. Guided tours of the Khutzeymateen operate out of Prince Rupert and Vancouver.

Useful Information
Adventure Canada, 1159 West Broadway, Vancouver, B.C., V6H 1G1 (736-7447 or 1-800-387-1483) offers guided trips into Khutzeymateen Valley from a "mother" ship anchored at the mouth of the river. Visitors, accompanied by a wildlife biologist, are taken by zodiac into the estuary each day. **Bluewater Adventures**, 202-1676 Duranleau St., Granville Island, Vancouver, B.C., V6H 3S5 (684-4575) may soon operate similar trips.

STEWART

The Stewart-Cassiar Highway, which begins at Kitwanga, 91 km (56 mi.) northeast of Terrace, connects the Yellowhead with the Alaska Highway, following the wide Nass River Valley north with views of distant ice-covered mountains. Meziadin Junction marks the intersection of Highway 37 with Highway 37A west to Stewart.

Stewart, Canada's most northerly ice-free port, is situated at the head of the Portland Canal. During the winter months, the 67-km (42-mi.) drive west from Meziadin Junction through avalanche chutes and steep rock cliffs is harrowing. And this is c-o-l-d country. So cold that Tide Lake, about 50 km (31 mi.) north of Stewart, used to hold the Guinness records title for snowfall in one year: 27 m (89 ft.) fell between May 16, 1971, and May 15, 1972. (Since that time, Stewart has been surpassed by Mount Rainier, Washington, where 30 m (99 ft.) fell in one year.) Four-metre (13-ft.) snowfalls are not uncommon in Stewart.

In summer, though, the drive from Meziadin Junction is a visual feast. From Meziadin Lake, with its excellent fishing, the road passes through the most spectacular mountain and glacier scenery in the province. On the way up to

Bear Pass, mountain sheep may be seen on the sheer rock faces, and the moving black bumps seen on the distant white slopes are probably black or grizzly bears. From the crest of Bear Pass, you can see the stunning Bear Glacier gleaming in the canyon below. The road winds down into the valley and passes within a stone's throw of the glacier, which has ice so dense that even at night it has a distinct blue glow. The road then continues through a granite canyon carved by the rushing waters of the Bear River to Stewart.

Stewart has recently been used as the location for several movies, including *Bear Island* and *Iceman*. Some props from *Iceman* are displayed in the yard of the local museum.

Travellers to Stewart invariably end up being "Hyderized" in the Glacier Inn of nearby Hyder, Alaska, a few miles and one time zone away from Stewart. This quaint custom involves drinking a shot of Clear Spring, a 190 proof Kentucky grain alcohol. The bartender will often drop some of the liquid on the counter and then set it alight. Don't miss this northern rite of passage!

NORTH TO THE YUKON:
Iskut Lakes, Spatsizi Plateau, Mount Edziza Park and the Stikine

Superlatives come easily when writing about the North, particularly the area sandwiched between the 55th and 56th parallels. Containing Mount Edziza Park, Spatsizi Plateau Wilderness Park and the Iskut Lake Chain, this is prime adventuring country for hearty hikers, paddlers and horse-packers.

Kinaskan Lake, the southernmost lake of the Iskut chain, is 195 km (120 mi.) north of Meziadin Junction along the Stewart-Cassiar Highway, now a good gravel road. En route you can spot remnants of the famous Telegraph Trail, which was constructed in 1866 with the intention of connecting North America with Europe via Alaska, the Bering Strait and Siberia. The project was abandoned in 1867 when the transatlantic cable was installed. Watch out also for the large trucks (called trains) hauling asbestos from Cassiar to Stewart; pull over to the side of the road to avoid the gravel spray from these vehicles. Make sure that your spare tire is in good shape and that you have a full tank of gas before you start out, as there are few gas stations or other services along the way.

The Iskut Lakes

Anglers claim you can "limit out" in no time in the lovely paddling country of the Iskut Lakes, which lie between Mount Edziza and Spatsizi Wilderness parks. Centred around Iskut, a Tahltan Indian community near the lakes, this area of forests, mountains, glaciers, lakes and streams offers endless opportunities for the adventurous traveller.

Look out for B.C.'s largest huckleberry patch on the Iskut Burn, a 31,566-ha (78,000-a.) area decimated by a forest fire in 1958.

Camping is permitted anywhere along the roadside as well as at the 36 sites at Kinaskan Lake Provincial Park, a popular base for both boaters and anglers. Other accommodation on the Iskut Lakes is available at Tatogga Lake Resort, a few miles north of the park, Iskutine Resort, at Eddontenajon Lake, and Ealue Lake Resort, 12 km (7 mi.) east of Tatogga. Canoes can be rented at Tatogga Lake Resort. Horse-packers can explore the area from the A-E Guest Ranch, which is equipped with camping facilities and cabins.

Eddontenajon Lake forms the headwaters of the Iskut chain. Its name comes from the Tahltan Indian phrase meaning "little boy drowned." According to legend, a small boy stood on the lakeshore, trying to imitate the cry of the loon. Though warned by his mother that if he continued to copy the bird he might fall into the water, he persisted, fell into the lake and was drowned.

Paddlers can travel from Eddontenajon through the entire chain to Natadesleen Lake in the south, but plan your trip carefully and be prepared for wilderness camping and river running. Be sure to have your angler's licence so you can fish for rainbow trout en route; local lore maintains that the biggest fish inhabit Natadesleen.

Useful Information

For information on Kinaskan Lake Park or on canoeing the Iskut lakes, contact the Visitor Services Coordinator, BC Parks, Skeena District, Bag 5000, Smithers, B.C., V0J 2N0 (847-7565).

Contact the **Tatogga Lake Resort**, Iskut, B.C., V0J 1K0 (234-3526) for information on accommodation and boat rentals.

Write to **A-E Guest Ranch**, General Delivery, Iskut, B.C., V0J 1K0 (no phone) for information on accommodation or horse-riding trips.

The Spatsizi Plateau

A true wilderness park, where minimum-impact camping and travel are advocated, Spatsizi Park includes the Gladys Lake Ecological Reserve and is second in size only to Tweedsmuir.

Approximately 300 km (186 mi.) north of Smithers and 50 km (32 mi.) east of Highway 37, this 6500-sq.-km (2500-sq.-mi.) park originated primarily as a result of the intensive lobbying work of Tommy Walker and his wife, Marion. In 1948 the Walkers rode 1500 km (945 mi.) from the coastal town of Bella Coola in search of a unique, remote valley, which they discovered surrounding Cold Fish Lake, 1067 m (3500 ft.) up on the Spatsizi Plateau. Here they built outfitting cabins, still in use today, facing down lake towards the Eaglenest

Mountains. Modern-day adventurers head into Spatsizi either with professionally guided groups or on extremely well-organized and planned individual treks. A favourite time to visit the park is fall, when the woodland caribou rut and spectacular yellow, orange and deep red slashes of autumnal dwarf birch (also known as buckbrush) sash the hillsides.

Most travellers begin at Iskut, midway between Edziza and Spatsizi on the Stewart-Cassiar Highway. From here, you can charter float planes, which fly regularly in summer from Tatogga and Eddontenajon lakes to Cold Fish Lake, 80 km (50 mi.) to the east in the park's north-central region. Rates vary depending on passenger load. Flying in is the best way to eliminate some of the drudgery that a trek-in to Spatsizi entails.

More rugged hikers head in to Cold Fish Lake along McEwan Creek, east of Ealue Lake, or along Eaglenest Creek to the south. Numerous trails and routes within the park allow access to a great variety of wilderness hiking on the plateau and in the alpine areas, which are covered with a cornucopia of species, including purple gentian, blue forget-me-nots, red Indian paintbrush, pale pink and purple columbines and various berry bushes.

Cold Fish Lake camp has become a popular bunk spot for hikers, horseback riders and hunters, although popular is a bit of a misnomer in this case, since fewer than 500 visitors come to Spatsizi in an average year. From Cold Fish Lake, hiking trails lead to Black Fox Creek, Caribou Mountain, Ice Box Canyon and Bates Mountain.

Binoculars are obligatory equipment on your Spatsizi trip, since the countryside here teems with animals and over 140 species of birds, including horned larks, gyrfalcons, all three of B.C.'s ptarmigan species and gulls. Woodland caribou, moose, grizzlies and stone sheep (a dark version of Dall's sheep) roam the trails while shaggy white mountain goats (those that have not rolled in red iron-oxide dust) look down casually from tiny, vertigo-inducing shelves in the mountains. Arctic ground squirrels live here at the southern extremity of their range.

Anglers catch rainbow, lake and Dolly Varden trout; the latter's bright red and orange spots seem to get more fluorescent the farther north you go. Mountain whitefish and Arctic grayling are also abundant.

Gladys Lake Ecological Reserve, the largest of the 132 such designations in the province, is a popular hiking destination. Just south of Cold Fish Lake, Gladys Lake is a prime viewing area for stone sheep and mountain goats, whose populations continue to increase significantly.

While Cold Fish Lake is the usual base destination in Spatsizi, travellers also fly south to Tuaton Lake, one of the most scenic wilderness lakes in the park.

The Spatsizi River runs through the park, providing a paddling opportunity for canoeists and kayakers. Access is via a 5-km (3-mi.) trail that leads to the confluence of the river and Didene and Kluayetz creeks from the B.C. Rail grade at Klappan. While the river is relatively easy to navigate, its wild surroundings and fluctuating water levels require that some members of your group have advanced canoe (or kayak) and wilderness skills. After 70 km (43 mi.), the river joins the Stikine and the trip then continues down to the takeout at the Stewart-Cassiar highway crossing.

Spatsizi is remote, but Tatlatui Provincial Park (its name comes from the Tahltan Indian word meaning "headwater") is even farther removed from civilization. Located at the southeastern tip of the Spatsizi Plateau, the park is accessible only by float plane. Its main claim to fame is unbeatable fishing on the main section of the Firesteel River (rumours abound of trout caught on every cast). Paddlers can canoe all the lakes in the park, but should beware of sudden winds that turn inland lakes into rough seas. As with Spatsizi, float planes can usually make it in during the ice-free months from early June to mid-October.

Useful Information

Contact the Visitor Services Coordinator, BC Parks, Skeena District, Bag 5000, 3726 Alfred St., Smithers, B.C., V0J 2N0 (847-7320) for information about Spatsizi and Tatlatui parks, and ask for a copy of the Spatzizi park brochure with its trail map.

Contact **Iskut River and Trail Adventures**, Iskut, B.C., V0J 1K0 (234-3331) for information on their horse-packing trips into Spatzizi. **Stikine Canyon Trail Rides**, General Delivery, Dease Lake, B.C., V0J 1L0 (771-4301) offers similar trips.

Hummingbird Nature Tours, 31-227374 Lougheed Highway, Maple Ridge, B.C., V2X 2T5 (467-9219) offers guided hiking trips in Spatsizi.

Contact **Northern Sun Tours**, Box 2522, Smithers, B.C., V0J 2N0 (847-4419) for information on their canoe trips on the Spatsizi and Stikine rivers.

Trans-Provincial Airlines, Box 280, Prince Rupert, B.C., V8J 3P6 (627-1341) or Terrace (635-6516) or Iskut (234-3411) runs float-plane charters into Spatsizi and Tatlatui.

Every traveller to the park should read Tommy Walker's book *Spatsizi*, which describes his search for an unspoiled wilderness home and his efforts to safeguard the unique ecology of the Spatsizi area.

Mount Edziza Provincial Park and Recreation Area

Eight, possibly nine thousand years ago, the Tahltan Indians would travel every summer in family groups up to the Tahltan plateau below 2787-m (9143-ft.) Mount Edziza to quarry obsidian, a form of rapidly cooled lava that crystallizes into hard, black volcanic glass. As keen as surgical steel when sharpened, obsidian cutting tools were traded with other tribes from Alaska to the Queen Charlotte Islands in the shadow of the place the Tahltan called "ice mountain."

Nowadays one of the best ways to explore this 230,000-ha (568,336-a.) wilderness is on horseback, guided by the descendants of these early Tahltan people. Edziza is not for the faint of heart—it's tough, treacherous country requiring skill and stamina. But if extraordinary volcanic countryside and sightings of moose, grizzly bears, Osborn caribou and stone sheep appeal to you, then Edziza is well worth the effort.

Since there is no road access into Mount Edziza Park, travellers come in by float plane to one of the 5 lakes that form the park's eastern boundary or to Buckley Lake on the northern border. The nearest community for horsepackers and hikers is Telegraph Creek, located on the west bank of the Stikine River. To get there, follow Highway 37 north to Dease Lake, then drive 118 km (71 mi.) to the southwest.

The park's central peak, Mount Edziza, erupted over 4 million years ago, spreading lava east, south and west over a 1625-sq.-km (600-sq.-m.) area. Subsequent small eruptions have pushed up 30 cinder cones, including the perfectly symmetrical Eve Cone, which rises 150 m (500 ft.) above the lava plateau, and Coffee and Cocoa craters, so young (only 1300 years old) that they are bare of vegetation and basically unaltered by erosion.

Within park boundaries to the south lies the Spectrum mountain range, separated from Edziza by Raspberry Pass. Lava flows formed these mountains. Erosion of the rhyolite, a various-coloured volcanic rock, and staining by sulphurous waters have created their vibrant red, yellow, white and purple rock faces.

North of the park boundary, the Stikine (Tlingit for "great river") has carved a Grand Canyon through the volcanic and sedimentary rock deposits.

Park valley floors contain wetlands replete with black moss, ferns and fungi, juxtaposed with moonscapes where the occasional orange-blossomed stonecrop, part of the saxifrage family, peeks out. (*Saxifraga* literally means "rock breaker.") Up on the Edziza plateau, you'll find the swirling pumice dust, fine as beach sand, from which the park takes its name (*edziza* is the Tahltan word for "cinders").

A hike across the park takes 2 weeks, with the best time being between July 1 and September 15. Be prepared for sudden changes in weather—warm clothing and rain gear are essential. Marked trails are nonexistent, so you'll need a compass to complement your topographical maps. Bear bells are handy for an Edziza hike; you may see gaping holes in the mountainside where grizzlies have dug out gopher dinners! Again, we strongly emphasize that you need stamina and skill to complete this journey. Contact the Parks and Outdoor Recreation divisions in Smithers or Prince George before attempting any trip into Edziza.

Some horse-packers travel in west from Iskut to Buckley Lake and then ride south past Edziza to the Spectrum Range.

Useful Information

Contact the Visitor Services Coordinator, BC Parks, Skeena District, Bag 5000, 3726 Alfred St., Smithers, B.C., V0J 2N0 (847-7320) for information about the park, advice on access and a copy of the park brochure with its trail map.

Stikine Canyon Trail Rides, General Delivery, Dease Lake, B.C., V0J 1L0 (771-4301) offers horse-packing trips into Edziza, as does **Iskut River and Trail Adventures**, Iskut, B.C., V0J 1K0 (234-3331). **Stikine Riversong Lodge and Cafe**, Telegraph Creek, B.C., V0J 2W0 (235-3196) runs guided hiking trips into the park.

Contact **Trans-Provincial Airlines**, Box 280, Prince Rupert, B.C., V8J 3P6 (627-1341) or in Terrace (635-6516) or Iskut (234-3411) regarding their float-plane charters into Edziza. **Tel Air** also operates charter flights into the park; contact them at Telegraph Creek, B.C., V0J 2W0 (235-3296) for further information.

The Stikine

The great Stikine River is a challenge for ardent advanced canoeists, kayakers and rafters: no one has yet run the full length of its treacherous waters. It begins in an ice cave high in the Cassiar Mountains, rises in the southern part of Spatsizi Park, flows east, arcs north, travels west to curl down through the Grand Canyon northeast of Telegraph Creek, then flows south to fan out into its great salmon spawning delta north of Wrangell, Alaska.

The Grand Canyon, Canada's largest, is 96 km (60 mi.) long, a place where towering volcanic cliffs 300 m (1000 ft.) high flank roaring waters. All 5 species of Pacific salmon run below Telegraph Creek and every summer, as they have for thousands of years, Tahltan families travel up-country to fish camps to smoke the river's harvest.

Most paddlers join the Stikine at Tuaton Lake or Laslui Lake, flying in from nearby Eddontenajon Lake or from Watson Lake, just north of the Yukon border. From Tuaton and Laslui the river stretches 640 km (400 mi.) and drops 1370 m (4500 ft.) to the ocean. The 260 km (160 mi.) from Tuaton Lake to the Grand Canyon are good rafting and canoeing waters. Take-out for this upper Stikine trip is at the Highway 37 bridge. Travel on the Stikine between the bridge and Telegraph Creek, farther west, is obstructed by the impassable waters of the Grand Canyon. Allow 2 weeks for the trip.

The Spatsizi, the Stikine's major tributary, runs through Spatsizi Park from south to north, flowing in a series of oxbows and providing about 70 km (43 mi.) of good canoeing and rafting waters, with only a couple of minor rapids, before flowing into the larger river. River travellers report frequent sightings of moose grazing on the banks.

Paddlers wishing to continue down the lower Stikine put in at Telegraph Creek, after the Grand Canyon, and can arrange for float-plane pick-up at Stikine on the Alaska border. Another option is to continue paddling the further 65 km (40 mi.) across the border to Wrangell, Alaska. From here, float planes can be chartered for the trip back to Iskut or to Telegraph Creek, or paddlers can take a ferry service south to Prince Rupert.

The lower Stikine is deeper, wider and straighter than the upper section, exuding a gentler quality. Travellers on the river should stop for food at the Stikine Riversong Lodge and Cafe in Telegraph Creek, at one time a Hudson's Bay Company post and now a small centre for river-raft trips and riverboat and aircraft charters.

Richard Wright's book *Canoe Routes B.C.*, now out of print, is an excellent reference, and travellers on any portion of the Stikine should get hold of a library copy. Rafters can contact Iskut River and Trail Adventures, who raft both the upper and lower Stikine and the Spatsizi River.

Useful Information

Contact **Northern Sun Tours**, Box 2522, Smithers, B.C., V0J 2N0 (847-4419) for information on canoe trips along the Spatsizi and Stikine rivers.

Talugga Triangle Services, c/o Mike Jones, General Delivery, Iskut, B.C., V0J 1K0 (234-3526) offers canoe rentals and car ferry services for canoeists.

Contact **Iskut River and Trail Adventures**, Iskut, B.C., V0J 1K0 (234-3331) for information on their raft trips down the Stikine.

Information on canoe and raft trips, boat and aircraft charters as well as accommodation can be obtained from **Stikine Riversong Lodge**, General Delivery, Telegraph Creek, B.C., V0J 2W0 (235-3196).

DEASE LAKE AND DEASE RIVER

Dease Lake is located 120 km (81 mi.) north of Iskut on the Stewart-Cassiar Highway. Along with the Dease River, it was once part of a major transportation route into the north for Hudson's Bay Company traders and trappers.

Now popular with modern-day paddlers, the Dease flows out of Dease Lake through the Cassiar Mountains and north to the Liard River, offering a rich panorama of moose, stone sheep, mountain goats, black and grizzly bears, and, for bird watchers, great horned owls, kingfishers, loons and bald eagles. The slow-moving waters of the Dease are ideal for families or novice paddlers, with excellent opportunities for fishing and photography, but talk with locals about the occasional rapids which should be scouted. Allow a week for the 265-km

(167-mi.) trip. Put-in is at Dease Lake. Paddlers can also fly in to the lake from Watson Lake, Yukon Territory. Take-out is at Lower Post on the Alaska Highway just south of the Yukon border.

Northern Sun Tours, Box 2522, Smithers, B.C., V0J 2N0 (847-4419) runs canoe trips on Dease Lake and Dease River.

BOYA LAKE PROVINCIAL PARK

Continue about 150 km (93 mi.) north of Dease Lake along the Stewart-Cassiar Highway to get to Boya Lake Provincial Park. Canoeists and kayakers making the Dease River trip will pass through the park en route to Lower Post.

Boya Lake is also good for paddlers and harbours plenty of excellent fishing holes for such species as lake char and grayling. Hikers can expect to spot moose and plenty of beaver lodges.

The shoreline of Boya Lake consists of ridges of gravel, known as eskers, formed 8000 years ago during the last ice age. As the ice melted, streams flowed beneath the ice sheets, depositing rock, gravel, sand and silt along the way. When the ice disappeared completely, these deposits were exposed. While this glacial action has created mostly rocky beaches, there are 5 sandy beaches along the lake's eastern shores. During July, the water can warm to a swimmable 18° C (64° F). Contact the Visitor Services Coordinator, BC Parks, Skeena District, Bag 5000, Smithers, B.C., V0J 2N0 (847-7320) for a copy of the Boya Lake Park brochure.

ATLIN

If you were to fly 238 km (148 mi.) due west of Boya Lake you would reach the northern town of Atlin, but most visitors come in by bus or car from Whitehorse in the Yukon. Atlin sits beside a turquoise lake of the same name backed by snow-capped mountains. Sailboats and the occasional houseboat explore the lake's many islands, while float planes lift off regularly in summer for wilderness fishing and hiking areas. The movie *Never Cry Wolf*, based on the Farley Mowat novel, was filmed in the vicinity.

At the end of the 19th century many prospectors, crossing part of Alaska and northern B.C. to reach the Klondike goldfields, headed instead for Atlin, 50 km (31 mi.) south of the Yukon border, when German miner Fritz Miller staked a lucrative claim in the area. Rumour has it that Miller and his brother George decided to investigate this area northeast of Juneau, Alaska, after a dying prospector staggered into town, dragging a sack of gold and a rough map of his discovery.

By freeze-up in 1898 about 3000 people had arrived in Atlin to prospect and stake every stream. At both Atlin and Discovery (now a ghost town 9.5 km/ 6 mi. to the east), communities sprang up seemingly overnight. By 1899 Atlin had a telegraph line, a telephone system, a post office and—most importantly—a brewery. Wooden buildings shot up amongst the hundreds of tents. But in 1900, a major fire, the perennial scourge of gold-rush settlements, demolished a good part of town, including hotels, stores, offices, homes and 40 cases of champagne—all uninsured.

Nevertheless, the good life continued. An opera society thrived and the prestigious Atlin Club included in its membership roster such notables as King Edward VII and Sir Wilfrid Laurier. But gold production fell in 1907, the club disbanded and the population of the Atlin area fell steadily from an all-time high of 5000 to a low of 100 in the 1960s.

Today, Atlin's permanent population of 400 inhabits the most northwesterly town in British Columbia, ten degrees of latitude north of Vancouver. Each year on June 21 the sun rises over the 100-km (60-mi.) length of Atlin Lake at 4:35 A.M. and sets at 11:18 P.M., giving residents 18 hours and 42 minutes of sunlight, with enough light remaining at midnight for taking photographs. When the land cools down in fall, the pyrotechnics of the northern lights puncture an indigo sky, crackling and twinkling during long winter nights.

Visitors to Atlin follow in the footsteps of the Tlingit people, who called the area *ahtlah*, meaning "big lake." The area was originally an important hunting ground for caribou.

The only way to reach Atlin by road is from the north. Travellers driving along the Alaska Highway should turn south at Jakes Corner and follow the scenic all weather Highway 7 for 100 km (60 mi.) to its end. Since Atlin is only a 2½-hour drive south of Whitehorse, the town has become popular with Yukoners. The Atlin Express Company also runs buses from Whitehorse along this route. Air travellers can reach Atlin via a short flight from Juneau, Alaska.

Travellers coming in from Whitehorse should pick up a copy of the "Travellers' Guide to Yukon Government Campgrounds" at the Whitehorse tourist information office. Handy campgrounds exist at Tagish Bridge and at Snarfu and Tarfu lakes. There are also several small B.C. Forestry Service campgrounds at McDonald Lake, Warm Bay (on Atlin Lake) and Palmer Lake.

Be sure to pick up the excellent little walking tour booklet produced by the Atlin Historical Society, available at the tourist information centre, located in the Atlin Historical Museum, an old schoolhouse built in 1902. Take time to stroll through the Pioneer Cemetery, a mile east of town, for a sombre hint of a

more rugged era. Here tombstone epitaphs graphically recall tough times—
"Died of gunshot wounds: mistaken for a bear. Age, 16 years."
    During spring migration, keep an eye out for arctic loons, Barrow's gold-
eneye, old squaws, white-winged scoters, ospreys, gyrfalcons, herring gulls
and arctic terns, all of which breed in this area.
    Hikers who want to range farther afield might enjoy an initial hike on Mon-
arch Mountain to get the lay of the land. To reach trailhead, travel 4.8 km
(3 mi.) south of town on the Warm Bay Road, past Creek Bridge on the left-
hand side. A sign marks the beginning of this moderately strenuous (steep in
sections) trail, which takes approximately 2 hours to complete. Views and
plenty of wildflowers characterize the trail in summer. In August death camas
and monkshood bloom at the summit.
    From the mountaintop, you can see Atlin Lake and the numerous islands of
Atlin Park to the southwest. Directly west of Monarch, on Teresa Island, lies
Birch Mountain, claimed to be the highest mountain above fresh water in the
world. With a pair of binoculars you can see why Teresa Island is also known
as Goat Island, as you spot goats gingerly crossing the snows below Birch
Peak. To the northwest lie the Chilkoot Pass, Tagish Lake and, due north, latitude 60°, the Yukon boundary, which slices off the northernmost waters of
Atlin Lake.
    Since there are no published guides to other hikes in the Atlin area, we list
below some of the better ones, provided by the local tourist information centre.
The very hospitable local folks are super at giving additional directions.
    Warm Springs: Atlin Lake's waters are too cold for swimming but a 25-km
(16.75-mi.) drive from town will take you to Warm Springs, a natural pool that
maintains a constant 29° C (84° F). The springs are located a short walk from
the landing at the south end of Warm Bay.
    Birch Mountain, Teresa Island: Canoe or kayak across Atlin Lake from
Warm Bay to a point on the eastern side of the island. There is no established
trail, so some bushwhacking may be necessary to reach timber line. The
elevation gain is over 1370 m (4500 ft.), so the entire trip will take a full day.
    Sloko Trail: There is no road access to this trailhead, which is at the head of
Sloko Inlet at the southern end of Atlin Lake. The .6-km (1-mi.) trail goes up
the east side of the valley to the gravel flats at Sloko Lake. Two other trails in
the area are routes to the Llewellyn Glacier, one from the western arm of Sloko
Inlet and the other over the gravel flats just west of Sloko Inlet.
    Sloko Island: Many possible landing sites allow boaters to ramble along
the ridges to 3 small lakes. There is also a trail across the isthmus.
    Main trail to Llewellyn Glacier: The trailhead lies in the middle of the
cove at the head of Llewellyn Inlet.
    Copper Island: The best landing spot for boaters is at the southwest corner
of the island, and a hike to the summit provides great views. In early times, the

island was a source of mature copper slabs.

Rock Glacier, Atlin Mountain: From Torres Channel the route leads up a valley on the south side of the mountain and then west to the summit at 2029 m (6656 ft.).

Scotia Bay to Taku: The wagon road, later the narrow gauge railway bed, may be followed west to the old landing at Taku on Graham Inlet. Here you will find the old freight shed, with what's left of the jetty supporting the remains of three flatcars.

Winter trail to Talaha Bay of Taku Arm: This trail heads northwest past Jones Lake. It can involve an excessive amount of bushwhacking on the flat.

Mount Minto: This conspicuous, 2107-m (6913-ft.) dome towards the north end of Atlin Lake often wears a cloud cap. Timber line is approximately 1220 m (6913 ft.). Weather conditions permitting, you can follow an established route to the summit.

In honour of its gold mining past, Atlin has set aside a "Keep All You Find" gold panning claim area east of town on Spruce Creek. The folks at the Atlin Museum are happy to give directions to the mother lode.

Houseboats and canoes can be rented in town and provide a great way for adventurers to fan out across Atlin Lake. But the winds do whip up unexpectedly on this vast inland sea, so boaters should exercise caution.

For experienced canoeists or kayakers, we recommend a 5-day trip from put-in 27 km (17 mi.) south of Atlin at Warm Bay. Keep close to the small islands, since the wind can churn up 1.2-m (4-ft.) waves in a matter of minutes on open stretches of water. Many wilderness camping spots dot the route down to final camp at Taku Inlet, where you can make the 4.8-km (3-mi.) hike to Llewellyn Glacier.

Less strenuous canoeing is available on Gladys Lake, a great fishing hole for grayling. The lake can be reached via Fourth of July Road, which starts 6 km (4 mi.) north of the town of Atlin.

To get an inkling of why the Atlin area was dubbed "the Switzerland of the North" by tourists of the roaring twenties and thirties, adventurers can head across Atlin Lake by boat to a site that evokes an earlier era. Guide-outfitter Bruce Johnson of Atlin is one of the best people to contact if you want to make this pilgrimage to Ben-My-Chree (Manx, language of the Isle of Man, for "girl of my heart") at the south end of nearby Tagish Lake.

Once serviced by the sternwheeler S.S. *Tutshi*, which bought visitors the 138 km (86 mi.) down Tagish Lake from Carcross, Ben-My-Chree was the country retreat of the Partridges, founders of the Bennett Lake and Klondike Navigation Company. Their spacious two-storey home, surrounded by .8 ha (2 a.) of flower gardens once containing 40 different kinds of flowers, is set against a craggy mountain backdrop. Illustrious visitors to Ben-My-Chree, including the Prince of Wales and President Roosevelt, came to take tea and listen to Mrs. Partridge pick out some tunes on her organ (brought in on foot over the Chilkoot Pass!), and be regaled by her husband, Otto, with tales of the gold rush.

After both Partridges died in the thirties, the Yukon and White Pass Railway maintained this oasis of gracious living until Pacific Steamships changed its schedules in 1955, making the *Tutshi* trips no longer feasible. Today, the Partridge estate is private property, a tangle of alder, fireweed and arctic poppies. Camping is permitted on a sandbar farther down the lake.

In the Tagish Highlands of the Coast Mountain chain, which totally surround the toe of Atlin Lake, lies Atlin Provincial Park. One-third of this 271,140-ha (670,000-a.) undeveloped park is covered by the massive Llewellyn and Willison glaciers.

Atlin Park is home to the only population of white Dall sheep in the province, plus the usual contingent of stone sheep, mountain goats, Osborn caribou and cinnamon (a colour phase of black) and grizzly bears. Bird watchers can count on spotting bald eagles, spruce grouse and possibly ptarmigans. It's hardy country and hikers here basically bushwhack since there are no established trails.

Both float planes and water taxis bring adventurers to Pike Bay, where most of the camping in the area is done. From Pike Bay, hikers can reach Atlin Park's alpine meadows via Simpson Creek. This whole area was formerly well used by the Tagish Indians and almost 40 archaeological sites have been catalogued here.

In winter, skiers can fly in by ski-equipped plane or by helicopter to the Llewellyn Glacier for a day of telemarking or for a traverse to Juneau, Alaska.

Useful Information

For further information about Atlin Park, contact the Visitor Services Coordinator, BC Parks, Skeena District, Bag 5000, Smithers, B.C., V0J 2N0 (847-7565). There are no park brochures but the Visitor Services Coordinator can provide up-to-date information on access and a list of local guides and outfitters who could assist with a trip into the park.

A copy of the "Travellers' Guide to Yukon Government Campgrounds" can be obtained from the Whitehorse Tourist Office or by writing to Tourism Yukon, Box 2703, Whitehorse, Yukon, Y1A 2C6 (403-667-5340).

Bruce Johnson, **North by Dog Adventures**, Box 14, Atlin, B.C, V0W 1A0 (radio phone via Whitehorse, ask for White Mountain channel 2M-5017) runs summer trips on Atlin and Tagish lakes, including visits to Ben-My-Chree. Winter dog-sled trips are also offered. **Chilkoot Boat Tours**, R. R. #1, Site 20, Comp. 34, Whitehorse, Yukon, Y1A 4Z6 (403-668-7766) also offers trips on Tagish Lake to Ben-My-Chree.

Norsemen Adventures, Box 184, Atlin, B.C., V0W 1A0 (651-7535 or 826-2559) rents houseboats and canoes.

Atlin Air, Box 300, Atlin, B.C., V0W 1A0 (651-7635), flies canoeists, kayakers and rafters to local lakes and rivers. In winter, skiers can arrange charter flights to the Llewellyn Glacier.

THE CHILKOOT TRAIL

Ninety km (57 mi.) due west of Atlin as the crow flies lies trailhead for one of B.C.'s legendary hikes—the Chilkoot Trail. Like the West Coast Trail on Vancouver Island, the Chilkoot has become a symbol of an earlier time, in this case the Klondike gold rush to the Yukon, which peaked in 1898. Used for centuries by native traders, the Chilkoot Trail was the most popular route for prospectors heading to the Klondike gold fields. After a trip by steamer from Seattle, the trail took stampeders from tidewater at Dyea, Alaska, and over the Chilkoot Pass to the headwaters of the Yukon River at Lindeman Lake and on to Lake Bennett. At either Lindeman or Bennett miners built boats or rafts and were able to complete the rest of their trip to Dawson City on water. Sadly, by the time most of the 30,000 to 40,000 hopefuls arrived in Dawson, all claims had been staked.

What made an already gruelling (due to the weather and the topography) trail so grim was the passing of a law that required every prospector to bring a year's supply of food into Canada, a measure introduced to counteract the lawlessness and squalor spawned by gold booms. A North-West Mounted Police station was established at the summit of the pass to enforce this regulation.

For the miners, the new law meant hauling nearly 900 kg (a ton) of food across the border, a process that took the average prospector 3 months as he packed gear back and forth from cache to cache. Once the goods were finally in Canada, miners had to pay duty on the lot!

Murders, suicides, spinal meningitis outbreaks, hypothermia, avalanches and heartbreak—the Chilkoot Trail dished it up in spades. The miners' legacies litter the trail, a humble reminder to modern hikers. The law protects all gold rush artifacts and memorabilia, down to the last rusted tin can.

Today, the rugged 53-km (33-mi.) trail provides a challenge to even the most seasoned hiker. Although there is the occasional patch of good weather, blinding snow, ice, sleet, fog and gale-force winds can occur at any time of year. Nevertheless, the 4- to 5-day trek is well worth the effort.

To tackle the Chilkoot Trail, you should be totally self-sufficient and should expect to backpack about 20 kg (44 lb.) of gear, including wool and waterproof clothing, food and survival equipment with a comprehensive (but light) first-aid kit.

Your camping gear should include a good-quality tent with waterproof fly, a warm sleeping bag and a lightweight camp stove suitable for extreme conditions, plus fuel (open fires are prohibited on the trail). We recommend taking mainly dried food and high-energy snacks which can be supplemented along the way at lower elevations by a variety of high- and low-bush cranberries, blueberries, salmonberries, wild currants and gooseberries. Water is available along the route, but you might want to pack some purifier tablets as a precaution.

Other invaluable gear includes a walking stick for balance and a pair of gaiters (zippered, waterproof lower-leg protectors that prevent saturation in snow and water). Woollen toques and mitts, sunglasses and a down or polarguard vest or jacket are necessities, since good weather is rare and hypothermia a constant possibility. For early- or late-season hikes when snow might be encountered, you may want to consider taking crampons (spikes that attach to hiking boots) to get you over icy patches and/or snowshoes. Though the summit is only 989 m (3246 ft.) high—the same elevation as the city of Calgary—you do slog up from sea level. The western face of the hike receives the brunt of Pacific weather; the leeward side lies partially in a rain shadow. Most hikers travel the route from Dyea, Alaska, northeast to Bennett, British Columbia. You will have the weather and the wind at your back and it is easier and less treacherous to climb up the Golden Stairs to the pass than to climb down. The busiest times on the trail are between mid-July and mid-August following the arrival of the Alaska Marine Highway ferries in Skagway. If you want to avoid the rush, try a June or early September hike, but be prepared for snow above the timber line.

Purists who wish to follow the whole gold rush trail from Seattle to Dawson City can take a selection of ferries and buses up Vancouver Island and then catch the B.C. ferry to Prince Rupert from Port Hardy. Many backpackers sleep on deck on this leg of the trip. At Prince Rupert, hikers change to the Alaska ferry system for the final ocean lap to Skagway.

Once home to 10,000 permanent inhabitants, Skagway now houses a population of 1000. The Skagway Visitor Center provides lots of information on gold rush lore and the latest details on trail conditions and transportation to trailhead. You can also get directions to the local bus depot where you can arrange to ship extra gear by bus to Whitehorse. Skagway's most famous native son, the con artist Soapy Smith, lies buried in the Gold Rush Cemetery. If you have time, Skagway makes a good base for day hikes into the mountains above town and offers a lively nightlife when you return.

Mile Zero of the Chilkoot Trail is a 13-km (8-mi.) cab ride or hitchhike from Skagway via the steel bridge over the Taiya River. Leading at the beginning through lush timber country filled with berries, wildflowers and brilliantly coloured mushrooms, the trail passes near the old townsite of Dyea with its slide cemetery where 60 prospectors are buried, victims of the Palm Sunday avalanche of April 3, 1898. Up-to-the-minute trail conditions and other relevant information are available from the Dyea ranger station.

Four clearly designated public shelters exist along the trail and campsites are also well marked. No sleeping is permitted inside any of the shelters during June, July and August. The first shelter, a log building near some waterfalls, is at Canyon City, at km 12.4 (mile 7.75). Facilities here once included restaurants, hotels, saloons, repair shops and a steam-driven power plant.

En route to Sheep Camp (km 20.8/mile 13), the trail ascends steeply. In summer you'll probably spot hummingbirds flitting through the alders and hovering over brightly coloured camping gear. No bear attack has so far occurred on the trail, and hikers are encouraged to preserve that record by storing food up out of temptation's way at night.

The hike from Sheep Camp to the summit, at km 26.4 (mile 16.5), is hard work. Trees thin quickly as you leave the campsite and you will find yourself scrambling over slick granite boulders and snow patches. In the distance, waterfalls pour out of stony mountains; rusted cooking utensils, old boots and animal skeletons lie close at hand at the Scales, where packers used to reweigh their loads and renegotiate their contracts before the final pitch to the summit. Here Soapy Smith and his Skagway con men encouraged weary miners to squander their supplies in gambling games. Those who held on to their money could use it to have supplies routed up to the summit on the aerial tramway.

The 30° incline from the Scales to the summit was known as the Golden Stairs for the steps carved by the boots of hundreds of prospectors in the ice and snow. Anyone who fell out of the single-file line ascending the stairs would often have to wait a day in a blizzard for a chance to get back on track.

Today, no buffalo-coated North-West Mounted Police are there to meet you as you enter British Columbia at the summit. After a well-deserved rest, you might want to take a 10-minute hike south along the ridge to view the remains of old collapsible canvas-sided canoes, complete with wooden frames.

The elation of reaching the top is soon replaced by the need to keep going down to your next camp. The trail descends sharply and crosses a perpetual snow field; keep right as the trail carves its way around the steep side of electric-blue Crater Lake. After crossing a few streams, you reach Happy Camp, at km 33 (mile 20.5), a large, flat area suitable for camping. A couple of kilometres farther on lies another campsite at Deep Lake.

Scenery on the Canadian side of the Chilkoot Trail is less sombre than that to the west. The trail leads down through miniature willow, heather, spruce and alder on the rounded lower mountains to Lindeman Lake, end of the land journey for many of the original stampeders who embarked here for the lake and river trip to Dawson. The Lindeman Lake campsite, staffed by Parks Canada, offers an excellent exhibition of trail memorabilia, photos and diaries.

Allow 4 hours for the final leg of your trail, the 11.3 km (7 mi.) to Bennett. If you are really dedicated to recreating the gold rush past you can pre-arrange to rent a canoe and paddle down Lake Bennett, then the Yukon River to Whitehorse. It will take about 3½ days, so a motor does come in handy! Otherwise, a boat runs passengers down Lake Bennett to Carcross, some 42 km (26 mi.) away. From there, Alaskon Express (Gray Line) buses regularly take passengers to Whitehorse and Skagway.

The White Pass & Yukon Route runs a mobile track motorcar service from Bennett to Log Cabin or Fraser on the Klondike Highway. Buses to Whitehorse or Skagway can be flagged down at either place. At Fraser, you can also connect with the White Pass & Yukon Route steam train back to Skagway. An alternative for people wishing to reach the Klondike Highway at Log Cabin is to take the cutoff trail about halfway down Lindeman Lake on the way to Bennett. This route goes close to the railroad track and WP&YR have expressed a concern about hikers using their right of way. They have adopted a "No Trespassing" policy and hikers should respect this.

Hikers travelling from south to north are required to pre-clear Canadian customs. This can be done by reporting, either in person or by phone, to Canada Customs and Canada Employment and Immigration at Fraser, B.C. (403-821-4111) or Whitehorse (403-667-6471). Note that firearms may not be brought into Canada and are strongly discouraged on the U.S. portion of the trail. Hikers travelling from north to south are required to report to U.S. Customs in Skagway.

Successful nordic ski and snowshoe crossings of the Chilkoot Trail have been made in winter. Be warned, though—it can snow upwards of 21 m (70 ft.), creating a deceptive, avalanche-prone, meringue-like landscape. The recommended route for this trip, which should be undertaken only by experienced winter travellers, is via Petterson rather than the Golden Stairs, an avalanche hazard at this time of year. Crampons are essential since the snow freezes into boilerplate. If you are going to ski the Chilkoot in winter, be sure to allow several days' leeway for "weather waiting."

Useful Information

If you want advance information about the Chilkoot Trail, write or call the Superintendent, Chilkoot Trail National Historic Park, 204 Range Rd., Whitehorse, Yukon, Y1A 5H4 (403-668-2116) or the Superintendent, Klondike Gold Rush National Historic Park, Box 517, Skagway, Alaska 99840 (407-983-2921), who both provide an excellent information package.

Guided hiking trips of the Chilkoot Trail are offered by **Arctic Edge Expeditions**, Box 4850, Whitehorse, Yukon, Y1A 4N6 (403-633-5470).

Chilkoot Boat Tours, R. R. #1. Site 20, Comp 34, Whitehorse, Yukon, Y1A 4Z6 (403-668-7766) operates a hiker pick-up service at Bennett with boat transportation to Carcross. **Nares Boat Charters**, Box 78, Carcross, Yukon, Y0B 1B0 (403-821-3131) offers a similar service.

Information about rail service can be obtained from **White Pass Yukon Route**, Box 435, Skagway, Alaska 99840 (907-983-2217; 1-800-343-7373 toll free from U.S. or 1 800-478-7373 toll free from B.C/Yukon).

Contact **Alaskon Express** (Gray Line of Alaska), 300 Elliott Ave. West, Seattle, Washington 98119 (1-800-544-2206) or **Gray Line**, 2191 2nd Ave., Whitehorse, Yukon, Y1A 3T8 (403-667-2223) for information on bus schedules.

Archie Satterfield's *Chilkoot Pass* gives a history of the trail together with a description of the route today.

THE TATSHENSHINI

While the Chilkoot Pass provides an adventure for hikers in this northwest corner of the province, paddlers can experience a similar challenge by exploring the magnificent Tatshenshini/Alsck river watershed. Due west of the Chilkoot, the visually spectacular Tatshenshini is rated as one of the 7 best white-water rafting and kayaking trips in the world. Kayaked for the first time in 1976, this river of glaciers and grizzlies rises from a series of lakes in the southwestern Yukon. It then flows south through the northwestern corner of B.C., bisecting the massive Saint Elias and Fairweather mountain ranges to join with the Alsek River, which in turn empties into the ocean at Dry Bay, Alaska, just north of famous Glacier Bay. The Tat carries more water than the Colorado, even though it is in fact a mere tributary of the larger Alsek River. Pristine and raw, it presents the ultimate practical lesson in glacial topography to those who travel its length.

Tat country is rife with grizzlies. In the upper reaches of the river, bears gather to feast on berries, so be sure to make a lot of noise or wear bear bells when hiking the river banks. Farther south, where the Tat enters Alaska, grizzlies are more concerned with grabbing the up to 22 kg (50 lb.) of salmon they can eat in one day. In the Carmine Mountains keep an eye out for white woolly mountain goats, which clamber over a landscape sculpted by powerful glaciers.

Birds along the Tat include semipalmated plovers, spotted sandpipers, northern phalaropes, water pipits, pine siskins, tree swallows, Canada geese, hawks, falcons and willow ptarmigans. Where the river crosses the B.C./ Yukon border, look out for what is possibly the greatest concentration of bald eagles in the world.

Where the Tat merges with its main tributary, the McConnell, it picks up speed and volume until it equals that of the Colorado River through the Grand Canyon at medium water. Past the Melbern Glacier, the river winds through countryside where you can find such natural edibles as sour grass, wild cucumber, wild celery and low-bush cranberry. When the Tatshenshini runs into the Alsek, their combined waters slide through an area that has been described as sheer geology in action. Here glaciers calve house-sized chunks of ice into the river. Boaters negotiating the bergs are often simultaneously rewarded with unpredictable light shows of the aurora borealis, the northern lights. The combination of floating icebergs and exploding purples, reds, greens and yellows makes for quite a spectacle. The Alsek enters Alaska at Glacier Bay National Park and surges south in ice-clogged rapids before entering Dry Bay.

Guided canoe, kayak and raft trips on portions of the Tatshenshini/Alsek are offered by B.C.-, Yukon- and Alaska-based companies, and vary in length from 3 days to 3 weeks.

Useful Information

Canadian River Expeditions, Suite 10, 3524 West 16th Ave., Vancouver, B.C., V6R 3C1 (738-4449) offers 12-day rafting trips on the Tat/Alsek, as does **Ecosummer Expeditions**, 1516 Duranleau St., Granville Island, Vancouver, B.C., V6H 3S4 (669-7741).

Arctic Edge Expeditions, Box 4850, Whitehorse, Yukon, Y1A 4N6 (403-633-5470) offers 10-day rafting trips on the Tat/Alsek as well as expediting and rental services for those wishing to do it themselves. The company will also arrange transportation to put-in and take-out by passenger van and air charter.

Tatshenshini Expediting, 1602 Alder St., Whitehorse, Yukon, Y1A 3W8 (403-633-2742) offers both 1-day and 10-day rafting trips on the Tat/Alsek as well as complete canoe, kayak and raft rentals.

CHAPTER 10

Peace River/Alaska Highway

North of the Yellowhead Highway, reaching right to the borders of the Yukon and the Northwest Territories, lies the vast chunk of northeastern B.C. known as the Peace District after its main river.

Visitors to B.C. are often surprised to discover that a large part of the province lies east of the Rocky Mountains, and in fact a good portion of the Peace is rolling plainland that extends uninterrupted into Alberta. Since the Rocky Mountain Trench splits off the agriculturally rich Peace River district from Spatsizi and Edziza (covered in Chapter 9, "North by Northwest") and other points west, residents of the Peace maintain close ties with their Alberta neighbours. Until recently, if you bought farmland in some areas of the Peace, you lodged title with the land titles office in Edmonton, Alberta, rather than with the equivalent bureau in Victoria, B.C.

The main artery of the Peace River district, the Alaska Highway, runs from the town of Dawson Creek near the Alberta border in a steady northwestern arc through Fort St. John, Fort Nelson and Stone Mountain and Muncho Lake parks to Watson Lake in the Yukon. Built by Canadian and American army units in only nine months in 1942, the highway is the pathway to many northern adventures.

For years before Caucasian exploration, territorial boundaries shifted constantly in this vast northeastern portion of the province. The Athapaskan people, including the Slave (who lived around Fort Nelson) and the Beaver and the Sekani (who lived along the Peace River) skirmished with the Plains Cree. In 1790 the Cree and Beaver ended their war by setting a boundary at Peace Point near Lake Athabasca, three years before Sir Alexander Mackenzie, working for the North West Company, passed through the area on his famous trip to the Pacific.

When passing the mouth of what is now the Pine River, near the present site of Fort St. John, Mackenzie noted that the area would be suitable for the establishment of a trading post. Recent research indicates that John Finlay, travelling through the area the following year, may have established Rocky Mountain Fort for the NWC. In any event, by 1798 the fort was well entrenched, complete with storage cellar, houses, flagpole and fur-press. Five Indian lodges were located nearby.

Peace River/Alaska Highway

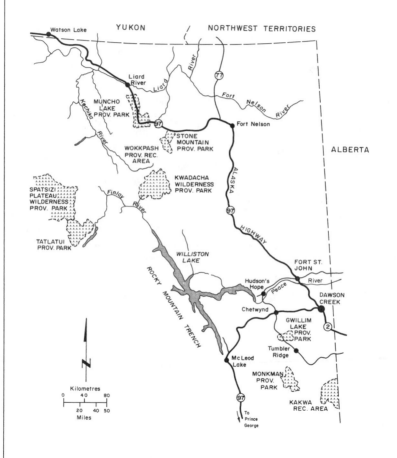

Today, the Peace is still pioneer country. Residents ranch and practise some logging, yet vast tracts of northeastern B.C. remain little used except by hunters and self-sufficient explorers. Williston Lake, the province's largest, occupies 250 km (155 mi.) of the Rocky Mountain Trench. The Peace River is so popular for canoeing that in some sections it is not unusual to spot upwards of twenty craft on a long weekend. Other great rivers of the North include the Liard, the Gataga-Kechika and the Besa-Prophet systems.

Winters here are cold but sunny, and summers are hot. Bugs are heavy in the area in June and July. Snows come early to the North, so our favourite times to explore are August and September, when fall colours are prime.

The many parks and waterways of the Peace District provide lots of exciting opportunities for adventurers. We begin our trip through this region by heading north from Dawson Creek to Fort St. John. From there, we make a brief detour to explore the parks south of the city before returning to the Alaska Highway and heading north to Stone Mountain, the Wokkpash Canyon and Muncho Lake Park, and Liard Hot Springs. Major centres are few and far between in this marvellous country, so you need to plan your trip carefully.

We recommend that all travellers to the Peace District arm themselves with Map 16 in the Outdoor Recreation Maps of British Columbia series published jointly by the Outdoor Recreation Council and the Peace River-Liard Regional District. The map splits the area into two sections. The northern portion, on a scale of 1 cm=6 km, stretches north of Fort St. John to the borders of the Yukon and the Northwest Territories and includes the Liard Plateau and Stone Mountain and Kwadacha Wilderness parks. The southern portion, on a scale of 1 cm=2.5 km, includes the city of Fort St. John and covers the area to the south as far as Monkman Park, south of Tumbler Ridge. The map can be obtained from the Outdoor Recreation Council of B.C., 1367 West Broadway, Vancouver, B.C., V6H 4A9 (737-3058 or 737-3000) and from many outdoor stores.

An alternative map is "Northern Parks of B.C.," published by BC Parks. Order a copy from the Visitor Services Coordinator, BC Parks, Peace-Liard District, 9512-100th St., Fort St. John, B.C., V1J 3X6 (787-3407) or pick it up at travel infocentres around the province.

DAWSON CREEK AND FORT ST. JOHN

The Alaska Highway starts at Dawson Creek, 412 km (256 mi.) north of Prince George on Highway 97. Dawson Creek (pop. 12,000) serves an agricultural community, and Peace River honey is one of the delicacies of the area. A delightful reminder of the town's rural roots is the Dawson Creek Art Gallery, housed inside the Alberta Pool Elevators building, an old grain elevator saved from demolition. Other sights in town include the historic

Station Museum, which is devoted to railways, agriculture and dinosaurs. Mile Zero of the Alaska Highway is on 10th Street. Four km (2.5 mi.) south of town, some cross-country ski routes radiate out from the Bear Mountain downhill facilities.

The highway continues 75 km (47 mi.) north from Dawson Creek to Fort St. John (pop. 13,000), one of the oldest pioneer settlements in B.C. Here the excellent North Peace Museum gives you an insight into the fur-trading life of earlier times, as well as documenting mining activities. Fort St. John's present economy hinges on oil and gas exploration.

Outside of town, Beatton Provincial Park includes 30 km (19 mi.) of trails. Another 30-km (19-mi.) network loops out in the Dinosaur Heights area near Hudson's Hope, west of Fort St. John.

PARKS SOUTH OF FORT ST. JOHN

Since space precludes us from talking about every park in the area, we concentrate here on parks that offer a wide range of adventuring activities. We urge parkaholics to get a copy of Maggie Paquet's *Parks of British Columbia and the Yukon.*

Contact the Visitor Services Coordinator, BC Parks, Peace-Liard District, 9512-100th St., Fort St. John, B.C., V1J 3X6 (787-3407) for copies of brochures on the parks in this region and for further information on trails and access. The Forest Service Recreation Site maps are also useful references. Copies can be obtained from the Ministry of Forests, Prince George Region, 1011-4th Ave., Prince George, B.C., V2L 3H9 (565-6193).

Crooked River Provincial Park

Crooked River Provincial Park, only 70 km (43 mi.) north of Prince George, is a popular destination for paddlers, hikers and nordic skiers. Since no hunting or power boating is allowed in this 1016-ha (2510-a.) park, kayakers in particular can enjoy uninterrupted game viewing.

Paddlers can travel the length of Crooked River north from Summit Lake, just north of Prince George, to McLeod Lake, and then have the option of going on farther through Tudyah Lake and down the Pack River to Parsnip Reach. Some portages may be necessary along the first part of the river, from Summit Lake to Bear Lake Park, because of numerous beaver dams. Watch for powerboats beyond Davie Lake.

There are three Forest Service campsites along the banks of the Crooked River and the fishing is excellent. Be sure to get a copy of the Forest Service brochure about Crooked River recreation sites.

Crooked River Park is also popular in winter. *B.C. Cross Country Ski Routes* contains a comprehensive map of the 25-km (15-mi.) network of marked trails that loop out from park headquarters in the extreme northeast, just west of Highway 97. (The book is unfortunately out of print, but you may be able to get copies in libraries or used bookstores.) Skiers may be lucky enough to see trumpeter swans on the river. Trout lurk under the ice of Bear, Skeleton, Hart and Squaw lakes for the winter angler.

A pleasant one-week paddle can be made down the Salmon River, which runs through the Nechako plateau north of Prince George and east of Fort St. James. Paddlers can arrange to fly in to Great Beaver Lake from Prince George or follow the Salmon River road to where the Salmon meets the Muskeg River. A remote river, the Salmon is a great place for spotting wildlife and birds. Black and grizzly bears scout its banks together with moose, mule deer and a wide variety of ducks and birds of prey. Canoeists planning to make this journey should consult *Canoe Routes B.C.* since specific logjams must be portaged on the lower two-thirds of the Salmon. You'll have to search libraries and used bookstores for a copy of this title too.

Carp Lake Provincial Park

Canoeists, wilderness campers, hikers and anglers gravitate to Carp Lake Provincial Park, which lies 141 km (89 mi.) north of Prince George on a heavily glaciated till plain in the Nechako plateau at an elevation of 823 m (2700 ft.). A 32-km (20-mi.) gravel road leads southwest from McLeod Lake on Highway 97 to park headquarters at the northern tip of Carp.

Carp Lake is connected by an 8-km (5-mi.) section of the McLeod River to War Lake. This route allows kayakers and canoeists to retrace the path of some of Simon Fraser's voyageurs, who used to fish the trout-filled waters of Carp Lake to replenish their supplies. Paddlers will be entranced by the frequent sight of moose swimming between the Carp Lake islands.

Summers up here are relatively cool (between 12° C/54° F and 18° C/64° F in July) and the nights can get pretty chilly.

Gwillim Lake Provincial Park

The appeal of Gwillim Lake Provincial Park, 56 km (35 mi.) southeast of Chetwynd on Highway 29, is predominantly scenic. Because of the high percentage of deciduous trees within its boundaries, the park is especially nice to visit in the fall. Gwillim Lake contains trout, lake char, arctic grayling and other species. A mere half-hour drive from either Chetwynd or Tumbler Ridge, Gwillim is increasingly frequented by nordic skiers in winter.

Monkman Provincial Park

Monkman Provincial Park, a 32,000-ha (79,073-a.) gem 130 km (80 mi.) directly southwest of Dawson Creek, is characterized by spectacular falls, lakes, rapids and rivers. Access is via a 100-km (62-mi.) rough gravel road best suited to four-wheel-drive vehicles. Check with the travel infocentre in Fort St. John before heading to Monkman to get the most up-to-date road conditions. If fate is on your side and access to Monkman is feasible, you will enjoy some of the most superb alpine scenery in the Rocky Mountains.

One of the highlights of the park is Kinuseo Falls, at the northern tip of Monkman. Here the Murray River plunges 69 m (226 ft.) en route to its confluence with the Peace River below Fort St. John. A 22.5-km (14-mi.) semideveloped trail links the falls with Monkman Lake, a shallow body of water in the middle of the park. The seven waterfalls of Monkman Creek are also worth seeing. If you are hiking at higher elevations, be aware that grizzlies do frequent the alpine meadows, but don't let that prevent you from enjoying the wild white rhododendrons that proliferate during summer.

NORTHEASTERN WATERS

On a relief map, the river systems of northeastern British Columbia resemble the lines on an old, weatherbeaten palm. Though many waterways in the area remain unexplored, our overview of navigable rivers in the Peace district includes several serviced by outfitters. We give thumbnail sketches of river routes in the area, but we recommend that anyone wanting a rapid-by-rapid description try to obtain a copy of that trusty guide *Canoe Routes B.C.* by Richard Wright, now out of print but available in most public libraries.

Paddlers who want to canoe the **Peace River** usually put in at Hudson's Hope, on Highway 29 between Chetwynd and Fort St. John, and take out 3 days later at Taylor on the Alaska Highway. It is also possible to travel farther east along the river to the Alberta border, 45 km (28 mi.) away, or on to Vermilion, Alberta, another 595 km (370 mi.).

When the W. A. C. Bennett Dam was built at Mountain Portage, the Peace lost its status as the only navigable river to cross the Rockies and its importance as the main artery north from the interior of the province. Because of the possibility of sudden flooding caused by the dam, always camp well above the water line when paddling this river.

Another 3-day journey takes canoeists down a section of the **Pine River**, from East Pine bridge, 56 km (35 mi.) west of Dawson Creek on the Hart Highway, to Taylor.

Fur traders, trappers, prospectors and explorers all used part of the **Fort Nelson River**, which flows north past Fort Nelson, joins the Liard River at Nelson Forks and then flows into the Northwest Territories to eventually join the Mackenzie River. Most paddlers on this river put in at Fort Nelson and take out at Fort Liard in the Northwest Territories. Prior to setting out, you can arrange to be flown back from Fort Liard to your starting point when your trip is over. Richard Wright's description of this route is comprehensive. The Fort Nelson is not noted for its rapids or mountain scenery but has a strong appeal since it runs through wilderness full of moose and caribou. Black bears and grizzlies have been spotted in the Nelson Forks area where the Fort Nelson and Liard rivers converge, and the spot is also noted for its mosquitoes!

The **Liard River**, named by voyageurs after the cottonwood trees along its banks, rises in the Yukon, flows through part of northern B.C. and merges with the Mackenzie River at Fort Simpson in the Northwest Territories. The entire river is rarely canoed since it would take about a month to cover its 1400 km (882 mi.), but canoeists can refer to *Canoe Routes Yukon* (out of print now, but available in libraries) as a guide to shorter trips.

Early explorers cursed the Liard River as the "river of malediction" since its rapids were considered as difficult as those on the Colorado. Today, travellers can float down the river in the comfort of a raft, selecting the rapids they wish to run and soaking in hot springs en route. Tatshenshini Expediting offers 9-day rafting excursions on the Liard; the fall colours in August and early September are a visual treat. The trips start at Fireside, 40 km (24.8 mi) south of the Yukon on the Alaska Highway. Take-out is on the Grayling River, from which you are flown to Watson Lake or Whitehorse.

Kayaking, canoeing and rafting trips on three other northeastern British Columbian rivers can be organized using the charter-flight services of Liard Tours, which operates out of the northern city of Fort Nelson, flying travellers to their point of departure.

The **Tuchodi River** rises in Kwadacha Wilderness Park and flows through the Tuchodi (Slave for "the place of big water") Lakes, which are located in a mountain valley 128 km (80 mi.) southwest of Fort Nelson. The river runs relatively fast, dropping 305 m (1000 ft.) in the first 64 km (40 mi.) past the lakes to join the Muskwa River; paddlers can travel downstream from the lakes all the way back to Fort Nelson. Fishing is good in the lakes for trout, Dolly Varden and Arctic char. Liard Tours suggests a river travel time for this trip of 3 to 8 days.

The **Gataga River** rises in the northern peaks of the Rocky Mountains and runs between the Rockies and the Kechika Range to the Kechika River, which flows north through the Rockies to join the Liard. Travelling this river can take from 1 to 3 weeks. Depending on your skills, you can start either at the South Gataga lakes or approximately 40 km (25 mi.) downstream, then travel through a mountain valley to Fireside or to Liard River Lodge where the Alaska Highway crosses the Liard. The confluence of the Kechika and the Liard is known as Skook Davidson's country, after a legendary northern guide and horseman; Skook's Landing on the Liard is named after him.

Liard Tours can also provide information on a 10- to 14-day trip for paddlers on the **Besa-Prophet** river systems, which converge on Fort Nelson as the Prophet River. Air transportation is provided to put-in at Redfern Lake (a good fishing hole). Both the Gataga-Kechika and the Besa-Prophet systems are prime spots for viewing goats, bears, elk, moose and caribou.

Useful Information
Contact **Liard Tours**, Box 3190, Fort Nelson, B.C., V0C 1R0 (774-2909) for information on transportation and canoeing routes.

For information on their raft trips on the Liard, contact **Tatshenshini Expediting**, 1602 Alder St., Whitehorse, Yukon, Y1A 3W8 (403-633-2742).

PARKS NORTH OF FORT ST. JOHN

Four unique parks occur along the Alaska Highway between Fort Nelson and Watson Lake. They are a well-deserved reward for travellers who manage all 2400 km (1500 mi.) of this legendary highway. Driving the highway isn't quite the endurance feat it used to be, but you should still be prepared for trouble. Make sure your vehicle is equipped with a good spare tire, an emergency repair kit and extra water. Drive with your headlights on and watch for flying gravel churned up by other vehicles.

Contact the Visitor Services Coordinator, BC Parks, Peace-Liard District, 9512-100th St., Fort St. John, B.C., V1J 3X6 (787-3407) for brochures on the parks in this area and for further information on trails and access.

Liard Tours, Box 3190, Fort Nelson, B.C., V0C 1R0 (774-2909) offers float-plane charters into Stone Mountain and Kwadacha Wilderness parks.

Stone Mountain Provincial Park and Wokkpash Recreation Area

One hundred and fifty km (93 mi.) west from Fort Nelson lies Stone Mountain Provincial Park, the first in the necklace of parks that studs this section of the Alaska Highway. Adventurers keen to do some climbing and fairly strenuous hiking should plan a visit to this 25,691-ha (63,481-a.) wilderness park, which encompasses part of the Stoney Range of the Rocky Mountains. The Wokkpash Recreation Area abuts the southern boundary of the park and adds an additional 37,800 ha (93,405 a.) to the unit.

Summit Pass, at 1275 m (4183 ft.) the highest point on the Alaska Highway, lies within park boundaries. The deep blue waters of Summit Lake, the park's largest, are stocked with trout and so provide a favourite resting place for migrating birds. Another pit stop for birds is Rocky Crest Lake, on the west side of Summit Pass. An easy hike from the Rocky Crest picnic area to the hoodoos on Erosion Pillars Trail makes it clear that this is indeed glacier country.

Stunning scenery and great back-country hiking are two of the main draws of Stone Mountain Park, and there are prime lookouts and possibilities for game viewing at the southern Wokkpash Valley end of the park. Despite a lack of groomed trails, nordic skiing is gaining in popularity in the park.

North of the highway, easily accessible alpine bowls circle Mount St. Paul, and the majority of hikes in this area of the park afford picture-postcard views of alpine lakes and rugged peaks.

Though it has yet to gain the popularity of the Chilkoot or West Coast trails, we predict that in time the 70-km (43-mi.) 5- to 7-day Wokkpash Trek will vie with these two famous hikes. The trek starts in Stone Mountain Park and continues into the adjacent recreation area.

Locals advise that this hike is only for the experienced and energetic. Since access is unpredictable, check with BC Parks staff in Fort St. John or with outfitters such as Liard Tours based in Fort Nelson for latest conditions. One way of exploring the Wokkpash is to take the old Churchill Mine Road, which leaves the Alaska Highway at km 643, about 18 km (11 mi.) beyond the Summit Lake campground. Cross MacDonald Creek (no bridge here), where there is good fishing for grayling and Dolly Varden, then follow the mine road south to Wokkpash Creek. Continue up the creek for 3 km (1.8 mi.) to a ford. Be cautious—the creek is subject to flash flooding and the ford may be impassable. (For this reason, the BC Parks brochure warns that people should always start this hike at Churchill Mine Road rather than attempting to travel in the reverse direction.) The trail loops through different kinds of terrain, including bare rocky ground and alpine meadows, and at the highest points snowstorms are a possibility year-round. A wooden staff will come in very handy for frequent creek crossings.

In addition to browsing caribou, so trusting they come up almost to within arm's reach to investigate strangers, the lure of the Wokkpash is its lunar landscape of hoodoos. These great columns of hard rock, eroded by wind and rain into fantastic shapes, form an other-worldly landscape.

The hoodoos edge the creek for about 5 km (3 mi.), then lead the hiker, via Wokkpash Lake, into another interesting geological formation: Forlorn Gorge, a miniature Grand Canyon 25 m (80 ft.) wide and 150 m (490 ft.) deep. The trail loops back north to MacDonald Creek and the Alaska Highway.

Kwadacha Wilderness Provincial Park

Directly south of Stone Mountain Park lies the Kwadacha Wilderness Provincial Park, 155 km (98 mi.) southwest of Fort Nelson. Inaccessible by road, Kwadacha is located at the northern end of the Rocky Mountains. Its main visitors are horse-packers and hikers who come in by float plane to camp, hike and fish. The Fort Nelson Travel Infocentre, Bag Service 399, Fort Nelson, B.C., V0C 1R0 (774-2541) can provide up-to-date information on local outfitters.

There are several trails in Kwadacha (the Sekani word for "white water"). Most of them have been established by hunting guides and connect the Finlay, Kwadacha and Warneford rivers to Chesterfield Lake and to the other main bodies of water in the park, Haworth and Quentin lakes.

Some of the mountain peaks here are named in honour of dead leaders, including Mount Churchill (3201 m/10,500 ft.) and Mounts Roosevelt and Stalin (both at 2896 m/9500 ft.).

Kwadacha is home to at least 70 species of birds, as well as the usual northern contingent of mammals such as grizzlies, Siberian lemmings, stone sheep and caribou.

Muncho Lake Provincial Park

About 60 km (38 mi.) northwest of Stone Mountain Park lies Muncho Lake Provincial Park, bisected by the Trout and Toad rivers, which flow into the Liard. The Alaska Highway cuts through this park for more than 90 km (55 mi.) and this stretch is considered by many to be the most scenic of the drive north.

Muncho's reputation as one of the province's most beautiful areas is cemented by Muncho Lake, a 12-km (7-mi.) jewel whose stunning blue-green colour is caused by copper oxides leached from the lake bedrock. Spruce and pine cover the slopes of the 2515-m (8250-ft.) mountains surrounding the lake. Anglers fish for artic char in June and early July; this is also prime lake-trout fishing time, with recorded catches in the 14-20 kg. (30-50 lb.) range. Summertime also attracts windsurfers to Muncho Lake. Wetsuits are recommended at all times since waters stay cool year-round.

Northern travel expert Anne Tempelman-Kluit particularly recommends a trip to Muncho Lake in the spring when, in her words, "the lake surface shimmers with 'candle ice,' melting ice that separates into millions of thin slivers, held vertical by sheer numbers. The wind funneling down the valley gently bumps the ice candles against each other, creating musical chimes that fill the valley."

Muncho is a great place to hike, despite the comparative lack of marked trails, since the park is renowned for its wildlife. Moose range the Toad River Valley on the park's eastern boundary. Mineral licks attract Stone sheep and caribou a few kilometres in from the western boundary. Wherever creeks spill into Muncho Lake, wildflowers such as rare yellow lady's slipper orchids, bog orchids, kinnikinnick and wild rose flourish. Naturalists recommend visiting Muncho in late June to see the orchids blooming. Higher up, alpine meadows are brilliant fields of primary colours in July. By mid-September fall colours are particularly appealing, but be prepared for early snow flurries.

Except in summer, the campsites at Strawberry Flats and MacDonald are virtually deserted, save for the occasional angler from Fort Nelson.

Liard Hot Springs Provincial Park

In the early part of the century rumours circulated about a "banana belt" hidden in this northern stretch of turf, replete with parrots, monkeys and other jungle creatures and vegetation. The reality is, in a sense, just as exciting. Liard Hot Springs Provincial Park, located at km 800 (east of the 500-mi. post) on the Alaska Highway, has a unique microclimate caused by a batch of hot springs that ostensibly well up from 5000 m (16,404 ft.) below the earth's crust to create thermal waters (54° C/130° F at source).

Ostrich ferns and extra-tall larch thrive on the banks of the steaming pools and springs, as do three insect-eating plants. the purple butterwort and the reddish-brown sundew trap insects on their sticklike leaves, while the aquatic bladderwort filters shrimp and algae through its many tiny bladders, digesting what it needs and squirting out the rest. The springs elevate the ambient temperature and humidity, creating hospitable conditions for more than 80 species of plants, many of them uncommon to an area that is typically cold and harsh. Summer visitors might enjoy teaming up with the resident park naturalist, who conducts short hikes around the area.

Alpha and Beta, the two main hot-spring pools, lie a 10-minute walk from the campground. A boardwalk takes you across a swamp where dragonflies swoop and dart; this species of dragonfly, otherwise unknown west of southern Saskatchewan, stopped evolving 6000 years ago. The tiny warm-water snails often found close to the children's pool beside Alpha are characterized by shell spirals that coil in the opposite direction to those of all other snails. Endemic to the park is a species of small lake chub that swim the waters near the boardwalk and are reputedly an isolated pocket of fish left over from the last ice age, 10,000 years ago.

Even in winter, pool waters are a comfortable 43° C (110° F). Tiny waterfalls cascade down the moss-covered tufa (porous rock) terraces, providing a stunning all-season backdrop.

Early evening is prime time to watch the algae-munching moose, who nonchalantly ignore bathers. Black bears are not so casual and have been a nuisance in the past, so we strongly recommend stringent care with any sort of food or garbage.

CHAPTER 11

Queen Charlotte Islands

The Queen Charlotte Islands off B.C.'s west coast are considered to be one of the most special places in the world. Misty, often storm-lashed and replete with archaeological and wilderness treasures, the 150-island, dagger-shaped archipelago is known as Haida Gwaii, "islands of the people," to the native Haida people.

Located 130 km (80 mi.) west of Prince Rupert across treacherous Hecate Strait, Haida Gwaii has been called the Canadian Galapagos. Since the islands escaped the last ice age, temperate rain forests thrived and strange creatures evolved. The ancient forests here still contain some of the largest trees on earth, including giant red cedar, western hemlock, yellow cypress and Sitka spruce so massive it can take 11 people to encircle one. A certain kind of yellow daisy (*Senecio newcombei*) is found only in the alpine meadows of the Charlottes. The island chain also contains a number of alpine mosses usually found only in the Himalayas or the high mountains of China.

As many as 218 bird species live on these windswept islands, including tiny saw-whet owls, hairy woodpeckers, the largest population of bald eagles in Canada and the highest density of breeding Peale's peregrine falcons in the world. One quarter of B.C.'s seabirds nest in the Charlottes.

An extraordinary evolved stickleback fish lives here, as do half of the province's population of sea lions and some of the biggest black bears in North America. (The bears' particularly large teeth, an evolutionary trait, make very efficient crab-shell crackers.) Other unique forms of land mammals include deer mice, pine martens, ermine and dusky shrews.

According to the Haida creation story, Nai-kun, at the far northeastern tip of the islands, is the place where it all began. A strand extending into the converging currents of Dixon Entrance and Hecate Strait, Nai-kun, or Rose Spit, as it is now known, exudes mystery and spirituality. It was here over 10,000 years ago that Raven, wandering along the beach after the Big Flood, discovered a clamshell full of people struggling to emerge. Cajoling them with his smooth trickster's tongue, he pried open the shell and introduced the Haida to life on earth.

Campfire charcoal recovered from Kiusta on Graham Island dates human habitation on the Charlottes back 10,400 years. Early European navigation brought Juan Pérez on a Spanish voyage of discovery to the islands in 1774. Captain James Cook's trip in 1778 was followed by Captain George Dixon's in

Queen Charlotte Islands

Langara
Island

GRAHAM

ISLAND

Masset

Rose
Spit

NAIKOON
PROV. PARK

Port
Cléments

Tlell

Rennell
Sound

Skidegate

Ferry to
Prince Rupert

Queen
Charlotte
City

Sandspit

MORESBY

Louise
Island

ISLAND

Lyell
Island

GWAII HAANAS /
SOUTH MORESBY
NATIONAL PARK
RESERVE

Kilometres

0   40

Miles

25

Skungwai
(Anthony Island)

Kunghit
Island

N

1787. Dixon named the islands after Queen Charlotte, the wife of England's King George III. The Haida people of the Charlottes became involved in the sea otter trade to satisfy the great demand for furs in China. Many of them fell prey to Western diseases, and by 1915 their numbers were greatly reduced.

Haida society was divided into two moieties ("halves"), the Eagle and the Raven, with descent traced through the mother. A man inherited his rank and ceremonial privileges through his mother's brothers. Elaborate tattoos covered the bodies of men and women of rank. All pierced their ears, nobles in as many as six places.

Traditionally considered the preeminent canoeists of the Pacific Northwest, the Haida were, and still are, skilled carvers and master canoe builders. Likened by some anthropologists to the Vikings of northwestern Europe, the Haida used war canoes to travel up and down the coast, trading and raiding for slaves. These war canoes, which measured up to 18 m (60 ft.) long, were made from cedar logs, steamed enough to be spread to a seaworthy shape.

Haida homes, situated close to shore, were made of fine cedar planks and accommodated several related families. The people moved several times a year to seasonal camps but winter village houses were permanent. The Haida made several kinds of totem poles, including house frontal poles, memorial poles and specially carved mortuary poles in which they placed their high-status dead.

Haida art, carvings and jewellery have a worldwide appeal. One famous contemporary carver is Bill Reid, whose superb *Raven and the First Men* is the focus of the Museum of Anthropology at the University of British Columbia in Vancouver. Haida artists exaggerate and accentuate special attributes of each animal drawn and carved. So the tail and front teeth of the beaver, its principal tools for work, would be emphasized, as would the huge dorsal fin and sharp teeth of a killer whale.

From the cauldron of the Pacific Ocean the Haida have always caught their salmon. They got tasty oolichan oil (the main form of seasoning for northwest native food) from their great northern neighbours on the mainland, the Tsimshian.

Today about 2000 Haida people live on the islands, still steeped in a rich cultural tradition that involves living in harmony with the land. As Miles Richardson, President of the Council of the Haida Nation, describes it, "When we were first put on Haida Gwaii, our home, we weren't put here alone. We were put here with the great swimmers, the salmon: with the forests, the oceans, the birds. And we were given instructions to live with respect for the equality of all of us, and to give thanks for what we took, and to restore that balance." Haida families continue to fish every spring on the Yakoun River, close to the site of an original village called Had'aiwes or "place of light plentiful." Close to 400 Haida archaeological sites exist on Haida Gwaii. The abandoned village of Ninstints, on southern Anthony Island, contains the highest number of original standing totem poles in the world and was declared a UNESCO World Heritage

Site in 1981. Traces of principal villages also remain at Cumshewa, Chaatl and Kaisum on Moresby Island, Skedans on Louisa Island and Tanu on the island of the same name.

Inextricably involved with the successful struggle to save the South Moresby Wilderness Area, the Haida now look to the clearcuts fringing the Yakoun River and have spoken out against possible gold mining in the area, cautioning pollution and earthquake problems. (The strongest recorded earthquake in Canada, measuring 8.1 on the Richter scale, occurred in 1949 off the west coast of the Charlottes.)

As scientist David Suzuki put it in one of his *Vancouver Sun* columns, "Haida Gwaii's remoteness is a great advantage to the people who live there. They have a sense of connection with and respect for land and sea because they depend on them.... For city dwellers, a visit to the islands provides a chance to rethink our values and priorities."

The Charlottes have a population of 6000 people. Only 150 km (94 mi.) of paved highway connects the main communities of Haida, Masset, Port Clements, Tlell, Skidegate and Queen Charlotte City, on Graham Island, and Sandspit, on Moresby Island. Thousands of kilometres of logging roads supplement the main road to link other areas; one of the most dramatic logging routes leads southwest from the town of Port Clements to Rennell Sound on the west coast of Graham Island.

The entire west coast of the Queen Charlottes is rugged, rocky, deserted and pounded by Pacific storms. Sand dunes and long, empty beaches characterize the east coast. Precipitation blankets the west coast 200 days of the year, while the east side of the islands gets an average of 125 cm (50 in.) of rain annually. The months of May and August boast the least average amounts of rainfall, and patches of sunny weather do occur right through the summer months.

Air transport to the Queen Charlotte Islands is on small charter aircraft from Prince Rupert or on scheduled Canadian International Airlines flights, which jet in twice daily from Vancouver to Sandspit on northern Moresby Island. Cars and trucks can be rented in Sandspit, Queen Charlotte City and Masset. A small open-deck ferry runs regularly between the two biggest islands, Graham and Moresby.

One of the nicest ways of getting to the Charlottes is on the provincial car-ferry service from Prince Rupert on the mainland. Depending on the weather, this fully serviced trip takes 6 to 8 hours. The summer schedule runs from June 1 to September 30 and car reservations are imperative. The ferry makes a 6-hour stopover in Skidegate, so there is enough time for the casual visitor to take in the museum and Indian village, but most people prefer to stay longer. A 15-hour day cruise up the Inside Passage on the *Queen of the North*, running from Bear Cove, near Port Hardy on Vancouver Island, to Prince Rupert, may also be made between June and September.

Access from Graham and Moresby to other islands is by boat or air. Float-plane charters and helicopter services operate out of Sandspit and the sea-plane base at Masset, and many organized boat tours to South Moresby Island are available. If you are planning on visiting the southern Charlottes, we strongly suggest that you make all your travel and charter transportation bookings prior to arrival.

Accommodation on the Queen Charlotte Islands ranges from hotels to private homes to camping. The B.C. Ministry of Tourism's annual *Accommodation Guide* is a reliable source of information.

If you plan some logging-road travel, you might want to time your trip to coincide with MacMillan Bloedel's regular two-week mid-August break, when roads are much safer for recreational traffic. A call to their head office will clarify the exact dates. Otherwise, routinely there is no logging between 6:00 P.M. Friday and 6:00 A.M. Monday.

Probably the most popular method of exploring the Charlottes is by ocean kayak, which can stand up to rough seas much better than a canoe. *Sea Kayaking Canada's West Coast* by John Ince and Hedi Kottner provides comprehensive information for anyone planning such a trip.

Scuba diving in the islands is excellent, but there are limited facilities, so divers should make arrangements through an established dive shop prior to arrival.

Remember to bring rain gear with you to the Queen Charlottes, since this is rain-forest country. And one final tip: bring plenty of cash, as not all places take credit cards and the islands have only one credit union and no banks.

Useful Information

For ferry reservations to the Queen Charlottes, call 735-6626 in Nanaimo, 669-1211 in Vancouver or 386-3431 in Victoria, or write to the B.C. Ferry Corporation, 1112 Fort St., Victoria, B.C., V8V 4V2.

MacMillan Bloedel Ltd., Queen Charlotte Division, Box 10, Juskatla, B.C., V0T 1J0 can provide information and maps on logging road travel. **Budget Rent A Car** in Queen Charlotte City (559-4675) rents four-wheel drive vehicles.

Contact **Trans-Provincial Airlines** (626-3911 in Masset or 627-1341 in Prince Rupert) for information on scheduled and charter flights between Prince Rupert and communities on the islands.

Kallahin Expeditions and Travel Services, Box 131, Queen Charlotte City, B.C., V0T 1S0 (559-4746) acts as a booking service for any tours you may plan on the Queen Charlottes.

Some excellent in-depth guidebooks about the Queen Charlottes are Neil Carey's *A Guide to the Queen Charlotte Islands*, Dennis Horwood and Tom Parkin's *Islands for Discovery*, and *Guide to the Queen Charlottes*, published each spring by Observer Publishing Co., Box 9, Tlell, B.C., V0T 1Y0 (559-

4680). Other interesting titles include *The Queen Charlotte Islands* (only Volume II of this three-volume work is currently available) by K. E. Dalzell, *Islands at the Edge* by the Islands Protection Society (lovely photos), and *Ninstints, Museum Note No. 12* by G. F. MacDonald. Emily Carr's *Klee Wyck* describes her painting trips to the islands. *Paradise Won* by Elizabeth May is an in-depth account of the successful struggle to save the South Moresby Wilderness Area and *Yakoun—River of Life* by the Council of the Haida Nation celebrates the Yakoun's harvests.

GRAHAM ISLAND

Graham Island, the largest of the Queen Charlottes group, lends itself to back-roads exploration and sightseeing. Both the Haida village of Skidegate and Queen Charlotte City are easily reached from the B.C. ferry dock at Skidegate Landing on the south end of the island.

Home to Haida artists such as Rufus Moody, Skidegate is an important centre for carvers of argillite as well as jewellers working in gold and silver. Moody (a recipient of the Order of Canada) and other carvers regularly hike to the top of Slatechuck Mountain near Queen Charlotte City to obtain blocks of argillite weighing up to 50 kg (110 lb.). Freshly cut argillite gleams slate blue but acquires a soft black shine when polished. Argillite carvers find their medium softer than soapstone and therefore easier to carve.

On average, Moody's 52-cm (26-in.) argillite totem poles take about 100 hours to complete and sell for about $200 an inch. His clients are mainly doctors and lawyers from Canada and the United States who come to the Queen Charlottes primarily to fish. Moody's biggest totem, 2.7 m (8.7 ft.) high and weighing 227 kg (500 lb.), resides in Vancouver's Museum of Anthropology. A smaller, 1.2-m (4-ft.) totem is on display at the Parliament Buildings in Ottawa. At the Skidegate Arts Co-op, artists are happy to show visitors around, explaining and interpreting Haida carvings and other artwork.

Another point of local interest, the Queen Charlotte Islands Museum, is located just north of Skidegate Landing on a cliff overlooking the inlet. Many of the cedar totems in its collection are well over 100 years old. The longhouse here shelters a collection of Haida canoes, including the 15.4-m (50-ft.) *Loo-Taas* ("wave-eater") designed by master carver Bill Reid and painted by Sharon Hitchcock for display at Expo 86. When the world's fair ended, the canoe and 15 hardy paddlers made the 960-km (600-mi.) journey home from Vancouver. In September 1989, the *Loo-Taas* made an epic trip up the Seine River to the Museum of Man in Paris at the invitation of social anthropologist Claude Levi-Strauss. The canoe is occasionally used by Haida Gwaii Watchmen Tours on its 7- to 10-day trips to 8 different destinations in the Charlottes.

From late April into June, the museum is an ideal site from which to spot gray whales feeding in Skidegate Inlet en route from Mexico to Alaska on their annual spring migration.

Queen Charlotte City, known as Charlotte by the locals, is the administrative centre for the islands, servicing the major industries of logging and fishing. Heritage buildings in the city, such as the Premier Hotel, the old hospital, the old schoolhouse and the old sawmill site, convey the flavour of life here in the early part of this century. The travel infocentre is at Joy's Island Jewellers on the road into Charlotte from the ferry dock.

To travel up island, take Highway 16, an extension of the interprovincial Yellowhead Highway from Prince Rupert. The road leads north from Skidegate along the east coast to Tlell, providing views along the way of Hecate Strait and classic windswept spruce forests.

Visitors to Tlell usually beachcomb or walk the 4 km (2.5 mi.) to the wreck of the *Pesuta*, a log barge that sank in 1928. From Tlell, the highway continues around Naikoon Provincial Park to Port Clements. From here you can decide to head back to Queen Charlotte City via a web of gravel logging roads or keep following Highway 16 farther north. Before you leave Port Clements, be sure to view the Golden Spruce, a 50.8-m (165-ft.), 300-year-old tree covered with gold needles, located just south of town along the logging road to Juskatla. The tree is best viewed before noon, when the sun is behind the viewer. A rare mutation causes the Sitka spruce's needles to be bleached by sunlight. Cuttings taken from the tree turn bright yellow or gold when grown in direct sunlight, yellow-green when grown under moderate shade and green when grown under heavy shade.

From Port Clements, Highway 16 leads to the fishing community of Masset and the Haida village of Old Masset, from which a gravel road will take the traveller east towards the finger of Rose Spit.

Masset is the largest municipality (pop. 1565) on the islands. The travel infocentre at the entrance to town distributes a detailed brochure on the area.

Old Masset, 3.2 km (2 mi.) to the north, is home to about 600 Haida people, including some famous carvers like Claude Davidson. The Ed Jones Haida Museum here is well worth a visit. Set up in an old schoolhouse, this private museum houses an unusual assortment of items from pre- and post-contact periods, and is surrounded by numerous totem poles. A good selection of silver, gold and argillite carvings and jewellery is available from local artists.

The Delkatla Wildlife Sanctuary, just north of Masset, is the first major landfall for weary migrating birds on the Pacific Flyway. Unusual birds congregate here, particularly after gales; at last count 113 different species had been spotted, including puffins, petrels (named after St. Peter for their habit of walking on water), auklets and murrelets. Shore birds include red knot or marbled godwits, dowitchers and western sandpipers. Trumpeter swans winter in the sanctuary and sandhill cranes mate here in the spring. People often spot killer whales in Masset Inlet.

Useful Information

Contact the Travel Infocentre, Box 337, Queen Charlotte City, B.C., V0T 1S0 (559-4742) for local travel information. The infocentre is located at Joy's Island Jewellers, on the road into Queen Charlotte City from the ferry landing.

Contact the Queen Charlotte Islands Museum, Second Beach, Skidegate, B.C., V0T 1S0 (559-4643) for information on opening hours and cultural programs.

NAIKOON PROVINCIAL PARK

Naikoon, one of two provincial parks on the Charlottes, consists of 72,640 ha (179,493 a.) of low bog land and dunes, with forests occurring only along river valleys and on hills. In the beautiful, unspoiled rain forest, moss hangs heavily from spindly tree limbs, dark waters fester in creek beds, and marsh grasses, salal and cedars reach up from mossy beds. Naikoon (Haida for "long nose") reaches out into Hecate Strait and culminates in Rose Spit, an excellent spot for watching birds migrating south on the Pacific Flyway. Surging offshore currents churn up plenty of food here so you can spot birds rarely seen from shore. Sandhill cranes gather on the spit and nest in nearby bogs.

The park's headquarters and information office are in Tlell. If you only plan to spend a brief time here, you might want to make the 4.9-km (3-mi.) hike from the Tlell picnic ground to the ocean. The route follows the Tlell River, famous for its coho salmon and steelhead trout runs. From the river's mouth, you head north to the wreck of the *Pesuta*. When the log barge sank in a 1928 storm, its cargo was soon incorporated into local residents' homes.

Cutthroat trout are plentiful at Mayer Lake slightly to the west, where scientists are doing research into the evolution of twin-spined sticklebacks.

A 94-km (60-mi.) beach runs all the way from park headquarters to Rose Point in the extreme northeast apex of the park. You can hike the East Beach, as it is known, in 4 to 6 days, wading two streams and seeing remains of homesteads en route. You will pass superb sand dunes which stretch for miles along the shore. In some places the sand has moved into the forest, burying trees to a depth of 10 m (39 ft.). Three walk-in wilderness camping sites along the way protect hikers from vigorous Pacific squalls. The Misty Meadows campsite at Tlell gets top marks for the nicest, cleanest loos of any park we've visited. We particularly like the framed photos of Haida Gwaii that grace the back of each loo door.

From Rose Spit, North Beach curves west to the basalt columns of Tow Hill. Keep an eye out here for tufted puffins (black birds with brilliant orange beaks) who dive in the surf. You can beachcomb for agates on Agate Beach and then take the trail to the top of Tow Hill for excellent views along the coast and great

Agate Beach, Graham Island. *Photo by Lloyd Twaites*

whiffs of sea air. Halfway back down Tow Hill you can follow a branch trail to the beach to see a spectacular blow-hole where the ancient basalt rock has been sculpted into weird shapes by wind and water.

Popular with keen hikers is the Cape Fife Trail, which links East Beach with Tow Hill. This route is an overnight hike; you can make it a 3-day circle trip by taking in Rose Point, at the tip of Naikoon. The two ecological reserves set up near Tow Hill and Rose Spit to preserve dunes and peat bog are off-limits to campers, hunters and fishers, but there is a superb provincial park campsite directly west of Tow Hill.

Useful Information
The comprehensive BC Parks brochure and map of Naikoon Provincial Park includes trail descriptions. It is available from local information centres or from the Visitor Services Coordinator, BC Parks, Box 19, Tlell, B.C., V0T 1Y0 (557-4390).

Excellent trail descriptions of hikes in Naikoon Park can be found in *Islands for Discovery* by Dennis Horwood and Tom Parkin.

LANGARA ISLAND

Avid anglers will already know of Langara Island, north of Graham Island, whose waters are home to some of the most consistent fishing for giant salmon in B.C. Clients travel to Sandspit on Moresby Island by charter aircraft from Vancouver, then catch a float plane to Parry Passage, where Rick Bourne's floating lodge lies anchored in a cove at the south end of Langara, just 64 km (40 mi.) south of Alaska. Thousands of spawning salmon swim through this bottleneck and the statistics say it all: in 1988 Langara's 1200 guests landed 1450 tyee (spring salmon weighing 13.6 kg/30 lb. or more). For information on fishing and flights to Langara Island Fishing Lodge call their Vancouver office at 873-4228.

Langara Island and Frederick Island, off the west coast of Graham Island, are major nesting grounds for Peale's peregrine falcons, a species on the world's endangered list.

RENNELL SOUND

Rennell Sound, which indents the southwest coast of Graham Island, can be reached by logging road from either Queen Charlotte City or Port Clements. The back-roads trip over the hogback ridge between the Yakoun River and this Pacific fiord is not for the fainthearted. Check your brakes before making the steep descent down to the west coast, and try not to fall into your windshield! Once there, expect good fishing and spectacular sunsets. Lovely beaches line the sound itself, some featuring Forest Service campsites and trails.

MORESBY ISLAND

Moresby, the second of the two main Queen Charlotte islands, is triangular in shape, tapering into the Tangil peninsula at its southern tip. A large wilderness island with one main settlement at Sandspit, the location of the main airport for the islands, Moresby is famous for Gwaii Haanas/South Moresby National Park Reserve and for its many ancient abandoned Haida village sites. One hundred and sixty smaller islands lie scattered off Moresby's east coast, including such gems as All Alone Stone Island, Flower Pot Island and the Lost Islands.

A 25-minute ferry ride connects Alliford Bay on North Moresby with Skidegate Landing on Graham Island; ferries run approximately every hour from 7:00 A.M. to 10:30 P.M. Sandspit (pop. 700) can be reached by road, jet (from Vancouver), float plane (from Prince Rupert) and charter boat, helicopter and float plane from points on Graham Island. Plane travel to and from Sandspit airport is dependent on good weather. Keep in mind when planning your trip to the Charlottes that North Moresby is accessible in a way that South Moresby is not.

Since North Moresby has been heavily logged, with clear-cut areas now in the first stages of reforestation, it is riddled with logging roads. Directions and a map of open roads can be obtained from Fletcher Challenge's office in Sandspit. Remember: when driving logging roads, always leave your headlights on.

For an interesting circle tour, head south from Sandspit along a gravel road that skirts the coast to Copper Bay, a busy spring camp for Haidas from Skidegate. As you drive, keep an eye out for eagle nests. Continue south for a few kilometres until you see the turnoff to a lovely camping area on sandy Gray Bay beach, a location popular with body surfers who can handle frigid temperatures. From Gray Bay, the road runs along the north shore of Skidegate Lake and then to Moresby Camp, a jumping-off point for salmon fishers heading out to Cumshewa Inlet and kayakers paddling to South Moresby Island. Follow the road to the tip of Skidegate Inlet, farther north to Alliford Bay and then east back to Sandspit. This route can be completed in 2 to 3 hours, although it is a nice day trip.

If you want to stop for a longer period of time along the way, you can camp at the B.C. Forest Service site at Mosquito Lake, which is connected by river to Cumshewa Inlet. A 2- to 3-day wilderness hike on marked trails leads from the Gray Bay campground south along the coast for 32 km (20 mi.) to Cumshewa Inlet. Incidentally, Mosquito Lake is named not for the bugs but because spruce felled here was used to build the Mosquito fighter bombers of World War II.

You can charter a float plane or helicopter from Sandspit airport for a flight-seeing tour of Moresby Island. Another favourite method of exploring Moresby is by kayak.

Useful Information

Contact the Fletcher Challenge Canada office in Sandspit for information, maps of logging roads and details of summer tours of their logging territory; the address is Box 470, Sandspit, B.C., V0T 1T0 (637-5323 or, in summer, 637-5436).

Contact the Ministry of Forests, Queen Charlotte Islands District, Box 39, Queen Charlotte City, B.C., V0T 1S0 (559-8447) for information on Forest Service trails and campsites on Moresby Island.

For air charters from Sandspit and tours of the area, contact **South Moresby Air Charters**, Box 346, Queen Charlotte City, B.C., V0T 1S0 (559-4222); **Vancouver Island Helicopters** (637-5344; fax: 637-2223), based in Sandspit, and **Sandspit Heli-jet**, Box 192, Sandspit, B.C., V0T 1T0 (637-5707).

For complete kayak rental packages for the Charlottes, contact **Moresby Mountain Sports**, Box 735, Queen Charlotte City, B.C., V0T 1S0 (559-8234).

GWAII HAANAS/SOUTH MORESBY NATIONAL PARK RESERVE

In July 1987, after a long struggle by native people and environmental groups, the Canadian and B.C. governments signed a memorandum creating 147,000-ha (363,090-a.) Gwaii Haanas/South Moresby National Park Reserve, signalling the end of logging and mining in this remote wild land. Minimal development is planned within the park reserve, which encompasses 138 islands.

More than 500 abandoned Haida villages lie within park boundaries, including the remains at Cumshewa. Removing or rearranging material of any kind at these sites is prohibited. Fires are not permitted, and camping is not allowed on Anthony Island.

South Moresby's east coast is extraordinarily rich in intertidal life, particularly in sheltered spots like Darwin Sound, between Lyell and Moresby islands, Burnaby Narrows and, farther south, the shoals of Skincuttle Inlet. Snorkelling and scuba diving are prime in the clear waters of all three areas, and you can expect to see sea anemones, mussels, barnacles, algae, sea snails and other creatures. At zero tide in Burnaby Narrows, the channel empties to reveal a sea floor plastered with starfish.

Another strong claim to naturalist fame is the area's great variety of birds. One quarter of Canada's Pacific Coast population breeds on South Moresby and neighbouring islands. Sixty thousand pairs of ancient murrelets live on Lyell Island, while the East Rankine Islands, the Copper Islands and the Kerouards, off the southern end of Moresby, are home to outstanding sea-bird colonies of tufted puffins, auklets and storm petrels. Richardson Island and the Bischoff and Topping islands, as well as the area around Darwin Sound, have the highest concentration of bald eagles. Baldies like to make their nests—which can weigh up to 2 tonnes—in the surrounding old-growth Sitka spruce. More than 50 pairs of rare Peale's peregrine falcons nest in the Charlottes; this bird can apparently power-dive at 320 kph (200 mph)!

Birders who visit the islands are entranced by the fact that many birds show little fear of humans. The same is true of South Moresby's marine animals, particularly the large rookeries of seals that exist on the Tar Islands just east of Lyell Island. Huge numbers of Steller's sea lions dry out on the Skedans Islands off Louisa Island, and even more at their largest provincial breeding colony on the southern coast at Cape St. James. Orcas and humpbacks can be spotted year-round off South Moresby, as can gray whales during the migrating season.

Since Gwaii Haanas has no maintained roads, trails or public facilities, it really lends itself to exploration by kayak, but accurate and up-to-date marine charts are essential equipment. These are published by the Canadian Hydrographic Survey and can be obtained from Meegan's Store in Skidegate Landing and most marine supply stores. Although coverage of the Queen Charlotte Islands is complete, not all the charts are the same scale. Many areas of this coastline remain poorly charted, with unmarked shoals and reefs.

Parks Canada suggests that kayakers in the park follow a number of safety measures. Groups should consist of a minimum of 3 kayaks, and each group should be equipped with a VHF radio for marine weather forecasts and for sending emergency distress messages. A mandatory licence for operating the radio is issued by Communications Canada upon successful completion of a test. Other equipment should include an EPIRB (electronic positional beacon), which will trigger the signal for a search when activated. It is recommended you file your "sail plan" with Coastguard Radio in Prince Rupert; be sure to include the number in your party, vessel sizes, colours, etc.

A favourite trip for kayakers is along the east coast of Moresby Island. Most kayakers put in at Moresby Camp on Gillatt Arm of Cumshewa Inlet and travel to Anthony Island via Hotspring Island (which lies at the entrance to Juan Perez Sound). Others charter a Grumman Goose from Sandspit or Queen Charlotte City to transport them, along with their kayaks and gear, to the waters of Juan Perez Sound in the heart of Gwaii Haanas.

If you put in at Moresby Camp, you will paddle down Cumshewa Inlet to the abandoned Haida village of Skedans. Skedans, at the northeast tip of Louisa Island, is home to some of the best-preserved totem poles still in existence and it was here in 1912 that Emily Carr painted the poles of Koona. Keep an eye out at Skedans too for the sea-lion caves in front of the village. Continuing south, you will reach Tanu and then Windy Bay, an exposed location on the outside east coast of Lyell Island, which many consider to be the soul of Gwaii Haanas.

The rain forest here is a maze of first-growth Sitka spruce and western red cedar, hung with thick lichens and carpeted with heavy mosses. The 1000-year-old trees, some as tall as 70 m (231 ft.), provided the focal point of the struggle for South Moresby when, in 1985, the Haida peacefully blocked logging roads to the threatened Windy Bay watershed. Now Blinking Eye House, a roofed shelter at Windy Bay, provides a welcome respite from bad weather.

Kayakers who put in at Juan Perez Sound can head to Hotspring Island for a dip in the hot pools before heading south. (The springs are periodically closed to visitors because of high coliform counts.) You must cross the sound in the early morning because it is completely exposed to southeast winds.

Travelling south from Hotspring Island, kayakers can head for Burnaby Strait, which connects the waters of Juan Perez Sound with Skincuttle Inlet. The strait tapers to 50-m (160-ft.) wide Burnaby Narrows, considered the greatest concentration of protein per square metre in the world. At low tide, brilliant bat starfish, crabs, sea anemones, sculpins and seaweed rival the northern lights in colour and intensity.

In their book *Islands for Discovery*, authors Dennis Horwood and Tom Parkin recall a night spent in Skincuttle Inlet, south of the narrows, watching the hilarious ground landings of a group of rhinoceros auklets coming home from a day's fishing at sea. Since their stubby bodies are designed for diving and swimming, their incoming technique consists of a "kamikaze dive into the trees near a burrow, and a prayer that they'll hit something soft...usually the mossy forest floor!"

Perhaps the most arduous paddle of the trip south will be the 5 km (3 mi.) of open ocean to Skungwai, or Red Cod Island (Anthony Island), which lies off the west coast of Kunghit Island.

A UNESCO World Heritage Cultural Site, Anthony Island contains the ruins of the village of Ninstints, which has the greatest number of in-situ totems in the world. The Kunghit Haida lived here until smallpox killed 90 per cent of the 300 inhabitants, and by 1900 Ninstints was abandoned. Many of the poles have open cavities at their tops; these were mortuary poles in which the bodies of Haida chiefs were placed for burial. The belief was that if physical remains were lifted up, the spirit was set free. The grass is tall around Ninstints and the earth spongy, making walking difficult, but the place retains a unique and extraordinarily poignant spiritual quality. Extra caution should be exercised not to damage the fragile fallen totems and house timbers, covered with moss, which can easily be mistaken for fallen trees.

(If you are not travelling by kayak, you can take an hour-long flight from Queen Charlotte City harbour to Rose Harbour, then travel for half an hour by

inflatable boat across the choppy waters to Anthony Island.)
Kayakers who camp down the east coast of South Moresby will find plenty
of driftwood for making fires. Dry cedar is best. Keep in mind the local
delicacies you can enjoy. Abalone can be sliced thin and fried briefly in butter,
while turban snails and California mussels cooked over hot Douglas fir coals are
delicious with hot garlic butter. Kayakers interested in hiking can capitalize on
day trips in the east-coast mountains.

South Moresby's west coast is rugged hiking terrain, exposed to fierce winds
and drenching rain and pounded by a murderous surf. It is also the most earth-
quake-prone part of Canada. Its few inlets are surrounded by mountains in the
600- to 900-m (2000- to 3000-ft.) range. Mosses thrive and are so deep in some
places that you can bury your arms in their velvet cushioning. Those hikers who
do explore here tend to head up the western face of the San Cristovals, characterized on their lower slopes by old-growth western hemlock, western red cedar
and Sitka spruce. At 800 m (2400 ft.), the terrain gives way to alpine meadows
often shrouded in mists. Since there are no developed trails, exploring here is
only for the fit, experienced wilderness adventurer.

A vast network of waterways and remote ranges, South Moresby provides a
test of any traveller's wilderness skills. Companies such as Kallahin Expeditions and Travel Services in Queen Charlotte City and Blue Heron Travel
Services in Sandspit can assist travellers in making arrangements for do-it-
yourself trips as well as offering organized tours. Tourist facilities on the island
are in a preliminary stage, so dealing through a local expert is the best way to
find out about rentals, accommodation, boat charters, etc. Once again, be sure to
plan any travel to South Moresby Island well in advance of your visit.

Some excellent organized tours of this spectacular region are also available.
Haida Gwaii Watchmen Tours runs a selection of trips to South Moresby,
paddling a traditional 15.5-m (50-ft.) canoe accompanied by a motorized escort
boat. Several companies offer kayak or sailing trips in the South Moresby area.
Vancouver Island Helicopters operates a South Moresby tour that stops at
Skedans Village, and Sandspit Heli-jet features tours taking in Skedans and
Lyell Island at reasonable rates.

Useful Information
Contact the Park Superintendent, Gwaii Haanas/South Moresby National Park
Reserve, Box 37, Queen Charlotte City, B.C., V0T 1S0 (559-8818) for further
information about the park.

Kayak trips are offered by **Pacific Rim Paddling**, Box 1840, Station E,
Victoria, B.C., V8W 2Y3 (384-6103) and **Ecosummer**, 1516 Duranleau St.,
Granville Island, Vancouver, B.C., V6H 3S4 (669-7741).

Ecosummer also offers sailing trips, as do **Eepo Yacht Charters**, 406-1755
Robson St., Vancouver, B.C., V6G 3B7 (290-8079), **Maple Leaf Adventures**,

4360 River Rd., Richmond, B.C., V7C 1A2 (644-4343) and **Bluewater Adventures**, 202-1676 Duranleau St., Granville Island, Vancouver, B.C., V6H 3S5 (684-4575).

Queen Charlotte Wilderness Expeditions, Suite 10, 3524 West 16th Ave., Vancouver, B.C., V6R 3C1 (738-4449) and **Haida Gwaii Watchmen Tours**, Box 609, Skidegate, B.C., V0T 1S0 (559-8225) run combined boat/camping trips.

South Moresby Charters, Box 174, Queen Charlotte City, B.C., V0T 1S0 (559-8383) and **Husband Charters**, Box 733, Queen Charlotte City, B.C., V0T 1S0 (559-4582) offer boat excursions on the east coast of South Moresby, customized tours and charter boat services.

Kallahin Expeditions and Travel Services, Box 131, Queen Charlotte City, B.C., V0T 1S0 (559-8455) and **Blue Heron Travel Services**, Box 331, 403 Beach Rd., Sandspit, B.C., V0T 1T0 (637-5430) offer expediting services in arranging kayak trips as well as other travel services.

Contact **Vancouver Island Helicopters** (637-5344; fax: 637-2223), based in Sandspit, and **Sandspit Heli-jet**, Box 192, Sandspit, B.C., V0T 1T0 (637-5707) for information on aerial tours of the islands. For air charters from Sandspit as well as tours of the area, contact **South Morseby Air Charters**, Box 346, Queen Charlotte City, B.C., V0T 1S0 (559-4222).

John Ince and Hedi Kottner's *Sea Kayaking Canada's West Coast* is a good reference book for kayakers. *Islands for Discovery* by Dennis Horwood and Tom Parkin is another useful guide, as is *Ninstints, Museum Note No. 12* by G. F. MacDonald.

USEFUL ADDRESSES

NATIONAL PARKS

For information on national parks in British Columbia, write or phone:

Pacific Rim National Park
    Park Superintendent, Pacific Rim National Park, Box 280,
    Ucluelet, B.C., V0R 3A0, 726-7721 or 726-4212.
Gwaii Haanas/South Moresby National Park Reserve
    Park Superintendent, Gwaii Haanas/South Moresby National
    Park Reserve, Box 37, Queen Charlotte City, B.C., V0T 1S0,
    559-8818.
Mount Revelstoke National Park
    Park Superintendent, Mount Revelstoke National Park, Box 350,
    Revelstoke, B.C., V0F 2S0, 837-5155.
Glacier National Park
    Park Superintendent, Glacier National Park, Box 350,
    Revelstoke, B.C., V0E 2S0, 837-5155.
Yoho National Park
    Park Superintendent, Yoho National Park, Box 99, Field, B.C., V0A 1G0,
    343-6324.
Kootenay National Park
    Park Superintendent, Box 220, Radium Hot Springs, B.C., V0A 1M0,
    347-9615.

PROVINCIAL PARKS

For general information on provincial parks in British Columbia, write
or phone:

Ministry of Parks, 4000 Seymour Place, Victoria, B.C., V8V 1X5,
    387-5002.

For information on specific parks, write or call the individual regional or district
offices:

South Coast Region
    Visitor Services Coordinator, BC Parks, 1610 Mount Seymour Rd.,
    North Vancouver, B.C., V7G 1L3, 929-1291.
Strathcona District
    Visitor Services Coordinator, BC Parks, Box 1479, Parksville,
    B.C., V0R 2S0, 755-2483 or 248-3931.

Malahat District
  Visitor Services Coordinator, BC Parks, 2930 Trans-Canada Highway,
  R. R. #6, Victoria, B.C., V8X 3X2, 387-4363.
Vancouver District
  Visitor Services Coordinator, BC Parks, Golden Ears Park,
  Maple Ridge, B.C., V2X 7G3, 463-3513.
Garibaldi/Sunshine Coast District
  Visitor Services Coordinator, BC Parks, Box 220, Brackendale,
  B.C., V0N 1H0, 898-3678 or 898-9313.
Fraser Valley District
  Visitor Services Coordinator, BC Parks, Box 10, Cultus Lake,
  B.C., V0X 1H0, 858-7161.
Southern Interior Region
  Visitor Services Coordinator, BC Parks, 101-1050 West Columbia St.,
  Kamloops, B.C., V2C 1L4, 828-4501.
Okanagan District
  Visitor Services Coordinator, BC Parks, Box 399, Summerland,
  B.C., V0H 1Z0, 494-0321.
Thompson River District
  Visitor Services Coordinator, BC Parks, 1265 Dalhousie Drive,
  Kamloops, B.C., V2C 5Z5, 828-4494.
West Kootenay District
  Visitor Services Coordinator, BC Parks, R. R. #3, Nelson,
  B.C., V1L 5P6, 825-4421 or 825-4422.
East Kootenay District
  Visitor Services Coordinator, BC Parks, Box 118, Wasa, B.C., V0B 2K0,
  422-3212 or 422-3213.
Northern Region
  Visitor Services Coordinator, 1011-4th Ave., Prince George,
  B.C., V2L 3H9, 565-6270.
Skeena District
  Visitor Services Coordinator, BC Parks, Bag 5000, Smithers,
  B.C., V0J 2N0, 847-7320 or 847-7565.
Cariboo District
  Visitor Services Coordinator, BC Parks, 540 Borland St.,
  Williams Lake, B.C., V2G 1R8, 398-4414.
Prince George District
  Visitor Services Coordinator, BC Parks, Box 2045, Prince George, B.C.,
  V2N 2J6, 565-6340.
Peace-Liard District
  Visitor Services Coordinator, BC Parks, 9512-100th St., Fort St. John, B.C.,
  V1J 3X6, 787-3407.

OUTDOOR RECREATION COUNCIL OF BRITISH COLUMBIA

The Outdoor Recreation Council provides a central resource and information centre for outdoor recreational activities in the province. It has over 40 affiliated clubs and associations. Contact the council at 1367 West Broadway, Vancouver, B.C., V6H 4A9, 737-3058 or 737-3000; fax 738-7157.

Some of the affiliated groups that can be contacted at the above address are the Bicycling Association of B.C., Cross Country B.C., Federation of Mountain Clubs of B.C., Recreation Canoeing Association of B.C., River Outfitters Association of B.C., Sea Kayaking Association of B.C. and Whitewater Canoeing Association of B.C.

Other useful addresses are:

B.C. Speleological Federation, Box 733, Gold River, B.C., V0P 1G0, 283-2691.

Dive B.C., 5824 Ash St., Powell River, B.C., V8A 4R4, 483-9740.

Alpine Club of Canada, Box 1026, Banff, Alberta, T0L 0C0, 403-762-4481.

Sierra Club of Western Canada, 314-626 View St., Victoria, B.C., V8W 1J4, 467-1766 or 386-5255.

Western Canada Wilderness Committee, 20 Water St., Vancouver, B.C., V6B 1A4, 683-8220.

TOURISM ASSOCIATIONS

For general information about the province or to obtain the free *Accommodations Guide* or provincial road maps, etc., write or call:

Tourism BC, 1117 Wharf St., Victoria, B.C., V8W 2Z2, 387-1642 or 1-800-663-6000 (toll free within Canada and U.S.).

Ministry of Tourism, Parliament Buildings, Victoria, B.C., V8V 1X4, 387-1642.

For information about a particular area of the province, write or call:

Vancouver Island
Tourism Association of Vancouver Island, #302-45 Bastion Square, Victoria, B.C., V8W 1J1, 382-3551.

Southwestern B.C. and Vancouver
Tourism Association of Southwestern B.C., Box 48610, Bentall P.O.,
#101-1425 West Pender St., Vancouver, B.C., V6G 2S3,
688-3677.
Okanagan-Similkameen
Okanagan-Similkameen Tourist Association, #104-515 Highway 97 South,
Kelowna, B.C., V1Z 3J2, 769-5959.
Kootenay Country
Kootenay Country Tourist Association, 610 Railway St., Nelson,
B.C., V1L 1H4, 352-6033.
B.C. Rocky Mountains
B.C. Rocky Mountain Visitors Association, Box 10, 495 Wallinger Ave.,
Kimberley, B.C., V1A 2Y5, 427-4838.
High Country
High Country Tourist Association, #403-186 Victoria St.,
Box 962, Kamloops, B.C., V2C 5N4, 372-7770.
Cariboo-Chilcotin
Cariboo Tourist Association, Box 4900, 190 Yorston Ave.,
Williams Lake, B.C., V2G 2V8, 392-2226.
North by Northwest
North by Northwest Tourism Association, Box 1030, 2840 Alfred Ave.,
Smithers, B.C., V0J 2N0, 847-5227.
Peace River/Alaska Highway
Peace River/Alaska Highway Tourism Association, Box 6850,
#10631-100th St., Fort St. John, B.C., V1J 4J3, 785-2544.

FOREST SERVICE RECREATION AREAS

Information and maps of campsites are available free of charge by
writing to each of the 6 regional or 46 district offices of the Ministry of Forests.
Each region must be contacted individually for maps and information.

Vancouver Region
Ministry of Forests, Vancouver Forest Region, Regional
Recreation Officer, 4595 Canada Way, Burnaby B.C., V5G 4L9,
660-7608.
Brochures available: Campbell River Forest District,
Chilliwack-Hope, North Fraser Valley, South Vancouver Island,
Squamish-Pemberton, Sunshine Coast, Powell Forest Canoe Route
and Spruce Lake Trails area.

Campbell River District
Ministry of Forests, 370 Dogwood St., Campbell River, B.C. V9W 6Y7, 286-3282.
Brochures available: Sayward Forest Canoe Route and North Vancouver Island.
Prince Rupert Region
Ministry of Forests, 3726 Alfred St., Smithers, B.C., V0J 2N0, 847-7425.
Brochures available: Morice and Lakes Districts, Smithers and Hazelton area, Terrace-Nass and Cassiar.
Prince George Region
Ministry of Forests, 1011-4th Ave., Prince George, B.C., V2L 3H9, 565-6193.
Brochures available: Crooked River, Fort St. John-Blueberry, McBride-Goat River, Moberly-Sukunka, Murray-Kiskatinaw, Nation-Takla, Prince George West, Prince George East, Stuart Lake, Valemount-Blue River, Vanderhoof-Kluskus and Williston-Mackenzie.
Kamloops Region
Ministry of Forests, 515 Columbia St., Kamloops, B.C., V2C 2T7, 828-4137.
Brochures available: Clearwater and area, Kamloops and area, Lillooet and area, Merritt and area, and Penticton and area.
Nelson Region
Ministry of Forests, 518 Lake St., Nelson, B.C., V1L 4C6, 354-6286.
Brochures available: Boundary District, Golden and area, Invermere and area, Lower Arrow and Kootenay Lake area, Revelstoke area, Southeastern B.C. and Upper Arrow, Trout and Duncan lakes.
Cariboo Region
Ministry of Forests, 540 Borland St., Williams Lake, B.C., V2G 1R8, 398-4420.
Brochure available: Cariboo region.

MAPS

Topographic Maps

The MAPS B.C. office in Victoria no longer sells the federal National Topographic Maps (1:50,000 scale). It still distributes the smaller-scale provincial maps (1:100,000, 1:125,000 and 1:250,000).

The Canada Map Office in Ottawa will provide an NTS map index as well as a list of map distributors in B.C., some of which are listed below.

Canada Map Office, 615 Booth St., Ottawa, Ontario, K1A 0E9,
    613-998-9900 (NTS index, maps and B.C. distributor list).

MAPS B.C., Surveys and Mapping Branch, Parliament Buildings,
    Victoria, B.C., V8V 1X5, 387-1441 (provincial and parks maps).

World Wide Books and Maps, 736A Granville St., Vancouver, B.C., V6Z 1L3,
    687-3320 (NTS and provincial maps—mail order service).

Geological Survey of Canada, Sales Information Office, 6th floor,
    100 West Pender St., Vancouver, B.C., V6B 2R0, 666-0271 (NTS maps).

Nanaimo News and Charts, 8 Church St., Nanaimo, B.C., V9R 5H4,
    754-2513 (NTS, provincial and park maps—mail order service).

Marine Charts

Marine charts and tide tables are available from most marine stores and from the Canadian Hydrographic Service, Department of Fisheries and Oceans, Institute of Ocean Sciences, 9860 West Saanich Rd., Box 6000, Sidney, B.C., V8L 4B2, 356-6358, fax 356-6390 (marine charts, tide tables and other marine publications).

The central branch of the Vancouver Public Library at 750 Burrard Street has copies of most NTS and marine charts of the province. If only a portion of a map or chart is required, it may be easier, and cheaper, to photocopy the one in the library.

The Outdoor Recreation Council of B.C. publishes a very useful series of B.C. outdoor recreation maps, available from the Outdoor Recreation Council or from local sporting goods stores. Maps currently available are: 100 Mile House region; Windermere Lake region; Whistler/Garibaldi region; Greater Kamloops region; Central Okanagan region; Campbell River region; Shuswap Lake region; Princeton/Manning/Cathedral region; Princeton/Merritt region; Nicola Valley region; Chilliwack/Hope/Skagit region; North Okanagan region; South Okanagan region; Greater Vancouver/Lower Fraser Valley region; Greater Victoria/Gulf Islands/Nanaimo region and Peace River/Liard region.

Canoe Sport B.C. sells a B.C. Canoe Route map, obtainable from the Outdoor Recreation Council.

RECOMMENDED READING

Akrigg, G. P. V. and Helen B. *British Columbia Place Names*. Victoria: Sono Nis, 1986.

Bentley, Mary and Ted. *Gabriola: Petroglyph Island*. Victoria: Sono Nis, 1990.

Blier, Richard. *Island Adventures: An Outdoor Guide to Vancouver Island*. Victoria: Orca Books, 1989.

Blix, Einar. *Trails to the Timberline in West Central British Columbia*. Smithers, B.C: Fjelltur Books, 1989.

Bovey, Robin. *Birds of Vancouver*. Vancouver: Lone Pine Publishing, 1990.

British Columbia Recreational Atlas. Victoria: Province of British Columbia, Ministry of Environment and Informap, 1990.

Bryson, Sandy. *Vancouver Island Traveler*. Juneau: Windham Bay Press, 1989.

Campbell, Wayne. *The Birds of British Columbia. Vol. I, parts I and II*. Victoria: Royal British Columbia Museum, 1990.

Carey, Neil G. *A Guide to the Queen Charlotte Islands, 1989-90*. Anchorage: Alaska Northwest Books, 1989.

Carr, Emily. *Klee Wyck*. Don Mills, Ontario: Stoddart, 1989.

Chettleburgh, Peter. *An Explorer's Guide: Marine Parks of British Columbia*. Vancouver: Special Interest Publications, 1985.

Christie, Jack. *Day Trips from Vancouver*. Vancouver: Brighouse Press, 1989.

Clark, Lewis J. *Lewis Clark's Field Guide to the Wild Flowers of Field and Slope in the Pacific Northwest*. Vancouver: Douglas & McIntyre, 1984.

Clark, Lewis J. *Lewis Clark's Field Guide to the Wild Flowers of Forest and Woodland in the Pacific Northwest*. Vancouver: Douglas & McIntyre, 1984.

Clark, Lewis J. *Lewis Clark's Field Guide to the Wild Flowers of Marsh and Waterway in the Pacific Northwest*. Vancouver: Douglas & McIntyre, 1984.

Clark, Lewis J. *Lewis Clark's Field Guide to the Wild Flowers of the Arid Flatlands in the Pacific Northwest*. Vancouver: Douglas & McIntyre, 1984.

Clark, Lewis J. *Lewis Clark's Field Guide to the Wild Flowers of the Mountains in the Pacific Northwest*. Vancouver: Douglas & McIntyre, 1984.

Cousins, Jean and Robinson, Heather. *Easy Hiking Around Vancouver*. Vancouver: Douglas & McIntyre, 1990.

Cummings, Al and Bailey-Cummings, Jo. *Gunkholing in the Gulf Islands*. Edmonds, Washington: Norwesting Inc., 1989.

Darling, Dr. Jim. *Wild Whales*. Vancouver: Whitecap Books, 1987.

Dalzell, K. E. *The Queen Charlotte Islands, Book 2 of Places and Names*. Madeira Park, B.C.: Harbour Publishing, 1989.

Dorst, Adrian and Young, Cameron. *Clayoquot: On the Wild Side*. Vancouver: Rainforest, 1990.

Eberts, Tony and Grass, Al. *Exploring the Outdoors (Southwestern B.C.)* Vancouver: Hancock House, 1984.

Fairley, Bruce. *A Guide to Climbing and Hiking in Southwestern British Columbia*. Vancouver: Gordon Soules Publishing, 1986.

Fleming, June. *The Well-Fed Backpacker*. Portland: Victoria House, 1978.

Foster, David and Aitken, Wayne. *Blisters and Bliss*. Seattle Cloudcap, 1989.

Freeman, Roger and Ethel. *Exploring Lynn Canyon and Lynn Headwaters Park*. Vancouver: Federation of Mountain Clubs of British Columbia, 1986.

Freeman, Roger and Ethel. *Exploring Vancouver's North Shore Mountains*. Vancouver: Federation of Mountain Clubs of British Columbia, 1985.

Gibson, Nancy and Whittaker, John. *The Lone Pine Picnic Guide for British Columbia*. Vancouver: Lone Pine Publishing, 1990.

Gordon, David. *Field Guide to the Orca*. Vancouver: Rainforest, 1990.

Gould, Ed. *Ralph Edwards of Lonesome Lake*. Vancouver: Hancock House, 1979.

Gould, Stephen Jay. *Wonderful Life: The Burgess Shale and the Nature of History*. New York: Viking, 1989.

Goward, Trevor and Hickson, Cathie. *Nature Wells Gray*. Kamloops: The Friends of Wells Gray Park, 1987. (Box 1386, Kamloops, B.C. V2C 6L7)

Harris, Bob. *The Best of B.C.'s Hiking Trails*. Surrey: Heritage House/B.C. Outdoors, 1986.

Hill, Beth. *Exploring the Kettle Valley Railway*. Winlaw, B.C.: Polestar, 1989.

Hobson, Richmond P. *Grass Beyond the Mountains*. Toronto: McClelland & Stewart, 1978.

Hobson, Richmond P. *Nothing Too Good for a Cowboy*. Toronto: McClelland & Stewart, 1989.

Hobson, Richmond P. *The Rancher Takes a Wife*. Toronto: McClelland & Stewart, 1978.

Holman, Wendy and Nowlan, Sheila K. *Where To Stay and Play Along the Pacific Coast*. Seattle: Northwest Beachcomber Publishers, 1990.

Horse Council of British Columbia. *Horse Trail Guide: Southwestern B.C.* Vancouver: Horse Council of British Columbia, 1989.

Horwood, Dennis and Parkin, Tom. *Islands for Discovery: An Outdoors Guide to British Columbia's Queen Charlotte Islands*. Victoria: Orca Books, 1989.

Hosie, R. C. *Native Trees of Canada*. Markham: Fitzhenry & Whiteside, 1979.

Ince, John and Kottner, Hedi. *Sea Kayaking Canada's West Coast*. Vancouver: Raxas Books, 1982.

Islands Protection Society. *Islands at the Edge*. Vancouver: Douglas and McIntyre, 1984.

Kennedy, Dorothy and Bouchard, Randy. *Sliammon Life, Sliammon Lands*. Vancouver: Talonbooks, 1983.

Kunelius, Rick and Biederman, Dave. *Ski Trails in the Canadian Rockies*. Banff: Summerthought, 1981.

Lyons, C. P. *Okanagan Valley*. Surrey: Heritage House, 1985.

Lyons, C. P. *Trees, shrubs and flowers to know in British Columbia*. Toronto: Dent, 1952.

Macaree, Mary and David. *103 Hikes in Southwestern British Columbia.* Vancouver: Douglas & McIntyre, 1987.

Macaree, Mary and David. *109 Walks in British Columbia's Lower Mainland.* Vancouver: Douglas & McIntyre, 1990.

Mark, Shannon and McLean, Heather. *Hiking in the Rain Forest—Prince Rupert and Terrace.* Prince Rupert, B.C.: Bookmark, 1986.

Maud, Ralph. *A Guide to B.C. Indian Myth and Legend.* Vancouver: Talonbooks, 1982.

May, Elizabeth. *Paradise Won: The Struggle for South Moresby.* Toronto: McClelland & Stewart, 1989.

M'Gonigle, Michael and Wickwire, Wendy. *Stein: The Way of the River.* Vancouver: Talonbooks, 1988.

Moyes, Robert. *Victoria: The Insider's Guide.* Victoria: Orca Books, 1990.

National Geographic Society. *Field Guide to Birds of North America.* Second edition. Washington, D.C.: National Geographic, 1989.

Neave, Roland. *Exploring Wells Gray Park.* Third edition. Kamloops: The Friends of Wells Gray Park, 1988. (Box 1386, Kamloops, B.C. V2C 6L7)

Obee, Bruce. *The Gulf Islands Explorer—The Complete Guide.* Vancouver: Whitecap Books, 1990.

Obee, Bruce. *The Pacific Rim Explorer.* Vancouver: Whitecap Books, 1986.

Oltmann, Ruth. *Lizzie Rummel: Baroness of the Rockies.* Exshaw, Alberta: Ribbon Creek Publishing Company, 1984.

Outdoor Club of Victoria. *Hiking Trails I—Victoria and Vicinity.* Victoria: Outdoor Club of Victoria, 1987. (Box 1875, Victoria, B.C., V8W 2Y3)

Outdoor Club of Victoria. *Hiking Trails II—Southeastern Vancouver Island.* Victoria: Outdoor Club of Victoria, 1988. (Box 1875, Victoria, B.C., V8W 2Y3)

Outdoor Club of Victoria. *Hiking Trails III—Central and Northern Vancouver Island.* Victoria: Outdoor Club of Victoria, 1986. (Box 1875, Victoria, B.C., V8W 2Y3)

Paquet, Maggie. *Parks of British Columbia and the Yukon.* North Vancouver: Maia Publishing, 1990.

Patterson-Z., Tanna. *Exploring the Creston Valley.* Vancouver: Waterwheel Press, 1989.

Patton, Brian and Robinson, Bart. *The Canadian Rockies Trail Guide —A Hiker's Manual to the National Parks.* Banff: Summerthought, 1989.

Peterson, Roger Tory. *Western Birds.* Boston: Houghton Mifflin, 1990.

Pratt-Johnson, Betty. *141 Dives in the Protected Waters of Washington and British Columbia.* Vancouver: Gordon Soules Publishing, 1977.

Pratt-Johnson, Betty. *Whitewater Trips and Hot Springs, West and East Kootenays, for Kayakers, Canoeists and Rafters in British Columbia.* Vancouver: Adventure Publishing, 1989.

Pratt-Johnson, Betty. *Whitewater Trips for Kayakers, Canoeists and Rafters on Vancouver Island*. Vancouver: Gordon Soules Publishing, 1983.

Pratt-Johnson, Betty. *Whitewater Trips for Kayakers, Canoeists and Rafters in British Columbia: Greater Vancouver through Whistler, Okanagan and Thompson River Regions*. Vancouver: Adventure Publishing, 1986.

Priest, Simon and Klint, Kimberley. *Bicycling Southwestern British Columbia and the Sunshine Coast*. Vancouver: Douglas & McIntyre, 1985.

Priest, Simon and Klint, Kimberley. *Bicycling Vancouver Island and the Gulf Islands*. Vancouver: Douglas & McIntyre, 1984.

Ragsdale, John G. *Camper's Guide to Outdoor Cooking*. Toronto: Gulf Publishing, 1989.

Rogers, Fred. *Shipwrecks of British Columbia*. Vancouver: Douglas & McIntyre, 1980.

St. Pierre, Paul. *Boss of the Namko Drive*. Vancouver: Douglas & McIntyre, 1986.

St. Pierre, Paul. *Breaking Smith's Quarter Horse*. Vancouver: Douglas & McIntyre, 1984.

St. Pierre, Paul. *Chilcotin Holiday*. Vancouver: Douglas and McIntyre, 1984.

St. Pierre, Paul. *Smith and Other Events*. Vancouver: Douglas and McIntyre, 1985.

Satterfield, Archie. *Chilkoot Pass*. Bothell, Wa.: GTE Alaska Northwest Publishing Co., 1990.

Scott, R. Bruce. *Barkley Sound*. Victoria: Sono Nis, 1990.

Scotter, George W. and Flygare, Halle. *Wildflowers of the Canadian Rockies*. Edmonton: Hurtig, 1986.

Shewchuk, Murphy. *Backroads Explorer Vol. 1: Thompson—Cariboo*. Vancouver: B.C. Outdoors, 1985.

Shewchuk, Murphy. *Backroads Explorer Vol. 2: Similkameen & south Okanagan*. Surrey: Hancock House, 1988.

Shewchuk, Murphy. *Coquihalla Country*. Merritt, B.C.: Sonotek Publishing, 1990.

Shewchuk, Murphy. *Fur, Gold and Opals: A Guide to the Thompson River Valleys*. Surrey: Hancock House, 1975.

Sierra Club of Western Canada. *The West Coast Trail and Nitinat Lakes: A Trail Guide*. Vancouver: Douglas & McIntyre, 1989.

Snively, Gloria. *Exploring the Seashore in B.C., Washington and Oregon*. Vancouver: Gordon Soules Publishing, 1989.

Snowden, Mary Ann. *Island Paddling. (A Paddler's Guide to the Gulf Islands and Barkley Sound.)* Victoria: Orca Books, 1990.

Southern, Karen. *Sunshine and Salt Air—A Recreation Guide to the Sunshine Coast*. Madeira Park: Harbour Publishing, 1987.

Stewart, Anita. *The Lighthouse Cookbook*. Madeira Park: Harbour Publishing, 1990.

Stoltmann, Randy. *A Hiking Guide to the Big Trees of Southwestern British Columbia.* Vancouver: Western Canada Wilderness Committee, 1987.

Strom, Erling. *Pioneer on Skis.* Banff: Summerthought, 1978.

Tempelman-Kluit, Anne. *Green Spaces of Vancouver.* Vancouver: Brighouse Press, 1990.

Tippett, Maria and Cole, Douglas. *From Desolation to Splendour.* Don Mills, Ontario: Stoddart, 1976.

Thomas, Carolyn and Stewart, Jill. *Island Treasures (Vancouver Island, Gulf Islands and Victoria).* Madeira Park: Harbour Publishing, 1990.

Vancouver Natural History Society. *Nature West Coast.* Victoria: Sono Nis, 1990.

Vernon Outdoor Club. *Hiking Trails Enjoyed by the Vernon Outdoor Club.* Vernon: Vernon Outdoor Club, 1989. (Box 1241, Vernon, B.C. V1T 6N6)

Walker, T. A. *Spatsizi.* Madeira Park: Harbour Publishing, 1983.

Watmough, Don. *Cruising Guide to British Columbia. Vol. IV: West Coast Vancouver Island, Cape Scott to Sooke.* Vancouver: Whitecap Books, 1984.

Wells, R. E. *A Guide to Shipwrecks along the West Coast Trail.* 1990. (Box 817, Sooke, B.C. V0S 1N0)

Wershler, Terri. *The Vancouver Guide.* Third edition. Vancouver: Douglas & McIntyre, 1991.

Wilson, Ethel. *Swamp Angel.* Toronto: McClelland & Stewart, 1990.

Wilson, Ian and Sally. *Wilderness Seasons: Life and Adventure in Canada's North.* Vancouver: Gordon Soules Publishing, 1987.

Wolferstan, Bill. *Cruising Guide to British Columbia. Vol. I: Gulf Islands and Vancouver Island from Sooke to Courtenay.* Vancouver: Whitecap Books, 1987.

Wolferstan, Bill. *Cruising Guide to British Columbia. Vol. II: Desolation Sound to Discovery.* Vancouver: Whitecap Books, 1981.

Wolferstan, Bill. *Cruising Guide to British Columbia. Vol. III: Sunshine Coast, Fraser Estuary and Vancouver to Jervis Inlet.* Vancouver: Whitecap Books, 1982.

Woodcock, George. *British Columbia: A History of the Province.* Vancouver: Douglas & McIntyre, 1990.

Woods, John G. *Glacier Country: A Guide to Mount Revelstoke and Glacier National Parks.* Vancouver: Douglas & McIntyre, 1987.

Woodworth, John and Flygare, Halle. *Trail Guide: In the Steps of Alexander MacKenzie.* Toronto: The Nature Conservancy of Canada, 1987.

Wright, Richard T. *Backroads Guide: Volume I—Bridge River Country.* Surrey: Heritage House, 1980.

Wright, Richard T. *The Bowron Lakes—A Year Round Guide.* Surrey: Heritage House, 1985.

Wright, Richard T. *Discover Barkerville: A Gold Rush Adventure.* Vancouver: Special Interest Publications, 1984.

INDEX